Holt Literature & Language Arts

P9-CBY-797

UNIVERSAL ACCESS Interactive Reading

- **Word Analysis, Fluency, and Systematic Vocabulary Development**
- **Reading Comprehension**
- **Literary Response and Analysis**

HOLT, RINEHART AND WINSTON

A Harcourt Education Company

Austin • Orlando • Chicago • New York • Toronto • London • San Diego

Credits

Editorial

Project Directors: Kathleen Daniel, Juliana Koenig
Editor: Amy Fleming
Managing Editor: Mike Topp
Manager of Editorial Services: Abigail Winograd
Senior Product Manager: Don Wulbrecht
Editorial Staff: Victoria Moreland, Pamela Thompson Baggett, Brenda Sanabria, Jan Watson-Collins
Project Administration: Elizabeth LaManna
Editorial Support: Renée Benitez, Louise Fernandez, Bret Isaacs, Laurie Muir
Editorial Permissions: David Smith, Carrie Jones

Art, Design, and Production

Director: Athena Blackorby
Senior Design Director: Betty Mintz
Series Design: Proof Positive/Farrowlyne Associates, Inc.
Design and Electronic Files: Proof Positive/Farrowlyne Associates, Inc.
Photo Research: Proof Positive/Farrowlyne Associates, Inc.
Production Manager: Catherine Gessner
Production Coordinator: Joseph Padial

Printed in the United States of America
ISBN 0-03-065094-1

17 18 19 20 21 0956 12 11 10 09

Contents

• PART ONE •
LITERATURE AND INFORMATIONAL READINGS

CHAPTER 1 The Anglo-Saxons (449–1066)
Songs of Ancient Heroes

CHAPTER 5 The Romantic Period (1798–1832)
The Quest for Truth and Beauty

CHAPTER 6 The Victorian Period (1832–1901)
Paradox and Progress

CHAPTER 7   The Modern World (1900 to the Present)
A Remarkable Diversity

• PART TWO •
CONSUMER, WORKPLACE, AND PUBLIC DOCUMENTS

To the Student

A Book for You

Reading a book is like re-writing it for yourself. . . . You bring to a novel, anything you read, all your experience of the world. You bring your history and you read it in your own terms.
—Angela Carter, English novelist and short-story writer

Imagine this: a book full of stories you want to read and informational articles that are really interesting. Make it a book that actually tells you to write in it, circling, underlining, jotting down responses. Fill it with graphic organizers that encourage you to think a different way. Make it a size that's easy to carry around. That's *Interactive Reading*—a book created especially for you.

A Book Designed for Your Success

Interactive Reading is designed to accompany *Holt Literature and Language Arts,* Sixth Course. Like *Holt Literature and Language Arts,* its purpose is to help you interact with the selections and master the California English–Language Arts Content Standards. The chart below shows you how your book is organized.

Part One Literature and Informational Readings	Part Two Consumer, Workplace, and Public Documents
Literary and informational selections from *Holt Literature and Language Arts*	New selections that help you learn how to read various kinds of documents

When you read documents such as technical directions or a Web site, you usually read to "get the facts." When you read literature, you need to go beyond "the facts" and read between the lines of a poem or a story to discover the writer's meaning. No matter what kind of reading you do, *Interactive Reading* will help you practice the skills you need to become an active and successful reader. Here's how . . .

Part One: Literature and Informational Readings

Interactive Reading will help you respond to, analyze, evaluate, and interpret literature. These skills will increase your understanding of the literature you read, which is a major goal of the California language arts standards.

In Part One of *Interactive Reading,* here is what you will find in each chapter.

- Every chapter begins with a **historical essay** that provides highlights of the period. A more detailed version of this essay can be found in the corresponding chapter of *Holt Literature and Language Arts.* This historical introduction is divided into short, easy-to-read sections. The interactive notes in the side column will guide you through each section, so that you come to understand the people, events, and ideas that shaped the life and literature of that period.

- Following the historical essay are **literary and informational selections.** These pieces were selected from *Holt Literature and Language Arts,* Sixth Course. They are reprinted in a single column and in larger type to give you the room you need to mark up the text and respond to the interactive notes in the side column.

The following features appear with the selections in Part One:

- A **Before You Read** page that teaches a literary focus and provides you with a reading skill to help you read the selection successfully and master the standards
- **Interactive notes** in the side column to guide your reading and help you respond to the selection
- A **Practice and Review graphic organizer** that helps you understand the reading skill and literary focus for the selection
- A **Vocabulary Development** page that provides practice with selection vocabulary (in cases where selection vocabulary is taught)

Part Two: Consumer, Workplace, and Public Documents

Reading various kinds of documents is another important goal of the California language arts standards. To help you master how to read these kinds of materials, Part Two contains:

- A **Before You Read** page that introduces you to the special features of the type of document you will be reading and teaches you the informational focus for the selection
- **New selections** accompanied by notes in the side column (as in Part One) to guide your reading and help you respond to the text
- A **Standards Review** page that helps you practice test-taking skills while applying the standards

At the back of your book, following Part Two, you will find more special features to help you keep track of what you have read and what you have learned:

- A **Checklist for Standards Mastery** that helps you track your progress by checking off the skills you have acquired
- A **Vocabulary Development** guide that explains how to read the pronunciation respellings provided with vocabulary and word study notes

. . . .

What is reading but silent conversation?
—Walter Savage Landor, English poet and essayist

. . . .

Reading is an interactive process, like a conversation. This book is designed to help you interact with the selections you read by marking them up, asking your own questions, taking notes, recording your own ideas, and responding to the questions of others. The more you "talk" to the text in this way, the more you will make valuable connections between your reading and your own life.

A Walk Through the Book

The Anglo-Saxons (449–1066)

David Adams Leeming

The following essay provides highlights of the historical period.
For a more detailed version of this essay,
see *Holt Literature and Language Arts*, pages 6–17.

Reading Standard 3.7c Evaluate the philosophical, political, religious, ethical, and social influences of the historical period that shaped the characters, plots, and settings.

The Spirit of the Celts

When Greek travelers visited what is now Great Britain in the fourth century B.C., they found an island inhabited by tall blond warriors who called themselves Celts. Among these island Celts was a group called the Britons who left their permanent stamp in one of the names (Britain) eventually adopted by the land they settled.

10   The Celts saw spirits everywhere—in rivers, trees, stones, ponds, fire, and thunder. These spirits or gods controlled all aspects of existence, and they had to be constantly satisfied. Priests called Druids acted as go-betweens between the gods and the people.

The Celtic Heroes and Heroines: A Magical World

The mythology of the Celts has influenced British and Irish writers to this day. Sir Thomas Malory, in the fifteenth century, gathered together the Celtic legends about a warrior named Arthur. He mixed those stories to produce *Le Morte d'Arthur*, about the legendary King Arthur.

20   Early in the twentieth century, William Butler Yeats used the Celtic myths in his poetry and plays in an attempt to make the Irish aware of their lost heroic past.

IDENTIFY
Pause at line 7. Who were the Celts?

IDENTIFY
Pause at line 22. According to this essay, what did the writings of Sir Thomas Malory and William Butler Yeats have in common?

The Anglo-Saxons   **3**

The Battle with Grendel translated by Burton Raffel

BEFORE YOU READ

REVIEW SKILLS
As you read *Beowulf*, look for ways in which the following literary device makes the story rich and memorable.

IMAGERY
Language that appeals to the senses.

LITERARY FOCUS: THE EPIC HERO

An **epic** is a long, involved story that tells of the great deeds of a larger-than-life hero. The central character in an epic—the **epic hero**—embodies the values and ideals of a particular society. Most epic heroes undertake a long, dangerous journey, or quest, to achieve something of great value to themselves or their people.

Beowulf is an **archetype**, or perfect example, of an epic hero. He possesses superhuman strength and reflects the highest ideals of his culture—the Anglo-Saxon culture of ancient England. The heroic archetype that Beowulf represents is that of the dragon slayer: In his quest, the hero must protect a community by defeating a gruesome monster that seeks to destroy it.

What Makes a Hero? In the left-hand column of the chart below, create your own list of heroes. In the right-hand column, write at least one detail or characteristic that proves each hero is truly heroic.

My List of Heroes	Proof of Heroism

Reading Standard 3.6 Analyze the way in which authors through the centuries have used archetypes.

Reading Standard 3.7 (Grade 9–10 Review) Recognize and understand the significance of various literary devices, including figurative language, imagery, allegory, and symbolism, and explain their appeal.

READING SKILLS: IDENTIFYING DETAILS

Beowulf demonstrates a number of characteristics that identify him as an **archetype** of the **epic hero**. These characteristics, listed below, are revealed in details about Beowulf himself or about events connected with the battle.

Characteristics of an Epic Hero

- Is significant and glorified
- Is on a quest
- Has superior or superhuman strength, intelligence, and/or courage
- Is ethical

- Risks death for glory or for the greater good of society
- Is a strong and responsible leader
- Performs brave deeds
- Reflects the ideals of a particular society

Use the Skill As you read the selection, underline or highlight details that describe Beowulf as an epic hero. Refer to the list above for hints.

10   **Part 1**   Chapter 1: The Anglo-Saxons

Historical Essay
This essay is a shortened version of the one that appears in *Holt Literature and Language Arts*. The short, easy-to-read sections will help you understand the political, religious, ethical, and social influences of the historical period.

Reading Standards
The California reading standards that are covered in the essay are listed here.

Side-column Notes
This essay, and each selection that follows, is accompanied by interactive notes in the side columns. The notes are designed to help you master the California standards that are listed with each selection. The notes guide your interaction with the text. Many notes ask you to circle or underline in the text itself. Others provide lines on which you can write your responses to questions.

Before You Read
This feature explains important elements of the selection you are about to read and sets the stage for reading.

Literary Focus
Here, you learn about the literary focus for the selection—the same focus that is covered in *Holt Literature and Language Arts*. Often, an activity is included to help you connect with and understand the literary focus.

Reading Standards
The California standards covered with the selection (both grade level and review) are listed here.

Reading Skills
This feature provides a reading skill for you to apply to the selection. Each skill ties into and supports the literary focus so that you can make sense of the text while mastering the California standards.

Review Skills
When a review standard is taught with a selection, definitions of key elements from the standard are given here.

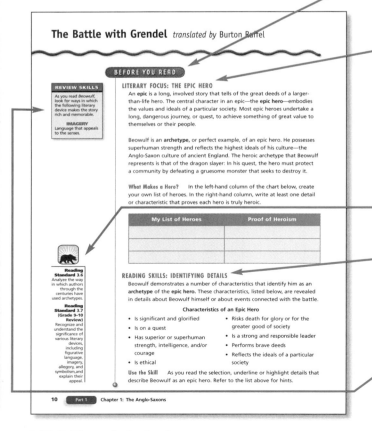

The Death of Hector
from the Iliad

Homer *translated by* **Robert Fagles**

The *Iliad* begins when the war between the Greeks and the Trojans has already lasted for nearly ten years. Each army fights bravely and receives help from the gods. The god Apollo assists Hector and the Trojans. Apollo is the god of the sun and is also called Phoebus. The goddess Athena aids Achilles and the Greeks, who are also called the Achaeans or the Argives. Earlier in the story, Hector kills Achilles' best friend, a soldier named Patroclus. Hector strips Patroclus of his armor and leaves his body exposed and unburied. Achilles is enraged and seeks revenge, because the Greeks believed that a soul could not find rest until the body was buried with the proper rituals. In this section of Book 22, the exhausted Trojans have taken refuge behind the walls of their city, but their hero, Hector, remains outside the gates. Achilles orders his men to hold back so that he can fight Hector by himself.

And swift Achilles kept on coursing Hector, nonstop
as a hound in the mountains starts a fawn from its lair,
hunting him down the gorges, down the narrow glens
and the fawn goes to ground, hiding deep in brush
5   but the hound comes racing fast, nosing him out
until he lands his kill. So Hector could never throw
Achilles off his trail, the swift racer Achilles—
time and again he'd make a dash for the Dardan Gates,[1]
trying to rush beneath the rock-built ramparts, hoping
10 men on the heights might save him, somehow, raining spears
but time and again Achilles would intercept him quickly,
heading him off, forcing him out across the plain
and always sprinting along the city side himself—
endless as in a dream . . .

INTERPRET

Lines 1–6 contain an **epic simile.** Achilles is said to be "coursing" (tracking) Hector, just as a hound hunts down a fawn. If Achilles is like the hound, then who is like the fawn? *(Grade 9–10 Review)*

IDENTIFY CAUSE & EFFECT

Find the cause-and-effect relationship in lines 6–14. Underline the effect, and circle the cause.

"The Death of Hector" from *The Iliad* by Homer, translated by Robert Fagles. Copyright © 1990 by Robert Fagles. Reprinted by permission of **Viking Penguin,** a division of Penguin Putnam Inc. Electronic format by permission of **Georges Borchardt, Inc.**

---

1. **Dardan Gates:** gates of Troy. Dardania, a city built near the foot of Mount Ida, became part of Troy.

The Death of Hector   **31**

PRACTICE AND REVIEW
The Death of Hector

Reading Skills: Visualizing Imagery   Look back over the passages you underlined or highlighted in "The Death of Hector" that help you visualize the characters and events. Look especially for the words and phrases you marked within the **epic similes** listed in the first column of the chart below. Complete the second column by writing at least four vivid words or phrases that helped you create a mental picture of the images. Most of those words or phrases will appeal to the sense of sight, but some of them might also appeal to another sense, such as hearing or touch.

Epic Simile	Vivid Words and Phrases
Comparison of Achilles with a hunting dog, and Hector with a fawn (lines 1–6)	
Comparison of Hector with an attacking eagle (lines 142–144)	
Comparison of Hector's soul with a winged being (lines 203–206)	

Interactive Selections from *Holt Literature and Language Arts*

The literary and informational selections in Part One also appear in *Holt Literature and Language Arts,* Sixth Course. The selections are reprinted in a single column and in larger type to give you the room you need to mark up the text.

Headnote

This feature gives you background information about the selection and, in some cases, about the author. For selections that are excerpts of much longer works, the headnote will lead you into the story, explaining what has happened so far.

Side-column Notes

Each selection is accompanied by notes in the side columns. The notes help you—
- interpret, analyze, and evaluate the text
- understand literary elements
- build vocabulary
- develop word knowledge
- build fluency
- master the California grade-level and review standards

Footnotes

Difficult or unusual terms are defined in footnotes.

Practice and Review

After each selection, a **graphic organizer** gives you a visual way to organize, interpret, and understand the reading skill and literary focus of the selection.

The Death of Hector

VOCABULARY
DEVELOPMENT

VOCABULARY IN CONTEXT

DIRECTIONS: Write words from the Word Box in the blanks to complete the paragraph below. Use each word only once.

Word Box
fawning
gallant
groveling
scourge

The war between Greece and Troy was a (1) _____ that cost the lives of many young soldiers. These soldiers were often (2) _____, noted for their bravery and courtesy. Such heroes would not be found (3) _____ in the dust, begging an authority figure for a favor. Nor were they likely to be found (4) _____ over anyone else, using flattery or sweet, begging words to get their way.

CONNOTATIONS

A word's **denotation** is its dictionary definition. Some words also have **connotations,** the attitudes or emotional overtones that a word suggests. For example, *assertive* and *bossy* have similar denotations. *Bossy,* however, implies meanness, while *assertive* suggests a person who calmly gets what he or she wants.

DIRECTIONS: The chart below lists sentences about "The Death of Hector." In the second column, write down the ideas or images you associate with each boldface word. Then, decide whether the word carries positive (**Pos.**) or negative (**Neg.**) connotations, and check the appropriate column.

Sentence About the Story	Word Associations	Pos.	Neg.
Apollo couldn't save Hector even by **groveling** at Zeus' feet.			
Hector made a **gallant** suggestion for honoring the loser's body.			
Achilles called Hector's behavior cowardly and **fawning.**			

Reading Standard 1.2 (Grade 9–10 Review) Distinguish between the denotative and connotative meanings of words and interpret the connotative power of words.

☑ Check your Standards Mastery at the back of this book.

The Death of Hector   **43**

Checklist for Standards Mastery

Each time you read, you learn something new. Track your growth as a reader and your progress toward success by checking off skills you have acquired. If you read all the selections in this book and complete the sidenote questions and activities, you will be able to check off, at least once, all the standards for success listed below.

☑	California Reading Standard (Grade 9–10 Review)	Selection
☐	**1.1** Identify and use the literal and figurative meanings of words and understand word derivations.	
☐	**1.2** Distinguish between the denotative and connotative meanings of words and interpret the connotative power of words.	
☐	**2.1** Analyze the structure and format of functional workplace documents, including the graphics and headers, and explain how authors use the features to achieve their purposes.	
☐	**2.3** Generate relevant questions about readings on issues that can be researched.	
☐	**2.5** Extend ideas presented in primary or secondary sources through original analysis, evaluation, and elaboration.	
☐	**2.6** Demonstrate use of sophisticated learning tools by following technical directions (e.g., those found with graphic calculators and specialized software programs and in access guides to World Wide Web sites on the Internet).	
☐	**2.7** Critique the logic of functional documents by examining the sequence of information and procedures in anticipation of possible reader misunderstandings.	

Vocabulary Development

After selections in which vocabulary words are taught in the side-column notes, you will find this page of vocabulary development activities. These activities reinforce your understanding of the words' meanings and provide you with instruction and practice on a vocabulary skill.

Checklist for Standards Mastery

Use this chart at the back of your book to track your progress as you acquire reading skills.

Part One

Literature and Informational Readings

Chapter 1

The Anglo-Saxons

(449–1066)

Songs of Ancient Heroes

Stonehenge, consisting of large sandstone blocks and smaller bluestone pillars.

The Anglo-Saxons (449–1066)

David Adams Leeming

The following essay provides highlights of the historical period.
For a more detailed version of this essay,
see *Holt Literature and Language Arts,* pages 6–17.

Reading Standard 3.7c
Evaluate the philosophical, political, religious, ethical, and social influences of the historical period that shaped the characters, plots, and settings.

The Spirit of the Celts

When Greek travelers visited what is now Great Britain in the fourth century B.C., they found an island inhabited by tall blond warriors who called themselves Celts. Among these island Celts was a group called the Britons who left their permanent stamp in one of the names (Britain) eventually adopted by the land they settled.

The Celts saw spirits everywhere—in rivers, trees, stones, ponds, fire, and thunder. These spirits or gods controlled all
10 aspects of existence, and they had to be constantly satisfied. Priests called Druids acted as go-betweens between the gods and the people.

The Celtic Heroes and Heroines: A Magical World

The mythology of the Celts has influenced British and Irish writers to this day. Sir Thomas Malory, in the fifteenth century, gathered together the Celtic legends about a warrior named Arthur. He mixed those stories to produce *Le Morte d'Arthur,* about the legendary King Arthur.
20 Early in the twentieth century, William Butler Yeats used the Celtic myths in his poetry and plays in an attempt to make the Irish aware of their lost heroic past.

> **IDENTIFY**
>
> Pause at line 7. Who were the Celts?

> **IDENTIFY**
>
> Pause at line 22. According to this essay, what did the writings of Sir Thomas Malory and William Butler Yeats have in common?

COMPARE & CONTRAST

Re-read lines 23–28. Circle details that describe Celtic stories. Underline the description of Anglo-Saxon stories.

WORD STUDY

Dominion (line 32) is a noun meaning "governed territory or country." It is related to the verb *dominate,* meaning "to rule or control." Look for a related adjective two paragraphs ahead. Circle it.

IDENTIFY

Re-read lines 30–36. What did the Romans accomplish in Britain? Circle that information.

IDENTIFY CAUSE & EFFECT

The paragraph beginning on line 40 explains a cause-and-effect relationship. Re-read the paragraph, and circle the cause. Underline the effect.

The Celtic stories are very different from the Anglo-Saxon tales that came later. Celtic stories, unlike the later, brooding Anglo-Saxon stories, leap into the sunlight (no matter how much blood is spilled). Full of fantastic animals, passionate love affairs, and fabulous adventures, the Celtic myths take you to enchanted lands where magic and the imagination rule.

The Romans: The Great Administrators

30 Beginning with an invasion led by Julius Caesar in 55 B.C., the Celts were finally conquered by the legions of Rome. Using the administrative genius that enabled them to achieve dominion over much of the known world, the Romans provided the armies and organization that prevented further serious invasions of Britain for several hundred years. They built a network of roads and a great defensive wall seventy-three miles long. During Roman rule, Christianity, which would later become a unifying force, gradually took hold under the leadership of European missionaries. The old Celtic religion began to vanish.

40 Early in the fifth century, the Romans, under attack by invaders on many fronts, were forced to evacuate their troops from Britain. They left roads, walls, villas, and great public baths, but no central government. The result was weakness, which made the island ripe for a series of successful invasions by non-Christian peoples from the Germanic regions of Continental Europe.

The Anglo-Saxons Sweep Ashore

In the middle of the fifth century, invaders from Germany, the Angles and the Saxons, and Jutes from Denmark, crossed
50 the North Sea to Britain. They drove out the old Britons before them and eventually settled the greater part of Britain. The language of the Anglo-Saxons became the dominant language in the land that was to become known as England, meaning "land of the Angles."

King Sweyn and his Danish troops arrive in England, from a manuscript (c. 14th century).
The British Library, London.

IDENTIFY

Pause at line 57. Who put up resistance when the Anglo-Saxons invaded Britain?

_____

_____

_____

_____

WORD STUDY

A *prow* (prou) is a forward part of a ship or boat. What would a "dragon-prowed" boat be (lines 68–69)?

_____

_____

_____

_____

_____

_____

_____

_____

_____

_____

_____

_____

_____

The newcomers did not have an easy time of it. The Celts put up a strong resistance before they retreated into Wales in the far west of the country. There, traces of their culture, especially their language, can still be found. One of the heroic Celtic leaders was a Welsh chieftain called Arthur, who devel-

60 oped in legend as Britain's "once and future king."

Unifying Forces: Alfred the Great and Christianity

For a long time after the invasions, Anglo-Saxon England was divided into a number of small kingdoms. It was not until King Alfred of Wessex, also known as Alfred the Great, led the Anglo-Saxons against the invading Danes that England became in any true sense a nation. The Danes were one of the fierce Viking peoples who crossed the cold North Sea in their dragon-prowed boats in the eighth and ninth centuries. Plundering and

70 destroying everything in their path, the Danes eventually took over and settled in parts of northeast and central England.

It is possible that even King Alfred would have failed to unify the Anglo-Saxons had it not been for the gradual reemergence

**IDENTIFY
CAUSE & EFFECT**

What effect did the acceptance of Christianity have on Britain (lines 72–83)?

_____

_____

_____

_____

_____

_____

IDENTIFY

Pause at line 83. What happened in 1066?

_____

_____

_____

INFER

Re-read lines 86–96. What were the heroic ideals of Anglo-Saxon Britain?

_____

_____

_____

WORD STUDY

Communal (kə·myōo′nəl), line 102, is an adjective meaning "shared by all." Look for a related word later in this paragraph. Circle it.

of Christianity in Britain. Irish and Continental missionaries converted the Anglo-Saxon kings, whose subjects converted also. Christianity linked England to Europe. Under Christianity and Alfred, Anglo-Saxons fought to protect their people, their culture, and their church from the ravages of the Danes. Alfred's reign began the shaky dominance of Wessex kings in southern

80 England. Alfred's descendents carried on his battle against the Danes. The battle continued until both the Anglo-Saxons and the Danes were defeated in 1066 by William, duke of Normandy, and his invading force of Normans from northwestern France.

Anglo-Saxon Life: The Warm Hall, the Cold World

The Anglo-Saxons were not barbarians, though they are frequently depicted that way. Their lives, however, were anything but luxurious. Warfare was the order of the day. As _Beowulf_ shows, law and order, at least in the early days, were the respon-

90 sibility of the leader in any given group, whether family, clan, tribe, or kingdom. Fame and success, even survival, were gained only through loyalty to the leader, especially during war, and success was measured in gifts from the leader. Beowulf, as you will see in the story that follows, makes his name and gains riches by defeating the monsters who try to destroy King Hrothgar.

This pattern of loyalty grew out of a need to protect the group from the terrors of an enemy-infested wilderness— a wilderness that became particularly frightening during the long, bone-chilling nights of winter. In most of England,

100 the Anglo-Saxons tended to live close to their animals in single-family homesteads, wooden buildings that surrounded a communal court or a warm, fire-lit chieftain's hall. This cluster of buildings was protected by a wooden stockade fence. The arrangement contributed to a sense of security and to the close relationship between leaders and followers. It also encouraged the Anglo-Saxon tendency toward community discussion and rule by consensus.

The Anglo-Saxon Religion: Gods for Warriors

Despite the influence of Christianity, the old Anglo-Saxon
religion with its warrior gods persisted. A dark, fatalistic
religion, it had been brought by the Anglo-Saxons from
Germany and had much in common with what we think of
as Norse or Scandinavian mythology.

One of the most important Norse gods was Odin, the god
of death, poetry, and magic. The Anglo-Saxon name for Odin
was Woden (from which we have *Wednesday*, "Woden's day").
Woden could help humans communicate with spirits, and he
was associated especially with burial rites and ecstatic trances,
important for both poetry and religious mysteries. The Anglo-
Saxon deity named Thunor was essentially the same as Thor,
the Norse god of thunder and lightning. His sign was the
hammer and possibly also the twisted cross we call the swastika,
which is found on so many Anglo-Saxon gravestones. (Thor's
name survives in *Thursday*, "Thor's day.")

On the whole, the religion of the Anglo-Saxons seems to
have been more concerned with ethics than with mysticism—
with the earthly virtues of bravery, loyalty, generosity, and
friendship.

The Bards: Singing of Gods and Heroes

The Anglo-Saxon communal hall, besides offering shelter and
a place for holding council meetings, provided space for
storytellers and their audience. As in other parts of the world,
skilled storytellers, or bards, sang of gods and heroes. The
Anglo-Saxons did not regard these bards as inferior to warriors.
To the Anglo-Saxons, creating poetry was as important as fighting, hunting, and farming.

110

120

130

IDENTIFY

Re-read lines 114–124. Who
were Woden and Thunor?

_____
_____
_____
_____
_____
_____
_____
_____

IDENTIFY

Pause at line 128. What
earthly virtues did the
religion of the Anglo-Saxons
value? Underline the passage
that tells you.

IDENTIFY

How did the Anglo-Saxons
regard bards and poetry?

_____
_____
_____
_____
_____
_____
_____

Hope in Immortal Verse

Anglo-Saxon literature contains many works that stress the fact that life is hard and ends only in death. For the non-Christian
140   Anglo-Saxons, whose religion offered them no hope of an after-life, only fame and its commemoration in poetry could provide a defense against death. Perhaps that is why the Anglo-Saxon bards, gifted with the skill to preserve fame in the people's memory, were such honored members of their society.

A Light from Ireland

Ireland had historical good luck in the fifth century. Isolated and surrounded by wild seas, it was not, like England and the rest of Europe, overrun by Germanic invaders. Then, in 432, the whole of Celtic Ireland was converted to Christianity by a Romanized
150   Briton named Patricius (Patrick). Patrick had been seized by Irish slave traders when he was a teenager and had been held in bondage by a sheepherder in Ireland for six years. He escaped captivity, became a bishop, and returned to convert his former captors. While Europe and England sank into constant warfare, confusion, and ignorance, Ireland experienced a Golden Age. The Irish monks founded monasteries that became sanctuaries of learning for refugee scholars from Europe and England. Thus it was in Ireland that Christianity, in the words of Winston Churchill, "burned and gleamed through the darkness."

160   ## The Christian Monasteries: The Ink Froze

In the death-shadowed world of the Anglo-Saxons, the poets or bards provided one element of hope: the possibility that heroic deeds might be preserved in people's memories. Another kind of hope was supplied by Christianity. The monasteries served as centers of learning in this period. In England the cultural and spiritual influence of the monasteries existed right alongside the older Anglo-Saxon religion. In fact, the monasteries preserved not only the Latin and Greek classics but also great works of the Anglo-Saxon bards, such as *Beowulf*.

170   Monks assigned to the monastery's scriptorium, or writing room, probably spent almost all their daylight hours copying manuscripts by hand. The scriptorium was in a covered walkway open to a court. Makeshift walls of oiled paper or glass helped somewhat, but the British Isles in winter are cold; the ink could freeze. Picture a shivering scribe, hunched over sheepskin "paper," pressing with a quill pen, obeying a rule of silence: That's how seriously the Church took learning.

The Rise of the English Language

Latin alone remained the language of serious study in England
180   until the time of King Alfred. During his reign, Alfred instituted the *Anglo-Saxon Chronicle,* a lengthy running history of England that covered the earliest days and continued until 1154. Partly because of King Alfred's efforts. English began to gain respect as a language of culture. Only then did the Old English stories and poetry preserved by the monks come to be recognized as great works of literature.

WORD STUDY

Within the word *scriptorium* (line 170) is a smaller word that hints at its meaning. Circle that clue. Lines 170–171 contain a context clue that actually tells you what a *scriptorium* is. Find and underline the context clue.

IDENTIFY

Pause at line 177. How did the monasteries of Ireland and England help preserve ancient learning?

_____

_____

_____

_____

_____

_____

_____

_____

_____

_____

_____

_____

IDENTIFY CAUSE & EFFECT

Re-read lines 178–186, in which you learn about the importance of the *Anglo-Saxon Chronicle.* Circle the two effects brought about by its publication.

The Battle with Grendel *translated by* Burton Raffel

REVIEW SKILLS

As you read *Beowulf,* look for ways in which the following literary device makes the story rich and memorable.

IMAGERY
Language that appeals to the senses.

LITERARY FOCUS: THE EPIC HERO

An **epic** is a long, involved story that tells of the great deeds of a larger-than-life hero. The central character in an epic—the **epic hero**—embodies the values and ideals of a particular society. Most epic heroes undertake a long, dangerous journey, or quest, to achieve something of great value to themselves or their people.

Beowulf is an **archetype,** or perfect example, of an epic hero. He possesses superhuman strength and reflects the highest ideals of his culture—the Anglo-Saxon culture of ancient England. The heroic archetype that Beowulf represents is that of the dragon slayer: In his quest, the hero must protect a community by defeating a gruesome monster that seeks to destroy it.

What Makes a Hero?   In the left-hand column of the chart below, create your own list of heroes. In the right-hand column, write at least one detail or characteristic that proves each hero is truly heroic.

My List of Heroes	Proof of Heroism

READING SKILLS: IDENTIFYING DETAILS

Beowulf demonstrates a number of characteristics that identify him as an **archetype** of the **epic hero.** These characteristics, listed below, are revealed in details about Beowulf himself or about events connected with the battle.

Characteristics of an Epic Hero

- Is significant and glorified
- Is on a quest
- Has superior or superhuman strength, intelligence, and/or courage
- Is ethical
- Risks death for glory or for the greater good of society
- Is a strong and responsible leader
- Performs brave deeds
- Reflects the ideals of a particular society

Use the Skill   As you read the selection, underline or highlight details that describe Beowulf as an epic hero. Refer to the list above for hints.

Reading Standard 3.6
Analyze the way in which authors through the centuries have used archetypes.

Reading Standard 3.7 (Grade 9–10 Review)
Recognize and understand the significance of various literary devices, including figurative language, imagery, allegory, and symbolism, and explain their appeal.

THE BATTLE WITH GRENDEL

from Beowulf

translated by Burton Raffel

At the beginning of the epic, we are introduced to King Hrothgar, ruler of the Danes. He has recently built the great hall Herot to commemorate his many victories. As Hrothgar's people enjoy life in Herot, however, a monster called Grendel lurks in the swamps nearby, seething with hatred for humans. Eventually Grendel attacks Herot and kills thirty of Hrothgar's men. This marks the beginning of Grendel's reign of terror over the Danes, which lasts for twelve years.

A great warrior named Beowulf hears of Hrothgar's troubles. Beowulf, who comes from the land of the Geats (Sweden), decides to journey to Denmark with some of his strongest men to do battle with Grendel. Beowulf meets King Hrothgar and announces that he will fight the monster that night without weapons. After a celebration feast, Beowulf and his men take the place of Hrothgar's followers and lie down to sleep in Herot. Beowulf is awake, however, and eager to meet his enemy. He is not kept waiting long.

1

Out from the marsh, from the foot of misty

Hills and bogs, bearing God's hatred,

Grendel came, hoping to kill

Anyone he could trap on this trip to high Herot.

5   He moved quickly through the cloudy night,

Up from his swampland, sliding silently

Toward that gold-shining hall. He had visited Hrothgar's

Home before, knew the way—

But never, before nor after that night,

10 Found Herot defended so firmly, his reception

So harsh. He journeyed, forever joyless,

Straight to the door, then snapped it open,

Tore its iron fasteners with a touch,

IDENTIFY

Circle the words in lines 1–7 that describe the **setting**. What two places are described?

Describes Herot, and swampland.

INTERPRET

Re-read lines 11–18, in which Grendel's entrance into Herot is vividly described. Circle the verbs and draw boxes around adjectives and adverbs. What effect does this **imagery** have on you? *(Grade 9–10 Review)*

It makes you think how mad he would be

And rushed angrily over the threshold.

15　He strode quickly across the inlaid

Floor, snarling and fierce: His eyes

Gleamed in the darkness, burned with a gruesome

Light. Then he stopped, seeing the hall

Crowded with sleeping warriors, stuffed

20　With rows of young soldiers resting together.

And his heart laughed, he relished the sight,

Intended to tear the life from those bodies

By morning; the monster's mind was hot

With the thought of food and the feasting his belly

Bronze plaque showing a warrior killing a monster.
Statens Historiska Museer, Stockholm.

25   Would soon know. But fate, that night, intended

Grendel to gnaw the broken bones

Of his last human supper. Human

Eyes were watching his evil steps,

Waiting to see his swift hard claws.

30   Grendel snatched at the first Geat

He came to, ripped him apart, cut

His body to bits with powerful jaws,

Drank the blood from his veins, and bolted

Him down, hands and feet; death

35   And Grendel's great teeth came together,

Snapping life shut. Then he stepped to another

Still body, clutched at Beowulf with his claws,

Grasped at a strong-hearted wakeful sleeper

—And was instantly seized himself, claws

40   Bent back as Beowulf leaned up on one arm.

       That shepherd of evil, guardian of crime,

Knew at once that nowhere on earth

Had he met a man whose hands were harder;

His mind was flooded with fear—but nothing

45   Could take his talons and himself from that tight

Hard grip. Grendel's one thought was to run

From Beowulf, flee back to his marsh and hide there:

This was a different Herot than the hall he had emptied.

But Higlac's follower° remembered his final

50   Boast and, standing erect, stopped

The monster's flight, fastened those claws

In his fists till they cracked, clutched Grendel

Closer. The infamous killer fought

For his freedom, wanting no flesh but retreat,

55   Desiring nothing but escape; his claws

Had been caught, he was trapped. That trip to Herot

Was a miserable journey for the writhing monster!

° **Higlac's follower:** Beowulf. Higlac is Beowulf's leader.

IDENTIFY CAUSE & EFFECT

Find the cause-and-effect relationship in the sentence in lines 25–27. Underline the effect, and circle the cause.

INTERPRET

Circle the verbs in lines 30–34. What do Grendel's actions suggest about his character and about the task facing Beowulf?

Beowolf is facing a savage beast.

ANALYZE

Underline details in lines 41–53 that indicate that Beowulf possesses super-human strength.

IDENTIFY

Pause at line 57. What does Grendel want to do? What is preventing him from doing so?

wants to escape but his claws are preventing

FLUENCY

Read the boxed passage aloud twice. Focus on conveying simple meaning the first time around. During your second reading, strive to bring the images to life by paying special attention to the descriptive words you have underlined.

WORD STUDY

Ancestral (an·ses′trəl), in line 85, is an adjective meaning "inherited from an ancestor or forebear." The word *ancestor* is made of the Latin prefix *ante-,* meaning "before," and *cedere,* meaning "to go."

The high hall rang, its roof boards swayed,
And Danes shook with terror. Down
60　The aisles the battle swept, angry
And wild. Herot trembled, wonderfully
Built to withstand the blows, the struggling
Great bodies beating at its beautiful walls;
Shaped and fastened with iron, inside
65　And out, artfully worked, the building
Stood firm. Its benches rattled, fell
To the floor, gold-covered boards grating
As Grendel and Beowulf battled across them.

Hrothgar's wise men had fashioned Herot
70　To stand forever; only fire,
They had planned, could shatter what such skill had put
Together, swallow in hot flames such splendor
Of ivory and iron and wood. Suddenly
The sounds changed, the Danes started
75　In new terror, cowering in their beds as the terrible
Screams of the Almighty's enemy sang
In the darkness, the horrible shrieks of pain
And defeat, the tears torn out of Grendel's
Taut throat, hell's captive caught in the arms
80　Of him who of all the men on earth
Was the strongest.

2

That mighty protector of men
Meant to hold the monster till its life
Leaped out, knowing the fiend was no use
To anyone in Denmark. All of Beowulf's
85　Band had jumped from their beds, ancestral
Swords raised and ready, determined
To protect their prince if they could. Their courage
Was great but all wasted: They could hack at Grendel
From every side, trying to open

90 A path for his evil soul, but their points

Could not hurt him, the sharpest and hardest iron

Could not scratch at his skin, for that sin-stained demon

Had bewitched all men's weapons, laid spells

That blunted every mortal man's blade.

95 And yet his time had come, his days

Were over, his death near; down

To hell he would go, swept groaning and helpless

To the waiting hands of still worse fiends.

Now he discovered—once the afflictor

100 Of men, tormentor of their days—what it meant

To feud with Almighty God: Grendel

Saw that his strength was deserting him, his claws

Bound fast, Higlac's brave follower tearing at

His hands. The monster's hatred rose higher,

105 But his power had gone. He twisted in pain,

And the bleeding sinews deep in his shoulder

Snapped, muscle and bone split

And broke. The battle was over, Beowulf

Had been granted new glory: Grendel escaped,

110 But wounded as he was could flee to his den,

His miserable hole at the bottom of the marsh,

Only to die, to wait for the end

Of all his days. And after that bloody

Combat the Danes laughed with delight.

115 He who had come to them from across the sea,

Bold and strong-minded, had driven affliction

Off, purged Herot clean. He was happy,

Now, with that night's fierce work; the Danes

Had been served as he'd boasted he'd serve them; Beowulf,

120 A prince of the Geats, had killed Grendel,

Ended the grief, the sorrow, the suffering

Forced on Hrothgar's helpless people

By a bloodthirsty fiend. No Dane doubted

The victory, for the proof, hanging high

IDENTIFY

Pause at line 94. Why can't Beowulf's men harm Grendel?

_____

_____

_____

_____

_____

WORD STUDY

Afflictor, in line 99, is a noun based on the Latin verb *afflictare,* meaning "to injure." With that knowledge and the word's context, tell what *afflictor* means. Also look for the related word *affliction,* in line 116.

_____

_____

_____

_____

_____

IDENTIFY

Pause at line 117. Who wins the battle? Where does Grendel go after the battle?

• Beowolf wins.

• Bottom of Mash

_____

_____

_____

Beowulf hangs Grendel's torn-off shoulder and arm high in the rafters of Herot. Why do you think he does this?

They say they won the Battle

Pause at line 136. How do the Danes feel about Grendel's defeat? What does their reaction reveal about their sense of right and wrong?

125   From the rafters where Beowulf had hung it, was the monster's
        Arm, claw and shoulder and all.

(Left) the Germanic hero Weland at his forge and (right) the adoration of the Magi (8th century), from the Franks Casket. Whalebone.
British Museum © Michael Holford.

3

        And then, in the morning, crowds surrounded
        Herot, warriors coming to that hall
        From faraway lands, princes and leaders
130   Of men hurrying to behold the monster's
        Great staggering tracks. They gaped with no sense
        Of sorrow, felt no regret for his suffering,
        Went tracing his bloody footprints, his beaten
        And lonely flight, to the edge of the lake
135   Where he'd dragged his corpselike way, doomed
        And already weary of his vanishing life.
        The water was bloody, steaming and boiling
        In horrible pounding waves, heat
        Sucked from his magic veins; but the swirling
140   Surf had covered his death, hidden

Deep in murky darkness his miserable

End, as hell opened to receive him.

    Then old and young rejoiced, turned back

From that happy pilgrimage, mounted their hard-hooved

145   Horses, high-spirited stallions, and rode them

Slowly toward Herot again, retelling

Beowulf's bravery as they jogged along.

And over and over they swore that nowhere

On earth or under the spreading sky

150   Or between the seas, neither south nor north,

Was there a warrior worthier to rule over men.

(But no one meant Beowulf's praise to belittle

Hrothgar, their kind and gracious king!) . . .

ANALYZE

Re-read lines 137–142. Circle the **imagery** describing the lake Grendel vanished into. How does this imagery help convey the Anglo-Saxons' idea of hell? *(Grade 9–10 Review)*

_____

_____

_____

_____

_____

_____

_____

_____

_____

_____

_____

_____

_____

_____

_____

_____

_____

_____

_____

The Battle with Grendel

Reading Skills: Identifying Details   Review the details you highlighted or underlined in "The Battle with Grendel" that show Beowulf is an **epic hero.** Then, complete this chart with details that illustrate each of the characteristics of an epic hero.

Characteristics of an Epic Hero	Details from "The Battle with Grendel"
1. Is significant and glorified	
2. Is on a quest	
3. Has superior or superhuman strength, intelligence, and/or courage	
4. Is ethical	
5. Risks death for glory or for the greater good of society	
6. Is a strong and responsible leader	
7. Performs brave deeds	
8. Reflects the ideals of a particular society	

 Check your Standards Mastery at the back of this book.

from **Gilgamesh** *retold by* Herbert Mason

LITERARY FOCUS: THE FOIL

What would a hero do without ordinary people to admire his or her extraordinary accomplishments? In literature the hero is often paired with a **foil**—a character of ordinary abilities that contrast with the hero's abilities.

Like Beowulf (page 10), Gilgamesh is an **epic hero.** Gilgamesh is on a quest with his friend Enkidu to battle the monster Humbaba. Despite their close friendship, however, Gilgamesh and Enkidu have different character traits. The character of Enkidu acts as a foil, or opposite, to the character of Gilgamesh. Enkidu's presence helps us recognize the unique characteristics of the hero Gilgamesh and relate to his strengths and weaknesses.

Foiled Again! Think about some popular heroes and their foils, or sidekicks. One pairing might be the "Dynamic Duo," Batman and Robin. Another example from literature and film is the famous detective Sherlock Holmes and his trusted colleague, Dr. Watson. In the chart below, list at least two examples of a hero and his or her foil. In the last column, provide details that show how the hero and the foil differ from each other.

Hero	Foil	How Do They Differ?

READING SKILLS: COMPARING AND CONTRASTING

In this excerpt from *Gilgamesh,* Enkidu and Gilgamesh reveal their differences at several points in their journey. We see the contrast between them in their opinions about whether to fight the monster Humbaba, in their differing states of mind when they reach Humbaba's forest, in their attitudes during the battle, and even in the way the two friends relate to each other.

Use the Skill As you read the selection, highlight or underline details that reveal differences between Enkidu and Gilgamesh. Use a different color for each character.

REVIEW SKILLS

Look for examples of the following literary devices as you read *Gilgamesh.*

FIGURATIVE LANGUAGE
Words or phrases that describe one thing in terms of another and that are not meant to be taken literally.

IMAGERY
Language that appeals to the senses.

Reading Standard 3.1
Analyze characteristics of subgenres that are used in poetry, prose, plays, novels, short stories, essays, and other basic genres.

Reading Standard 3.7 (Grade 9–10 Review)
Recognize and understand the significance of various literary devices, including figurative language, imagery, allegory, and symbolism, and explain their appeal.

from Gilgamesh
A Verse Narrative

retold by Herbert Mason

> At the beginning of the epic, we meet Gilgamesh, the king of Uruk. Part god and part human, Gilgamesh is a mighty warrior who performs glorious deeds. He is also strong-willed and treats his people harshly. In response to the prayers of the people, the gods send an uncivilized wild man named Enkidu as a match for Gilgamesh. The two become close friends. In hopes of gaining fame and glory, the friends embark on a quest to a cedar forest guarded by the evil giant Humbaba. There they intend to battle the monster and destroy the forest.
>
> As this part of the story opens, Enkidu is terrified of meeting the monster. Gilgamesh urges him on.

ANALYZE

Pause at line 10. How does Gilgamesh feel about death?

_____

_____

_____

_____

COMPARE & CONTRAST

Pause at line 16. Based on these words of Gilgamesh, in what ways do he and Enkidu differ?

_____

_____

_____

_____

_____

Why are you worried about death?
Only the gods are immortal anyway,
Sighed Gilgamesh.
What men do is nothing, so fear is never
5 Justified. What happened to your power
That once could challenge and equal mine?
I will go ahead of you, and if I die
I will at least have the reward
Of having people say: He died in war
10 Against Humbaba. You cannot discourage me
With fears and hesitations.
I will fight Humbaba,
I will cut down his cedars.
Tell the armorers to build us two-edged swords
15 And double shields and tell them
I am impatient and cannot wait long.

Thus Gilgamesh and Enkidu went
Together to the marketplace

To notify the Elders of Uruk

20   Who were meeting in their senate.
     They too were talking of Humbaba,
     As they often did,
     Edging always in their thoughts
     Toward the forbidden.

25   The one you speak of, Gilgamesh addressed them,
     I now must meet. I want to prove
     Him not the awesome thing we think he is
     And that the boundaries set up by gods
     Are not unbreakable. I will defeat him

30   In his cedar forest. The youth of Uruk
     Need this fight. They have grown soft
     And restless.

                The old men leaned a little forward
     Remembering old wars. A flush burned on

35   Their cheeks. It seemed a little dangerous
     And yet they saw their king
     Was seized with passion for this fight.
     Their voices gave the confidence his friend
     Had failed to give; some even said

40   Enkidu's wisdom was a sign of cowardice.
     You see, my friend, laughed Gilgamesh,
     The wise of Uruk have outnumbered you.

     Amidst the speeches in the hall
     That called upon the gods for their protection,

45   Gilgamesh saw in his friend that pain
     He had seen before and asked him what it was
     That troubled him.

     Enkidu could not speak. He held his tears
     Back. Barely audibly he said:

50   It is a road which you have never traveled.

IDENTIFY

Re-read lines 25–32. Under-line three reasons Gilgamesh gives the elders for wanting to fight Humbaba.

IDENTIFY CAUSE & EFFECT

Pause at line 42. Why do the elders support Gilgamesh's wish to battle Humbaba?

_____

_____

_____

_____

_____

_____

_____

_____

_____

_____

_____

_____

_____

_____

_____

_____

VOCABULARY

austere (ô·stir′) *adj.:*
restrained; unemotional.

PREDICT

Circle the words of the
people that **foreshadow** the
coming battle (lines 55–59).
Based on their words, what
do you predict will happen?

_____

_____

_____

_____

_____

**COMPARE &
CONTRAST**

Pause at line 65. Although
Gilgamesh had earlier boasted about his intention of
destroying Humbaba, when
he reaches the forest's edge
he is suddenly afraid. How is
his sudden change of heart
different from Enkidu's feelings at this point?

_____

_____

_____

_____

_____

_____

_____

_____

The armorers brought to Gilgamesh his weapons

And put them in his hand. He took his quiver,

Bow and ax, and two-edged sword,

And they began to march.

55   The Elders gave their **austere** blessing

And the people shouted: Let Enkidu lead,

Don't trust your strength, he knows the forests,

The one who goes ahead will save his friend.

May Shamash[1] bring you victory.

✻ ✻ ✻ ✻ ✻ ✻ ✻

60   After three days they reached the edge

Of the forest where Humbaba's watchman stood.

Suddenly it was Gilgamesh who was afraid,

Enkidu who reminded him to be fearless.

The watchman sounded his warning to Humbaba.

65   The two friends moved slowly toward the forest gate.

When Enkidu touched the gate his hand felt numb,

He could not move his fingers or his wrist,

His face turned pale like someone's witnessing

                             a death,

He tried to ask his friend for help

70   Whom he had just encouraged to move on,

But he could only stutter and hold out

His paralyzed hand.

It will pass, said Gilgamesh.

Would you want to stay behind because of that?

75   We must go down into the forest together.

Forget your fear of death. I will go before you

And protect you. Enkidu followed close behind

So filled with fear he could not think or speak.

Soon they reached the high cedars.

---

1. **Shamash** (shä′mäsh): god associated with the sun and human laws.

80 They stood in awe at the foot

Of the green mountain. Pleasure

Seemed to grow from fear of Gilgamesh.

As when one comes upon a path in woods

Unvisited by men, one is drawn near

85 The lost and undiscovered in himself;

He was revitalized by danger.

They knew it was the path Humbaba made.

Some called the forest "Hell," and others "Paradise";

What difference does it make? said Gilgamesh.

90 But night was falling quickly

And they had no time to call it names,

Except perhaps "The Dark,"

Before they found a place at the edge of the forest

To serve as shelter for their sleep.

95 It was a restless night for both. One snatched

At sleep and sprang awake from dreams. The other

Could not rest because of pain that spread

Throughout his side. Enkidu was alone

With sights he saw brought on by pain

100 And fear, as one in deep despair

May lie beside his love who sleeps

And seems so unafraid, absorbing in himself the phantoms

That she cannot see—phantoms diminished for one

When two can see and stay awake to talk of them

105 And search out a solution to despair,

Or lie together in each other's arms,

Or weep and in exhaustion from their tears

Perhaps find laughter for their fears.

But alone and awake the size and nature

110 Of the creatures in his mind grow monstrous,

Beyond resemblance to the creatures he had known

Before the prostitute had come into his life.

FLUENCY

Read the boxed passage aloud twice. Use punctuation clues to guide your reading.

INTERPRET

Pause at line 86. Enkidu is filled with fear as he and Gilgamesh enter the forest. How does Gilgamesh react?

_____

_____

_____

_____

_____

COMPARE & CONTRAST

Re-read lines 95–98. How does Gilgamesh spend the night? How does Enkidu spend the night?

_____

_____

_____

_____

_____

_____

_____

_____

_____

Babylonian sculpture of head of Humbaba carved to resemble intestines (c. 1800–1600 B.C.).
British Museum, London. The Bridgeman Art Library.

INTERPRET

Re-read lines 115–123, and circle the words and phrases that describe Enkidu's feelings of paralysis. What might Enkidu's experience **symbolize**?

_____

_____

_____

_____

_____

_____

He cried aloud for them to stop appearing over him

Emerging from behind the trees with phosphorescent[2] eyes

115　Brought on by rain. He could not hear his voice

But knew he screamed and could not move his arms

But thought they tried to move

As if a heavy weight he could raise

Or wriggle out from underneath

120　Had settled on his chest,

Like a turtle trapped beneath a fallen branch,

Each effort only added to paralysis.

He could not make his friend, his one companion, hear.

---

2. **phosphorescent** (fäs′fə·res′ənt) *adj.:* giving off light after being exposed to heat.

Gilgamesh awoke but could not hear

125 His friend in agony, he still was captive to his dreams

Which he would tell aloud to exorcise:

I saw us standing in a mountain gorge,

A rockslide fell on us, we seemed no more

Than insects under it. And then

130 A solitary graceful man appeared

And pulled me out from under the mountain.

He gave me water and I felt released.

Tomorrow you will be victorious,

Enkidu said, to whom the dream brought chills

135 (For only one of them, he knew, would be released)

Which Gilgamesh could not perceive in the darkness

For he went back to sleep without responding

To his friend's interpretation of his dream.

Did you call me? Gilgamesh sat up again.

140 Why did I wake again? I thought you touched me.

Why am I afraid? I felt my limbs grow numb

As if some god passed over us drawing out our life.

I had another dream:

This time the heavens were alive with fire, but soon

145 The clouds began to thicken, death rained down on us,

The lightning flashes stopped, and everything

Which rained down turned to ashes.

What does this mean, Enkidu?

That you will be victorious against Humbaba,

150 Enkidu said, or someone said through him

Because he could not hear his voice

Or move his limbs although he thought he spoke,

And soon he saw his friend asleep beside him.

At dawn Gilgamesh raised his ax

155 And struck at the great cedar.

WORD STUDY

The verb *exorcise* in line 126 means "drive out or away evil spirits or thoughts."

CLARIFY

Re-read lines 133–138. Underline Enkidu's interpretation of Gilgamesh's dream. Why does the dream terrify Enkidu?

_____

_____

_____

_____

_____

_____

_____

IDENTIFY

Gilgamesh has a second dream (lines 143–153). Circle the **images** he describes. How does Enkidu interpret this dream? *(Grade 9–10 Review)*

_____

_____

_____

_____

_____

_____

_____

VOCABULARY

decreed (dē·krēd′) *v.*: ordered; commanded.

contortion (kən·tôr′shən) *n.*: twisted shape or motion.

INTERPRET

Re-read lines 161–171. Circle the two **figures of speech** that are used to describe Humbaba. What do these figures of speech tell you about him? *(Grade 9–10 Review)*

_____

_____

_____

INTERPRET

Find the **metaphor** in lines 170–171 that describes Humbaba. What effect does this metaphor have on you, the reader?

_____

_____

_____

_____

INTERPRET

Pause at line 183. What is happening here? What is ironic about Gilgamesh's situation?

_____

_____

_____

When Humbaba heard the sound of falling trees,

He hurried down the path that they had seen

But only he had traveled. Gilgamesh felt weak

At the sound of Humbaba's footsteps and called to Shamash

160   Saying, I have followed you in the way **decreed;**

Why am I abandoned now? Suddenly the winds

Sprang up. They saw the great head of Humbaba

Like a water buffalo's bellowing down the path,

His huge and clumsy legs, his flailing arms

165   Thrashing at phantoms in his precious trees.

His single stroke could cut a cedar down

And leave no mark on him. His shoulders,

Like a porter's[3] under building stones,

Were permanently bent by what he bore;

170   He was the slave who did the work for gods

But whom the gods would never notice.

Monstrous in his **contortion,** he aroused

The two almost to pity.

But pity was the thing that might have killed.

175   It made them pause just long enough to show

How pitiless he was to them. Gilgamesh in horror saw

Him strike the back of Enkidu and beat him to the ground

Until he thought his friend was crushed to death.

He stood still watching as the monster leaned to make

180   His final strike against his friend, unable

To move to help him, and then Enkidu slid

Along the ground like a ram making its final lunge

On wounded knees. Humbaba fell and seemed

To crack the ground itself in two, and Gilgamesh,

185   As if this fall had snapped him from his daze,

Returned to life

And stood over Humbaba with his ax

Raised high above his head watching the monster plead

---

3. **porter** *n.*: person who carries things for other people.

In strangled sobs and desperate appeals

190   The way the sea contorts under a violent **squall.**

I'll serve you as I served the gods, Humbaba said;

I'll build you houses from their sacred trees.

Enkidu feared his friend was weakening

And called out: Gilgamesh! Don't trust him!

195   As if there were some hunger in himself

That Gilgamesh was feeling

That turned him momentarily to yearn

For someone who would serve, he paused;

And then he raised his ax up higher

200   And swung it in a perfect arc

Into Humbaba's neck. He reached out

To touch the wounded shoulder of his friend,

And late that night he reached again

To see if he was yet asleep, but there was only

205   Quiet breathing. The stars against the midnight sky

Were sparkling like mica[4] in a riverbed.

In the slight breeze

The head of Humbaba was swinging from a tree.

VOCABULARY

squall (skwôl) *n.:* violent storm that doesn't last very long.

INTERPRET

Why does Gilgamesh hesitate before killing Humbaba (line 198)? Why does he decide to kill Humbaba despite his second thoughts?

_____

_____

_____

_____

_____

_____

_____

_____

_____

_____

_____

_____

_____

_____

_____

_____

_____

_____

_____

_____

---

4.   **mica** *n.:* kind of thin, crystalline mineral.

from Gilgamesh

Reading Skills: Comparing and Contrasting   Look back over the details that you highlighted or underlined that show the differences between Enkidu and Gilgamesh. Then, read the points of comparison listed in the first column below. Complete the chart by describing how Gilgamesh and Enkidu differ.

Points of Comparison	Gilgamesh/Hero	Enkidu/Foil
Attitude about fighting Humbaba		
Attitude upon arriving at the edge of Humbaba's forest		
Responsiveness to his friend's feelings and opinions		
Courage and determination during the battle		

Evaluate   Review the details you recorded in the chart above. What **character traits** of Gilgamesh might not have been as obvious if Enkidu had not been part of the story?

_____

_____

_____

_____

_____

from **Gilgamesh**

VOCABULARY DEVELOPMENT

VOCABULARY IN CONTEXT

DIRECTIONS: Write a vocabulary word from the Word Box in each blank to complete the paragraph below. Use each word only once.

Word Box

austere

squall

decreed

contortion

The sound of heavy rain and gusting wind was evidence of the fury of the (1) _____. Taking shelter in a cave, the two weary warriors watched as the light from the fire created a strange (2) _____ of twisted shapes on the rock walls. So far, they had failed in their mission to find and destroy a terrible monster that lived in the forest. Betraying no emotion at all, their faces remained (3) _____ as they tried to figure out what to do next. Finally, the older warrior (4) _____ that as soon as the storm ended they should get their weapons ready and continue their search.

ANALOGIES: RECOGNIZING SYNONYM AND ANTONYM PAIRS

In an **analogy,** the words in one pair relate to each other in the same way as the words in a second pair. Often, the words in each pair are **synonyms** (words having similar meanings) or **antonyms** (words having opposite meanings). In the analogy below, for example, the words in each pair are synonyms. Read each colon (:) as "is to" and the double colon (::) as "as." The sequence below therefore translates to "*furious* is to *enraged* as *worried* is to *anxious*."

FURIOUS : ENRAGED :: worried : anxious

DIRECTIONS: Study each incomplete analogy below to determine whether the word pairs are antonyms or synonyms. Then, fill each blank with the appropriate word from the Word Box above.

1. REFUSED : REJECTED :: _____ : ordered

2. CHEERFUL : DEPRESSED :: _____ : emotional

3. COURAGEOUS : BRAVE :: _____ : storm

4. RICHES : WEALTH :: _____ : deformity

Reading Standard 1.3 Discern the meaning of analogies encountered, analyzing specific comparisons as well as relationships and inferences.

 Check your Standards Mastery at the back of this book.

from Gilgamesh: A Verse Narrative   **29**

The Death of Hector by Homer

REVIEW SKILLS

As you read "The Death of Hector," look for examples of figurative language.

FIGURATIVE LANGUAGE
Words or phrases that describe one thing in terms of another and that are not meant to be taken literally. Figurative language includes all **figures of speech,** such as similes and metaphors.

Reading Standard 3.1
Analyze characteristics of subgenres that are used in poetry.

Reading Standard 3.4
Analyze ways in which poets use imagery, personification, figures of speech, and sounds to evoke readers' emotions.

Reading Standard 3.11 (Grade 9–10 Review)
Evaluate the aesthetic qualities of style, including the impact of diction and figurative language on tone, mood, and theme, using the terminology of literary criticism.

LITERARY FOCUS: THE EPIC AND THE EPIC SIMILE

The *Iliad* is an **epic,** a long story that tells of the great adventures of larger-than-life heroes who embody in some way the values of their civilization. The *Iliad* tells the story of the Trojan War, a great conflict between the Greeks and the Trojans that began about 1200 B.C. Two main characters are at the center of the story: Achilles, the bravest and handsomest warrior in the Greek army, and his enemy Hector, the honorable warrior-prince of the Trojans. In the selection that follows, the conflict between the two enemies reaches its tragic climax.

One of the most important features of the *Iliad* is Homer's use of **epic similes** (also known as **Homeric similes**). Homer's comparisons often extend over many lines and use the words *like* or *as.* These long **figures of speech** usually compare heroic actions to simple, everyday events that listeners who heard the *Iliad* recited out loud could easily understand.

Here is how Homer describes Achilles as he charges the city of Troy on foot: "he dashed toward the city, / . . . rushing on / like a champion stallion drawing a chariot full tilt, / sweeping across the plain in easy, tearing strides— / so Achilles hurtled on, driving legs and knees." Because Homer's audience was familiar with chariot races, this comparison of Achilles with a race horse helped them picture Achilles' great strength and speed.

READING SKILLS: VISUALIZING IMAGERY

Imagery is language that appeals to the senses. When you visualize imagery, you create mental images of what's being described—characters, settings, or events. Below are some image-filled phrases from "The Death of Hector." Read each phrase, and visualize its imagery.
- "raining spears"
- "his dark hair swirling round / that head"
- "tall Hector, helmet flashing"
- "his spear's long shadow flew"

Use the Skill   As you read the story, underline or highlight words that help you visualize a character, a situation, or an event. Watch especially for details that are used in **epic similes.**

The Death of Hector
from the Iliad

Homer *translated by* Robert Fagles

> The *Iliad* begins when the war between the Greeks and the Trojans has
> already lasted for nearly ten years. Each army fights bravely and receives help
> from the gods. The god Apollo assists Hector and the Trojans. Apollo is the
> god of the sun and is also called Phoebus. The goddess Athena aids Achilles
> and the Greeks, who are also called the Achaeans or the Argives. Earlier in the
> story, Hector kills Achilles' best friend, a soldier named Patroclus. Hector strips
> Patroclus of his armor and leaves his body exposed and unburied. Achilles is
> enraged and seeks revenge, because the Greeks believed that a soul could not
> find rest until the body was buried with the proper rituals. In this section of
> Book 22, the exhausted Trojans have taken refuge behind the walls of their
> city, but their hero, Hector, remains outside the gates. Achilles orders his men
> to hold back so that he can fight Hector by himself.

    And swift Achilles kept on coursing Hector, nonstop
as a hound in the mountains starts a fawn from its lair,
hunting him down the gorges, down the narrow glens
and the fawn goes to ground, hiding deep in brush
5 but the hound comes racing fast, nosing him out
until he lands his kill. So Hector could never throw
Achilles off his trail, the swift racer Achilles—
time and again he'd make a dash for the Dardan Gates,[1]
trying to rush beneath the rock-built ramparts, hoping
10 men on the heights might save him, somehow, raining spears
but time and again Achilles would intercept him quickly,
heading him off, forcing him out across the plain
and always sprinting along the city side himself—
endless as in a dream . . .

---

1. Dardan Gates: gates of Troy. Dardania, a city built near the foot of
Mount Ida, became part of Troy.

INTERPRET

Lines 1–6 contain an **epic simile.** Achilles is said to be "coursing" (tracking) Hector, just as a hound hunts down a fawn. If Achilles is like the hound, then who is like the fawn? *(Grade 9–10 Review)*

_____

_____

IDENTIFY CAUSE & EFFECT

Find the cause-and-effect relationship in lines 6–14. Underline the effect, and circle the cause.

Re-read lines 18–21. What god gives Hector the strength to stay ahead of Achilles?

_____

_____

_____

_____

_____

_____

_____

_____

_____

_____

_____

_____

Zeus uses his scales of judgment to decide the fates of Achilles and Hector (lines 25–31). Circle the name of the man who is doomed to die.

groveling (grăv′əl·iŋ) v. used as adj.: crawling; humiliating oneself in front of authority.

Athena is saying that Apollo, or Phoebus, can't help Hector, even by groveling at the feet of Zeus.

15 when a man can't catch another fleeing on ahead

and he can never escape nor his rival overtake him—

so the one could never run the other down in his speed

nor the other spring away. And how could Hector have fled

the fates of death so long? How unless one last time,

20 one final time Apollo had swept in close beside him,

driving strength in his legs and knees to race the wind?

And brilliant Achilles shook his head at the armies,

never letting them hurl their sharp spears at Hector—

someone might snatch the glory, Achilles come in second.

25 But once they reached the springs for the fourth time,

then Father Zeus held out his sacred golden scales:

in them he placed two fates of death that lays men low—

one for Achilles, one for Hector breaker of horses—

and gripping the beam mid-haft the Father raised it high

30 and down went Hector's day of doom, dragging him down

to the strong House of Death—and god Apollo left him.

Athena rushed to Achilles, her bright eyes gleaming,

standing shoulder-to-shoulder, winging orders now:

"At last our hopes run high, my brilliant Achilles—

35 Father Zeus must love you—

we'll sweep great glory back to Achaea's fleet,

we'll kill this Hector, mad as he is for battle!

No way for him to escape us now, no longer—

not even if Phoebus the distant deadly Archer

40 goes through torments, pleading for Hector's life,

groveling over and over before our storming Father Zeus.

But you, you hold your ground and catch your breath

while I run Hector down and persuade the man

to fight you face-to-face."

So Athena commanded

45 and he obeyed, rejoicing at heart—Achilles stopped,

leaning against his ashen spearshaft barbed in bronze.

And Athena left him there, caught up with Hector at once,

and taking the build and vibrant voice of Deiphobus[2]
stood shoulder-to-shoulder with him, winging orders:

50 "Dear brother, how brutally swift Achilles hunts you—
coursing you round the city of Priam in all his lethal speed!
Come, let us stand our ground together—beat him back."

"Deiphobus!"—Hector, his helmet flashing, called out to her—
"dearest of all my brothers, all these warring years,
55 of all the sons that Priam and Hecuba produced!
Now I'm determined to praise you all the more,
you who dared—seeing me in these straits—
to venture out from the walls, all for *my* sake,
while the others stay inside and cling to safety."

60 The goddess answered quickly, her eyes blazing,
"True, dear brother—how your father and mother both
implored me, time and again, clutching my knees,
and the comrades round me begging me to stay!
Such was the fear that broke them, man for man,
65 but the heart within me broke with grief for you.
Now headlong on and fight! No letup, no lance spared!
So now, now we'll *see* if Achilles kills us both
and hauls our bloody armor back to the beaked ships
or *he* goes down in pain beneath your spear."

70 Athena luring him on with all her immortal cunning—
and now, at last, as the two came closing for the kill
it was tall Hector, helmet flashing, who led off:
"No more running from you in fear, Achilles!
Not as before. Three times I fled around
75 the great city of Priam—I lacked courage then
to stand your onslaught. Now my spirit stirs me
to meet you face-to-face. Now kill or be killed!

---

2. **Deiphobus** (dē·if′ō·bəs): one of Hector's brothers.

PREDICT

Pause at the end of line 52. Athena has just tricked Hector by posing as Hector's brother and offering to help Hector fight Achilles. Since you know that Athena is really on Achilles' side, what do you think she might be planning to do?

_____

_____

_____

_____

_____

INTERPRET

Re-read lines 60–69. Restate Athena's persuasive "pep talk" to Hector in your own words.

_____

_____

_____

_____

_____

_____

_____

_____

_____

IDENTIFY

Re-read lines 78–84. Underline the lines that spell out the terms of a pact, or agreement, that Hector proposes to Achilles.

IDENTIFY

Pause at line 89. Does Achilles agree to the pact? Circle the two comparisons Achilles uses to describe his relationship with Hector. *(Grade 9–10 Review)*

_____

_____

_____

_____

_____

_____

WORD STUDY

Some words in lines 90–92 appear in unusual order. Normal word order for "gluts with blood Ares" would be "gluts Ares with blood." Since Ares is the god of war, and the battle is likely to be very bloody, what must be meant by the word *gluts*?

_____

_____

_____

_____

_____

_____

Come, we'll swear to the gods, the highest witnesses—
the gods will oversee our binding pacts. I swear

80 I will never mutilate you—merciless as you are—
if Zeus allows me to last it out and tear your life away.
But once I've stripped your glorious armor, Achilles,
I will give your body back to your loyal comrades.
Swear you'll do the same."

                      A swift dark glance

85 and the headstrong runner answered, "Hector, stop!
You unforgivable, you . . . don't talk to me of pacts.
There are no binding oaths between men and lions—
wolves and lambs can enjoy no meeting of the minds—
they are all bent on hating each other to the death.

90 So with you and me. No love between us. No truce
till one or the other falls and gluts with blood
Ares who hacks at men behind his rawhide shield.
Come, call up whatever courage you can muster.
Life or death—now prove yourself a spearman,

95 a daring man of war! No more escape for you—

Hector and Menelaus fight over the body of Euphorbos (c. 600 B.C.).
The British Museum, London. The Bridgeman Art Library, New York.

Athena will kill you with my spear in just a moment.
Now you'll pay at a stroke for all my comrades' grief,
all you killed in the fury of your spear!"

                                With that,
shaft poised, he hurled and his spear's long shadow flew

100   but seeing it coming glorious Hector ducked away,
crouching down, watching the bronze tip fly past
and stab the earth—but Athena snatched it up
and passed it back to Achilles
and Hector the **gallant** captain never saw her.

105   He sounded out a challenge to Peleus' princely son:
"You missed, look—the great godlike Achilles!
So you knew nothing at all from Zeus about my death—
and yet how sure you were! All bluff, cunning with words,
that's all you are—trying to make me fear you,

110   lose my nerve, forget my fighting strength.
Well, you'll never plant your lance in my back
as I flee *you* in fear—plunge it through my chest
as I come charging in, if a god gives you the chance!
But now it's for you to dodge *my* brazen spear—

115   I wish you'd bury it in your body to the hilt.
How much lighter the war would be for Trojans then
if you, their greatest **scourge,** were dead and gone!"

      Shaft poised, he hurled and his spear's long shadow flew
and it struck Achilles' shield—a dead-center hit—

120   but off and away it glanced and Hector seethed,
his hurtling spear, his whole arm's power poured
in a wasted shot. He stood there, cast down . . .
he had no spear in reserve. So Hector shouted out
to Deiphobus bearing his white shield—with a ringing shout
he called for a heavy lance—

125   but the man was nowhere near
    him, vanished—
                  yes and Hector knew the truth in his heart

CLARIFY

Pause at line 132. What truths does Hector know "in his heart" when it seems that Deiphobus has vanished?

_____

_____

_____

_____

ANALYZE

The "distant deadly Archer" in line 134 is the sun god Apollo, son of Zeus. Why might Hector use this **figure of speech** to describe Apollo? *(Grade 9–10 Review)*

_____

_____

_____

_____

_____

_____

_____

IDENTIFY

Re-read lines 139–144. Underline the **epic simile** that describes Hector's attack. What creature is Hector compared with? Circle the words that most vividly show how that creature moves.

_____

_____

and the fighter cried aloud, "My time has come!
At last the gods have called me down to death.
I thought he was at my side, the hero Deiphobus—
130   he's safe inside the walls, Athena's tricked me blind.
And now death, grim death is looming up beside me,
no longer far away. No way to escape it now. This,
this was their pleasure after all, sealed long ago—
Zeus and the son of Zeus, the distant deadly Archer—
135   though often before now they rushed to my defense.
So now I meet my doom. Well let me die—
but not without struggle, not without glory, no,
in some great clash of arms that even men to come
will hear of down the years!"
                                        And on that resolve
140   he drew the whetted sword that hung at his side,
tempered, massive, and gathering all his force
he swooped like a soaring eagle
launching down from the dark clouds to earth
to snatch some helpless lamb or trembling hare.
145   So Hector swooped now, swinging his whetted sword
and Achilles charged too, bursting with rage, barbaric,
guarding his chest with the well-wrought blazoned shield,
head tossing his gleaming helmet, four horns strong
and the golden plumes shook that the god of fire
150   drove in bristling thick along its ridge.
Bright as that star amid the stars in the night sky,
star of the evening, brightest star that rides the heavens,
so fire flared from the sharp point of the spear Achilles
brandished high in his right hand, bent on Hector's death,
155   scanning his splendid body—where to pierce it best?
The rest of his flesh seemed all encased in armor,
burnished, brazen—*Achilles'* armor that Hector stripped
from strong Patroclus when he killed him—true,
but one spot lay exposed,

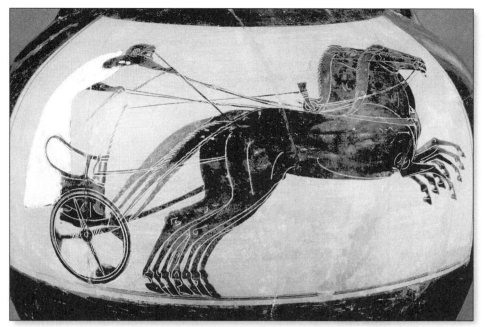

Chariot race depicted on black-figured amphora with white glaze (6th century B.C.).
Louvre, Paris. © Erich Lessing/Art Resource, New York.

INTERPRET

Pause for a moment to circle and then visualize the **imagery** in lines 145–155. What effect does this imagery have on your idea of Achilles?

_____

_____

_____

_____

_____

CLARIFY

Re-read lines 156–164. How is Achilles able to pierce Hector's armor and kill him?

_____

_____

_____

_____

_____

INTERPRET

Why does Achilles call Hector a "fool" (line 169)?

_____

_____

_____

_____

_____

_____

160   where collarbones lift the neckbone off the shoulders,
       the open throat, where the end of life comes quickest—*there*
       as Hector charged in fury brilliant Achilles drove his spear
       and the point went stabbing clean through the tender neck
       but the heavy bronze weapon failed to slash the windpipe—
165   Hector could still gasp out some words, some last reply . . .
       he crashed in the dust—
                              godlike Achilles gloried over him:
       "Hector—surely you thought when you stripped Patroclus'
          armor
       that you, you would be safe! Never a fear of me—
       far from fighting as I was—you fool!
170   Left behind there, down by the beaked ships
       his great avenger waited, a greater man by far—
       that man was I, and I smashed your strength! And you—
       the dogs and birds will maul you, shame your corpse
       while Achaeans bury my dear friend in glory!"

FLUENCY

Read the boxed speech aloud three times. With each reading, work to improve the way you express Hector's intense emotions.

VOCABULARY

fawning (fôn'in) *v.* used as *adj.:* cringing and pleading.

CLARIFY

How does Achilles respond to Hector's plea to be given to his countrymen for burial after his death (lines 185–194)?

175   Struggling for breath, Hector, his helmet flashing,

said, "I beg you, beg you by your life, your parents—

don't let the dogs devour me by the Argive ships!

Wait, take the princely ransom of bronze and gold,

the gifts my father and noble mother will give you—

180 but give my body to friends to carry home again,

so Trojan men and Trojan women can do me honor

with fitting rites of fire once I am dead."

   Staring grimly, the proud runner Achilles answered,

"Beg no more, you **fawning** dog—begging me by my parents!

185 Would to god my rage, my fury would drive me now

to hack your flesh away and eat you raw—

such agonies you have caused me! Ransom?

No man alive could keep the dog-packs off you,

not if they haul in ten, twenty times that ransom

190 and pile it here before me and promise fortunes more—

no, not even if Dardan Priam should offer to weigh out

your bulk in gold! Not even then will your noble mother

lay you on your deathbed, mourn the son she bore . . .

The dogs and birds will rend you—blood and bone!"

195   At the point of death, Hector, his helmet flashing,

said, "I know you well—I see my fate before me.

Never a chance that I could win you over . . .

Iron inside your chest, that heart of yours.

But now beware, or my curse will draw god's wrath

200 upon your head, that day when Paris and lord Apollo—

for all your fighting heart—destroy you at the Scaean Gates!"[3]

   Death cut him short. The end closed in around him.

Flying free of his limbs

his soul went winging down to the House of Death,

---

3. **Paris . . . Gates:** Hector is foretelling Achilles' ultimate fate. Achilles will later be slain by Paris, who will shoot an arrow into Achilles' heel, the only vulnerable part of his body.

205   wailing his fate, leaving his manhood far behind,

his young and supple strength. But brilliant Achilles

taunted Hector's body, dead as he was, "Die, die!

For my own death, I'll meet it freely—whenever Zeus

and the other deathless gods would like to bring it on!"

210   With that he wrenched his bronze spear from the corpse,

laid it aside and ripped the bloody armor off the back.

And the other sons of Achaea, running up around him,

crowded closer, all of them gazing wonder-struck

at the build and marvelous, lithe beauty of Hector.

215   And not a man came forward who did not stab his body,

glancing toward a comrade, laughing: "Ah, look here—

how much softer he is to handle now, this Hector,

than when he gutted our ships with roaring fire!"

        Standing over him, so they'd gloat and stab his body.

220   But once he had stripped the corpse the proud runner Achilles

took his stand in the midst of all the Argive troops

and urged them on with a flight of winging orders:

"Friends—lords of the Argives, O my captains!

Now that the gods have let me kill this man

225   who caused us agonies, loss on crushing loss—

more than the rest of all their men combined—

come, let us ring their walls in armor, test them,

see what recourse the Trojans still may have in mind.

Will they abandon the city heights with this man fallen?

230   Or brace for a last, dying stand though Hector's gone?

But wait—what am I saying? Why this deep debate?

Down by the ships a body lies unwept, unburied—

Patroclus . . . I will never forget him,

not as long as I'm still among the living

235   and my springing knees will lift and drive me on.

INTERPRET

Restate what Hector says in lines 196–201. (Paris, mentioned in line 200, is another Trojan warrior.)

_____

_____

_____

_____

_____

_____

_____

_____

_____

CLARIFY

Lines 210–218 tell how the other Achaean, or Greek, soldiers gather around Achilles and the body of his victim. Circle the information that explains what Achilles and the Greek soldiers did to Hector's body.

_____

_____

_____

_____

_____

_____

Though the dead forget their dead in the House of Death,
I will remember, even there, my dear companion.

Now,
come, you sons of Achaea, raise a song of triumph!
Down to the ships we march and bear this corpse on high—

The goddess Athena (c. 335 B.C.). Bronze statue.
National Archaeological Museum, Athens.
The Bridgeman Art Library.

240   we have won ourselves great glory. We have brought

magnificent Hector down, that man the Trojans

glorified in their city like a god!"

                           So he triumphed

and now he was bent on outrage, on shaming noble Hector.

Piercing the tendons, ankle to heel behind both feet,

245   he knotted straps of rawhide through them both,

lashed them to his chariot, left the head to drag

and mounting the car, hoisting the famous arms[4] aboard,

he whipped his team to a run and breakneck on they flew,

holding nothing back. And a thick cloud of dust rose up

250   from the man they dragged, his dark hair swirling round

that head so handsome once, all tumbled low in the dust—

since Zeus had given him over to his enemies now

to be defiled in the land of his own fathers.

IDENTIFY

In the middle of his victory speech (lines 223–242), Achilles pauses to remember someone. Who is the person, and why does Achilles think of him now?

_____

_____

_____

_____

_____

_____

_____

EVALUATE

Re-read lines 244–249, which describe the final cruelty that Achilles inflicts on the body of Hector. What effect does Achilles' final action have on your opinion of his character?

_____

_____

_____

_____

_____

_____

_____

_____

_____

---

4. **famous arms:** Hector's armor.

The Death of Hector

Reading Skills: Visualizing Imagery   Look back over the passages you underlined or highlighted in "The Death of Hector" that help you visualize the characters and events. Look especially for the words and phrases you marked within the **epic similes** listed in the first column of the chart below. Complete the second column by writing at least four vivid words or phrases that helped you create a mental picture of the images. Most of those words or phrases will appeal to the sense of sight, but some of them might also appeal to another sense, such as hearing or touch.

Epic Simile	Vivid Words and Phrases
Comparison of Achilles with a hunting dog, and Hector with a fawn (lines 1–6)	
Comparison of Hector with an attacking eagle (lines 142–144)	
Comparison of Hector's soul with a winged being (lines 203–206)	

The Death of Hector

VOCABULARY IN CONTEXT

DIRECTIONS: Write words from the Word Box in the blanks to complete the paragraph below. Use each word only once.

Word Box

- groveling
- gallant
- scourge
- fawning

The war between Greece and Troy was a (1) _____ that cost the lives of many young soldiers. These soldiers were often (2) _____, noted for their bravery and courtesy. Such heroes would not be found (3) _____ in the dust, begging an authority figure for a favor. Nor were they likely to be found (4) _____ over anyone else, using flattery or sweet, begging words to get their way.

CONNOTATIONS

A word's **denotation** is its dictionary definition. Some words also have **connotations,** the attitudes or emotional overtones that a word suggests. For example, *assertive* and *bossy* have similar denotations. *Bossy,* however, implies meanness and pushiness, while *assertive* suggests confidence and getting what one wants.

DIRECTIONS: The chart below lists sentences about "The Death of Hector." In the second column, write down the ideas or images you associate with each boldface word. Then, decide whether the word carries positive (**Pos.**) or negative (**Neg.**) connotations, and check the appropriate column.

Sentence About the Story	Word Associations	Pos.	Neg.
Apollo couldn't save Hector, even by **groveling** at Zeus's feet.			
Hector made a **gallant** suggestion for honoring the loser's body.			
Achilles called Hector's behavior cowardly and **fawning.**			

Reading Standard 1.2 (Grade 9–10 Review) Distinguish between the denotative and connotative meanings of words and interpret the connotative power of words.

 Check your Standards Mastery at the back of this book.

Chapter 2

The Middle Ages

(1066–1485)

The Tales They Told

*The Alcazar, a medieval castle in Segovia, Spain.
This famous castle-palace, built in the eleventh century,
was home to many Spanish kings and queens.*

The Middle Ages
(1066–1485)

David Adams Leeming

The following essay provides highlights of the historical period.
For a more detailed version of this essay,
see *Holt Literature and Language Arts,* pages 94–107.

Reading Standard 3.7c
Evaluate the philosophical, political, religious, ethical, and social influences of the historical period that shaped the characters, plots, and settings.

In October 1066, a daylong battle near Hastings, England, changed the course of history. There, Duke William of Normandy, France, defeated and killed King Harold of England, the last of the Anglo-Saxon kings. So began the Norman Conquest, an event that radically affected English history, the English character, and the English language. Unlike the Romans, the Normans never withdrew from England.

William the Conqueror and the Norman Influence

10 Duke William of Normandy, who came to be called William the Conqueror, was an efficient and ruthless soldier, but he wanted to rule the Anglo-Saxons, not eliminate them. Today, as a result, rather than a Norman, French-speaking England (and United States), we find a culture and a language that combine Norman and Anglo-Saxon elements. To the Anglo-Saxons' more democratic and artistic tendencies, the Normans brought administrative ability, an emphasis on law and order, and cultural unity.

One of William's great administrative feats was an inventory of nearly every piece of property in England—land, cattle,
20 buildings—in the Domesday Book. For the first time in European history, taxes were based on what people owned.

IDENTIFY

Pause at line 7. What happened at the battle near Hastings that changed the course of history?

_____

_____

_____

_____

_____

_____

IDENTIFY

What three influences did the Normans bring to Anglo-Saxon society (lines 10–17)? Circle that information.

IDENTIFY CAUSE & EFFECT

Re-read lines 18–21. What is the Domesday Book? Underline that information. Circle the effect it had on European history.

CLARIFY

Pause at line 31. How did the French language and the social system of feudalism come to be introduced to England?

_____

_____

_____

_____

_____

_____

_____

_____

WORD STUDY

Caste (kast), line 33, is a noun, used here as an adjective, that refers to a strict grouping of people into social classes based on birth, wealth, or occupation.

CLARIFY

Read lines 33–44 carefully. What is a vassal? Circle that information. Then, list the positions or social groups within the feudal system in order of their rank, beginning with the king.

_____

_____

_____

Suit of medieval armor standing beneath a Gothic archway.
Tony Garcia.

The Normans Change England

Although the Normans did not erase Anglo-Saxon culture, they did bring significant changes to England. William and many of his successors remained dukes of Normandy as well as kings of England, bringing England into mainstream European civilization in a new way. For example, William divided the holdings of the fallen English landowners among his own followers. These men and their families brought to England not only a new language—

30 French—but also a new social system—feudalism—which displaced the old Nordic social structure described in *Beowulf*.

Feudalism: From the Top Down

More than simply a social system, **feudalism** was also a caste system, a property system, and a military system. Ultimately, it was based on a religious concept of rank, with God as the supreme overlord. In this sense even a king held land as a **vassal**—a dependent tenant—by "divine right." A king as powerful as William the Conqueror could stand firmly at the top of the pyramid. He could appoint certain barons as his immediate

40 vassals, allotting them portions of his land in return for their economic or military allegiance—or both. In turn, the barons could appoint vassals of their own. The system operated all the way down to the landless knights and to the **serfs,** who were not free to leave the land they tilled.

The feudal system did not always work. Secure in a well-fortified castle, a vassal might choose not to honor his obligations to a weak overlord. The ensuing battles between iron-clad knights around moated castles account for one of the enduring images of the Middle Ages.

50 The feudal system carried with it a sense of form and manners that influenced all aspects of the life, art, and literature of the Middle Ages. This sense of formalism came to life most fully in the institution of knighthood and in the related practice, or code, of chivalry.

Knights in Shining Armor

We cannot think of the medieval period without thinking of knights. Since the primary duty of males above the serf class was military service to their lords, boys were trained from an early age to become warriors. Often their training took place in houses
60 other than their own, to be sure that the training was strict. When a boy's training was completed, he was dubbed, or ceremonially tapped on his shoulder. Once knighted, the youth became a man with the title "Sir" and the full rights of the warrior caste.

Knighthood was grounded in the feudal ideal of loyalty, and it was based on a complex system of social codes. Breaking any one of those codes would undermine not only the knight's position but also the very institution of knighthood.

Women in Medieval Society: No Voice, No Choice

70 Since they were not soldiers, women had no political rights in a system that was primarily military. A woman was always

IDENTIFY

Re-read lines 45–49. Why did the feudal system sometimes fail to work?

_____

_____

_____

_____

INTERPRET

Re-read lines 56–67. What was the primary duty of a knight?

_____

_____

_____

_____

WORD STUDY

Dubbed (line 61) is a verb that is defined by nearby context clues. Locate and circle the clues.

CLARIFY

Pause at line 71. Why didn't women have political rights within the feudal system?

_____

_____

_____

_____

IDENTIFY

Re-read lines 82–87. What is chivalry? Underline that information. Circle three rules of chivalry that are listed here.

COMPARE & CONTRAST

Re-read lines 88–96. How is the idea of courtly love different from modern ideas of love?

_____

_____

_____

_____

_____

_____

_____

_____

_____

_____

_____

_____

_____

_____

IDENTIFY

Underline the details that tell you what a romance hero does (lines 98–105).

subservient to a man, whether husband, father, or brother. Her husband's or father's social standing determined the degree of respect she commanded. For peasant women, life was a ceaseless round of childbearing, housework, and hard fieldwork. Women of higher stations were occupied with childbearing and household supervision. Such women might even manage entire estates while their men were away on business or at war, but the moment the men returned, the women had to give up their

80 temporary powers.

Chivalry and Courtly Love: Ideal but Unreal

Chivalry was a system of ideals and social codes governing the behavior of knights and gentlewomen. The rules of chivalry included taking an oath of loyalty to the overlord and observing certain rules of warfare, such as never attacking an unarmed opponent. In addition, adoring a particular lady (not necessarily one's wife) was seen as a means of self-improvement.

The idea that adoring a lady would make a knight braver and nobler was central to one aspect of chivalry, courtly love.

90 **Courtly love** was, in its ideal form, nonsexual. A knight might wear his lady's colors in battle, he might glorify her in words and be inspired by her, but the lady always remained pure and out of reach. She was set above her admirer, just as the feudal lord was set above his vassal. The fact that such a concept flew in the face of human nature provided a perfect subject for poets and story-tellers, as the King Arthur sagas illustrate.

The Rise of the Romance

Chivalry brought about an idealized attitude toward women, but it did little to improve their actual position. Chivalry did

100 give rise to a new form of literature, the **romance.** The greatest English example of the romance is *Sir Gawain and the Green Knight.* The romance hero—who often has the help of magic— undertakes a quest to conquer an evil enemy. J.R.R. Tolkien's

trilogy *The Lord of the Rings* shows that the romance is still alive and well today.

The New City Classes: Out from Under the Overlords

For the most part, medieval society centered on the feudal castle, but as the population grew, an increasing number of people
110 lived in towns and cities. Eventually those population centers would make the feudal system obsolete.

The emerging merchant class had its own tastes in the arts and the ability to pay for what it wanted. As a result, much medieval art is not aristocratic; it is middle class, even "people's art." The people of the cities were free, tied neither to the land nor to knighthood and chivalry. Their point of view was expressed in **ballads,** in mystery and miracle plays, and even in great cathedrals and municipal buildings.

The Great Happenings

120 Against the backdrop of the feudal system imported from the Continent, several events radically influenced the course of English history, as well as English literature.

■ The Crusades: Bloodbath Over the Holy Land

The **Crusades** (1095–1270) were a series of holy wars waged by European Christians against Muslims. In 1095, the head of the Catholic Church in Rome, Pope Urban II, sent out a plea to the Christians of Europe. He upheld that it was their duty to wage war against Muslims occupying Jerusalem and other places in the Middle East that were considered holy to Christians. The pope's
130 call for help set off a series of disastrous military expeditions that came to be known as the Crusades. Even children were swept up in the cause, during the Children's Crusade in 1212. Although the Europeans failed to hold Jerusalem, they benefited enormously from the contact with the sophisticated civilization of the Middle

IDENTIFY CAUSE & EFFECT

Re-read lines 108–111. What eventually made the feudal system obsolete, or no longer in use? Underline that information.

INFER

What is a "merchant class" (line 112)?

_____

_____

_____

_____

IDENTIFY

Re-read lines 112–118. What medieval forms of art were produced by the middle classes living in the cities? Circle your answer.

CLARIFY

Pause at line 129. Why did European Christians lead crusades against the Muslims?

_____

_____

_____

_____

_____

_____

_____

East. Their exposure to Eastern mathematics, astronomy, architecture, and crafts made possible the rich, varied life we find in Chaucer's *The Canterbury Tales.*

■ **The Martyrdom of Thomas à Becket: Murder in the Cathedral**

When Chaucer's pilgrims set out for Canterbury, their goal was
140 the shrine of Saint Thomas à Becket (c. 1118–1170). Thomas, a Norman, had risen to great power as chancellor (prime minister) under his friend King Henry II (reigned 1154–1189). By appointing his trusted friend Thomas archbishop of Canterbury (head of the Catholic Church in England), Henry hoped to gain the upper hand in disputes with the Church. The independent Thomas took the pope's side more than once, though, infuriating the king. In December 1170, Henry raged, "Will no one rid me of this turbulent priest?" Taking his words literally, four of Henry's knights murdered Becket—right in his own cathedral. Public
150 outrage at Becket's murder led to devotion to Saint Thomas the Martyr and created a backlash against Henry, a significant setback for the monarchy in its power struggles with Rome.

At its worst this setback led to corruption in the Church— corruption that the state was in no position to correct. Yet the medieval Church did have one positive effect: It fostered cultural unity—a system of beliefs and symbols that transcended the national cultures of Europe. The Church continued to be the center of learning. Its monasteries were the libraries and publishers of the time, and its language, Latin, remained the
160 international language of educated Europeans. Its leader, the pope, was king of all kings—and his kingdom had no boundaries.

■ **The Magna Carta: Power to (Some of) the People**

The event that most clearly heralded a return to older, democratic tendencies in England was the signing of the **Magna Carta** ("Great Charter") by King John in 1215, at Runnymede. The vicious but pragmatic John was strongly backed by the pope, but the English barons forced him to sign the document. The signing was a defeat for central papal power. As aristocrats writing for

IDENTIFY

Pause at line 137. How did the Europeans benefit from contact with the Middle East during the Crusades? Underline that information.

IDENTIFY CAUSE & EFFECT

Re-read lines 139–152. What effect did the murder of Thomas à Becket have on the monarchy? Underline your answer.

WORD STUDY

The verb *foster,* used in the past tense in line 155, means "to help develop" or "to promote." It comes from the Old English *fostrian,* which means "to nourish."

PARAPHRASE

Re-read lines 153–161. Restate in your own words the positive effects the Church had on medieval society.

The Magna Carta.
© Bettmann/CORBIS.

aristocrats, the barons had no interest in the rights of the common
170   people. Still, the Magna Carta later became the basis of English
constitutional law, in which such rights as trial by jury and
legislative taxation were established.

■ The Hundred Years' War (1337–1453): The Arrow Is Mightier Than the Armor

What might be called the first national war was waged by
England against France. Fought on the Continent, the **Hundred Years' War** was based on weak claims to the throne of France by
two English kings: Edward III (reigned 1327–1377) and Henry V
(reigned 1413–1422).

IDENTIFY

Pause at line 172. What
two elements of English
constitutional law were
introduced in the Magna
Carta? Circle your answer.

IDENTIFY

Pause at line 179. What
two nations fought in the
Hundred Years' War? Circle
your answer.

IDENTIFY

Pause at line 188. Who were the yeomen? Why were they important after the war? Underline the reason.

_____

_____

_____

_____

_____

_____

_____

_____

_____

_____

IDENTIFY CAUSE & EFFECT

Re-read lines 192–198. The Black Death caused a chain of events that contributed to the collapse of the feudal system. Underline those events.

_____

_____

_____

_____

_____

_____

_____

_____

180   This long war was militarily unsuccessful for the English, but it was an important factor in the gradual development of a British national consciousness. During the war the knight in shining armor came to be replaced by the green-clad **yeoman** (small landowner) with his longbow. These English yeomen had formed the nucleus of the English armies in France. Their yard-long arrows could fly over castle walls and pierce the armor of knights. These small landowners now became a dominant force in the new society that grew up from the ruins of feudalism. The old ideals of chivalry lived on only in stories, such as the

190   King Arthur legends.

■ **The Black Death**

The **Black Death,** or bubonic plague, which struck England in 1348–1349, delivered another blow to feudalism. Highly contagious and spread by fleas from infected rats, the disease reduced the nation's population by a third—causing a labor shortage and giving the lower classes more bargaining power against their overlords. One long-term result was the serfs' freedom, which knocked out feudalism's last support. By the time King Henry VII's 1486 marriage reconciled the warring

200   Houses of York and Lancaster, the Middle Ages were ending in England. Henry, a strong king, began the Tudor line that would lead to Elizabeth I. England's Renaissance was about to begin.

from The Prologue *to* The Canterbury Tales by Geoffrey Chaucer

LITERARY FOCUS: CHARACTERIZATION

Interesting characters are what make certain stories so memorable and vivid. The process by which writers reveal the personality of a character is called **characterization.** To describe his characters, Chaucer used the same methods and techniques that writers still use today. Chaucer—

- Tells us directly what characters are like

- Describes characters' looks and clothing

- Tells us what characters say and do

- Reveals characters' thoughts and feelings

- Shows how other people react to characters

Cast of Characters   When we describe a person, we try to choose the most telling details to create a vivid portrait of that person. In the chart below, write the name of a person you know well. Then, list details about his or her appearance or behavior that suggest what the person is like. Look at the methods of characterization listed above for ideas.

Name	Details

READING SKILLS: ANALYZING KEY DETAILS

Chaucer uses very specific details to help you visualize and understand the various characters who are on their way to Canterbury. Here are some details Chaucer uses to describe two different characters in the Prologue:

- "Bold was her face, handsome, and red in hue. / . . . and on her head a hat / As broad as is a buckler or a shield . . . " (lines 94, 106–107)

- "He could heave any door off hinge and post . . . / His mighty mouth was like a furnace door . . ." (lines 118, 127)

Use the Skill   As you read the selection, underline or highlight details that help bring each character to life. Be on the lookout for details that suggest how the narrator feels about each character.

from The Prologue *to*

The Canterbury Tales

Geoffrey Chaucer, *translated by* Nevill Coghill

The Canterbury Tales is a collection of stories told by people traveling together on a pilgrimage, a religious journey made to some holy place. The group of pilgrims is making the 55-mile journey on horseback, from London to the burial place of the martyr Saint Thomas à Becket at Canterbury Cathedral in southeastern England. These pilgrims are of all different ages, occupations, and economic means. Their stories give us a fascinating picture of life during the Middle Ages.

The Canterbury Tales begins with a Prologue. The host of the inn suggests that the pilgrims exchange stories to pass the time on their long journey. This sets up the frame story—the main story of the pilgrimage that includes each pilgrim's story. Now the pilgrim narrator (whom many consider to be Chaucer himself) describes his fellow pilgrims.

We have included only portions of the Prologue here.

WORD STUDY

Engendering (line 4) is based on the Latin verb *ingenerare*, meaning "to beget," and is related to the verb *generate*. With that knowledge and the word's context, tell what you think *engendering* means.

_____

_____

IDENTIFY CAUSE & EFFECT

The opening paragraph (lines 1–18) is a single long sentence that is built on this cause-effect pattern: *When "x" happens, then "y" follows.* Re-read the paragraph. What do the people long to do in April? Circle that information.

The Prologue

When in April the sweet showers fall

And pierce the drought of March to the root, and all

The veins are bathed in liquor of such power

As brings about the engendering of the flower,

5   When also Zephyrus[1] with his sweet breath

Exhales an air in every grove and heath

Upon the tender shoots, and the young sun

His half-course in the sign of the *Ram*[2] has run,

And the small fowl are making melody

10   That sleep away the night with open eye

(So nature pricks them and their heart engages)

Then people long to go on pilgrimages

---

1. **Zephyrus** (zef′ə·rəs): in Greek mythology, god of the west wind.
2. **Ram:** Aries, first sign of the zodiac. The time is mid-April.

And palmers[3] long to seek the stranger strands

Of far-off saints, hallowed in sundry lands,

15 And specially, from every shire's end

Of England, down to Canterbury they wend[4]

To seek the holy blissful martyr, quick

To give his help to them when they were sick.

      It happened in that season that one day

20 In Southwark, at *The Tabard,* as I lay

Ready to go on pilgrimage and start

For Canterbury, most devout at heart,

At night there came into that hostelry

Some nine and twenty in a company

25 Of sundry folk happening then to fall

In fellowship, and they were pilgrims all

That towards Canterbury meant to ride.

The rooms and stables of the inn were wide:

They made us easy, all was of the best.

30 And, briefly, when the sun had gone to rest,

I'd spoken to them all upon the trip

And was soon one with them in fellowship,

Pledged to rise early and to take the way

To Canterbury, as you heard me say.

35   But none the less, while I have time and space,

Before my story takes a further pace,

It seems a reasonable thing to say

What their condition was, the full array

Of each of them, as it appeared to me,

40 According to profession and degree,

And what apparel they were riding in;

And at a Knight I therefore will begin.

IDENTIFY

Pause at line 27. According to the narrator, who has arrived at the inn?

_____

_____

_____

_____

_____

_____

_____

_____

_____

_____

_____

_____

_____

_____

IDENTIFY

Re-read lines 35–42. What is the narrator going to tell you about his fellow pilgrims? Underline the answer.

_____

_____

_____

---

3. **palmers** *n. pl.:* people who had visited the Holy Land and wore palm fronds to show it.
4. **wend** *v.:* go; travel.

The Knight

IDENTIFY

Chivalry (line 45) refers to a code of conduct by which knights should live. Read on to line 46, and circle the qualities or ideals associated with chivalry.

There was a *Knight,* a most distinguished man,

Who from the day on which he first began

45 To ride abroad had followed chivalry,

Truth, honor, generousness, and courtesy.

He had done nobly in his sovereign's war

And ridden into battle, no man more,

As well in Christian as in heathen[5] places,

50 And ever honored for his noble graces.

    When we took Alexandria,[6] he was there.

He often sat at table in the chair

Of honor, above all nations, when in Prussia.

In Lithuania he had ridden, and Russia,

55 No Christian man so often, of his rank.

When, in Granada, Algeciras sank

Under assault, he had been there, and in

North Africa, raiding Benamarin;

In Anatolia he had been as well

60 And fought when Ayas and Attalia fell,

For all along the Mediterranean coast

He had embarked with many a noble host.

In fifteen mortal battles he had been

And jousted for our faith at Tramissene

65 Thrice in the lists, and always killed his man.

This same distinguished knight had led the van

Once with the Bey of Balat, doing work

For him against another heathen Turk;

He was of sovereign value in all eyes.

70 And though so much distinguished, he was wise

And in his bearing modest as a maid.

He never yet a boorish thing had said

In all his life to any, come what might;

INFER

Re-read lines 51–68, in which we learn about the Knight's long and distinguished career. What does this information tell you about life in the Middle Ages?

_____

_____

_____

_____

ANALYZE

In lines 69–74, underline the narrator's description of the Knight's character. What is the narrator's **tone**, or attitude, toward the Knight? *(Grade 9–10 Review)*

_____

_____

_____

WORD STUDY

In Chaucer's day, the term *gentle* (line 74) meant "well bred and considerate." What term similar to *gentle-knight* do we still use today to refer to a well-mannered, courteous man?

_____

---

5. **heathen** *n:* pagan. Chaucer here is referring to non-Christians.
6. **Alexandria:** city in Egypt captured by the Crusaders in 1365. In the next few lines, Chaucer is indicating the Knight's distinguished and extensive career.

John Lydgate and the Canterbury pilgrims leaving Canterbury, from a volume of Lydgate's poems (early 16th century).
MS Royal 18 D 11, fol. 148. British Library, London.

He was a true, a perfect gentle-knight.

75   Speaking of his equipment, he possessed

Fine horses, but he was not gaily dressed.

He wore a fustian[7] tunic stained and dark

With smudges where his armor had left mark;

Just home from service, he had joined our ranks

80   To do his pilgrimage and render thanks. . . .

___

7.   fustian (fus'chən) *adj.:* coarse cloth made of linen and cotton.

Notes ___

The Wife of Bath

CLARIFY

Pause at line 84. What is the Wife's profession?

_____

_____

_____

_____

IDENTIFY

Re-read lines 81–94. Circle the words and phrases that help you visualize the Wife of Bath.

INTERPRET

What generalization can you make about the Wife of Bath from the details the narrator provides in lines 99–104?

_____

_____

_____

_____

_____

_____

_____

_____

_____

_____

_____

_____

A worthy *woman* from beside *Bath* city
Was with us, somewhat deaf, which was a pity.
In making cloth she showed so great a bent
She bettered those of Ypres and of Ghent.[8]
85   In all the parish not a dame dared stir
Towards the altar steps in front of her,
And if indeed they did, so wrath was she
As to be quite put out of charity.
Her kerchiefs were of finely woven ground;[9]
90   I dared have sworn they weighed a good ten pound,
The ones she wore on Sunday, on her head.
Her hose were of the finest scarlet red
And gartered tight; her shoes were soft and new.
Bold was her face, handsome, and red in hue.
95   A worthy woman all her life, what's more
She'd had five husbands, all at the church door,
Apart from other company in youth;
No need just now to speak of that, forsooth.
And she had thrice been to Jerusalem,
100   Seen many strange rivers and passed over them;
She'd been to Rome and also to Boulogne,
St. James of Compostella and Cologne,
And she was skilled in wandering by the way.
She had gap-teeth,[10] set widely, truth to say.
105   Easily on an ambling horse she sat
Well wimpled[11] up, and on her head a hat
As broad as is a buckler or a shield;
She had a flowing mantle that concealed
Large hips, her heels spurred sharply under that.

---

8. **Ypres (ē′pr′) and of Ghent:** Flemish centers of the wool trade.
9. **ground** *n.:* type of cloth.
10. **gap-teeth:** In Chaucer's time, gap-teeth on a woman were considered a sign of boldness and were said to indicate an aptitude for love and travel.
11. **wimpled** *adj.:* A wimple is a linen covering for the head and neck.

110 In company she liked to laugh and chat

And knew the remedies for love's mischances,

An art in which she knew the oldest dances. . . .

The Miller

The *Miller* was a chap of sixteen stone,[12]

A great stout fellow big in brawn and bone.

115 He did well out of them, for he could go

And win the ram at any wrestling show.

Broad, knotty, and short-shouldered, he would boast

He could heave any door off hinge and post,

Or take a run and break it with his head.

120 His beard, like any sow or fox, was red

And broad as well, as though it were a spade;

And, at its very tip, his nose displayed

A wart on which there stood a tuft of hair

Red as the bristles in an old sow's ear.

125 His nostrils were as black as they were wide.

He had a sword and buckler at his side,

His mighty mouth was like a furnace door.

A wrangler and buffoon, he had a store

Of tavern stories, filthy in the main.

130 His was a master-hand at stealing grain.

He felt it with his thumb and thus he knew

Its quality and took three times his due—

A thumb of gold, by God, to gauge an oat![13]

He wore a hood of blue and a white coat.

135 He liked to play his bagpipes up and down

And that was how he brought us out of town. . . .

---

12. **sixteen stone:** 224 pounds.
13. **thumb . . . oat:** In other words, he pressed on the scale with his thumb to increase the weight of the grain.

INFER

Re-read lines 137–147. Circle details that describe the Summoner. What can you infer about his **character** based on his physical appearance? *(Grade 9–10 Review)*

_____

_____

_____

_____

_____

_____

_____

_____

_____

_____

_____

_____

_____

_____

_____

_____

_____

The Summoner, from the Ellesmere manuscript.
Fol. 81r. By permission of The Huntington Library, San Marino, California.

The Summoner

    There was a *Summoner* with us at that Inn,

His face on fire, like a cherubim,[14]

For he had carbuncles.[15] His eyes were narrow,

140   He was as hot and lecherous as a sparrow.

Black scabby brows he had, and a thin beard.

Children were afraid when he appeared.

No quicksilver, lead ointment, tartar creams,

No brimstone, no boracic, so it seems,

145   Could make a salve that had the power to bite,

Clean up, or cure his whelks[16] of knobby white

Or purge the pimples sitting on his cheeks.

Garlic he loved, and onions too, and leeks,

And drinking strong red wine till all was hazy.

150   Then he would shout and jabber as if crazy,

And wouldn't speak a word except in Latin

When he was drunk, such tags as he was pat in;

He only had a few, say two or three,

That he had mugged up out of some decree;

155   No wonder, for he heard them every day.

And, as you know, a man can teach a jay[17]

---

14. **cherubim** *n.:* in medieval art, a little angel with a rosy face.
15. **carbuncles** (kär′bun′kəlz) *n. pl.:* pus-filled skin inflammations, something like boils.
16. **whelks** *n. pl.:* pus-filled sores.
17. **jay** *n.:* type of bird.

To call out "Walter" better than the Pope.

But had you tried to test his wits and grope

For more, you'd have found nothing in the bag.

160   Then "*Questio quid juris*"[18] was his tag.

He was a noble varlet[19] and a kind one,

You'd meet none better if you went to find one.

Why, he'd allow—just for a quart of wine—

Any good lad to keep a concubine

165   A twelvemonth and dispense him altogether!

And he had finches of his own to feather:[20]

And if he found some rascal with a maid

He would instruct him not to be afraid

In such a case of the Archdeacon's curse

170   (Unless the rascal's soul were in his purse)

For in his purse the punishment should be.

"Purse is the good Archdeacon's Hell," said he.

But well I know he lied in what he said;

A curse should put a guilty man in dread,

175   For curses kill, as shriving brings, salvation.

We should beware of excommunication.

Thus, as he pleased, the man could bring duress

On any young fellow in the diocese.

He knew their secrets, they did what he said.

180   He wore a garland set upon his head

Large as the holly-bush upon a stake

Outside an ale-house, and he had a cake,

A round one, which it was his joke to wield

As if it were intended for a shield.

INTERPRET

Re-read lines 150–159. (Lines 150–155 mean that the Summoner would rattle off quotations he had heard in court.) What point is the narrator making about the Summoner's "wits," or intelligence?

_____

_____

_____

_____

_____

_____

_____

_____

_____

_____

_____

CLARIFY

What does the Summoner do when he catches people sinning (lines 167–171)?

_____

_____

WORD STUDY

Duress (dŏŏ·res′), line 177, is a noun that means "force or pressure," as in blackmail.

---

18. ***Questio quid juris*** (kwest′ē·ō kwid yŏŏ′ris): Latin for "I ask what point of the law [applies]." The Summoner uses this phrase to stall and dodge the issue.
19. **varlet** (vär′lit) *n.:* scoundrel.
20. **finches . . . feather:** a maxim that means roughly the same as "feathering one's nest"—taking care of one's own interests.

The Pardoner,
from the Ellesmere manuscript.
Fol. 138r. By permission of The Huntington
Library, San Marino, California.

The Pardoner

IDENTIFY

Re-read lines 185–190.
Underline words or phrases
that suggest the Pardoner
and the Summoner have a
lot in common.

INTERPRET

Re-read lines 191–200, and
circle details about the
Pardoner's appearance.
How do these details
affect your understanding
of this **character**?

185 He and a gentle *Pardoner* rode together,

A bird from Charing Cross of the same feather,

Just back from visiting the Court of Rome.

He loudly sang *"Come hither, love, come home!"*

The Summoner sang deep seconds[21] to this song,

190 No trumpet ever sounded half so strong.

This Pardoner had hair as yellow as wax,

Hanging down smoothly like a hank of flax.

In driblets fell his locks behind his head

Down to his shoulders which they overspread;

195 Thinly they fell, like rat-tails, one by one.

He wore no hood upon his head, for fun;

The hood inside his wallet had been stowed,

He aimed at riding in the latest mode;

But for a little cap his head was bare

200 And he had bulging eye-balls, like a hare.

He'd sewed a holy relic[22] on his cap;

---

21. **deep seconds:** harmonies.
22. **relic** *n.:* remains of a saint.

His wallet lay before him on his lap,

Brimful of pardons[23] come from Rome, all hot.

He had the same small voice a goat has got.

205 His chin no beard had harbored, nor would harbor,

Smoother than ever chin was left by barber.

I judge he was a gelding, or a mare.

As to his trade, from Berwick down to Ware

There was no pardoner of equal grace,

210 For in his trunk he had a pillow-case

Which he asserted was Our Lady's veil.

He said he had a gobbet[24] of the sail

Saint Peter had the time when he made bold

To walk the waves, till Jesu Christ took hold.

215 He had a cross of metal set with stones

And, in a glass, a rubble of pigs' bones.

And with these relics, any time he found

Some poor up-country parson to astound,

In one short day, in money down, he drew

220 More than the parson in a month or two,

And by his flatteries and prevarication[25]

Made monkeys of the priest and congregation.

But still to do him justice first and last

In church he was a noble ecclesiast.[26]

225 How well he read a lesson or told a story!

But best of all he sang an Offertory,[27]

For well he knew that when that song was sung

He'd have to preach and tune his honey-tongue

And (well he could) win silver from the crowd.

230 That's why he sang so merrily and loud.

IDENTIFY

Relics are the remains of a holy person, such as bones, hair, or clothing. Re-read lines 210–222. Circle the relics that the Pardoner claims to have. Underline the information that reveals the Pardoner is a cheat.

IDENTIFY

According to lines 226–230, what is the Summoner good at?

_____

_____

_____

_____

_____

_____

_____

_____

_____

_____

_____

_____

_____

_____

_____

_____

---

23. **pardons** *n. pl.:* small strips of parchment with papal seals attached. They were sold as indulgences (pardons for sins), with the proceeds supposedly going to a religious house.
24. **gobbet** *n.:* fragment.
25. **prevarication** (pri·var′i·kā′ sһən) *n.:* telling lies.
26. **ecclesiast** (e·klē′zē·ast) *n.:* practitioner of church ritual.
27. **Offertory** *n.:* hymn sung while offerings are collected in church.

CLARIFY

Re-read lines 231–240. The narrator has now taken us back to the Tabard Inn. Draw a box around the section in which the narrator explains how he will organize the rest of his story.

INTERPRET

Pause at line 252. According to the narrator, who is to blame if some of the tales offend his readers? Why?

Now I have told you shortly, in a clause,

The rank, the array, the number, and the cause

Of our assembly in this company

In Southwark, at that high-class hostelry

235   Known as *The Tabard,* close beside *The Bell.*

And now the time has come for me to tell

How we behaved that evening; I'll begin

After we had alighted at the Inn,

Then I'll report our journey, stage by stage,

240   All the remainder of our pilgrimage.

But first I beg of you, in courtesy,

Not to condemn me as unmannerly

If I speak plainly and with no concealings

And give account of all their words and dealings,

245   Using their very phrases as they fell.

For certainly, as you all know so well,

He who repeats a tale after a man

Is bound to say, as nearly as he can,

Each single word, if he remembers it,

250   However rudely spoken or unfit,

Or else the tale he tells will be untrue,

The things pretended and the phrases new.

He may not flinch although it were his brother,

He may as well say one word as another.

255   And Christ Himself spoke broad in Holy Writ,

Yet there is no scurrility[28] in it,

And Plato says, for those with power to read,

"The word should be as cousin to the deed."

Further I beg you to forgive it me

260   If I neglect the order and degree

And what is due to rank in what I've planned.

I'm short of wit as you will understand.

---

28. scurrility (skə·ril'ə·tē) *n.:* indecency.

The Host

                Our *Host* gave us great welcome; everyone

        Was given a place and supper was begun.

265   He served the finest victuals you could think,

        The wine was strong and we were glad to drink.

        A very striking man our Host withal,

        And fit to be a marshal in a hall.

        His eyes were bright, his girth a little wide;

270   There is no finer burgess in Cheapside.[29]

        Bold in his speech, yet wise and full of tact,

        There was no manly attribute he lacked,

        What's more he was a merry-hearted man.

        After our meal he jokingly began

275   To talk of sport, and, among other things

        After we'd settled up our reckonings,

        He said as follows: "Truly, gentlemen,

        You're very welcome and I can't think when

        —Upon my word I'm telling you no lie—

280   I've seen a gathering here that looked so spry,

        No, not this year, as in this tavern now.

        I'd think you up some fun if I knew how.

        And, as it happens, a thought has just occurred

        To please you, costing nothing, on my word.

285   You're off to Canterbury—well, God speed!

        Blessed St. Thomas answer to your need!

        And I don't doubt, before the journey's done

        You mean to while the time in tales and fun.

        Indeed, there's little pleasure for your bones

290   Riding along and all as dumb as stones.

        So let me then propose for your enjoyment,

        Just as I said, a suitable employment.

        And if my notion suits and you agree

        And promise to submit yourselves to me

295   Playing your parts exactly as I say

---

29. Cheapside: district of medieval London.

WORD STUDY

The word *victuals* (line 265) is pronounced (vit"lz). Circle the context clue in line 264, and tell what *victuals* means.

_____

WORD STUDY

Context can also help with word pronunciation. The pattern of rhyming words at the ends of lines tells you that the word *withal* (line 267) must rhyme with the word *hall* (line 268). How should *withal* be pronounced?

_____

_____

_____

INTERPRET

Underline the details the narrator uses to describe the Host (lines 267–273). How would you describe the narrator's **tone**, or attitude, toward the Host? *(Grade 9–10 Review)*

_____

_____

CLARIFY

Re-read lines 282–292. What is the Host going to reveal to the pilgrims?

_____

_____

_____

Read aloud the boxed portion of the Host's speech at least twice, and make sure you understand what he is suggesting. Imagine you are the Host trying to interest the pilgrims in your offer. Read the rhyming lines in a natural, conversational way.

INTERPRET

Review the Host's speech (lines 307–322), and briefly **summarize** the rules he proposes for the storytelling competition.

Tomorrow as you ride along the way,

Then by my father's soul (and he is dead)

If you don't like it you can have my head!

Hold up your hands, and not another word."

300　　　　Well, our opinion was not long deferred,

It seemed not worth a serious debate;

We all agreed to it at any rate

And bade him issue what commands he would.

"My lords," he said, "now listen for your good,

305　　And please don't treat my notion with disdain.

This is the point. I'll make it short and plain.

Each one of you shall help to make things slip

By telling two stories on the outward trip

To Canterbury, that's what I intend,

310　　And, on the homeward way to journey's end

Another two, tales from the days of old;

And then the man whose story is best told,

That is to say who gives the fullest measure

Of good morality and general pleasure,

315　　He shall be given a supper, paid by all,

Here in this tavern, in this very hall,

When we come back again from Canterbury.

And in the hope to keep you bright and merry

I'll go along with you myself and ride

320　　All at my own expense and serve as guide.

I'll be the judge, and those who won't obey

Shall pay for what we spend upon the way.

Now if you all agree to what you've heard

Tell me at once without another word,

325　　And I will make arrangements early for it."

　　　　Of course we all agreed, in fact we swore it

Delightedly, and made entreaty[30] too

That he should act as he proposed to do,

Become our Governor in short, and be

---

30. entreaty n.: urgent request.

330   Judge of our tales and general referee,

And set the supper at a certain price.

We promised to be ruled by his advice

Come high, come low; unanimously thus

We set him up in judgment over us.

335   More wine was fetched, the business being done;

We drank it off and up went everyone

To bed without a moment of delay.

        Early next morning at the spring of day

Up rose our Host and roused us like a cock,

340   Gathering us together in a flock,

And off we rode at slightly faster pace

Than walking to St. Thomas' watering-place;

And there our Host drew up, began to ease

His horse, and said, "Now, listen if you please,

345   My lords! Remember what you promised me.

If evensong and matins will agree[31]

Let's see who shall be first to tell a tale.

And as I hope to drink good wine and ale

I'll be your judge. The rebel who disobeys,

350   However much the journey costs, he pays.

Now draw for cut[32] and then we can depart;

The man who draws the shortest cut shall start."

31. **If . . . agree:** in other words, if you feel the same way in the
     evening (at evensong, or evening prayers) as you do in the
     morning (at matins, or morning prayers).
32. **draw for cut:** in other words, draw straws.

IDENTIFY

Re-read lines 326–331. How do the pilgrims react to the Host's offer? Underline that information.

IDENTIFY

Who will be first to tell a story (line 352)?

_____

_____

_____

_____

_____

_____

_____

_____

_____

_____

_____

_____

_____

_____

_____

_____

_____

from The Prologue *to* **The Canterbury Tales**

Reading Skills: Analyzing Key Details   Chaucer uses several methods of **characterization** to describe the pilgrims, choosing colorful details to make each character come alive. For example, two methods he uses to characterize the Summoner are—

- *Directly telling us what he is like:* If you test his wits, you find nothing there (lines 158–159); he is greedy to feather his own nest (line 166).
- *Describing his looks and clothing:* He has boils, pimples, narrow eyes, scabby eyebrows, and a thin beard (lines 139–147); he wears a garland on his head (line 180).

Re-read the passages about the Wife of Bath and the Miller, and review the details you marked as you read. Complete the chart below with at least one detail that shows the method of characterization listed in column one. You may want to make similar charts for the other pilgrims as well.

Method of Characterization	The Wife of Bath (lines 81–112)	The Miller (lines 113–136)
Directly telling us what the character is like		
Describing the character's looks and clothing		
Showing how other people react to the character		
Presenting what the character says and does		
Revealing the character's thoughts and feelings		

 Check your Standards Mastery at the back of this book.

Federigo's Falcon by Giovanni Boccaccio

BEFORE YOU READ

LITERARY FOCUS: SITUATIONAL IRONY

One form of irony is **situational irony,** when what actually happens is the opposite of what is expected or appropriate. Situational irony always involves an unexpected turn of events. The Greek myth about King Midas, for example, is full of situational irony. Midas values wealth so much that he is happy to gain the power to turn anything he touches to gold. However, his "golden touch" soon leaves him starving and filled with grief: It turns food, drink, and even his beloved daughter into gold—certainly not what the king expected or desired.

That's So Ironic!   Think of an experience in your life in which a situation turned out very differently from what you expected. In the chart below, briefly describe the situation and the unexpected outcome.

What I Expected to Happen	What Actually Happened

READING SKILLS: EVALUATING HISTORICAL CONTEXT

Literature often reflects ideas, prejudices, and values of a particular time and place. Although Boccaccio's story resembles a modern love story, it also reflects the fourteenth-century world in which he lived. During the Middle Ages:

- Women were dependent on male family members for everything.
- Men of noble rank were expected to perform knightly deeds to honor a lady and win her love.
- Courtly love—idolizing women, even married women, from afar—was accepted and considered a compliment.
- Hawking—the use of a trained bird to hunt small prey—was a popular sport among the upper classes.
- Many people died young because the causes and cures for diseases were poorly understood.

Use the Skill   As you read the story, underline or highlight details that reveal historical details of the Middle Ages. Then, think about how the time period affects the characters' actions.

REVIEW SKILLS

As you read "Federigo's Falcon," expect the unexpected—in the form of irony.

IRONY
A contrast between expectations and reality—between what is expected and what actually happens.

Reading Standard 3.3 Analyze the ways in which irony achieves specific rhetorical purposes.

Reading Standard 3.7b Relate literary works and authors to the major themes and issues of their eras.

Reading Standard 3.7c Evaluate the political, religious, ethical, and social influences of the historical period that shaped the characters, plots, and settings.

Reading Standard 3.8 (Grade 9–10 Review) Interpret and evaluate the impact of ambiguities, subtleties, contradictions, ironies, and incongruities in a text.

Federigo's Falcon
from the Decameron

Giovanni Boccaccio, *translated by* Mark Musa *and* Peter Bondanella

In the *Decameron,* ten wealthy young people from Florence, Italy, flee to a large house outside the city to escape a deadly outbreak of the plague. To pass the time, they decide that for each of ten days they will name a king or queen, who, in turn, will choose a theme upon which the others must tell a story. "Federigo's Falcon" is the ninth story told on the fifth day, a day devoted to stories with happy endings.

WORD STUDY

Prowess (prou'is), line 3, means "superior ability." Circle the context clue that helps you figure out the word's meaning.

IDENTIFY

What happens when Federigo tries to win the love of Monna Giovanna (lines 7–13)? Underline that information.

There was once in Florence a young man named Federigo, the son of Messer[1] Filippo Alberighi, renowned above all other men in Tuscany for his prowess in arms and for his courtliness. As often happens to most gentlemen, he fell in love with a lady named Monna[2] Giovanna, in her day considered to be one of the most beautiful and one of the most charming women that ever there was in Florence; and in order to win her love, he participated in jousts and tournaments, organized and gave feasts, and spent his money without restraint; but she, no less virtuous than beautiful,
10 cared little for these things done on her behalf, nor did she care for him who did them. Now, as Federigo was spending far beyond his means and was taking nothing in, as easily happens he lost his wealth and became poor, with nothing but his little farm to his name (from whose revenues he lived very meagerly) and one falcon which was among the best in the world.

More in love than ever, but knowing that he would never be able to live the way he wished to in the city, he went to live at

---

1. **Messer** (mes'ər): title of address similar to *sir.*
2. **Monna** (mō'nə): In Italian, *Monna* is an abbreviation for *Madonna* (mə·dän'ə), a formal title for a woman, similar to *madam.*

"Fifth Day, Ninth Story" (retitled "Federigo's Falcon") from *The Decameron* by Giovanni Boccaccio, translated by Mark Musa and Peter Bondanella. Translation copyright © 1982 by Mark Musa and Peter Bondanella. Reprinted by permission of **W. W. Norton & Company, Inc.**

Campi,[3] where his farm was. There he passed his time hawking whenever he could, asked nothing of anyone, and endured his
20 poverty patiently. Now, during the time that Federigo was reduced to **dire** need, it happened that the husband of Monna Giovanna fell ill, and realizing death was near, he made his last will. He was very rich, and he made his son, who was growing up, his heir, and, since he had loved Monna Giovanna very much, he made her his heir should his son die without a legitimate heir; and then he died.

Monna Giovanna was now a widow, and as is the custom among our women, she went to the country with her son to spend a year on one of her possessions very close by to Federigo's
30 farm, and it happened that this young boy became friends with Federigo and began to enjoy birds and hunting dogs; and after he had seen Federigo's falcon fly many times, it pleased him so much that he very much wished it were his own, but he did not dare to ask for it, for he could see how dear it was to Federigo. And during this time, it happened that the young boy took ill, and his mother was much grieved, for he was her only child and she loved him enormously. She would spend the entire day by his side, never ceasing to comfort him, and often asking him if there was anything he desired, begging him to tell her what it
40 might be, for if it were possible to obtain it, she would certainly do everything possible to get it. After the young boy had heard her make this offer many times, he said:

"Mother, if you can arrange for me to have Federigo's falcon, I think I would be well very soon."

When the lady heard this, she was taken aback for a moment, and she began to think what she should do. She knew that Federigo had loved her for a long while, in spite of the fact that he never received a single glance from her, and so, she said to herself:

50 "How can I send or go and ask for this falcon of his which is, as I have heard tell, the best that ever flew, and besides this,

---

3. **Campi** (käm′pē): small town set in the mountains northwest of Florence. *Campi* literally means "fields."

VOCABULARY

dire (dīr) *adj.:* extreme; desperate.

CLARIFY

Re-read lines 20–26. Underline the terms of the last will made by Monna Giovanna's husband. What circumstances would make Monna Giovanna his heir?

ANALYZE

Re-read lines 27–34. Underline information that suggests how Monna Giovanna's actions after her husband's death were influenced by the time and place in which she lived.

CONNECT

Pause at line 41. How would you describe Monna Giovanna's relationship with her son?

Detail from Frederick II's *Treatise on Falconry.*
Ms. Pal. Lat. 1071, fol. 5v. Apostolic Library, Vatican City, Rome.

Pause at line 57, and consider the **historical context** of the story. Why is Monna Giovanna certain that Federigo will give her his falcon if she asks him for it?

his only means of support? And how can I be so insensitive as to wish to take away from this gentleman the only pleasure which is left to him?"

And involved in these thoughts, knowing that she was certain to have the bird if she asked for it, but not knowing what to say to her son, she stood there without answering him. Finally the love she bore her son persuaded her that she should make him happy, and no matter what the consequences might
60 be, she would not send for the bird, but rather go herself for it and bring it back to him; so she answered her son:

"My son, take comfort and think only of getting well, for I promise you that the first thing I shall do tomorrow morning is to go for it and bring it back to you."

The child was so happy that he showed some improvement that very day. The following morning, the lady, accompanied by another woman, as if going for a stroll, went to Federigo's modest house and asked for him. Since it was not the season for it, Federigo had not been hawking for some days and was in his orchard, attending to certain tasks. When he heard that Monna Giovanna was asking for him at the door, he was very surprised and happy to run there. As she saw him coming, she greeted him with feminine charm, and once Federigo had welcomed her courteously, she said:

"Greetings, Federigo!" Then she continued: "I have come to **compensate** you for the harm you have suffered on my account by loving me more than you needed to; and the compensation is this: I, along with this companion of mine, intend to dine with you—a simple meal—this very day."

To this Federigo humbly replied: "Madonna, I never remember having suffered any harm because of you. On the contrary, so much good have I received from you that if ever I have been worth anything, it has been because of your merit and the love I bore for you; and your generous visit is certainly so dear to me that I would spend all over again that which I spent in the past; but you have come to a poor host."

And having said this, he received her into his home humbly, and from there he led her into his garden, and since he had no one there to keep her company, he said:

"My lady, since there is no one else, this good woman here, the wife of this workman, will keep you company while I go to set the table."

Though he was very poor, Federigo, until now, had never before realized to what extent he had wasted his wealth; but this morning, the fact that he found nothing with which he could honor the lady for the love of whom he had once entertained

IDENTIFY

Re-read lines 65–74. How does Federigo react when he hears that Monna Giovanna is at his door? Underline that information.

VOCABULARY

compensate (käm′pən·sāt′) v.: make up for; make up (for or to).

Circle the word later in this paragraph that is the noun form of compensate.

ANALYZE

Pause at line 79. Underline the form of "compensation" that Monna Giovanna is offering to Federigo. Would her offer seem strange or normal if this story took place in the twenty-first century?

_____

_____

INTERPRET

Re-read Federigo's reply (lines 80–86). Does he regret the loss of his money? Explain.

_____

_____

_____

_____

Pause at line 111. Why does Federigo kill his prize falcon for dinner? Underline the reasons for his action.

INTERPRET

Re-read lines 112–115. In what way is this meal an example of **situational irony**? *(Grade 9–10 Review)*

_____

_____

_____

_____

_____

_____

_____

_____

_____

_____

_____

_____

_____

_____

VOCABULARY

presumption (prē·zump′shən) *n.:* act of taking too much for granted.

countless men in the past gave him cause to reflect. In great anguish, he cursed himself and his fortune and, like a man beside himself, he started running here and there, but could find

100 neither money nor a pawnable[4] object. The hour was late and his desire to honor the gracious lady was great, but not wishing to turn for help to others (not even to his own workman), he set his eyes upon his good falcon, perched in a small room; and since he had nowhere else to turn, he took the bird, and finding it plump, he decided that it would be a worthy food for such a lady. So, without further thought, he wrung its neck and quickly gave it to his servant girl to pluck, prepare, and place on a spit to be roasted with care; and when he had set the table with the whitest of tablecloths (a few of which he still had left), he

110 returned, with a cheerful face, to the lady in his garden, saying that the meal he was able to prepare for her was ready.

The lady and her companion rose, went to the table together with Federigo, who waited upon them with the greatest devotion, and they ate the good falcon without knowing what it was they were eating. And having left the table and spent some time in pleasant conversation, the lady thought it time now to say what she had come to say, and so she spoke these kind words to Federigo:

"Federigo, if you recall your past life and my virtue, which

120 you perhaps mistook for harshness and cruelty, I do not doubt at all that you will be amazed by my **presumption** when you hear what my main reason for coming here is; but if you had children, through whom you might have experienced the power of parental love, it seems certain to me that you would, at least in part, forgive me. But, just as you have no child, I do have one, and I cannot escape the common laws of other mothers; the force of such laws compels me to follow them, against my own will and against good manners and duty, and to ask of you a gift which I know is most precious to you; and it is naturally so,

---

4. **pawnable** *adj.:* able to be given as security in return for a loan of money or goods.

August: Departure for the Hunt with Falcons, from the calendar for the *Très riches heures du duc de Berry* by the Limbourg brothers.
Ms. 65/1284, fol. 8v. Musée Condé, Chantilly, France.

130   since your extreme condition has left you no other delight, no other pleasure, no other consolation; and this gift is your falcon, which my son is so taken by that if I do not bring it to him, I fear his sickness will grow so much worse that I may lose him. And therefore I beg you, not because of the love that you bear for me, which does not oblige you in the least, but because of your own nobility, which you have shown to be greater than that

_____

_____

_____

_____

_____

_____

_____

_____

_____

Federigo refers to "Fortune" as feminine (lines 149–156). Circle the pronouns that show this. In Roman mythology the goddess of fortune, or fate, was named Fortuna. As you might expect, the word *fortune* comes from the Latin word *fortuna* and refers to a power or being that some believe determines whether people have good or bad luck.

Notice that the boxed speech is one long sentence. Read the speech aloud several times. Circle the semicolons that separate each idea. With each reading, improve the smoothness of your delivery.

console (kən·sōl′) *v.*: comfort.

reproached (ri·prōcht′) *v.*: expressed disapproval.

of all others in practicing courtliness, that you be pleased to give it to me, so that I may say that I have saved the life of my son by means of this gift, and because of it I have placed him in your
140   debt forever."

    When he heard what the lady requested and knew that he could not oblige her since he had given her the falcon to eat, Federigo began to weep in her presence, for he could not utter a word in reply. The lady, at first, thought his tears were caused more by the sorrow of having to part with the good falcon than by anything else, and she was on the verge of telling him she no longer wished it, but she held back and waited for Federigo's reply after he stopped weeping. And he said:

    "My lady, ever since it pleased God for me to place my love
150   in you, I have felt that Fortune has been hostile to me in many things, and I have complained of her, but all this is nothing compared to what she has just done to me, and I must never be at peace with her again, thinking about how you have come here to my poor home where, while it was rich, you never deigned to come, and you requested a small gift, and Fortune worked to make it impossible for me to give it to you; and why this is so I shall tell you briefly. When I heard that you, out of your kindness, wished to dine with me, I considered it fitting and right, taking into account your excellence and your worthiness, that I should
160   honor you, according to my possibilities, with a more precious food than that which I usually serve to other people; therefore, remembering the falcon that you requested and its value, I judged it a food worthy of you, and this very day I had it roasted and served to you as best I could; but seeing now that you desired it in another way, my sorrow in not being able to serve you is so great that I shall never be able to **console** myself again."

    And after he had said this, he laid the feathers, the feet, and the beak of the bird before her as proof. When the lady heard and saw this, she first **reproached** him for having killed such a
170   falcon to serve as a meal to a woman; but then to herself she commended the greatness of his spirit, which no poverty was

able or would be able to diminish; then, having lost all hope of getting the falcon and, perhaps because of this, of improving the health of her son as well, she thanked Federigo both for the honor paid to her and for his good will, and she left in grief, and returned to her son. To his mother's extreme sorrow, either because of his disappointment that he could not have the falcon, or because his illness must have necessarily led to it, the boy passed from this life only a few days later.

180   After the period of her mourning and bitterness had passed, the lady was repeatedly urged by her brothers to remarry, since she was very rich and was still young; and although she did not wish to do so, they became so insistent that she remembered the merits of Federigo and his last act of generosity—that is, to have killed such a falcon to do her honor—and she said to her brothers:

"I would prefer to remain a widow, if that would please you; but if you wish me to take a husband, you may rest assured that I shall take no man but Federigo degli Alberighi."

190   In answer to this, making fun of her, her brothers replied:

"You foolish woman, what are you saying? How can you want him; he hasn't a penny to his name?"

To this she replied: "My brothers, I am well aware of what you say, but I would rather have a man who needs money than money that needs a man."

Her brothers, seeing that she was determined and knowing Federigo to be of noble birth, no matter how poor he was, accepted her wishes and gave her in marriage to him with all her riches. When he found himself the husband of such a great lady,

200   whom he had loved so much and who was so wealthy besides, he managed his financial affairs with more prudence than in the past and lived with her happily the rest of his days.

ANALYZE

Circle the two reasons Monna Giovanna's brothers want her to remarry (line 182). In the **historical context** of the Middle Ages, why does the opinion of her brothers matter so much?

_____

_____

_____

_____

_____

IDENTIFY

Pause at line 186. What single act of Federigo's finally impresses Monna Giovanna and causes her to think well of him? Underline that information.

CONNECT

Re-read the story's final paragraph. "Federigo's Falcon" was told on a day reserved for stories with happy endings. Briefly, describe this story's happy ending.

_____

_____

_____

_____

_____

_____

_____

Federigo's Falcon

Reading Skills: Evaluating Historical Context   By looking at story details, you can learn about what life was like in a certain time and place. Match each passage from the story with information it reveals about life in the Middle Ages. Write the letter of each passage before the item of historical information it exemplifies.

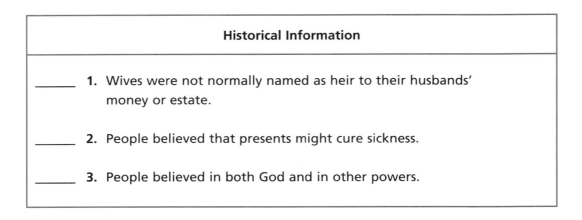

Historical Information
_____ **1.** Wives were not normally named as heir to their husbands' money or estate.
_____ **2.** People believed that presents might cure sickness.
_____ **3.** People believed in both God and in other powers.

Story Passages
a. "[I need] to ask of you a gift which I know is most precious to you; . . . and this gift is your falcon, which my son is so taken by that if I do not bring it to him, I fear his sickness will grow so much worse that I may lose him." (lines 128–133)
b. "He was very rich, and he made his son, who was growing up, his heir, and since he had loved Monna Giovanna very much, he made her his heir should his son die without a legitimate heir". . . . (lines 23–26)
c. "My lady, ever since it pleased God for me to place my love in you, I have felt that Fortune has been hostile to me in many things, and I have complained of her, but all this is nothing compared to what she has just done to me . . ." (lines 149–152)

Federigo's Falcon

VOCABULARY IN CONTEXT

DIRECTIONS: Write a word from the Word Box in each blank to complete the paragraph below. Use each word only once.

Word Box

dire
compensate
presumption
console
reproached

Noblemen of the Middle Ages did all they could to win over the women they loved. Some efforts, like the knightly sport of jousting, could involve (1) _____ consequences, such as broken bones or even death. The (2) _____ was that a heroic performance would win a favor from a special lady. If a gentleman won a joust, he often regarded a smile from his lady as enough to (3) _____ for his bruises. Even if he lost, he never blamed the lady; instead he (4) _____ himself for performing poorly. Either way, he could (5) _____ himself with the happy thought that he had proven his love.

ETYMOLOGIES

The **etymology** of a word is the history of its development. Etymology traces a word's history to its original and earliest use. Dictionaries usually present a word's etymology right after the pronunciation of the word.

DIRECTIONS: Match each word from "Federigo's Falcon" with its etymology.

_____ 1. falcon

_____ 2. comfort

_____ 3. arrange

_____ 4. companion

_____ 5. gracious

a. from Latin *gratus,* meaning "pleasing"

b. from Latin *falc–,* meaning "sickle" or "sythe"

c. from Old French *a–* + *rengier,* "to set in a row"

d. from Latin *com–* meaning "with" + *fortis,* meaning "strong"

e. from Latin *com–* meaning "with" + *panis,* meaning "bread" or "food"

Reading Standard 1.1 (Grade 9–10 Review) Identify and use the literal and figurative meanings of words and understand word derivations.

 Check your Standards Mastery at the back of this book.

The Renaissance

(1485–1660)

A Flourish of Genius

Galileo at Work (c. 1630). Galileo Galilei (1564–1642) was an Italian astronomer, mathematician, and natural philosopher.

The Renaissance (1485–1660)

C. F. Main

The following essay provides highlights of the historical period. For a more detailed version of this essay, see *Holt Literature and Language Arts,* pages 238–256.

What do you think people living a hundred years from now will call the age we live in today? Will they say we lived in the space age, the age of computers, the age of anxiety, the age of violence? We might be given a label we can't even imagine.

Just as we don't know what people of the future will think of us, the people of Europe living in the 1400s, 1500s, and 1600s didn't know that they were living in the Renaissance. Historical periods are historians' inventions, useful labels for complex phenomena. The changes in people's values, beliefs, and behavior
10 that marked the emerging Renaissance occurred gradually. Much that could be called medieval lingered on long after the period known as the Middle Ages was past.

Rediscovering Ancient Greece and Rome

The term **renaissance** is a French word meaning "rebirth." It refers particularly to renewed interest in classical learning—the writings of ancient Greece and Rome. During the Middle Ages, few ordinary people could read. Those who could read were encouraged to study texts explaining Church doctrine. In the Renaissance, however, people discovered the marvels of old
20 Greek and Latin classics—books that had been forgotten for hundreds of years.

The Spirit of Rebirth

Some people became more curious about themselves and their world than people in general had been in the Middle Ages.

Reading Standard 3.7c Evaluate the philosophical, political, religious, ethical, and social influences of the historical period that shaped the characters, plots, and settings.

Reading Standard 2.3 (Grade 9–10 Review) Generate relevant questions about readings on issues that can be researched.

IDENTIFY

Pause at line 12. What happened during the Renaissance that distinguishes it as a historical period? Circle that information.

IDENTIFY

What does *renaissance* mean? Underline the answer.

IDENTIFY

Re-read lines 14–28. In what two ways did people in the Renaissance differ from people in the Middle Ages? Underline your answer.

_____

_____

_____

IDENTIFY

Pause at line 34. What kinds of creative people lived and worked in Italy during the Renaissance? Circle that information.

CLARIFY

Re-read lines 35–45. What part did the Roman Catholic Church play in regard to the new art and learning of the Renaissance?

_____

_____

_____

_____

_____

_____

_____

_____

_____

_____

_____

_____

_____

_____

_____

_____

_____

_____

_____

_____

Gradually there was a renewal of the human spirit—a renewal of curiosity and creativity. New energy seemed to be available for creating beautiful things and thinking new, even daring, thoughts.

It All Began in Italy: A Flourish of Genius

30 The Renaissance began in Italy in the fourteenth century and lasted into the sixteenth. Extraordinary people flourished in this period—artists such as Leonardo da Vinci and Michelangelo, explorers such as Christopher Columbus, and scientists such as Galileo.

Almost everyone in Europe and Britain at this time was Roman Catholic, so the Church was very rich and powerful. Many of the popes were generous supporters of artists, architects, and scholars. Pope Julius II, for example, commissioned the artist Michelangelo to paint gigantic scenes from the Bible 40 on the ceiling of the Sistine Chapel, a small church in the pope's "city," called the Vatican. Michelangelo's bright, heroic figures, which are still admired by thousands of visitors to Rome each year, show individual human beings who are noble and capable of perfection. This optimistic view of humanity was also expressed by many other Renaissance painters and writers.

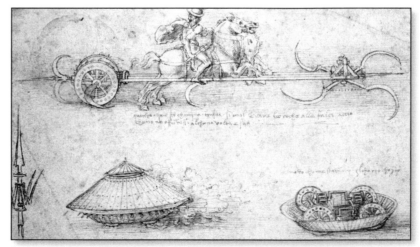

Leonardo da Vinci, one of the great geniuses of the Renaissance, was a master painter, sculptor, scientist, and military engineer. A brilliant inventor, he drew ideas for many new machines, like these sketches of tanks.
© Edimédia/CORBIS.

Humanism: Questions About the Good Life

Refreshed by the classics, the new writers and artists were part of an intellectual movement known as **humanism.** The humanists went to the old Latin and Greek classics to discover new answers

50 to such questions as "What is a human being?" "What is a good life?" and "How do I lead a good life?" Of course, Christianity provided complete answers to these questions, answers that the Renaissance humanists accepted as true. They sought to harmonize the Bible and the classics. Their aim was to use the classics to strengthen, not discredit, Christianity.

The humanists' first task was to recover accurate copies of these ancient writings. Their searches through Italian monasteries turned up writers and works whose very existence has been forgotten. Their next task was to share their findings. So they became

60 teachers, especially of the young men who would become the next generation's rulers—wise and virtuous rulers, they hoped.

The New Technology: A Flood of Print

The printing press transformed the way information was exchanged during the Renaissance. Before this, all books were laboriously written out by hand—you can imagine how difficult and expensive this was and how few books were available.

The inventor of printing with movable type was a German named Johannes Gutenberg (1400–1468). He printed the first complete book, an immense Latin Bible, at Mainz, Germany,

70 around 1455. From there, the art and craft of printing spread to other cities in Germany and beyond. By 1500, relatively inexpensive books were available throughout western Europe. In 1476, printing reached England. In that year, William Caxton (1422–1491), a merchant, diplomat, and writer, set up a printing press in Westminster (now part of London). In all, Caxton's press issued about one hundred different titles, initiating a flood of print in English that is still increasing.

IDENTIFY

Re-read lines 47–55. Underline questions that interested the humanist thinkers.

IDENTIFY

The humanists faced two tasks in their study of Latin and Greek writings (lines 56–61). Underline what those tasks were. What did they do once those tasks were completed?

_____

_____

_____

_____

IDENTIFY CAUSE & EFFECT

Name two major effects of the invention of the printing press with movable type (lines 63–77).

_____

_____

_____

_____

_____

_____

_____

Two Friends—Two Humanists

Desiderius Erasmus (1466?–1536) is today perhaps the best known
80   of all the Renaissance humanists. Erasmus was a Dutch monk, but
he lived outside the monastery and loved to travel, visiting many
of the countries in Europe, including Italy, France, Germany, and
England. Because he wrote in Latin, he could address his many
writings to all the educated people of western Europe.

On his visits to England, Erasmus became friendly with
a number of important people, among them a young lawyer
named Thomas More (1477–1535). More and Erasmus had
much in common: They both loved life, laughter, and classical
learning, and they both were dedicated churchmen, though they
90   were impatient with some of the Church's corrupt practices at
that time.

Like Erasmus, More wrote in Latin—poems, pamphlets,
biographies, and his famous treatise on human society, *Utopia*
(yo͞o·tō′pē·ə). More held a number of important offices, rose to
the top of his profession, was knighted, and as lord chancellor,
became one of the king's chief ministers.

The Reformation: Breaking with the Church

While the Renaissance was going on throughout Europe, there
occurred in some countries another important series of events,
100   called the **Reformation.** In England these two vast movements
were closely related, and their forces were felt by all English
writers. Reformers rejected the authority of the pope and the
Italian churchmen. By the 1530s, an open break with the
Roman Catholic Church could no longer be avoided.

By then a number of circumstances made such a break
possible. Strong feelings of patriotism and national identity
made the English people resent the financial burdens imposed
on them by the Vatican—the pope, after all, was a foreign power
in far-off Italy. Moreover, new religious ideas were coming into

COMPARE & CONTRAST

What did the humanists
More and Erasmus have in
common (lines 85–93)?
Underline that information.

IDENTIFY

Pause at line 104. With
whom were the Reformers in
conflict? Circle your answer.

IDENTIFY

Read on, and pause at
line 114. Why were Martin
Luther's teachings considered
radical?

110 England from the Continent, especially from Germany. There, a monk named Martin Luther (1483–1546) was teaching a different kind of Christianity. His teachings were not based on what the pope said but rather on a personal understanding of the Bible. In addition, right at home in England, humanists like Thomas More and Desiderius Erasmus were ridiculing the ignorance and idleness of monks and the loose living and personal wealth of priest and bishops.

King Versus Pope: All for an Heir

The conflict between the pope and the king of England came
120 to a climax when Henry VIII wanted to get rid of his wife of twenty-four years. The Church did not allow divorce, so Henry needed a loophole. He asked Pope Clement VII to declare that he, Henry, was not properly married to his Spanish wife, Catherine of Aragon, because she had previously been married to his older brother Arthur, now dead. (It was against Church law to marry a dead sibling's spouse.)

Henry had two motives for wanting to get rid of Catherine. First, although she had borne him a daughter, she was too old to give him the male heir that he thought he must have. What is
130 more, the king now wished to marry Anne Boleyn, who had been his "favorite" for several years. The pope was not able to grant Henry the annulment of his marriage, even if he had wanted to, because the pope was controlled by Queen Catherine's nephew, the emperor of Spain. So when he received the pope's refusal in 1533, Henry appointed a new archbishop of Canterbury, who obligingly declared Henry's marriage to Catherine invalid. In 1534, Henry concluded the break with Rome by declaring himself head of the English Church.

CLARIFY

Re-read lines 105–117. What three circumstances made the break between England and the Roman Catholic Church possible? Underline that information.

INTERPRET

Re-read lines 119–138. Why did Henry appoint a new archbishop of Canterbury and declare himself head of the Church of England?

_____
_____
_____
_____
_____
_____
_____
_____
_____
_____
_____
_____
_____
_____
_____
_____
_____
_____
_____
_____

IDENTIFY

Pause at line 147. Underline the reason that Henry ordered the execution of Thomas More.

ANALYZE

Read lines 148–158 carefully. What is the connection between the teachings of Renaissance humanists and the founding idea of most Protestant churches?

_____

_____

_____

_____

_____

_____

_____

_____

_____

_____

_____

_____

_____

_____

_____

_____

_____

_____

_____

Portrait of King Henry VIII of England (c. 1540).
Henry VIII (1491–1547) ruled England from 1509 until his death.
© Hulton Archive.

The Protestant Reformation

140   Henry closed all of England's monasteries and sold the rich buildings and lands to his subjects. While the vast majority of his subjects agreed with Henry's changes in the Church, some of them did not. The best known of those who remained loyal to the pope was Sir Thomas More, the lord chancellor of England. More felt he could not legally recognize his friend Henry as head of the Church. For More's stubbornness, Henry ordered that More be beheaded.

This was the very beginning of Protestantism in England. Many people were dissatisfied with the new church for reasons
150   just the opposite of More's. They felt that it was not reformed

enough, that it was merely a copy of Catholicism, as in some ways it was. These people later became known as Puritans, Baptists, Presbyterians, Dissenters, and Nonconformists. Some of them said that religion was solely a matter between the individual and God. This idea, which is still the foundation of most Protestant churches, is closely related to the teachings of those Renaissance humanists who emphasized the freedom of all human beings.

Henry VIII: Renaissance Man and Executioner

160 Henry VIII (reigned 1509–1547) had six wives: After Catherine of Aragon and Anne Boleyn, there were Jane Seymour, Anne of Cleves, Catherine Howard, and Catherine Parr. The fates of these unfortunate women are summarized in a jingle:

> Divorced, beheaded, died,
> Divorced, beheaded, survived.

The sexual intrigues of the court trapped two of Henry's wives: The king could play around, but he couldn't tolerate suspicions of his wives' fidelity. Like Thomas More, Anne Boleyn and Catherine Howard lost their heads on the chopping block.

170 Despite his messy home life, Henry VIII was an important figure in history. He created the Royal Navy, which put a stop to foreign invasions of England and provided the means for the political power, language, and literature of England to spread all over the globe. Henry himself deserves the title Renaissance man. He wrote poetry and played many musical instruments well; he was a champion athlete and a hunter; and he supported the new humanistic learning. In his old age, however, Henry was also coarse, dissolute, arrogant, and a womanizer. He died without knowing that the child he ignored because she was female

180 would become the greatest ruler England ever had.

Notes _____

CONNECT

From what you have read about his actions and behavior (lines 170–180), do you think Henry VIII should be remembered as a good king?

The Boy King and Bloody Mary

Henry VIII was survived by three children: Mary, Elizabeth, and Edward. According to the laws of succession, a son had to be crowned first, and so at age nine the son of Henry and Jane Seymour became Edward VI (reigned 1547–1553). An intelligent but sickly boy, he ruled in name only while his relatives wielded the actual power.

When Edward died (of tuberculosis), he was followed by his half-Spanish half-sister, Mary (reigned 1553–1558). Mary
190   was a devout, strong-willed Catholic determined to avenge the wrongs done to her mother, Catherine of Aragon. She restored the pope's power in England and ruthlessly hunted down Protestants.

If she had lived longer and exercised better judgment, Mary might have undone all her father's accomplishments. She made a strategic error, however, when she burned about three hundred of her subjects at the stake. She further lost the support of her people when she married Philip II, king of Spain, a country England was beginning to fear and hate. Mary's executions earned
200   her the name Bloody Mary. Because she was childless, upon her death she was succeeded by her sister Elizabeth.

Elizabeth: The Virgin Queen

Elizabeth I (reigned 1558–1603) was one of the most brilliant and successful monarchs in history. Since she inherited a kingdom torn by fierce religious feuds, her first task was to restore law and order. She reestablished the Church of England and again rejected the pope's authority. The pope excommunicated her. To keep Spain happy, she pretended that she just might marry her widowed brother-in-law, King Philip.
210   Philip was the first of a long procession of noblemen, both foreign and English, who wanted to wed her. However, Elizabeth resisted marriage all her life and officially remained "the Virgin

IDENTIFY

Re-read lines 188–201. Underline the reasons Queen Mary came to be known as "Bloody Mary."

WORD STUDY

The verb *excommunicate* (eks·kə·myōō′ni·kāt), used in the past tense in line 207, is built on the Latin prefix *ex–*, meaning "without," and the Latin verb *communicare*, meaning "to share or impart." It is a religious term that refers to the official exclusion of a person from the rights and privileges of church membership.

Queen Elizabeth I of England (1533–1603) in a dress worn to a ceremony to thank her navy for the defeat of the Spanish Armada.
© Hulton Archive.

INFER

Re-read lines 216–225. Why was Mary, Queen of Scots, a threat to Queen Elizabeth and to Protestant England?

Queen." She knew that her strength lay in her independence and in her ability to play one suitor off against another.

A True Daughter

A truly heroic person, Elizabeth survived many plots against her life. Several of these plots were initiated by her cousin, another Mary—Mary Stuart, Queen of Scots. As Elizabeth had no children, Mary was heir to England's throne because she too
220 was a direct descendant of Henry VII. A Catholic, Mary was eventually deposed from her throne in Protestant Scotland. Put under house arrest, she lived as a royal exile in England, carefully watched by her cousin Elizabeth. Elizabeth endured Mary and her plots for twenty years and then, a true daughter of her father, sent her Scottish cousin to the chopping block.

IDENTIFY CAUSE & EFFECT

Re-read lines 228–338. What important event in England's history occurred in 1588? Circle this information. Underline the result of this event.

GENERATE QUESTIONS

Pause at line 249. Think about what you have learned so far about Queen Elizabeth. What further question do you have about the role of the monarchy in the politics and culture of England? Where would you look to find the answer? *(Grade 9–10 Review)*

_____

_____

_____

_____

_____

_____

_____

_____

COMPARE & CONTRAST

How was King James I of England different from Elizabeth I (lines 251–257)? Underline the words and phrases that describe James. Circle the words and phrases that describe Elizabeth.

The Spanish Armada Sinks: A Turning Point in History

King Philip of Spain, ever watchful for an opportunity to hammer at England, used Mary's execution as an excuse to invade
230   England. He assembled a vast fleet of warships for that purpose: the famous Spanish Armada. In 1588, England's Royal Navy, assisted greatly by nasty weather in the Irish Sea, destroyed the Armada. This victory assured England's and all of northern Europe's independence from the powerful Catholic countries of the Mediterranean. It was a great turning point in history and Elizabeth's finest moment. If Spain had prevailed, history would have been quite different: All of North America, like most of South America, might be speaking Spanish instead of English.

A Flood of Literature

240   What is the connection between these political events and English literature? With their own religious and national identity firmly established, the English started writing as never before. After the defeat of the Armada, Elizabeth became a beloved symbol of peace, security, and prosperity to her subjects, and she provided inspiration to scores of English authors. They represented her in poetry, drama, and fiction as a mythological figure. Literary works that did not directly represent her were dedicated to her because authors knew she was a lover of literature, a person of remarkably wide learning, and something of a writer herself.

250   ## A Dull Man Succeeds a Witty Woman

Elizabeth died childless. She was succeeded by her second cousin, James VI of Scotland, the son of Elizabeth's cousin Mary. As James I of England (reigned 1603–1626), he lacked Elizabeth's ability to resolve critical issues. James was a spendthrift where Elizabeth had been thrifty; he was thick-tongued and goggle-eyed where she had been glamorous and witty; he was essentially a foreigner where she had been a complete Englishwoman.

James I tried hard. He wrote learned books; he patronized Shakespeare; he sponsored a new translation of the Bible; and he was in many respects an admirable man and a benevolent, peaceful ruler. Yet his relationship with many of his subjects went from bad to worse.

The Decline of the Renaissance

James's son and successor, Charles I (reigned 1625–1649), turned out to be remote, autocratic, and self-destructive. Some of his most powerful subjects had him beheaded in 1649. For the next eleven years, England was ruled by Parliament and the Puritan dictator Oliver Cromwell, not by an anointed king. When Charles's son came to power eleven years later, in 1660, England had changed in many important ways.

Of course the Renaissance did not end in 1660 when Charles II returned from exile in France, just as it had not begun on a specific date. Renaissance values, which were primarily moral and religious, gradually eroded, and Renaissance energies gradually gave out. The last great writer of the English Renaissance was John Milton, who lived on into an age in which educated people were becoming more worldly in their outlook. Scientific truths were soon to challenge long-accepted religious beliefs.

The English Renaissance was over.

DRAW CONCLUSIONS

Re-read lines 264–270. The English monarchy was dealt a serious blow when Charles I was beheaded. What does his son's return to the throne, restoring the monarchy to England, tell you about English society at this time?

Sonnets 29 and 116 by William Shakespeare

REVIEW SKILLS

Look for examples of the following literary devices as you read Sonnets 29 and 116.

FIGURATIVE LANGUAGE
Words or phrases that describe one thing in terms of another and that are not meant to be taken literally.

IMAGERY
Language that appeals to the senses (sight, hearing, touch, taste, or smell).

LITERARY FOCUS: SHAKESPEAREAN SONNET

Sonnets are lyrics that are fourteen lines long. A **Shakespearean sonnet** is a fourteen-line poem with a particular rhyme scheme and **meter,** or rhythmic pattern. The Shakespearean sonnet's rhymes are arranged in three **quatrains,** rhyming groups of four lines each, followed by a final two-line **couplet.** The rhyme scheme of a Shakespearean sonnet looks like this: *abab* (first quatrain), *cdcd* (second quatrain), *efef* (third quatrain), and *gg* (couplet). The meter of the Shakespearean sonnet is called **iambic pentameter.** Each line has five unstressed syllables that alternate with five stressed syllables.

> Ĭ áll ălóne bĕwéep mý óutcăst státe,

The message of a Shakespearean sonnet is shaped by the poem's rhyming pattern. The three quatrains express related ideas, while the couplet at the end sums up the poem's message. Within the poem, a shift in the thought or mood occurs, often between lines 12 and 13. This change of focus is called the **turn,** meaning that the speaker in the poem is turning from one thing to another.

READING SKILLS: PARAPHRASING

When we **paraphrase** a story or poem, we retell it using our own words. If you were to tell a friend about one of Shakespeare's sonnets, you might restate its ideas, relating its **imagery** and tone without using quotations from the poem. For example, the first three lines of Shakespeare's Sonnet 30 are shown below on the left; on the right is a paraphrase of those lines.

Lines from Sonnet 30	Paraphrase
"When to the sessions of sweet silent thought / I summon up remembrance of things past, / I sigh the lack of many a thing I sought, . . . "	When I think quietly about the past, I'm sad as I remember the things I tried to get but didn't.

Use the Skill   Read each sonnet at least twice. As you read, pause after each four-line quatrain and after the final couplet. First, paraphrase lines and phrases that are difficult to understand. Then, paraphrase the ideas in each quatrain.

Reading Standard 3.1
Analyze characteristics of subgenres that are used in poetry, prose, plays, novels, short stories, and other basic genres.

Reading Standard 3.7 (Grade 9–10 Review)
Recognize and understand the significance of various literary devices, including figurative language, imagery, allegory, and symbolism, and explain their appeal.

Sonnet 29

William Shakespeare

When, in disgrace[1] with Fortune and men's eyes,

I all alone beweep my outcast state,

And trouble deaf heaven with my bootless[2] cries,

And look upon myself and curse my fate,

5   Wishing me like to one more rich in hope,

Featured like him, like him[3] with friends possessed,

Desiring this man's art,[4] and that man's scope,[5]

With what I most enjoy contented least;

Yet in these thoughts myself almost despising,

10   Haply[6] I think on thee, and then my state,

Like to the lark[7] at break of day arising

From sullen[8] earth, sings hymns at heaven's gate;

For thy sweet love remembered such wealth brings

That then I scorn to change my state with kings.

---

1. **disgrace** *n.:* loss of favor.
2. **bootless** *adj.:* useless; futile.
3. **one . . . him . . . him:** three men whom the speaker envies.
4. **art** *n.:* literary ability.
5. **scope** *n.:* power.
6. **haply** *adv.:* by chance.
7. **lark** *n.:* English skylark, a bird whose song seems to pour down from the sky.
8. **sullen** *adj.:* gloomy.

Sonnet 116

William Shakespeare

IDENTIFY

Pause at line 4, after the first quatrain. The rhyme scheme is *abab,* meaning there are two pairs of lines that end with rhyming words. Circle the *aa* rhymes, and underline the *bb* rhymes.

INTERPRET

In lines 5–7, the speaker uses a kind of figurative language called **metaphor** to compare true love to a landmark and to a star that guides ships at sea. What ideas about true love do you think the speaker is expressing here? *(Grade 9–10 Review)*

_____

_____

_____

_____

_____

_____

_____

INTERPRET

Re-read lines 9–12. What idea about love does the speaker reveal?

_____

_____

Let me not to the marriage of true minds

Admit impediments. Love is not love

Which alters when it alteration finds,

Or bends with the remover to remove.

5 Oh no! It is an ever-fixèd mark[1]

That looks on tempests and is never shaken.

It is the star to every wandering bark,[2]

Whose worth's unknown, although his height be taken.[3]

Love's not Time's fool, though rosy lips and cheeks

10 Within his bending sickle's compass[4] come.

Love alters not with his brief hours and weeks,

But bears it out[5] even to the edge of doom.

    If this be error and upon me proved,

    I never writ, nor no man ever loved.

---

1. **mark** *n.:* seamark; a prominent object on shore that serves as a landmark to guide sailors.
2. **bark** *n.:* boat.
3. **height be taken:** altitude measured to determine a ship's position.
4. **compass** *n.:* range; reach.
5. **bears it out:** survives.

Sonnets 29 and 116

Reading Skills: Paraphrasing   Restate the ideas expressed in each quatrain and couplet of Sonnets 29 and 116 in the chart below. Also, note where you find each sonnet's **turn** and explain how the turn changes the poem's message.

	Sonnet 29	Sonnet 116
First quatrain	Paraphrase:	Paraphrase:
Second quatrain	Paraphrase:	Paraphrase:
Third quatrain	Paraphrase:	Paraphrase:
Final couplet	Paraphrase:	Paraphrase:
Location of the turn		
How the message changes after the turn		

✓ Check your Standards Mastery at the back of this book.

Saint Crispin's Day Speech by William Shakespeare

BEFORE YOU READ

REVIEW SKILLS

As you read the Saint Crispin's Day Speech from Shakespeare's *Henry V,* think about what the message of the monologue is.

MONOLOGUE
A long speech made by one character in a play to another character or to the audience.

LITERARY FOCUS: MONOLOGUE AND SOLILOQUY

Most of what we learn about characters and events in a play we learn through conversations between characters. This conversation is called **dialogue.** Playwrights during the Renaissance used two other devices to reveal a character's thoughts and feelings—monologues and soliloquies:

- A **monologue** is a long, usually formal speech spoken by one character to the audience or to another character.

- A **soliloquy** (sə·lil'ə·kwē) is a more thoughtful kind of monologue in which the speaker, usually alone onstage, shares his or her inner thoughts and feelings directly with the audience.

READING SKILLS: USING PUNCTUATION CLUES

Shakespeare's verse can baffle even the best readers at first. One way to find meaning in Shakespeare's writing is to look for and use punctuation clues. Sentences can begin and end anywhere in the poetic lines. Here are some tips:

- Pay attention to capital letters and periods or other end punctuation to signal the beginning and end of sentences.

- Information contained in commas or within dashes may not be essential to the basic meaning of a sentence. Read the sentence once, omitting that material to find its basic meaning. Then, re-read the sentence, and include the material you left out the first time.

Use the Skill　As you read the selection, look for punctuation clues. You may want to highlight the beginning and end of each sentence as you read.

Reading Standard 3.1
Analyze characteristics of subgenres that are used in poetry, prose, plays, novels, short stories, essays, and other basic genres.

Reading Standard 3.4 (Grade 9–10 Review)
Determine characters' traits by what the characters say about themselves in narration, dialogue, dramatic monologue, and soliloquy.

Saint Crispin's Day Speech

William Shakespeare

In *Henry V,* Act IV, Scene 3, Henry V, king of England, delivers this speech to a group of English soldiers who are facing a very difficult battle. Henry believes that the crown of France rightfully belongs to him, and he has taken an army across the English Channel to France in hopes of winning the crown. The English army is sick, underfed, and outnumbered by the French troops. As they prepare for battle, an English nobleman, Westmorland, wishes aloud that more soldiers would arrive to help in the fight. King Henry answers him with a stirring speech that lifts the spirits of his tired men and inspires them to fight, and even die, for their country.

King.

What's[1] he that wishes so?

My cousin Westmorland? No, my fair cousin.

If we are marked to die, we are enough

To do our country loss; and if to live,

5   The fewer men, the greater share of honor.

God's will, I pray thee, wish not one man more.

By Jove, I am not covetous for gold,

Nor care I who doth feed upon my cost;

It yearns[2] me not if men my garments wear;

10   Such outward things dwell not in my desires.

But if it be a sin to covet honor

I am the most offending soul alive.

No, faith, my coz, wish not a man from England.

God's peace, I would not lose so great an honor

15   As one man more, methinks, would share from me

For the best hope I have. O, do not wish one more!

IDENTIFY CAUSE & EFFECT

Lines 3–5 contain two cause-and-effect relationships. Circle each cause, and underline each effect. Restate in your own words the idea that Henry expresses here.

_____

_____

_____

_____

_____

_____

_____

_____

_____

_____

_____

---

1. **what's:** who's.
2. **yearns** *v.:* saddens.

IDENTIFY

In lines 17–22, the king instructs Westmorland to tell any men who are afraid to fight that he will pay their way home. Underline the reason he gives for this.

FLUENCY

Read the boxed passage aloud at least twice. As you read, try to inspire "your" army to victory with these words telling of future glory. Speak the words in lines 29–31 with dramatic emphasis, and act out the gesture described in line 30.

WORD STUDY

Henry refers to a *vigil* (line 28), a special ritual observed before a holy day. During a vigil, people keep watch by staying awake during the time they would normally sleep. The word *vigil* comes from the Latin word for wakefulness, *vigilia*. A person who is alert and watchful may be called *vigilant*, meaning that he or she does not fall asleep on the job.

Rather proclaim it, Westmorland, through my host[3]

That he which hath no stomach to this fight,

Let him depart; his passport shall be made

20 And crowns for convoy put into his purse.

We would not die in that man's company

That fears his fellowship to die with us.

This day is called the Feast of Crispian.[4]

He that outlives this day and comes safe home

25 Will stand a-tiptoe when this day is named

And rouse him at the name of Crispian.

He that shall see this day and live old age

Will yearly on the vigil feast his neighbors

And say, "Tomorrow is Saint Crispian."

30 Then will he strip his sleeve and show his scars,

And say, "These wounds I had on Crispin's Day."

Andre Braugher as Henry V, performed for the New York Shakespeare Festival (1996).

3. **host** *n.:* army.
4. **Feast of Crispian:** Saint Crispin's Day, October 25. Crispinus and Crispianus were martyrs who fled Rome in the third century. Because they worked as shoemakers, they became that craft's patron saints after they were martyred.

Old men forget; yet all shall be forgot,

But he'll remember with advantages[5]

What feats he did that day. Then shall our names,

35   Familiar in his mouth as household words—

Harry the King, Bedford and Exeter,

Warwick and Talbot, Salisbury and Gloucester—

Be in their flowing cups freshly remembered.

This story shall the good man teach his son;

40   And Crispin Crispian shall ne'er go by,

From this day to the ending of the world,

But we in it shall be rememberèd—

We few, we happy few, we band of brothers.

For he today that sheds his blood with me

45   Shall be my brother; be he ne'er so vile,

This day shall gentle his condition.[6]

And gentlemen in England now abed

Shall think themselves accursed they were not here,

And hold their manhoods cheap whiles any speaks

50   That fought with us upon Saint Crispin's Day.

IDENTIFY

Re-read lines 32–42, in which Henry describes how soldiers who fought on Saint Crispin's Day will tell their stories when they are old. Underline the words or phrases that reveal Henry's belief that they will all go down in history for winning the battle.

INTERPRET

Re-read lines 43–50, and circle the phrase Henry uses to describe the relationship between the soldiers. What makes those lines so convincing or appealing to his listeners?

5.   **advantages** *n. pl.:* additions of his own.
6.   **gentle his condition:** bring him up to the position of gentleman.

Saint Crispin's Day Speech

Literary Focus: Monologue and Soliloquy   There are three basic ways to communicate a character's thoughts and feelings in a play: through **dialogue, monologue,** and **soliloquy.** Refer to the speech as you fill in the following chart.

Who is delivering the lines?	
Whom is he addressing?	
Is this speech an example of a monologue or a soliloquy, and why?	
List three main ideas given in the speech.	
What does the audience learn about the speaker?	
If in this play dialogue rather than a speech had been used to convey this information, how would its effect differ?	

Check your Standards Mastery at the back of this book.

A Valediction: Forbidding Mourning by John Donne

LITERARY FOCUS: METAPHYSICAL CONCEITS

Poets sometimes use surprising comparisons to get you to think about their subjects in a different way. John Donne uses complex and clever **figures of speech** called **metaphysical conceits** to compare things that you ordinarily wouldn't think of as being similar. The following poem contains perhaps the most famous metaphysical conceit of all time.

Full of Surprises   Many of the comparisons that writers make are familiar. For example, a tall person may be compared to a tree. A metaphysical conceit, on the other hand, makes a clever, surprising comparison that lets us see things in a new way. Here are some examples of unusual metaphysical conceits that writers have created:

a lover's tears	*are compared to*	newly minted coins
a king's court	*is compared to*	a bowling alley
a man	*is compared to*	a world

READING SKILLS: RECOGNIZING COMPARISONS AND CONTRASTS

In this poem, Donne compares and contrasts lovers with the two pointed legs of a compass, a tool used in geometry to draw circles (shown here). **Comparing** two objects shows the ways in which they are alike. **Contrasting** objects focuses on their differences. Donne's use of this metaphysical conceit is a special way to compare and contrast two things that, on the surface, seem very unlike.

Use the Skill   As you read the poem, look for other comparisons Donne makes.

REVIEW SKILLS

As you read "A Valediction: Forbidding Mourning," look for examples of the following:

STYLE
An author's unique way of expressing ideas. Style is closely connected to the author's word choice.

FIGURATIVE LANGUAGE
Words or phrases that describe one thing in terms of another and that are not meant to be taken literally. Figurative language includes all **figures of speech.**

Reading Standard 3.4
Analyze the ways in which poets use imagery, figures of speech, and sounds to evoke readers' emotions.

Reading Standard 3.11 (Grade 9–10 Review)
Evaluate the aesthetic qualities of style, including the impact of diction and figurative language on tone, mood, and theme, using the terminology of literary criticism.

A Valediction: Forbidding Mourning

John Donne

> **BACKGROUND**
> Saying goodbye to a loved one can be very difficult. In this poem, the speaker is about to take a long journey, and he says farewell ("valediction") to the woman he loves. He tells her not to cry or feel sad ("forbidding mourning"). Donne wrote this poem before he left on a trip to France, leaving behind his pregnant but unwell wife.

INTERPRET

In lines 1–8, the speaker uses a **metaphor** and urges his wife to part as quietly (and privately) as the soul leaves the body of a good man. According to lines 7–8, why should they part like this?

_____

_____

_____

INTERPRET

According to lines 9–12, which is greater, an earthquake or movement of the heavenly spheres? What does the speaker compare his love to?

_____

_____

_____

_____

As virtuous men pass mildly away,
    And whisper to their souls, to go,
Whilst some of their sad friends do say,
    The breath goes now, and some say, no:

5 So let us melt, and make no noise,
    No tear-floods, nor sigh-tempests move,
'Twere profanation[1] of our joys
    To tell the laity[2] our love.

Moving of th' earth[3] brings harms and fears,
10   Men reckon what it did and meant,[4]
But trepidation of the spheres,[5]
    Though greater far, is innocent.[6]

---

1. **profanation** *n.:* lack of reverence or respect.
2. **laity** *n.:* laypersons; here, those unable to understand the "religion" of true love.
3. **moving of th' earth:** earthquake.
4. **meant:** "What does it mean?" was a question ordinarily asked of any unusual phenomenon.
5. **trepidation of the spheres:** irregularities in the movements of remote heavenly bodies.
6. **innocent** *adj.:* unobserved and harmless compared with earthquakes.

Dull sublunary[7] lovers' love

    (Whose soul[8] is sense[9]) cannot admit

15 Absence, because it doth remove

    Those things which elemented[10] it.

But we by a love, so much refined,

    That ourselves know not what it is,

Interassurèd of the mind,

20   Care less eyes, lips, and hands to miss.

Our two souls therefore, which are one,

    Though I must go, endure not yet

A breach,[11] but an expansion,

    Like gold to airy thinness beat.

25 If they be two, they are two so

    As stiff twin compasses are two,

Thy soul the fixed foot, makes no show

    To move, but doth, if th' other do.

And though it in the center sit,

30   Yet when the other far doth roam,

It leans, and hearkens after it,

    And grows erect, as that comes home.

Such wilt thou be to me, who must

    Like th' other foot, obliquely[12] run;

35 Thy firmness[13] makes my circle just,[14]

    And makes me end, where I begun.

---

7. **sublunary** *adj.:* under the moon, therefore subject to change.
8. **soul** *n.:* essence.
9. **sense** *n.:* the body with its five senses; that is, purely physical rather than spiritual.
10. **elemented** *v.:* comprised; composed.
11. **breach** *n.:* break; split.
12. **obliquely** *adv.:* off course.
13. **firmness** *n.:* fidelity.
14. **just** *adj.:* perfect. A circle symbolizes perfection, hence wedding rings.

COMPARE & CONTRAST

Circle words or phrases that describe "sublunary" lovers (lines 13–16). What difference does the speaker see between sublunary lovers and the more "refined" love (line 17) he shares with his wife? (*Interassurèd* in line 19 means "jointly assured" or "certain.")

_____

_____

_____

_____

_____

_____

_____

ANALYZE

In lines 25–36, Donne uses a **metaphysical conceit** to compare two lovers to the two pointed legs of a compass. Underline words that describe what the "fixed foot" (line 27) of the compass does when the other foot moves. What does this comparison say about the kind of love the speaker is describing? *(Grade 9–10 Review)*

_____

_____

_____

_____

A Valediction: Forbidding Mourning

Reading Skills: Recognizing Comparisons and Contrasts   Look over the details in the poem that describe the lovers and the love they share, including the striking comparisons called **metaphysical conceits.** The first column below lists three comparisons or contrasts that Donne makes in the poem. Complete the chart by explaining the point Donne makes in each comparison. Then, briefly describe any comparisons you find unusual.

Comparison or Contrast	What Point the Comparison Makes	Is the Comparison Unusual? Explain.
The effects of an earthquake are contrasted with the movements of the spheres. (lines 9–12)		
The speaker and his lover are contrasted with "sublunary lovers." (lines 13–20)		
The speaker and his lover are compared to the two legs of a compass. (lines 25–36)		

 Check your Standards Mastery at the back of this book.

Meditation 17 by John Donne

LITERARY FOCUS: TONE

The **tone** of a work expresses the writer's attitude or feelings about the subject, the reader, or a character. Writers convey a certain tone by selecting particular words, images, and details. By looking closely at the language a writer uses, for example, you can tell whether a story about love is romantic and idealistic or bitter and unhappy.

Tuning Your Ear for Tone   Have you ever been aware of a particular tone you used when you tried to communicate your thoughts or feelings? Jot down an event, a person, a thing, or an experience in your life that you have strong feelings about. It could be something you own, a place you've visited, a book you've read, or a special person. Then, write some words or phrases that convey a tone, revealing your attitude or feelings about the example you've chosen.

Example	Words/Phrases That Convey Tone

READING SKILLS: UNDERSTANDING PATTERNS OF ORGANIZATION

In "Meditation 17" Donne shares his ideas about life and death. To make his ideas clear, persuasive, and memorable, he uses several patterns of organization. **Repetition** of words is one such pattern. The repetition of sentence structures is another pattern, called **parallelism.** An example of parallelism appears in lines 13–14: "Some pieces are translated by age, some by sickness, some by war, some by justice." Watch for these patterns of organization as you read "Meditation 17":

repetition	words and phrases that are repeated to create rhythm and emphasis
parallel structure	the use of words, phrases, or sentences that have the same grammatical structure
rhetorical questions	questions that are addressed to the audience to emphasize a point, not to be answered

REVIEW SKILLS

As you read "Meditation 17," analyze the ideas in the text.

ANALYSIS
A close examination of the elements of a text.

Reading Standard 2.2
Analyze the ways in which clarity of meaning is affected by the patterns of organization, hierarchical structures, syntax, and word choice in the text.

Reading Standard 2.5 (Grade 9–10 Review)
Extend ideas presented in primary or secondary sources through original analysis, evaluation, and elaboration.

Reading Standard 3.3
Analyze the ways in which tone achieves specific rhetorical purposes.

MEDITATION 17

John Donne

BACKGROUND

In 1624, when he was very ill, John Donne wrote a series of meditations, or thoughtful reflections, on the topic of death. "Meditation 17" repeatedly refers to the ringing of church bells. In Donne's time, church bells rang to announce the death of a church member.

INTERPRET

In lines 5–10, Donne states that he is affected by each person's birth and each person's death. Why are all births and deaths important to him?

_____

_____

_____

_____

_____

IDENTIFY

Donne develops a long **metaphor** that compares humanity to a book written by God (lines 10–17). Circle the words and phrases that he uses to make this comparison. What does Donne mean by the "Library" (line 16)?

_____

Nunc lento　　　　Now, this bell tolling softly

sonitu dicunt,　　for another, says to me,

Morieris.　　　　　Thou must die.

Perchance he for whom this bell tolls, may be so ill, as that he knows not it tolls for him; and perchance I may think myself so much better than I am, as that they who are about me, and see my state, may have caused it to toll for me, and I know not that. The Church is catholic, universal, so are all her actions; all that she does belongs to all. When she baptizes a child, that action concerns me; for that child is thereby connected to that Head[1] which is my Head too, and engrafted into that body, whereof I am a member. And when she buries a man, that action concerns

10　me: All mankind is of one Author, and is one volume; when one man dies, one chapter is not torn out of the book, but translated[2] into a better language; and every chapter must be so translated; God employs several translators; some pieces are translated by age, some by sickness, some by war, some by justice; but God's

---

1. **Head:** Christ.
2. **translated** *v.*: spiritually carried across from one realm to another.

hand is in every translation; and his hand shall bind up all our scattered leaves[3] again, for that Library where every book shall lie open to one another: As therefore the bell that rings to a sermon, calls not upon the preacher only, but upon the congregation to come; so this bell calls us all: but how much more

20 me, who am brought so near the door by this sickness. There was a contention as far as a suit[4] (in which both piety and dignity, religion and estimation,[5] were mingled), which of the religious orders should ring to prayers first in the morning; and it was determined, that they should ring first that rose earliest. If we understand aright the dignity of this bell that tolls for our evening prayer, we would be glad to make it ours, by rising early, in that application, that it might be ours, as well as his, whose indeed it is. The bell doth toll for him that thinks it doth; and though it intermit[6] again, yet from that minute, that that

30 occasion wrought upon him, he is united to God. Who casts not up his eye to the sun when it rises? but who takes off his eye from a comet when that breaks out?[7] Who bends not his ear to any bell, which upon any occasion rings? but who can remove it from that bell, which is passing a piece of himself out of this world? No man is an island, entire of itself; every man is a piece of the continent, a part of the main;[8] if a clod be washed away by the sea, Europe is the less, as well as if a promontory were, as well as if a manor of thy friends or of thine own were; any man's death diminishes me, because I am involved in mankind; and

40 therefore never send to know for whom the bell tolls; it tolls for thee. Neither can we call this a begging of misery or a borrowing of misery, as though we were not miserable enough of ourselves, but must fetch in more from the next house, in taking upon us the misery of our neighbors. Truly it were an excusable

---

3. **leaves** *n. pl.:* pages.
4. **contention . . . suit:** argument that went as far as a lawsuit.
5. **estimation** *n.:* self-esteem.
6. **intermit** *v.:* cease.
7. **comet . . . out:** Comets were regarded as signs of disaster to come.
8. **main** *n.:* mainland.

ANALYZE

In lines 17–20, Donne describes how the "bell calls us all" and refers to his own life-threatening sickness. What is Donne's **tone** in this passage?

_____

_____

_____

IDENTIFY

Re-read lines 28–35, and underline the series of rhetorical questions Donne poses. What effect does this use of **parallel structure** have on readers?

_____

_____

_____

_____

FLUENCY

Read the boxed passage aloud twice. Emphasize Donne's famous "No man is an island" image (line 35), and think about the spiritual connection he describes.

CLARIFY

Re-read lines 41–48. Why does Donne claim that affliction, or suffering, is "a treasure"? Underline his reasons.

ANALYZE

Re-read lines 44–58, and circle the word *affliction* each time it appears. What effect does Donne create with the **repetition** of this word?

_____

_____

_____

_____

_____

_____

_____

_____

INTERPRET

How would you describe the speaker's **tone**: solemn, sad, depressed, angry, or something else? Re-read the meditation, and put a star next to words and phrases that support your answer.

_____

_____

_____

_____

_____

_____

_____

covetousness if we did; for affliction[9] is a treasure, and scarce any man hath enough of it. No man hath affliction enough that is not matured, and ripened by it, and made fit for God by that affliction. If a man carry treasure in bullion, or in a wedge of gold, and have none coined into current monies, his treasure
50 will not defray[10] him as he travels. Tribulation is treasure in the nature of it, but it is not current money in the use of it, except we get nearer and nearer our home, Heaven, by it. Another man may be sick too, and sick to death, and this affliction may lie in his bowels, as gold in a mine, and be of no use to him; but this bell, that tells me of his affliction, digs out, and applies that gold to me; if by this consideration of another's danger I take mine own into contemplation, and so secure myself by making my recourse[11] to my God, who is our only security.

Marble effigy of John Donne in his shroud, from St. Paul's Cathedral, London.
© Woodmansterne Limited Watford.

---

9. **affliction** *n.:* suffering.
10. **defray** *v.:* pay for.
11. **making my recourse:** turning for aid.

Meditation 17

Reading Skills: Understanding Patterns of Organization   In the first column below are three examples of organizational patterns used in "Meditation 17." In the second column, identify whether the passage is an example of repetition, parallel structure, or rhetorical questions.

Examples	Pattern of Organization
"Perchance he for whom this bell tolls, may be so ill, as that he knows not it tolls for him; and perchance I may think myself so much better than I am, as that they who are about me, and see my state, may have caused it to toll for me, and I know not that." (lines 1–4)	
"God employs several translators; some pieces are translated by age, some by sickness, some by war, some by justice; . . ." (lines 13–14)	
"Who casts not up his eye to the sun when it rises? but who takes off his eye from a comet when that breaks out? Who bends not his ear to any bell, which upon any occasion rings? but who can remove it from that bell, which is passing a piece of himself out of this world?" (lines 30–35)	

✓ Check your Standards Mastery at the back of this book.

Tilbury Speech by Queen Elizabeth I

BEFORE YOU READ

LITERARY FOCUS: AUTHOR'S INTENT AND TONE

Queen Elizabeth's Tilbury Speech conveys how deeply she loved her country and her people. The queen's beliefs are revealed in her patriotic **tone**—the words, images, and details she uses to make her point. Elizabeth's powerful use of language and courageous tone is meant to inspire her listeners. She is prepared to take up arms alongside her people to drive out all threats to her kingdom.

Listening to Language   The tone an author uses can be described as serious or playful, formal or casual, threatening or comforting—or any number of other adjectives. Read the passages below and jot down some adjectives you would use to describe the tone in each.

Passage	Tone
The castle on the hill is a magnificent reminder of our nation's past. The sun shines on the old stones of the building, bringing to mind the dull glint of armor on the battlefields. The old kitchen garden within the castle wall still blooms sweet with lavender, sage, and thyme.	
The old castle stands on the hill, forbidding and cold, not to mention damp. The old stones form a crumbling barrier against a long forgotten enemy. The kitchen gardens are the only sign of life in a setting that has no real meaning in our world.	

READING SKILLS: DRAWING INFERENCES

Sometimes you must draw inferences in order to understand things a writer has not stated directly. An **inference** is a guess you make based on information in the text and on your own knowledge and experience. To draw an inference, focus on important details in the text and then combine that information with what you already know.

Use the Skill   As you read the Tilbury Speech, underline or highlight details that help you make inferences about Queen Elizabeth's beliefs.

REVIEW SKILLS

As you read, think about how Queen Elizabeth's tone in the Tilbury Speech helps her achieve her purpose.

TONE
Attitude toward a topic that is revealed by word choice.

Reading Standard 2.8 (Grade 9–10 Review) Evaluate the credibility of an author's argument or defense of a claim by critiquing the relationship between generalizations and evidence, the comprehensiveness of evidence, and the way in which the author's intent affects the structure and tone of the text.

Reading Standard 3.8 Analyze the clarity and consistency of political assumptions in a selection of literary works or essays on a topic. (Political approach)

Tilbury Speech

Queen Elizabeth I

BACKGROUND

Queen Elizabeth I of England (reigned 1558–1603) could speak and read six languages, and dazzled her court with both her superb literary skills and her political know-how. She wrote poems, letters, sermons, and masterful speeches, such as the Tilbury Speech.

In 1588, a fleet of warships called the Spanish Armada sailed from Spain to attack England. At Tilbury, Queen Elizabeth addressed the English army as they prepared for a dangerous battle.

My loving people: We have been persuaded by some that are careful of our safety to take heed how we commit ourself to armed multitudes for fear of treachery, but I assure you I do not desire to live to distrust my faithful and loving people. Let tyrants fear. I have always so behaved myself that, under God, I have placed my chiefest strength and safeguard in the loyal hearts and goodwill of my subjects. And therefore I am come amongst you, as you see, at this time, not for my recreation and disport, but being resolved in the midst and heat of the battle to live or die amongst you all,

10 to lay down for my God, and for my kingdom, and for my people, my honor and my blood, even in the dust. I know I have the body but of a weak and feeble woman, but I have the heart and stomach of a king—and of a king of England too—and think foul scorn that Parma, or Spain, or any prince of Europe should dare to invade the borders of my realm. To which, rather than any dishonor shall grow by me, I myself will take up arms, I myself will be your general, judge, and rewarder of every one of your virtues in the field. I know already for your forwardness you have deserved rewards and crowns, and we do assure you, in the

20 word of a prince, they shall be duly paid you.

INFER

Elizabeth uses the word *treachery* (line 3) and indicates that she is in danger. What can you **infer** about the queen's political situation?

_____

_____

ANALYZE

Re-read lines 1–7, and underline the words Elizabeth uses to describe her subjects. Why might she have chosen these words?

_____

_____

FLUENCY

Read the speech aloud. First, circle words that convey Elizabeth's **tone** as she promises to fight, and emphasize those words as you read. *(Grade 9–10 Review)*

Tilbury Speech

Reading Skills: Drawing Inferences   Elizabeth I's rousing speech contains details that hint at her intentions and beliefs. Answer the questions below by listing details from the text that help you find the answers. Then, answer each question by drawing an inference. Write your inference in the column at the right.

Question	Details in the Text	My Inference
How does Elizabeth feel about her relationship to her subjects?		
Are people trying to persuade Elizabeth to be more careful?		
What picture of herself as a leader does Elizabeth try to convey?		
What is Elizabeth's main point?		

 Check your Standards Mastery at the back of this book.

When I consider how my light is spent by John Milton

BEFORE YOU READ

LITERARY FOCUS: ALLUSION

An **allusion** is a reference to a statement, a person, a place, an event, or a thing that is known from literature, history, religion, mythology, politics, sports, science, or popular culture. In ordinary conversation, for example, we might make an allusion to a famous figure by calling an intelligent person an *Einstein* or by referring to a good baseball player as a *Babe Ruth.* These allusions are effective only if our audience knows that Albert Einstein was a genius or that Babe Ruth was a legendary baseball player.

To understand Milton's poetry, keep in mind that he often alludes to people and events in literature, religion, and history. Look up details from his poem that you suspect are allusions. Then, compare the information you find with details in the poem to understand why Milton chose to make that allusion.

Filling in the Blanks   The sentences below contain allusions. See if you can recognize the references.

Allusion	What Is the Reference?
It seems as if everything Simon touched turned to gold.	
By returning the wallet she found, Leah was an honest Abe.	

READING SKILLS: PARAPHRASING

Paraphrasing means restating a text using your own words. A paraphrase is different from a summary. A **summary** gives a general overview of the main points of a text. A summary is much shorter than the main text and does not cover every single detail in the text. A paraphrase, on the other hand, restates the entire text in simpler language. Because poetry uses condensed language, a paraphrase of a poem is often longer than the poem itself.

Use the Skill   To be sure you understand the poem that follows, try paraphrasing it line by line, sentence by sentence. Look for sentences that do not follow standard subject-verb-complement order, and rephrase them.

Reading Standard 3.4 Analyze ways in which poets use imagery, personification, figures of speech, and sounds to evoke readers' emotions.

WHEN I CONSIDER HOW MY LIGHT IS SPENT

John Milton

> **BACKGROUND**
> John Milton was completely blind by age forty-four, long before he had finished his life's work. He was a deeply religious man who firmly believed that everyone is accountable to God. In the first part of this sonnet, Milton asks, "How can I continue to do the work that God expects of me?" In the remainder of the sonnet, he proposes an answer to his question.

INTERPRET

Milton makes an **allusion** to the parable of the talents in the Bible (lines 3–4). Besides "coins," *talents* can mean "abilities or gifts." What gift might Milton be referring to as useless in line 4?

_____

_____

IDENTIFY

Pause at line 8. Underline the question the speaker asks. What does he want to know?

_____

_____

_____

CLARIFY

Re-read lines 8–14. According to Patience, who best serves God? Underline that information.

When I consider how my light is spent
    Ere half my days in this dark world and wide,
    And that one talent[1] which is death to hide
    Lodged with me useless, though my soul more bent
5 To serve therewith my Maker, and present
    My true account, lest He returning chide,
    "Doth God exact day-labor, light denied?"
    I fondly[2] ask. But Patience, to prevent
That murmur, soon replies, "God doth not need
10 Either man's work or His own gifts. Who best
    Bear His mild yoke, they serve Him best. His state
Is kingly: Thousands[3] at His bidding speed,
    And post o'er land and ocean without rest;
    They also serve who only stand and wait."

---

1. **talent** *n.:* reference to the parable of the talents (Matthew 25:14–30), in which a servant is scolded for burying his one talent, or coin, in the earth instead of putting it to good use.
2. **fondly** *adv.:* foolishly.
3. **thousands:** of angels.

When I consider how my light is spent

Reading Skills: Paraphrasing   Use the chart below to paraphrase Milton's poem. The lines of the poem are provided at the left. Write your paraphrase in the boxes at the right. The first line has been done for you.

Lines from Poem	Paraphrase
"When I consider how my light is spent / Ere half my days in this dark world and wide," (lines 1–2)	When I consider that I can no longer see before I have finished half of my days in this world
"And that one talent which is death to hide / Lodged with me useless, though my soul more bent / To serve therewith my Maker, and present / My true account, lest He returning chide, / 'Doth God exact day-labor, light denied?' / I fondly ask." (lines 3–8)	
"But Patience, to prevent / That murmur, soon replies, 'God doth not need / Either man's work or His own gifts.' " (lines 8–10)	
" 'Who best / Bear His mild yoke, they serve Him best.' " (lines 10–11)	
" 'His state / Is kingly: Thousands at His bidding speed, / And post o'er land and ocean without rest.' " (lines 11–13)	
" 'They also serve who only stand and wait.' " (line 14)	

✓ Check your Standards Mastery at the back of this book.

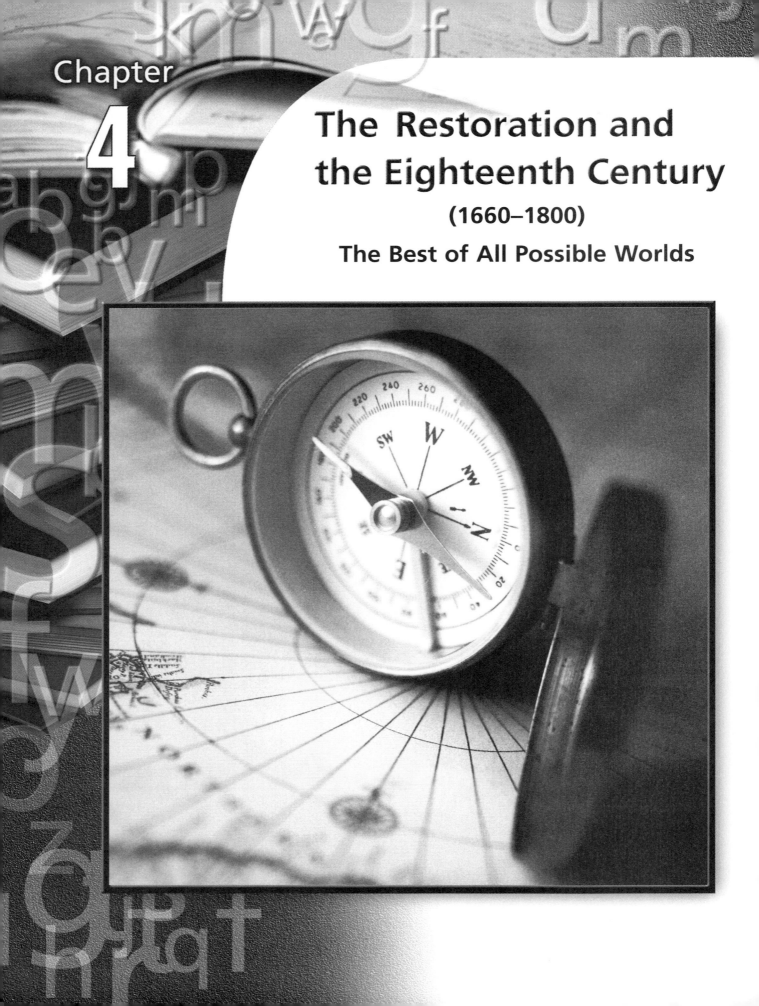

Chapter

4

The Restoration and the Eighteenth Century

(1660–1800)

The Best of All Possible Worlds

The Restoration and the Eighteenth Century
(1660–1800)

C. F. Main

The following essay provides highlights of the historical period. For a more detailed version of this essay, see *Holt Literature and Language Arts*, pages 412–426.

Reading Standard 3.7c Evaluate the philosophical, political, religious, ethical, and social influences of the historical period that shaped the characters, plots, and settings.

From 1660 to 1800, people from England and Europe were pouring into North America. These eager voyagers not only sought freedom from religious and political persecution, they also saw money to be made in the American continent's rich lands and forests. In 1775, these Colonies rebelled against British rule and eventually won their freedom. The United States was a raw, vigorous, brand-new nation. Across the Atlantic, however, things were very different.

From Tumult to Calm

10   In 1660, England was utterly exhausted from nearly twenty years of civil war. By 1700, it had lived through a devastating plague and a fire that left more than two thirds of Londoners homeless. By the middle of the eighteenth century, however, England had settled into a period of calm and order, at least among the upper classes. Despite the loss of the American Colonies, the renewed British military forces established new settlements around the globe. Though life for many was wretched, the middle class grew. Throughout this period, British men and women also produced many brilliant works of philosophy, art, and literature.

20   This long period of time in England—from 1660 to 1800—has been given several labels: the Augustan Age, the neoclassical

---

IDENTIFY CAUSE & EFFECT

According to lines 1–8, what were the two reasons that people from England and Europe came to North America?

_____

_____

_____

_____

_____

CLARIFY

Pause at line 12. What three disasters did England endure from the mid-1600s until 1700? Circle that information.

IDENTIFY

Re-read lines 13–19. What positive changes had occurred in England by the middle of the eighteenth century? Underline your answer.

IDENTIFY

Re-read lines 20–24. What four labels have been used to refer to the period from 1660 to 1800? Circle that information.

COMPARE & CONTRAST

Re-read lines 27–41. Underline three similarities between England during this period and ancient Rome during the reign of Octavian.

PARAPHRASE

Pause at line 48. Why were the Latin classics considered valuable? Restate that information in your own words.

period, the Enlightenment, and the Age of Reason. Each of these labels applies to some characteristics of these 140 years, but none applies to all.

Augustan and Neoclassical: Comparisons with Rome

Many people liked to find similarities between England in this period and ancient Rome, especially during the reign of the emperor Octavian (63 B.C.–A.D. 14). When he became emperor,
30 Octavian was given the high-sounding name *Augustus,* meaning "the exalted one." Augustus restored peace and order to Rome after Julius Caesar's assassination. Similarly, the Stuart monarchs of England restored peace and order to England after the civil wars that led to the execution of King Charles I in 1649—wars that continued even after the king was dead.

The people of both Rome and England were weary of war, suspicious of revolutionaries and radicals, and ready to settle down, make money, and enjoy life. The Roman Senate had hailed Augustus as the second founder of Rome; in 1660, the English
40 people brought back the son of Charles I from his exile in France, crowned him King Charles II, and hailed him as their savior.

In this age, many English writers consciously modeled their works on the old Latin classics, which they had studied in school and university. These writings that imitate Latin works were called **neoclassical**—"new classical." The classics, it was generally agreed, were valuable because they represented what was permanent and universal in human experience. All educated people knew the Latin classics better than they knew their own English literature.

Reason and Enlightenment:
50 ## From *Why?* to *How?*

Labels like the "Age of Reason" and the "Enlightenment" reveal how people were gradually changing their view of themselves and the world. For centuries people had believed that unusual events such as earthquakes, comets, and even babies born with malformations had some kind of meaning, and that they were sent as punishments for past misdoings or as warnings of future troubles. People did not ask, "*How* did this unusual event take place?" but "*Why* did this unusual event take place, and what does it *mean*?"

60 Throughout the Enlightenment, people gradually stopped asking *why?* questions and started asking *how?* questions, and the answers to those questions—about everything from the workings of the human body to the laws of the universe— became much less frightening and superstitious. For instance, the astronomer Edmond Halley (1656–1742) took the terror out of celestial phenomena by calculating when they were going to occur. He computed, with "immense labor," he said, the orbit of the comet that still bears his name. He predicted it would appear in 1758,

70 1834, 1910, and 1986—and it did. And how did he know it would reappear at seventy-six-year intervals? Because that was the time it took to complete its orbit. This reasonable explanation made no connection between the comet and human affairs.

Changes in Religion: More Questions

The new scientific and rational explanations of phenomena gradually began to affect some people's religious views. If comets

80 were not sent by God to warn people, perhaps God didn't interfere at all in human affairs. Perhaps the universe was like an immense piece of clockwork, set in motion by a Creator who more or less withdrew from this perfect mechanism and let it run by itself. Such a view, part of an ideology known as Deism, could make people feel self-satisfied and complacent, especially if they believed, as Alexander Pope noted, that "Whatever is, is

INTERPRET

Pause at line 64. What questions did people begin to ask during the Enlightenment?

_____

_____

_____

_____

_____

_____

_____

_____

Sir Isaac Newton's reflecting telescope (1688).
Royal Society, London.

WORD STUDY

Phenomena (fə·năm′ə·nə), line 66, is a plural noun. It refers to unusual events observable by the senses and of scientific interest. The singular form of this word is *phenomenon*.

IDENTIFY

Re-read lines 78–87. What idea of the universe was Deism based on? Underline that information.

_____

_____

_____

_____

_____

_____

_____

_____

_____

_____

_____

_____

_____

_____

_____

CLARIFY

Pause at line 112. Circle the religion that James II practiced. Why were most English people opposed to James? Underline that information.

IDENTIFY
CAUSE & EFFECT

Re-read lines 112–120. Find the causes for the return of Protestant rule to England, and circle them. Then underline the lasting result.

right." Other than a tiny minority of "enlightened" rationalists and materialists, most people, including great philosophers and scientists like Sir Isaac Newton (1642–1727) and John Locke
90 (1632–1704), remained religious. Christianity in its various forms continued to exercise an undiminished power over almost all Europeans in this period, just as it had in the Middle Ages and the Renaissance.

Religion and Politics: Repression of Minority Sects

Religion determined people's politics in this period. Charles II reestablished the Anglican Church as the official church of the country, which it continues to be in England to this day. (In the United States, it is called the Episcopal Church.) With the
100 approval of Parliament, the king attempted to outlaw all the various Puritan and Independent sects that had caused so much uproar during the preceding thirty years. Persecution of these various sects continued, in varying degrees, throughout the eighteenth century.

The Bloodless Revolution

Charles II had a number of illegitimate children, but no legal heir. When he died in 1685, he was succeeded by his brother, James II, a practicing Roman Catholic. Most English people were utterly opposed to James. After all, it was widely believed
110 that Roman Catholics had not only set fire to London and caused other disasters, but also were actively plotting to hand the country over to the pope. When James's queen produced a little boy—a Catholic heir—political leaders transferred power to James's daughter Mary, who was married to the Dutch William of Orange, a Protestant prince. Late in 1688, William attacked England. King James fled the country, and early in 1689 Parliament declared William and Mary king and queen, thus restoring Protestant rule. These events are known as the

Glorious (bloodless) Revolution. Ever since, the rulers of
120   England have been, at least in name, Anglicans.

Addicted to the Theater

For eighteen years, while the Puritans held power, the theaters
in England were closed. During the exile of the royal court
in France, Charles had become addicted to theatergoing, so
one of the first things he did after regaining his throne was to
repeal the ban on play performances, imposed in 1642. Charles
and his brother James supported companies of actors. Boys and
men no longer acted the female roles. The new theater had real
actresses, like the famous Nell Gwyn. The great witty comedies
130   produced during this period reflected the life of the rich and
leisured people of that time and their servants. In addition to
dramatists, a large number of prose and verse writers wrote not
for sophisticated people but solely for ordinary readers.

The Age of Satire: Attacks on Immorality and Bad Taste

Today, Alexander Pope and Jonathan Swift are regarded as the
most accomplished literary artists of the early eighteenth century.
During their own lifetimes, however, Pope and Swift were
frequently out of harmony with the values of the age, and
140   both often criticized it severely.

Although Pope addressed his works exclusively to the
educated and leisured classes, he also attacked the members of
these classes for their immorality and their bad taste. Pope loved
order, discipline, and craftsmanship; both he and Swift were
appalled by the squalor and shoddiness—in art, manners, and
morals—that lay beneath the polished surfaces of Augustan life.
Neither Swift nor Pope felt smug or satisfied with the world, as
many English people did. Both writers hated the corrupt politics
of the time and the growing commercialism and materialism of
150   the English people.

IDENTIFY

Pause at line 129. How were the new theaters different from earlier theaters? Underline that information.

IDENTIFY

Pause at line 133. What types of people were portrayed in the great comedies written during this period?

_____

_____

_____

_____

_____

_____

_____

_____

_____

CLARIFY

Re-read lines 141–150. Which two noted writers criticized Augustan life? Circle the things they objected to.

_____

_____

_____

_____

Pause at line 163. What did eighteenth-century journalists regard as part of their job? Underline your answer.

_____

_____

_____

_____

_____

_____

_____

Re-read lines 165–177. In what way did Pope's poetry differ from poetry that had come before?

_____

_____

_____

_____

_____

_____

_____

_____

_____

_____

Journalism: A New Profession

In contrast with Swift and Pope and their aristocratic values was a writer named Daniel Defoe (1660–1731), who stood for values that we think of as being middle class: thrift, prudence, industry, and respectability. Defoe had no interest in polished manners and social poise. Swift and Pope looked down their noses at him. "Defoe has written a vast many things," Pope once said, "and none bad, though none excellent."

160 Defoe, like the essayists Joseph Addison and Sir Richard Steele, followed a new profession: journalism. Eighteenth-century journalists did not merely describe contemporary political and social matters; they also saw themselves as reformers of public manners and morals.

A Poetry of Mind, Not of Soul

Today when we think of great poetry, we think of great lyrics. Poets such as Shakespeare, Wordsworth, John Donne, and Emily Dickinson reveal in their poems their innermost thoughts and feelings, their honest and original responses to life. "Genuine poetry," said Matthew Arnold, a nineteenth-century poet and 170 critic, "is conceived and composed in the soul."

Later critics like Matthew Arnold criticized the poetry of people such as Alexander Pope because, Arnold said, it was conceived and composed in their "wits"—that is, in their minds, not their souls. These so-called Augustan poets, however, did not define poetry in Arnold's way and so should not be judged by his standards. They had no desire to expose their souls; they thought of poetry as having a public rather than a private function.

A Public Poetry Conceived in Wit

Augustan poets would write not merely a poem but a particular 180 kind of poem. They would decide in advance the kind of poem, much as a carpenter decides on the kind of chair to make. Many of the popular kinds of poetry were inherited from classical antiquity.

If, for instance, an important person died, a poet would celebrate that dead person in an **elegy,** the appropriate kind of poem for the occasion. Augustan elegies did not tell the truth about a dead person, even if the truth could be determined; rather, they said the very best things that the poet could think of saying.

At the opposite extreme, a poet might decide that a certain type of behavior, or even a certain well-known person, should be exposed to public ridicule. The poet would then write a **satire,** a kind of writing that says the worst things about people and their behavior that the poet can think of saying.

Another important kind of poem was the **ode**—an ambitious, often pompous poem expressing a public emotion, like the jubilation felt after a great naval victory.

Regardless of its kind, every poem had to be carefully and artificially constructed in exact meter and rhyme. Poems were not to sound spontaneous and impromptu, just as people were not to appear in public except in fancy dress. Those who could afford it adorned themselves with vast wigs, ribboned and jeweled clothing, and red shoes with high heels. People's movements were dignified and stately in public. Nothing was what we would today call natural—neither dress nor manners nor poetry.

The First English Novels

By the mid-eighteenth century, people were writing long fictional narratives called novels ("something new"). These novels, which were a development of the middle class, were often broad and comical—the adventures, for example, of a handsome ne'er-do-well or lower-class beauty. They were frequently told in endless episodes or through a series of letters. Authorities disagree as to whether *Robinson Crusoe* and Defoe's other fictional narratives are true novels, but many agree that the novel began either with Defoe or with the writers of the next generation.

190

200

210

IDENTIFY

What were three popular kinds of poetry used by Augustan poets (lines 184–196)? Underline the information that describes each type.

_____

_____

_____

_____

_____

_____

COMPARE & CONTRAST

Re-read lines 197–204. Circle words and phrases that show how poetry was similar to fashion in the Augustan age. How would you describe the fashions of the time?

_____

_____

_____

_____

_____

_____

IDENTIFY

Pause at line 214. In what two formats were novels of the mid-eighteenth century frequently told? Circle your answer.

CONNECT

Pause at line 227. What can we learn by reading the novels of the eighteenth century? Underline that information.

GENERATE QUESTIONS

If you wanted to learn more about important historical events that occurred toward the end of the eighteenth century, what information in the last paragraph would you have questions about? Circle it. *(Grade 9–10 Review)*

The novels of one of the most prominent eighteenth-century novelists, Henry Fielding (1707–1754), are literally crammed with rough and rowdy incidents. Fielding's rollicking novel *Tom Jones* has even been made into an Oscar-winning movie, proof that his high-spirited characters are still fresh and

220   funny today. Samuel Richardson (1689–1761) was perhaps the first novelist to explore in great detail the emotional life of his characters, especially his heroines (in *Pamela* and *Clarissa*). The novels of Laurence Sterne (1713–1768) are experimental and whimsical—and still unique despite the efforts of many imitators to copy them. All these novels tell us something of what life at this time was like. They also help us understand the joys and disappointments of human experience in all ages.

Searching for a Simpler Life

By the last decade of the century, the world was changing in

230   disturbing ways. The Industrial Revolution was turning English cities and towns into filthy, smoky slums. Across the English Channel, the French were about to murder a king and set their whole society on a different political course. The eighteenth century was closing. Just as at the end of the twentieth century, people sensed that a new era was about to begin, so did people in England know that the age of elegance, taste, and reason was over.

Front cover of Daniel Defoe's novel Robinson Crusoe *(1881).* The Bridgeman Art Library.

A Modest Proposal by Jonathan Swift

LITERARY FOCUS: VERBAL IRONY

You use **verbal irony** whenever you say one thing but mean something completely different. When you speak, your tone of voice signals listeners that you don't really mean what you are saying. Writers don't have the option of using a sarcastic tone of voice to convey irony. Instead, they might make so many shocking or unbelievable statements that the reader can't possibly miss the point. Swift's essay is a classic example of verbal irony taken to the extreme.

Isn't It Ironic?   Look at the following examples of verbal irony. Then, create your own example in the space provided.

Situation	Verbal Irony (What You Say)
You trip and fall in front of a large group of people, your books and papers flying everywhere.	"Aren't I the picture of grace?" you ask as you struggle to your feet.
You have a bad case of the flu. A friend visits and asks, "How are you?"	You respond, "Never felt better!"

READING SKILLS: RECOGNIZING PERSUASIVE TECHNIQUES

"A Modest Proposal" is a type of persuasive writing called **satire.** Through satire, writers ridicule people or institutions in order to effect change. "A Modest Proposal" was written in 1729 to shock English society into an awareness of England's unjust policies toward the Irish. In it, Swift uses the types of **persuasive techniques** listed below to convince the reader that England's treatment of the Irish is heartless and immoral.

- **Logical appeals:** the use of facts or statistics to support a position.

- **Emotional appeals:** the use of words that stir up strong feelings.

- **Ethical appeals:** the use of details that will convince readers that the writer is fair and trustworthy.

Use the Skill   As you read the selection, highlight and identify the types of persuasive appeals used by Swift. Refer to the list above as a guide.

REVIEW SKILLS

As you read "A Modest Proposal," look for ways in which the use of verbal irony makes Swift's essay shocking— yet highly effective.

VERBAL IRONY The contrast between what a writer or speaker says and what is really meant.

Reading Standard 2.2 Analyze the way in which clarity of meaning is affected by the patterns of organization, hierarchical structures, repetition of the main ideas, syntax, and word choice in the text.

Reading Standard 3.3 Analyze the ways in which irony, tone, mood, the author's style, and the "sound" of language achieve specific rhetorical or aesthetic purposes or both.

Reading Standard 3.8 (Grade 9–10 Review) Interpret and evaluate the impact of ambiguities, subtleties, contradictions, ironies, and incongruities in a text.

A MODEST PROPOSAL

Jonathan Swift

FOR PREVENTING THE CHILDREN OF POOR PEOPLE IN IRELAND FROM BEING A BURDEN
TO THEIR PARENTS, AND FOR MAKING THEM BENEFICIAL TO THE PUBLIC

BACKGROUND

In the late 1720s, Ireland suffered from several years of poor harvests. Farmers had trouble paying the rents demanded by their English landlords. Many children and adults were forced to beg or starve. Most of the money collected by the landlords was sent to England; very little was spent in Ireland on locally produced goods.

Here, Swift pretends to be an economic planner who suggests a shocking solution to the problem. Watch for the sharp contrast between Swift's direct, logical style and the outrageous proposal he describes.

PARAPHRASE

Melancholy, in line 1, means "sad." Using that knowledge, paraphrase the first sentence.

_____

_____

_____

_____

_____

_____

_____

VOCABULARY

sustenance (sus'tə·nəns) *n.:* food or money to support life.

It is a melancholy object to those, who walk through this great town,[1] or travel in the country, when they see the streets, the roads, and cabin doors, crowded with beggars of the female sex, followed by three, four, or six children, all in rags, and importuning every passenger for an alms.[2] These mothers, instead of being able to work for their honest livelihood, are forced to employ all their time in strolling, to beg **sustenance** for their helpless infants, who, as they grow up either turn thieves for want[3] of work, or leave their dear native country to fight for the

10   Pretender[4] in Spain, or sell themselves to the Barbadoes.[5]

---

1. **this great town:** Dublin.
2. **importuning . . . alms:** asking passersby for a handout.
3. **want** *n.:* lack; need.
4. **the Pretender:** James Edward (1688–1766), son of England's last Catholic king, the deposed James II (1633–1701); James Edward kept trying to gain the English throne.
5. **sell . . . Barbadoes:** go to the West Indies and work as indentured servants.

I think it is agreed by all parties, that this prodigious number of children, in the arms, or on the backs, or at the heels of their mothers, and frequently of their fathers, is in the present deplorable state of the kingdom, a very great additional grievance; and therefore whoever could find out a fair, cheap, and easy method of making these children sound and useful members of the commonwealth would deserve so well of the public, as to have his statue set up for a preserver of the nation.

But my intention is very far from being confined to provide
20 only for the children of professed beggars; it is of a much greater extent, and shall take in the whole number of infants at a certain age, who are born of parents in effect as little able to support them, as those who demand our charity in the streets.

As to my own part, having turned my thoughts, for many years, upon this important subject, and maturely weighed the several schemes of other projectors,[6] I have always found them grossly mistaken in their computation. It is true a child, just dropped from its dam,[7] may be supported by her milk, for a solar year[8] with little other nourishment, at most not above the
30 value of two shillings, which the mother may certainly get, or the value in scraps, by her lawful occupation of begging, and it is exactly at one year old that I propose to provide for them, in such a manner, as, instead of being a charge upon their parents, or the parish, or wanting food and raiment[9] for the rest of their lives, they shall, on the contrary, contribute to the feeding and partly to the clothing of many thousands.

There is likewise another great advantage in my scheme, that it will prevent those voluntary abortions, and that horrid practice of women murdering their bastard children, alas! too
40 frequent among us, sacrificing the poor innocent babes, I doubt,[10]

---

6. **projectors** *n. pl.*: speculators; schemers.
7. **dam** *n.*: mother (ordinarily used only of animals).
8. **solar year**: from the first day of spring in one year to the last day of winter in the next.
9. **raiment** (rā′mənt) *n.*: clothing.
10. **doubt** *v.*: suspect.

WORD STUDY

The word *prodigious* (prō·dij′əs), in line 11, means "an enormous quantity."

IDENTIFY

Pause at line 18. What does Swift say is the problem facing the nation?

_____

_____

_____

_____

INFER

The word *dam* (line 28) means "female parent" and is usually used to refer to a domestic animal. What attitude toward poor women does this word choice suggest?

_____

_____

_____

_____

_____

IDENTIFY

Pause at line 36. At what age can children be made useful to society? Circle that information. Underline the way in which they can be of use.

more to avoid the expense, than the shame, which would move tears and pity in the most savage and inhuman breast.

The number of souls[11] in Ireland being usually reckoned one million and a half, of these I calculate there may be about two hundred thousand couples whose wives are breeders, from which number I subtract thirty thousand couples, who are able to maintain their own children, although I apprehend there cannot be so many under the present distresses of the kingdom, but this being granted, there will remain an hundred and seventy thousand

50 breeders. I again subtract fifty thousand for those women who miscarry, or whose children die by accident, or disease within the year. There only remain an hundred and twenty thousand children of poor parents annually born: The question therefore is, how this number shall be reared, and provided for, which, as I have already said, under the present situation of affairs, is utterly impossible by all the methods hitherto proposed, for we can neither employ them in handicraft,[12] or agriculture; we neither build houses (I mean in the country) nor cultivate land: They can very seldom pick up a livelihood by stealing until they

60 arrive at six years old, except where they are of towardly parts,[13] although, I confess they learn the rudiments much earlier, during which time, they can however be properly looked upon only as probationers,[14] as I have been informed by a principal gentleman in the county of Cavan,[15] who protested to me, that he never knew above one or two instances under the age of six, even in a part of the kingdom so renowned for the quickest proficiency in that art.[16]

I am assured by our merchants, that a boy or girl, before twelve years old, is no saleable commodity, and even when they

70 come to this age, they will not yield above three pounds, or three pounds and half a crown at most on the exchange, which cannot

---

11. **souls** *n. pl.:* people.
12. **handicraft** *n.:* manufacturing.
13. **of towardly parts:** exceptionally advanced or mature for their age.
14. **probationers** *n. pl.:* apprentices.
15. **Cavan:** inland county in Ireland that is remote from Dublin.
16. **that art:** stealing.

turn to account[17] either to the parents or the kingdom, the charge of nutriment and rags having been at least four times that value.

I shall now therefore humbly propose my own thoughts, which I hope will not be liable to the least objection.

I have been assured by a very knowing American[18] of my acquaintance in London, that a young healthy child well nursed is at a year old a most delicious, nourishing, and wholesome food, whether stewed, roasted, baked, or boiled, and I make no doubt that it will equally serve in a fricassee,[19] or ragout.[20]

I do therefore humbly offer it to public consideration, that of the hundred and twenty thousand children, already computed, twenty thousand may be reserved for breed, whereof only one-fourth part to be males, which is more than we allow to sheep, black cattle, or swine, and my reason is that these children are seldom the fruits of marriage, a circumstance not much regarded by our savages; therefore one male will be sufficient to serve four females. That the remaining hundred thousand may at a year old be offered in sale to the persons of quality, and fortune, through the kingdom, always advising the mother to let them suck plentifully in the last month, so as to render them plump, and fat for a good table. A child will make two dishes at an entertainment for friends, and when the family dines alone, the fore or hind quarter will make a reasonable dish, and seasoned with a little pepper or salt will be very good boiled on the fourth day, especially in winter.

I have reckoned upon a medium, that a child just born will weigh twelve pounds, and in a solar year if tolerably nursed increaseth to twenty-eight pounds.

---

17. **turn to account:** be profitable.
18. **American:** To Swift's readers this label would suggest a barbaric person.
19. **fricassee** (frik′ə·sē′) *n.:* stew with a light gravy.
20. **ragout** (ra·gōō′) *n.:* highly flavored stew.

Re-read lines 77–81. Circle the words Swift uses to describe a young, healthy child. Based on these details, what plan do you think he is about to propose to deal with Ireland's starving population?

IDENTIFY

The speaker provides details in support of his outrageous plan (lines 93–97). Underline those details.

An Irish cabin.
National Library of Ireland, Dublin.

I grant this food will be somewhat dear,[21] and therefore very proper for landlords, who, as they have already devoured[22] most of the parents, seem to have the best title to the children.

Infant's flesh will be in season throughout the year, but more plentiful in March, and a little before and after, for we are told by a grave author,[23] an eminent French physician, that fish being a prolific diet, there are more children born in Roman Catholic countries about nine months after Lent, than at any other season, therefore reckoning a year after Lent, the markets
110 will be more **glutted** than usual, because the number of popish[24] infants, is at least three to one in this kingdom, and therefore it will have one other collateral advantage by lessening the number of papists among us.

---

21. **dear** *adj.:* expensive.
22. **devoured** *v.:* made poor by charging high rents.
23. **grave author:** The French satirist François Rabelais. His work is comic, not "grave."
24. **popish** *adj.:* derogatory term meaning "Roman Catholic."

I have already computed the charge of nursing a beggar's child (in which list I reckon all cottagers,[25] laborers, and four-fifths of the farmers) to be about two shillings per annum,[26] rags included, and I believe no gentleman would repine to give ten shillings for the carcass of a good fat child, which, as I have said will make four dishes of excellent nutritive meat, when he hath only some particular friend, or his own family to dine with him. Thus the squire will learn to be a good landlord, and grow popular among his tenants, the mother will have eight shillings net profit, and be fit for work until she produceth another child.

Those who are more thrifty (as I must confess the times require) may flay[27] the carcass; the skin of which, artificially[28] dressed, will make admirable gloves for ladies, and summer boots for fine gentlemen.

As to our city of Dublin, shambles[29] may be appointed for this purpose, in the most convenient parts of it, and butchers we may be assured will not be wanting, although I rather recommend buying the children alive, and dressing them hot from the knife, as we do roasting pigs.

A very worthy person, a true lover of his country, and whose virtues I highly esteem, was lately pleased, in discoursing on this matter, to offer a refinement upon my scheme. He said, that many gentlemen of this kingdom, having of late destroyed their deer, he conceived that the want of venison might be well supplied by the bodies of young lads and maidens, not exceeding fourteen years of age, nor under twelve, so great a number of both sexes in every country being now ready to starve, for want of work and service:[30] and these to be disposed of by their parents if alive, or otherwise by their nearest relations. But with due

25. **cottagers** *n. pl.:* tenant farmers.
26. **per annum:** Latin for "by the year"; annually.
27. **flay** *v.:* remove the skin of.
28. **artificially** *adv.:* with great artifice; skillfully.
29. **shambles** *n.:* slaughterhouse.
30. **service** *n.:* employment as servants.

In discussing the economics of his proposal, what kind of appeal is the speaker making (lines 114–123)?

_____

_____

DRAW CONCLUSIONS

Re-read lines 128–132, in which the speaker suggests "dressing" children "hot from the knife." What effect do you think Swift expects this word choice to have on readers?

_____

_____

_____

_____

_____

_____

_____

IDENTIFY

Pause at line 142. What "refinement," or modification, of the author's plan is suggested in this paragraph? Underline the answer.

_____

_____

_____

deference (def′ər·əns) *n.:*
respect.

scrupulous (skrōō′pyə·ləs)
adj.: extremely careful and
precise in deciding what is
right or wrong.

censure (sen′shər) *v.:* condemn;
blame.

expedient (ek·spē′dē·ənt) *n.:*
convenient means to an end.

CONNECT

Pause at line 166, and read
footnote 32. How trustworthy
a source is Sallmanaazor?
Why do you think Swift uses
his ideas as an example?

deference to so excellent a friend, and so deserving a patriot, I cannot be altogether in his sentiments, for as to the males, my American acquaintance assured me from frequent experience, that their flesh was generally tough and lean, like that of our schoolboys, by continual exercise, and their taste disagreeable, and to fatten them would not answer the charge. Then as to the females, it would, I think with humble submission,[31] be a loss to

150 the public, because they soon would become breeders themselves: And besides it is not improbable that some **scrupulous** people might be apt to **censure** such a practice (although indeed very unjustly) as a little bordering upon cruelty, which, I confess, hath always been with me the strongest objection against any project, how well soever intended.

But in order to justify my friend, he confessed that this **expedient** was put into his head by the famous Sallmanaazor,[32] a native of the island Formosa, who came from thence to London, above twenty years ago, and in conversation told my

160 friend, that in his country when any young person happened to be put to death, the executioner sold the carcass to persons of quality, as a prime dainty, and that, in his time, the body of a plump girl of fifteen, who was crucified for an attempt to poison the emperor, was sold to his imperial majesty's prime minister of state, and other great mandarins[33] of the court, in joints[34] from the gibbet,[35] at four hundred crowns. Neither indeed can I deny, that if the same use were made of several plump young girls in this town, who, without one single groat to their fortunes, cannot stir abroad without a chair,[36] and appear at the play-

---

31. **with humble submission:** with all due respect to those who hold such opinions.
32. **Sallmanaazor:** George Psalmanazar (c. 1679–1763), a Frenchman who pretended to be from Formosa, an old Portuguese name for Taiwan. His writings were fraudulent.
33. **mandarins** (man′də·rinz) *n. pl.:* officials. The term comes from *mandarim,* the Portuguese word describing high-ranking officials in the Chinese Empire, with which the Portuguese traded.
34. **joints** *n. pl.:* large cuts of meat, including the bone.
35. **gibbet** (jib′it) *n.:* gallows.
36. **chair** *n.:* sedan chair; a covered seat carried by servants.

170   house, and assemblies in foreign fineries, which they never will pay for; the kingdom would not be the worse.

Some persons of a desponding spirit are in great concern about that vast number of poor people, who are aged, diseased, or maimed, and I have been desired to employ my thoughts what course may be taken, to ease the nation of so grievous an encumbrance. But I am not in the least pain upon that matter, because it is very well known, that they are every day dying, and rotting, by cold, and famine, and filth, and vermin,[37] as fast as can be reasonably expected. And as to the younger laborers they

180   are now in almost as hopeful[38] a condition. They cannot get work, and consequently pine away for want of nourishment, to a degree, that if at any time they are accidentally hired to common labor, they have not strength to perform it, and thus the country and themselves are in a fair way[39] of being soon delivered from the evils to come.

I have too long **digressed,** and therefore shall return to my subject. I think the advantages by the proposal which I have made are obvious and many as well as of the highest importance.

For first, as I have already observed, it would greatly lessen

190   the number of papists, with whom we are yearly overrun, being the principal breeders of the nation, as well as our most dangerous enemies, and who stay at home on purpose with a design to deliver the kingdom to the Pretender, hoping to take their advantage by the absence of so many good Protestants,[40] who have chosen rather to leave their country, than stay at home, and pay tithes[41] against their conscience, to an idolatrous Episcopal curate.

---

37. **vermin** *n. pl.:* pests such as lice, fleas, and bedbugs.
38. **hopeful** *adj.:* actually, hopeless. Swift is using the word with intentional irony.
39. **are in a fair way:** have a good chance.
40. **good Protestants:** that is, in Swift's view, bad Protestants, because they object to the Church of Ireland's bishops and regard them as "idolatrous."
41. **tithes** (tīthz) *n. pl.:* monetary gifts to the church equivalent to one tenth of each donor's income.

WORD STUDY

The word *encumbrance* (line 176) means "a burden, a hindrance, or a weight."

CLARIFY

Re-read lines 172–185. Why isn't the speaker concerned about the great number of other poor people in Ireland? Underline that information.

VOCABULARY

digressed (dī·grest′) *v.:* wandered off the subject.

IDENTIFY

The speaker lists the "advantages" of his proposal one by one. As you read lines 189–231, circle the word or phrase at the beginning of each paragraph that reveals the text's **pattern of organization**. Then, underline the "benefit" of each of the six proposals.

_____

_____

_____

_____

_____

_____

_____

VOCABULARY

procure (prō·kyoor') *v*.:
obtain; get.

_____
_____
_____
_____
_____
_____
_____
_____
_____
_____
_____

Secondly, the poorer tenants will have something valuable of their own, which by law may be made liable to distress,[42] and help to pay their landlord's rent, their corn and cattle being
200 already seized, and money a thing unknown.

Thirdly, whereas the maintenance of an hundred thousand children, from two years old, and upwards, cannot be computed at less than ten shillings apiece per annum, the nation's stock will be thereby increased fifty thousand pounds per annum, besides the profit of a new dish, introduced to the tables of all gentlemen of fortune in the kingdom, who have any refinement in taste, and the money will circulate among ourselves, the goods being entirely of our own growth and manufacture.[43]

Fourthly, the constant breeders, besides the gain of eight
210 shillings sterling per annum, by the sale of their children, will be rid of the charge of maintaining them after the first year.

Fifthly, this food would likewise bring great custom to taverns, where the vintners[44] will certainly be so prudent as to **procure** the best receipts[45] for dressing it to perfection, and consequently have their houses frequented by all the fine gentlemen, who justly value themselves upon their knowledge in good eating, and a skillful cook, who understands how to oblige his guests will contrive to make it as expensive as they please.

Sixthly, this would be a great inducement to marriage,
220 which all wise nations have either encouraged by rewards, or enforced by laws and penalties. It would increase the care and tenderness of mothers toward their children, when they were sure of a settlement for life to the poor babes, provided in some sort by the public to their annual profit instead of expense, we should soon see an honest emulation[46] among the married women, which of them could bring the fattest child to the

---

42. **liable to distress:** that is, the money from the sale of their children may be seized by their landlords.
43. **own growth and manufacture:** homegrown, edible children, not imported ones.
44. **vintners** (vint'nərz) *n. pl*.: wine merchants.
45. **receipts** *n. pl*.: archaic for "recipes."
46. **emulation** (em'yōō·lā'shən) *n*.: competition.

market, men would become as fond of their wives, during the time of their pregnancy, as they are now of their mares in foal, their cows in calf, or sows when they are ready to farrow,[47] nor offer to beat or kick them (as is too frequent a practice) for fear of a miscarriage.

Many other advantages might be enumerated. For instance, the addition of some thousand carcasses in our exportation of barreled beef. The propagation of swine's flesh, and improvement in the art of making good bacon, so much wanted among us by the great destruction of pigs, too frequent at our tables, which are no way comparable in taste, or magnificence to a well-grown, fat yearling child, which roasted whole will make a considerable figure at a Lord Mayor's feast, or any other public entertainment. But this, and many others I omit being studious of **brevity.**

Supposing that one thousand families in this city, would be constant customers for infants' flesh, besides others who might have it at merry meetings, particularly weddings and christenings, I compute that Dublin would take off annually about twenty thousand carcasses, and the rest of the kingdom (where probably they will be sold somewhat cheaper) the remaining eighty thousand.

I can think of no one objection, that will possibly be raised against this proposal, unless it should be urged that the number of people will be thereby much lessened in the kingdom. This I freely own, and it was indeed one principal design in offering it to the world. I desire the reader will observe, that I calculate my remedy for this one individual kingdom of Ireland, and for no other that ever was, is, or, I think, ever can be upon earth. Therefore let no man talk to me of other expedients:[48] *Of taxing our absentees*[49] *at five shillings a pound; of using neither clothes,*

---

47. **farrow** (far'ō) *v.:* produce piglets.
48. **other expedients:** At one time or another, Swift had advocated all these measures for the relief of Ireland, but they were all ignored by the government. This section was italicized in all editions printed during Swift's lifetime to indicate that Swift made these proposals sincerely rather than ironically.
49. **absentees** *n. pl.:* English landowners who refused to live on their Irish property.

INTERPRET

Explain the **irony** in the speaker's claim to "brevity" (line 240). *(Grade 9–10 Review)*

_____

_____

_____

_____

_____

IDENTIFY

Pause at line 254. What objection does the speaker anticipate (lines 248–250)? How does he answer the objection?

_____

_____

_____

_____

_____

_____

_____

_____

Re-read footnote 48 on page 135, which explains that Swift's essay is **ironic** except for this italicized passage. Why do you think Swift included this list of real solutions to the problems in Ireland?

_____

_____

_____

_____

_____

_____

_____

VOCABULARY

animosities (an′ə·mäs′ə·tēz) *n. pl.:* hostilities; violent hatreds or resentments.

_____

_____

_____

_____

_____

_____

_____

_____

_____

_____

_____

nor household furniture, except what is of our own growth and manufacture; of utterly rejecting the materials and instruments that promote foreign luxury; of curing the expensiveness of pride,

260 *vanity, idleness, and gaming[50] in our women; of introducing a vein of parsimony,[51] prudence, and temperance; of learning to love our country, wherein we differ even from Laplanders, and the inhabitants of Topinamboo;[52] of quitting our* **animosities,** *and factions,[53] nor act any longer like the Jews, who were murdering one another at the very moment their city[54] was taken; of being a little cautious not to sell our country and consciences for nothing; of teaching landlords to have at least one degree of mercy toward their tenants. Lastly of putting a spirit of honesty, industry, and skill into our shopkeepers, who, if a resolution could now be taken*

270 *to buy only our native goods, would immediately unite to cheat and exact[55] upon us in the price, the measure, and the goodness, nor could ever yet be brought to make one fair proposal of just dealing, though often and earnestly invited to it.*

Therefore I repeat, let no man talk to me of these and the like expedients, till he hath at least a glimpse of hope, that there will ever be some hearty and sincere attempt to put them in practice.

But as to myself, having been wearied out for many years with offering vain, idle, visionary thoughts, and at length utterly

280 despairing of success, I fortunately fell upon this proposal, which as it is wholly new, so it hath something solid and real, of no expense and little trouble, full in our own power, and whereby we can incur no danger in disobliging[56] England. For this kind

---

50. **gaming** *v.* used as *n.:* gambling.
51. **parsimony** (pär′sə·mō′nē) *n.:* thriftiness; economy.
52. **Topinamboo:** Swift is referring to a region of Brazil populated by native peoples collectively called the Tupinambá. Here, Swift suggests that if Brazilian peoples and Laplanders can love their seemingly inhospitable lands, the Irish should love Ireland.
53. **factions** *n. pl.:* political groups that work against the interests of other such groups or against the main body of government.
54. **their city:** Jerusalem, which the Roman emperor Titus destroyed in A.D. 70 while Jewish factions fought one another.
55. **exact** *v.:* force payment.
56. **disobliging** *v.* used as *adj.:* offending.

Judy O'Donnel's "home" under the bridge at Donnbeg, Clare, Ireland (1849).
The Illustrated London News Picture Library.

of commodity will not bear exportation, the flesh being of too tender a consistence, to admit a long continuance in salt, although perhaps I could name a country,[57] which would be glad to eat up our whole nation without it.

290   After all I am not so violently bent upon my own opinion, as to reject any offer, proposed by wise men, which shall be found equally innocent, cheap, easy, and effectual. But before something of that kind shall be advanced in contradiction to my scheme, and offering a better, I desire the author, or authors

---

57. a country: England.

IDENTIFY

In lines 293–305, the speaker offers two points for consideration. Re-read those lines, and underline the two points.

IDENTIFY

Re-read lines 305–311. According to the speaker, what miseries will be eliminated for poor people if his proposal is adopted? Draw a circle around that information.

ANALYZE

Re-read the closing paragraph of the essay. Underline words and phrases that show how the speaker tries to win over the reader. What type of **persuasive appeal** is the speaker making here?

will be pleased maturely to consider two points. First, as things now stand, how they will be able to find food and raiment for a hundred thousand useless mouths and backs. And secondly, there being a round million of creatures in human figure, throughout this kingdom, whose whole subsistence[58] put into a common stock would leave them in debt two millions of pounds sterling, adding those who are beggars by profession to the bulk
300 of farmers, cottagers, and laborers, with their wives and children, who are beggars in effect; I desire those politicians, who dislike my overture, and may perhaps be so bold to attempt an answer, that they will first ask the parents of these mortals, whether they would not at this day think it a great happiness to have been sold for food at a year old, in the manner I prescribe, and thereby have avoided such a perpetual scene of misfortunes, as they have since gone through, by the oppression of landlords, the impossibility of paying rent without money or trade, the want of common sustenance, with neither house nor clothes to cover them from
310 inclemencies of weather, and the most inevitable prospect of entailing[59] the like, or great miseries, upon their breed forever.

I profess in the sincerity of my heart that I have not the least personal interest in endeavoring to promote this necessary work, having no other motive than the public good of my country, by advancing our trade, providing for infants, relieving the poor, and giving some pleasure to the rich. I have no children, by which, I can propose to get a single penny; the youngest being nine years old, and my wife past childbearing.

---

58. **whole subsistence:** all their possessions.
59. **entailing** *v.* used as *n.:* passing on to the next generation.

A Modest Proposal

Reading Skills: Recognizing Persuasive Techniques   Each of the following excerpts from "A Modest Proposal" is an example of a **persuasive technique.** In the blank provided, write the type of appeal (logical, emotional, or ethical) that is used in the excerpt. The first one has been done for you.

---

1. "There is likewise another great advantage in my scheme, that it will prevent [women from] sacrificing the poor innocent babes." (lines 37–40)

   Type of appeal: _____ emotional appeal _____

---

2. "I profess in the sincerity of my heart that I have not the least personal interest . . . having no other motive than the public good of my country . . . I have no children, by which I can propose to get a single penny . . . and my wife past childbearing." (closing paragraph)

   Type of appeal: _____

---

3. "I do therefore humbly offer it to public consideration, that of the hundred and twenty thousand children, already computed, twenty thousand may be reserved for breed. . . ." (lines 82–84)

   Type of appeal: _____

Now, look back over the examples of persuasive techniques you highlighted or underlined in "A Modest Proposal." Choose an example not listed above, and write it in the space below. Identify the type of appeal that is used.

Example: _____

_____

_____

_____

_____

Type of appeal: _____

A Modest Proposal

VOCABULARY IN CONTEXT

DIRECTIONS: Write vocabulary words from the Word Box in the appropriate blanks. Not all words will be used.

Word Box

sustenance

glutted

deference

scrupulous

censure

expedient

digressed

procure

brevity

animosities

In "A Modest Proposal," Swift uses verbal irony to

(1) _____ the way England ignores Irish poverty.

Swift pretends to offer a suitable answer to the problem, but the

(2) _____ he suggests is shocking. Pointing out that

poor Irish people fill the streets everywhere one goes, Swift observes that

they have (3) _____ the kingdom with children. Irish

families who have a hard time providing their families with food are forced

to beg for their (4) _____. Swift pretends to show

(5) _____ for those who would profit from his plan,

but his use of irony reveals his true feeling of disgust.

WORD ORIGINS: SCIENTIFIC AND MATHEMATICAL TERMS

DIRECTIONS: Swift's essay is full of mathematical and scientific terminology. Study the chart on the left, which lists some common Greek and Latin roots and affixes. Use that information to match each mathematical or scientific word with its meaning.

Reading Standard 1.2
Apply knowledge of Greek, Latin, and Anglo-Saxon roots and affixes to draw inferences concerning the meaning of scientific and mathematical terminology.

Roots and Affixes
Greek, *melanos:* "dark; black"
Latin, *physica:* "natural science"
Greek, *geo–:* "ground; earth"
Latin, *com–:* "with" and *putare:* "to reckon"
Greek, *agros:* "field; soil; earth"

_____ 1. melancholy

_____ 2. geology

_____ 3. agriculture

_____ 4. physicist

_____ 5. computation

a. science of farming

b. mathematical calculation

c. study of the earth

d. characterized by dark depression

e. person who studies the natural sciences

 Check your Standards Mastery at the back of this book.

from An Essay on Man by Alexander Pope

LITERARY FOCUS: ANTITHESIS

"Give me liberty, or give me death."

or

"Give me liberty, or else kill me."

Which of the statements above is stronger? Which is more memorable? Of course, most people will choose the first statement, which happens to be an example of antithesis. An **antithesis** presents contrasting ideas in a grammatically balanced or parallel statement.

Alexander Pope regularly uses antithesis to express his thoughts. Look for examples of antithesis as you read the excerpt from *An Essay on Man.*

READING SKILLS: IDENTIFYING THE WRITER'S STANCE

You can identify a **writer's stance**—his or her views on a topic—because of things the writer either hints at or directly states. Like other writers of his time, Pope's purpose was to instruct his readers as well as entertain them. As a result, his poetry reflects his moral and social values. To express his views on human nature, education, and writing, Pope often uses the **heroic couplet** structure—two rhyming lines of iambic pentameter.

Here are some of Pope's heroic couplets:

- "Good nature and good sense must ever join;
  To err is human, to forgive, divine."

- "Hope springs eternal in the human breast:
  Man never is, but always to be blest."

- "Trust not yourself; but your defects to know,
  Make use of every friend—and every foe."

- "True ease in writing comes from art, not chance,
  As those move easiest who have learned to dance."

Use the Skill   As you read the excerpt from *An Essay on Man,* restate the heroic couplets in your own words. Mark examples of antithesis that you find. Think about what Pope's beliefs and values reveal about him as an individual and as a representative of the age in which he lived.

REVIEW SKILLS

As you read *An Essay on Man,* look for ways in which imagery helps the writer express his views on humanity.

IMAGERY
Language that appeals to the senses.

Reading Standard 2.5
Analyze an author's implicit and explicit philosophical assumptions and beliefs about a subject.

Reading Standard 3.4
Analyze the ways in which poets use imagery, figures of speech, and sounds to evoke readers' emotions.

Reading Standard 3.7 (Grade 9–10 Review)
Recognize and understand the significance of various literary devices, including figurative language, imagery, allegory, and symbolism, and explain their appeal.

from An Essay on Man

Alexander Pope

BACKGROUND

An Essay on Man is a long (1,304 lines) philosophical poem. Its subject is not just "man," by which Pope means the human race, but also the entire universe. It's important to know that the ideas in the poem are not only those of Pope and his friends. The ideas come from many authors, including Plato, Aristotle, St. Thomas Aquinas, Dante, Erasmus, Shakespeare, Bacon, and Milton.

In the following lines from the essay, Pope generalizes about humanity. "Man" (line 2) represents all people. As you read, see if you agree with Pope's statements.

INTERPRET

Re-read lines 1–2. What does this heroic couplet reveal about the **writer's stance**?

_____

_____

_____

_____

_____

VISUALIZE

An *isthmus* (line 3) is a small strip of land that links two larger bodies of land and is bordered on both sides by water. Re-read lines 3–7. Visualize the picture of man that Pope conjures up with his use of **imagery**. *(Grade 9–10 Review)*

Know then thyself,[1] presume not God to scan;[2]

The proper study of mankind is man.

Placed on this isthmus of a middle state,[3]

A being darkly wise, and rudely great:

5   With too much knowledge for the skeptic[4] side,

With too much weakness for the Stoic's pride,[5]

He hangs between; in doubt to act, or rest;

In doubt to deem himself a god, or beast;

In doubt his mind or body to prefer;

---

1. **Know . . . thyself:** moral precept of Socrates and other ethical philosophers.
2. **scan** *v.:* pry into; speculate about.
3. **middle state:** that is, having the rational intellect of angels and the physical body of beasts.
4. **skeptic** *n.* used as *adj.:* The ancient Skeptics doubted that humans can gain accurate knowledge of anything. They emphasized the limitations of human knowledge.
5. **Stoic's pride:** The ancient Stoics' ideal was a calm acceptance of life and an indifference to both pain and pleasure. Stoics are called proud because they refused to recognize human limitations.

10   Born but to die, and reasoning but to err;

Alike in ignorance, his reason such,

Whether he thinks too little, or too much:

Chaos of thought and passion, all confused;

Still⁶ by himself abused, or disabused;⁷

15   Created half to rise, and half to fall;

Great lord of all things, yet a prey to all;

Sole judge of truth, in endless error hurled:

The glory, jest, and riddle of the world!

ANALYZE

Underline examples of **antithesis** that you find in lines 10–18. Notice how Pope sounds both admiring and critical. What do these statements reveal about Pope's **stance,** or view, of humankind?

_____

_____

_____

_____

_____

_____

_____

_____

Alexander Pope. Portrait in oil.
Bryn Mawr College, Bryn Mawr, Pennsylvania.

FLUENCY

Read the poem aloud twice. On your first reading, be aware of marks of punctuation that signal you to make a full stop (a period), or a pause (a comma or a semicolon). If a line has no punctuation mark at its end, do not pause in your reading, but continue right on to the next line to complete the thought. On your second reading, try to use your voice to emphasize the grammatical repetitions (as in lines 5–6 and 8–9) and **antithesis.** Be aware of the rhymes, and decide how you will read them.

---

6.   **still** *adv.:* always; continually
7.   **disabused** *adj.:* undeceived.

from An Essay on Man

Reading Skills: Identifying the Writer's Stance   Find examples of **antithesis** in the excerpt from *An Essay on Man.* Fill in the chart below with those examples. Then, restate Pope's stance, or views, in your own words. One example has been done for you.

Examples of Antithesis	My Restatement of Pope's Views
Line 4: "A being darkly wise, and rudely great"	Humans are wise and great, but these qualities are mixed with flaws. We are wise about some things but ignorant about others. We can act in great and noble ways but also act "rudely," like animals.

 Check your Standards Mastery at the back of this book.

from **Don Quixote** by Miguel de Cervantes

LITERARY FOCUS: PARODY

Don Quixote is a parody of the medieval tales of romantic love and heroic knights that were extremely popular in Cervantes's day. A literary **parody** imitates another work of literature for amusement or instruction. Parodies often contain **exaggeration, verbal irony** (saying one thing and really meaning another thing), **incongruity** (deliberately pairing things that don't belong together, for example, a princess and a pig), and humorous imitation.

In *Don Quixote,* Cervantes makes fun of every aspect of medieval romances. Don Quixote is a poor, aging landowner who imagines himself to be a young, daring knight on a dangerous quest in honor of a lady. In reality, his armor is rusty, his horse is old, and the enemies he battles turn out to be windmills—all of which contribute to the story's comical effect.

All in Good Fun   Think of examples of novels, plays, comic strips, magazines, movies, or songs that use **parody** to ridicule someone or something. Jot down two examples, and briefly explain the target of the parody.

Examples of Parody	The Target of the Parody

READING SKILLS: IDENTIFYING DETAILS

Cervantes uses a number of techniques to poke fun at medieval romances. These techniques, listed below, are reflected in the details that describe Don Quixote's words and actions as well as other events in the story.

* exaggeration

* verbal irony (saying one thing but meaning another)

* incongruity (deliberately pairing things that don't belong together)

* humorous imitation

Use the Skill   As you read the story, underline or highlight details that illustrate techniques Cervantes uses in his parody. Refer to the list above for hints.

REVIEW SKILLS

As you read, look for ways in which Cervantes uses the following literary devices to add humor and meaning to the story of Don Quixote.

IRONY
A pointed contrast between reality and expectations.

INCONGRUITY
The deliberate pairing of things that don't belong together.

Reading Standard 3.1 Analyze characteristics of subgenres (e.g., satire, parody, allegory, pastoral) that are used in poetry, prose, plays, novels, short stories, essays, and other basic genres.

Reading Standard 3.8 (Grade 9–10 Review) Interpret and evaluate the impact of ambiguities, subtleties, contradictions, ironies, and incongruities in a text.

from *Don Quixote*

Miguel de Cervantes
translated by Samuel Putnam

Don Quixote is a middle-aged gentleman from the village of La Mancha.
He spends all his time reading books about knights, unlike other gentlemen,
who hunt and look after their property. Quixote's constant preoccupation
with these tales of adventure and enchantment drive him mad, and he
decides to become a knight-errant and go in search of adventure. He gets
out the rusty family armor and names his old horse Rocinante. He knows that
a knight-errant must have a fair lady to whom he can dedicate his dangerous
battles and noble deeds, so he chooses a country girl he barely knows,
Aldonza Lorenzo, and renames her Dulcinea del Toboso.

Don Quixote sets out to right the world's injustices, but his friends and family trick him into returning home. They prevent him from reading his beloved
books and treat him as if he were a lunatic. Back in his home village, Don
Quixote convinces a poor farmer he meets named Sancho Panza to serve as
his squire. One night, they secretly ride out in search of adventure.

The following excerpt from Chapter 8 of the novel tells what happens
when Don Quixote and Sancho Panza catch sight of a group of windmills.

IDENTIFY

Read on to line 14. Circle the
words that Don Quixote uses
to describe the windmills.
Underline the action he plans
to take.

_____

_____

_____

_____

_____

_____

from Chapter 8

*Of the good fortune which the valorous Don Quixote had in the
terrifying and never-before-imagined adventure of the windmills,
along with other events that deserve to be suitably recorded.*

At this point they caught sight of thirty or forty windmills
which were standing on the plain there, and no sooner had Don
Quixote laid eyes upon them than he turned to his squire and
said, "Fortune is guiding our affairs better than we could have
wished; for you see there before you, friend Sancho Panza, some
10   thirty or more lawless giants with whom I mean to do battle.

I shall deprive them of their lives, and with the spoils from this encounter we shall begin to enrich ourselves; for this is righteous warfare, and it is a great service to God to remove so accursed a breed from the face of the earth."

"What giants?" said Sancho Panza.

"Those that you see there," replied his master, "those with the long arms, some of which are as much as two leagues in length."

"But look, your Grace, those are not giants but windmills, and what appear to be arms are their wings which, when
20   whirled in the breeze, cause the millstone to go."

"It is plain to be seen," said Don Quixote, "that you have had little experience in this matter of adventures. If you are afraid, go off to one side and say your prayers while I am engaging them in fierce, unequal combat."

Saying this, he gave spurs to his steed Rocinante, without paying any heed to Sancho's warning that these were truly wind-mills and not giants that he was riding forth to attack. Nor even when he was close upon them did he perceive what they really were, but shouted at the top of his lungs, "Do not seek to flee,
30   cowards and vile creatures that you are, for it is but a single knight with whom you have to deal!"

At that moment a little wind came up and the big wings began turning.

"Though you flourish as many arms as did the giant Briareus,"[1] said Don Quixote when he perceived this, "you still shall have to answer to me."

He thereupon commended himself with all his heart to his lady Dulcinea, beseeching her to **succor** him in this peril; and, being well covered with his shield and with his lance at rest, he
40   bore down upon them at a full gallop and fell upon the first mill that stood in his way, giving a thrust at the wing, which was whirling at such a speed that his lance was broken into bits and both horse and horseman went rolling over the plain, very much

WORD STUDY

A league (lēg), line 17, is a unit of linear measurement that is usually thought to be about three miles.

INTERPRET

Underline what Quixote shouts at the windmills (lines 29–31). What is **ironic** about what he says? *(Grade 9–10 Review)*

_____

_____

_____

_____

VOCABULARY

succor (suk'ər) *v.:* help in time of distress.

INTERPRET

Underline details that describe Quixote's prepara-tion for battle with the windmills (lines 37–47). Circle details describing the out-come. What details **parody,** or make fun of, the typical medieval romance?

_____

_____

_____

_____

_____

---

1. **Briareus** (brī·är'ē·əs): in Greek mythology, a giant with a hundred arms who helped Zeus overthrow the Titans.

EVALUATE

Underline the reason Don Quixote gives for his failure (lines 52–60). What do you learn about Quixote from this explanation?

_____

_____

_____

_____

_____

_____

_____

_____

VOCABULARY

enmity (en'mə·tē) *n.*: hostility.

ANALYZE

Read lines 70–81 carefully. What does Quixote plan to replace his broken lance with? Circle that information. How does this detail demonstrate the use of **incongruity**? *(Grade 9–10 Review)*

_____

_____

_____

_____

_____

_____

_____

battered indeed. Sancho upon his donkey came hurrying to his master's assistance as fast as he could, but when he reached the spot, the knight was unable to move, so great was the shock with which he and Rocinante had hit the ground.

"God help us!" exclaimed Sancho, "did I not tell your Grace to look well, that those were nothing but windmills, a fact which

50   no one could fail to see unless he had other mills of the same sort in his head?"

"Be quiet, friend Sancho," said Don Quixote. "Such are the fortunes of war, which more than any other are subject to constant change. What is more, when I come to think of it, I am sure that this must be the work of that magician Frestón, the one who robbed me of my study and my books, and who has thus changed the giants into windmills in order to deprive me of the glory of overcoming them, so great is the **enmity** that he bears me; but in the end his evil arts shall not prevail against

60   this trusty sword of mine."

"May God's will be done," was Sancho Panza's response. And with the aid of his squire the knight was once more mounted on Rocinante, who stood there with one shoulder half out of joint. And so, speaking of the adventure that had just befallen them, they continued along the Puerto Lápice highway; for there, Don Quixote said, they could not fail to find many and varied adventures, this being a much-traveled thoroughfare. The only thing was, the knight was exceedingly downcast over the loss of his lance.

70   "I remember," he said to his squire, "having read of a Spanish knight by the name of Diego Pérez de Vargas, who, having broken his sword in battle, tore from an oak a heavy bough or branch and with it did such feats of valor that day, and pounded so many Moors, that he came to be known as Machuca,[2] and he and his descendants from that day forth have been called Vargas y Machuca. I tell you this because I too,

---

2. **Machuca** (mä·chōō'kä): literally, "the pounder," the hero of an old ballad.

The adventure with the windmills (c. 1868)
by Gustave Doré. Engraving.
The Bridgeman Art Library.

intend to provide myself with just such a bough as the one he
wielded, and with it I propose to do such exploits that you
shall deem yourself fortunate to have been found worthy to
80   come with me and behold and witness things that are almost
beyond belief."

    "God's will be done," said Sancho. "I believe everything that
your Grace says; but straighten yourself up in the saddle a little,
for you seem to be slipping down on one side, owing, no doubt,
to the shaking up that you received in your fall."

    "Ah, that is the truth," replied Don Quixote, "and if I do
not speak of my sufferings, it is for the reason that it is not
permitted knights-errant to complain of any wound whatsoever,
even though their bowels may be dropping out."

INFER

Re-read what Sancho says to
Quixote on pages 148 and
149. What can you infer about
Sancho from what he says?

IDENTIFY

Pause at line 89. Quixote
explains that knights are not
permitted to complain of
their wounds. Circle the
detail that is an example
of **exaggeration**.

CLARIFY

Underline words and phrases in lines 102–112 that reveal Sancho Panza's attitude toward the quest he is on with Don Quixote. Why does Sancho join Quixote on his journey?

_____

_____

_____

_____

_____

_____

_____

_____

_____

_____

_____

COMPARE & CONTRAST

Re-read lines 113–122. Underline words and phrases that describe how Quixote spent the night. Circle information that describes Sancho's night.

90   "If that is the way it is," said Sancho, "I have nothing more to say; but, God knows, it would suit me better if your Grace did complain when something hurts him. I can assure you that I mean to do so, over the least little thing that ails me—that is, unless the same rule applies to squires as well."

Don Quixote laughed long and heartily over Sancho's simplicity, telling him that he might complain as much as he liked and where and when he liked, whether he had good cause or not; for he had read nothing to the contrary in the ordinances[3] of chivalry. Sancho then called his master's attention

100   to the fact that it was time to eat. The knight replied that he himself had no need of food at the moment, but his squire might eat whenever he chose. Having been granted this permission, Sancho seated himself as best he could upon his beast, and, taking out from his saddlebags the provisions that he had stored there, he rode along leisurely behind his master, munching his **victuals** and taking a good, hearty swig now and then at the leather flask in a manner that might well have caused the biggest-bellied tavern-keeper of Málaga to envy him. Between drafts he gave not so much as a thought to any promise that

110   his master might have made him, nor did he look upon it as any hardship, but rather as good sport, to go in quest of adventures however hazardous they might be.

The short of the matter is, they spent the night under some trees, from one of which Don Quixote tore off a withered bough to serve him as a lance, placing it in the lance head from which he had removed the broken one. He did not sleep all night long for thinking of his lady Dulcinea; for this was in accordance with what he had read in his books, of men of arms in the forest or desert places who kept a wakeful **vigil,** sustained by the

120   memory of their ladies fair. Not so with Sancho, whose stomach was full, and not with chicory water.[4] He fell into a dreamless slumber, and had not his master called him, he would not have

---

3. **ordinances** (ôrd″n·əns·əz) *n. pl.:* authoritative commands.
4. **chicory water:** inexpensive coffee substitute.

been awakened either by the rays of the sun in his face or by the many birds who greeted the coming of the new day with their merry song.

Upon arising, he had another go at the flask, finding it somewhat more **flaccid** than it had been the night before, a circumstance which grieved his heart, for he could not see that they were on the way to remedying the deficiency within any very short space of time. Don Quixote did not wish any breakfast; for, as has been said, he was in the habit of nourishing himself on savorous memories. They then set out once more along the road to Puerto Lápice, and around three in the afternoon they came in sight of the pass that bears that name.

"There," said Don Quixote as his eyes fell upon it, "we may plunge our arms up to the elbow in what are known as adventures. But I must warn you that even though you see me in the greatest peril in the world, you are not to lay hand upon your sword to defend me, unless it be that those who attack me are rabble and men of low degree, in which case you may very well come to my aid; but if they be gentlemen, it is in no wise permitted by the laws of chivalry that you should assist me until you yourself shall have been dubbed a knight."

"Most certainly, sir," replied Sancho, "your Grace shall be very well obeyed in this; all the more so for the reason that I myself am of a peaceful **disposition** and not fond of meddling in the quarrels and feuds of others. However, when it comes to protecting my own person, I shall not take account of those laws of which you speak, seeing that all laws, human and divine, permit each one to defend himself whenever he is attacked."

"I am willing to grant you that," assented Don Quixote, "but in this matter of defending me against gentlemen you must restrain your natural impulses."

"I promise you I shall do so," said Sancho. "I will observe this precept as I would the Sabbath day. . . ."

130

140

150

VOCABULARY

flaccid (flas'id) *adj.:* limp; flabby.

disposition (dis'pə·zish'ən) *n.:* natural qualities of personality.

INFER

Quixote does not eat breakfast (lines 130–132). Circle the reason, and then restate it in your own words. What does this detail tell you about Quixote's state of mind?

_____

_____

_____

_____

_____

_____

_____

PREDICT

Re-read lines 144–155. Do you predict Sancho will keep his promise? Explain.

_____

_____

_____

_____

_____

from Don Quixote

Reading Skills: Identifying Details   Look back over the story to find details that **parody** medieval romances. Then complete this chart.

Techniques Used in Parodies	Details from *Don Quixote*
Exaggeration	
Incongruity (deliberately pairing things that don't belong together)	
Verbal irony (saying one thing but meaning another)	
Humorous imitation	

Evaluate   One of Cervantes's purposes in writing this parody was to amuse readers by poking fun at medieval romances. Another goal was to demonstrate the power of visions and dreams. Review the details you recorded in the chart above, and evaluate how well Cervantes succeeds in his purposes.

_____

_____

_____

from Don Quixote

VOCABULARY IN CONTEXT

DIRECTIONS: Write a word from the Word Box in each blank to complete the paragraph below. Not all words will be used.

Word Box

succor

enmity

victuals

vigil

flaccid

disposition

A medieval knight was expected to have a personality characterized by bravery, loyalty, and courtesy—in short, a practically perfect

(1) _____. When a knight saw people in danger or in

need, he would offer (2) _____ and comfort without

expecting anything in return. Sometimes knights went on quests

to slay dragons or other monsters, which required them to keep a constant

(3) _____ and be ever watchful for signs of danger.

Though gentlemanly toward the ladies, knights were capable of great

(4) _____ in the heat of battle.

ETYMOLOGIES

DIRECTIONS: The etymology of a word traces the history of its development to its earliest usage. Match the words from *Don Quixote* with their etymologies, listed at the right.

_____ **1.** prevail

_____ **2.** chivalry

_____ **3.** provisions

_____ **4.** quarrel

_____ **5.** knight

a. from Latin *queri:* "to complain; lament"

b. from Old English *cniht:* "boy"

c. from Latin *valere:* "to be strong"

d. from Middle English and Old French *cheval:* "horse"

e. from Latin *pro–:* "ahead" + *videre:* "to see"

Reading Standard 1.1 (Grade 9–10 Review) Identify and use the literal and figurative meanings of words and understand word derivations.

from **The Education of Women** by Daniel Defoe

REVIEW SKILLS

As you read Defoe's essay, pay special attention to how he uses **tone** to reinforce his argument.

TONE
The attitude a writer takes toward the reader, the subject, or a character. Tone is conveyed by a writer's word choice.

Reading Standard 2.4
Make warranted and reasonable assertions about the author's arguments by using elements of the text to defend and clarify interpretations.

Reading Standard 2.8 (Grade 9–10 Review)
Evaluate the credibility of an author's argument or defense of a claim by critiquing the relationship between generalizations and evidence, the comprehensiveness of evidence, and the way in which the author's intent affects the structure and tone of the text.

LITERARY FOCUS: WRITER'S ARGUMENT

An **argument** is a form of persuasion that aims to convince an audience to think in a certain way or to take a particular action. An argument appeals to the audience's reason, not to its emotions.

It is important to keep in mind that, even if a writer's argument is logical and well thought out, he or she may voice a particular value judgment or personal preference, called **bias**. The presence of bias means that the argument is not completely fair and impartial.

READING SKILLS: ANALYZING AN ARGUMENT

When you analyze an argument, you examine the persuasive techniques used by the writer. Here are some persuasive techniques used in argument:

- **rhetorical question:** The writer, for effect, asks a question for which an answer is not expected.

- **argument by analogy:** The writer points out a parallel between two subjects or situations in order to make a point.

- **repetition or restatement:** The writer repeats the main idea in different ways.

- **counterargument:** The writer anticipates the audience's objections or concerns and openly addresses them.

- **anecdote or example:** The writer uses a brief story or cites a particular case in order to support his or her point.

Use the Skill   As you read the selection, underline or highlight techniques that Defoe uses to develop his argument. Use the list above as a guide.

from
The Education of Women

Daniel Defoe

BACKGROUND
Writer Daniel Defoe (1660–1731) was a businessman and a spy at different times in his life. He wrote on a variety of subjects, from how to
choose a wife to the history of the devil. Despite writing on so many
different topics, Defoe is mainly remembered today for his novel
Robinson Crusoe (1719), the survival story of a shipwrecked sailor.
    In the essay that follows, Defoe shares his thoughts on the education
of women. In the eighteenth century, women in England were denied
access to formal education. They were not allowed to own property,
run a business, vote, or control their own lives or those of their children.

I have often thought of it as one of the most barbarous customs
in the world, considering us as a civilized and a Christian country,
that we deny the advantages of learning to women. We reproach
the sex every day with folly and impertinence; while I am confident, had they the advantages of education equal to us, they
would be guilty of less than ourselves.

    One would wonder, indeed, how it should happen that
women are conversible at all; since they are only beholden to
natural parts, for all their knowledge. Their youth is spent to
10   teach them to stitch and sew or make baubles. They are taught
to read, indeed, and perhaps to write their names, or so; and
that is the height of a woman's education. And I would but ask
any who slight the sex for their understanding, what is a man (a
gentleman, I mean) good for, that is taught no more? I need not
give instances, or examine the character of a gentleman, with a
good estate, or a good family, and with tolerable parts; and
examine what figure he makes for want of education.

ANALYZE

The word *barbarous* in
the first sentence means
"uncivilized." What does
Defoe's use of this word
suggest about his **tone,**
or attitude, toward the
education of women?
(Grade 9–10 Review)

_____

_____

_____

_____

IDENTIFY

What skills are women usually
taught (lines 9–12)? Circle
that information.

ANALYZE

Re-read lines 18–22. To what does Defoe compare the human soul? Underline this information. What point about the value of education does Defoe make with this **analogy**?

_____

_____

_____

_____

_____

_____

_____

ANALYZE

Underline the **rhetorical questions** in lines 23–34. What "answer" does Defoe expect to each question?

_____

_____

_____

_____

_____

_____

_____

INTERPRET

Re-read lines 35–41. What does Defoe suggest is the *real* reason women are not given an education? Underline that information.

The soul is placed in the body like a rough diamond; and must be polished, or the luster of it will never appear. And 'tis
20 manifest, that as the rational soul distinguishes us from brutes; so education carries on the distinction, and makes some less brutish than others. This is too evident to need any demonstration. But why then should women be denied the benefit of instruction? If knowledge and understanding had been useless additions to the sex, GOD Almighty would never have given them capacities; for he made nothing needless. Besides, I would ask such, What they can see in ignorance, that they should think it a necessary ornament to a woman? or how much worse is a wise woman than a fool? or what has the woman done to forfeit
30 the privilege of being taught? Does she plague us with her pride and impertinence? Why did we not let her learn, that she might have had more wit? Shall we upbraid women with folly, when 'tis only the error of this inhuman custom, that hindered them from being made wiser?

The capacities of women are supposed to be greater, and their senses quicker than those of the men; and what they might be capable of being bred to, is plain from some instances of female wit, which this age is not without. Which upbraids us with Injustice, and looks as if we denied women the advantages
40 of education, for fear they should *vie* with the men in their improvements. . . .

The Young Schoolmistress (1740) by Jean-Baptiste Chardin. Oil on canvas. The Bridgeman Art Library.

[They] should be taught all sorts of breeding suitable both to their genius and quality. And in particular, Music and Dancing; which it would be cruelty to bar the sex of, because they are their darlings. But besides this, they should be taught languages, as particularly French and Italian: and I would venture the injury of giving a woman more tongues than one. They should, as a particular study, be taught all the graces of speech, and all the necessary air of conversation; which our common education is

50   so defective in, that I need not expose it. They should be brought to read books, and especially history; and so to read as to make them understand the world, and be able to know and judge of things when they hear of them.

To such whose genius would lead them to it, I would deny no sort of learning; but the chief thing, in general, is to cultivate the understandings of the sex, that they may be capable of all sorts of conversation; that their parts and judgments being improved, they may be as profitable in their conversation as they are pleasant.

Women, in my observation, have little or no difference in

60   them, but as they are or are not distinguished by education. Tempers, indeed, may in some degree influence them, but the main distinguishing part is their Breeding. . . .

The great distinguishing difference, which is seen in the world between men and women, is in their education; and this is manifested by comparing it with the difference between one man or woman, and another.

And herein it is that I take upon me to make such a bold assertion, That all the world are mistaken in their practice about women. For I cannot think that GOD Almighty ever made them

70   so delicate, so glorious creatures; and furnished them with such charms, so agreeable and so delightful to mankind; with souls capable of the same accomplishments with men: and all, to be only Stewards of our Houses, Cooks, and Slaves.

IDENTIFY

What particular things does Defoe believe women should be taught (lines 42–53)? Underline that information.

FLUENCY

Read the boxed passage aloud twice. Focus on understanding simple meaning the first time around. The second time you read, pay special attention to marks of punctuation to guide the pace of your reading.

IDENTIFY CAUSE & EFFECT

Re-read lines 54–58. According to Defoe, what would be the positive effects of educating women? Underline that information.

ANALYZE

Circle the words Defoe uses to describe women (lines 67–73). What **bias** against women, if any, do you find in Defoe's argument?

_____

_____

_____

_____

_____

_____

_____

PARAPHRASE

Defoe clearly states his opinion on the education of women (lines 74–78). Restate it in your own words.

_____

_____

_____

_____

_____

_____

ANALYZE

What is the purpose of the **anecdote** told in this paragraph (lines 83–92)?

_____

_____

_____

_____

INTERPRET

Granted (line 93) means "acknowledged." What observation is Defoe making at the conclusion of his essay?

_____

_____

_____

_____

_____

Not that I am for exalting the female government in the least: but, in short, *I would have men take women for companions, and educate them to be fit for it.* A woman of sense and breeding will scorn as much to encroach upon the prerogative of man, as a man of sense will scorn to oppress the weakness of the woman. But if the women's souls were refined and improved by teaching,

80 that word would be lost. To say, the *weakness* of the sex, as to judgment, would be nonsense; for ignorance and folly would be no more to be found among women than men.

I remember a passage, which I heard from a very fine woman. She had wit and capacity enough, an extraordinary shape and face, and a great fortune: but had been cloistered up all her time; and for fear of being stolen, had not had the liberty of being taught the common necessary knowledge of women's affairs. And when she came to converse in the world, her natural wit made her so sensible of the want of education, that she gave

90 this short reflection on herself: "I am ashamed to talk with my very maids," says she, "for I don't know when they do right or wrong. I had more need go to school, than be married.". . .

'Tis a thing will be more easily granted than remedied.

from The Education of Women

Reading Skills: Analyzing an Argument   Look back over the techniques of argument that you underlined or highlighted in Defoe's essay. Complete the chart below by writing examples in the right-hand column that illustrate each of the techniques listed in the left-hand column.

Techniques of Argument	Examples from "The Education of Women"
Rhetorical question: The writer, for effect, asks a question for which an answer is not expected.	
Argument by analogy: The writer points out a parallel between two subjects or situations in order to make a point.	
Repetition or restatement: The writer repeats the main idea in different ways.	
Counterargument: The writer anticipates the audience's objections or concerns and openly addresses them.	
Anecdote or example: The writer uses a brief story or cites a particular case in order to support his or her point.	

Check your Standards Mastery at the back of this book.

The Romantic Period

(1798–1832)

The Quest for Truth and Beauty

The Wanderer Above the Sea of Clouds
(1818) by Caspar David Friedrich. Oil on canvas.

The Romantic Period
(1798–1832)

Harley Henry

The following essay provides highlights of the historical period.
For a more detailed version of this essay,
see *Holt Literature and Language Arts,* pages 522–533.

Reading Standard 2.3 (Grade 9–10 Review) Generate relevant questions about readings on issues that can be researched.
Reading Standard 3.7c Evaluate the philosophical, political, religious, ethical, and social influences of the historical period.

During the spring of 1798, two young English poets sold some of their poems to raise money for a trip to Germany. Each had published books of poetry, but their new joint work was to be anonymous. As Samuel Taylor Coleridge, the younger of the pair, told the printer: "Wordsworth's name is nothing . . . mine *stinks.*"

Soon after they left England, their book, *Lyrical Ballads, with a Few Other Poems,* appeared. Among the "few other poems" was Coleridge's long narrative *The Rime of the Ancient Mariner* and a last-minute addition, Wordsworth's "Lines Composed a Few
10 Miles Above Tintern Abbey." Both of these works are now among the most important poems in English literature.

So began what is now called the "Romantic period" in England. Literary historians have found other important events to mark its beginning and end, but we should remember the casual, modest appearance of *Lyrical Ballads* as we consider the Romantic period and the writers associated with it.

Turbulent Times, Bitter Realities

Another way to date the Romantic period is to say that it started with the French Revolution in 1789 and ended with the
20 Parliamentary reforms of 1832 that laid the political foundations for modern Britain. It was a turbulent, revolutionary age, marked by important historical developments—an age in which England changed from an agricultural society to an industrial nation.

INTERPRET

Re-read Coleridge's remark in line 5. What did he mean by it?

_____

_____

_____

_____

_____

_____

_____

IDENTIFY

Which "few other poems" ended up becoming among the most famous in the English language? Underline their titles (lines 6–11).

IDENTIFY

Re-read lines 18–23. What other event and what year is sometimes considered the beginning of the Romantic era? Circle the event and year.

IDENTIFY
CAUSE & EFFECT

What were some effects of
the age of revolution that
swept across western Europe
(lines 24–28)? Underline that
information.

WORD STUDY

The word *repercussions*
(rē'pər·kush'ənz), line 33,
is a noun built on the Latin
verb *repercutere*, meaning
"to rebound or strike back."
It refers to the sweeping
and sometimes unforeseen
effects or reactions to an
event or action.

CLARIFY

Re-read lines 30–38. Why did
the ruling classes of England
view the French Revolution
as threatening?

_____

_____

_____

_____

_____

_____

_____

IDENTIFY
CAUSE & EFFECT

Re-read lines 44–56. What
event disillusioned many
people and helped lead to
war between England and
France? Underline that
information.

We think about this era in terms of some important historic developments. Beginning in America in 1776, an age of revolution swept across western Europe. During the next century, new political, economic, and social forces produced some of the most radical changes ever experienced in human life.

The French Revolution

30 A radical revolution started in France with the storming of the prison called the Bastille on July 14, 1789. Unlike the American Revolution, the more radical French Revolution had threatening repercussions for England. For the English ruling classes, the French Revolution came to represent their worst fears: the overthrow of an anointed king by a democratic mob. To English conservatives, the French Revolution meant the triumph of radical principles, and they feared that the revolutionary fever would spread across from France to England.

The "New Regime"

40 Democratic idealists and liberals felt exhilarated by the events in France. During the revolution's early years, they even made trips to France to view the "new regime" firsthand, as if it were a tourist attraction like the Acropolis in Greece.

Many became disillusioned, however, when in 1792 the "September massacre" took place in France. Hundreds of French aristocrats and some members of the clergy—with only the slightest ties to the regime of King Louis XVI—had their heads severed from their bodies by a grisly new invention, the guillotine (gil'ə·tēn *or* gē'ə·tēn).

50 In 1793, France and England declared war on each other. Many English liberals, including Wordsworth and Coleridge, turned against France. In the midst of the turmoil, control of the French government changed hands again. Napoleon Bonaparte, an officer in the French army, emerged first as dictator and then, in 1804, as emperor of France. In the end, Napoleon became as ruthless as the executed king himself had been.

The Conservatives Clamp Down

The bewildering changes in western Europe prompted conservatives in England to institute severe repressive measures. The

60 English outlawed collective bargaining and kept suspected spies or agitators in prison without a trial. After a brief peace in 1802–1803, England began a long war against Napoleon. The English first defeated Napoleon's navy at the Battle of Trafalgar and, finally—in 1815 with the help of allies—conquered Napoleon's army at Waterloo, Belgium.

The conservatives in England felt they had saved their country from a tyrant and from chaos; the early supporters of the revolution felt betrayed. For them, Waterloo was simply the defeat of one tyrant by another. Still, the Romantics clung

70 to their hopes for the "dawn of a new era" through peaceful change—hopes provoked and shaped by upheavals in English life brought about by the Industrial Revolution.

The Industrial Revolution Finds a Foothold

England was the first nation in the world to experience the effects of the Industrial Revolution. Previously, goods had been made by hand, at home. Now, production switched to factories, where machines worked many times faster than human beings could work by hand. Since factories were in cities, the city populations increased, resulting in desperate living conditions that would

80 horrify even the most hardened social worker today.

In addition, the land once shared by small farmers was taken over by individual owners and converted into private parks or privately held fields. This resulted in large numbers of landless people. Just as some unemployed and homeless people do today, these landless people moved to cities in search of work, or relied on the forms of charity of the time, the poorhouse and begging.

WORD STUDY

Collective bargaining (line 60) is a term meaning "negotiation between workers and employers for reaching agreement on wages, hours, working conditions, and so on."

IDENTIFY

Re-read lines 58–72. Circle what the English achieved at Waterloo in 1815. After Napoleon's defeat, what hopes did the Romantics cling to? Underline that information.

DRAW CONCLUSIONS

Pause at line 80. Why do you think that rapid population growth in cities resulted in such horrible living conditions?

_____

_____

_____

_____

_____

_____

IDENTIFY

Re-read lines 81–87. What did small farmers who suddenly found themselves without land do? Underline that information.

**IDENTIFY
CAUSE & EFFECT**

Underline the idea behind the economic policy of laissez faire (lines 89–99). Circle three effects of this policy.

IDENTIFY

Pause at line 107. Circle the names of the six poets most often identified with the Romantic era.

CLARIFY

Re-read lines 107–117. What goal were the Romantics dedicated to? How did their poetry differ from poetry that had come before?

_____

_____

_____

_____

_____

_____

_____

_____

_____

_____

_____

_____

The Tyranny of Laissez Faire

90 The economic philosophy that kept all this misery going was a policy called **laissez faire** (les′ā·fer′), a French term meaning "let (people) do (as they please)." According to this policy, the new economic forces should be allowed to operate freely without government interference. The result of laissez faire was that the rich grew richer, and the poor suffered even more. The system, of course, had its most tragic effects on the helpless, especially children. Small children of the poor were often used as beasts of burden. In the coal pits, for example, very small children were even harnessed to carts for dragging coal, just as if they had been small donkeys.

The Rebellion of the Romantic Poets

100 The Romantic era has been most often identified with six poets. Three of them (William Blake, William Wordsworth, and Samuel Taylor Coleridge) were born before the period began and lived through most or all of it. The other three (the "second generation" of Percy Bysshe Shelley, John Keats, and George Gordon, Lord Byron) began their short careers in the second decade of the new century but died before 1825. All six poets were, in their own ways, deeply aware of their revolutionary times and dedicated to bringing about change. They had no
110 illusions about their very limited political power, but they believed in the force of literature. Frustrated by England's resistance to political and social change that would improve conditions, the Romantic poets turned from the formal, public verse of the eighteenth-century Augustans to a more private, spontaneous, lyric poetry. These lyrics expressed the Romantics' belief that imagination, rather than mere reason, was the best response to the forces of change.

What Does "Romantic" Mean?

The word *romantic* comes from the term *romance,* one of the
120 most popular genres of medieval literature. Later, Romantic
writers self-consciously used the elements of romance in an
attempt to go back to older types of writing that they saw as
more "genuine" than neoclassical literature. The romance genre
also allowed writers to explore new, more psychological and
mysterious aspects of human experience.

Today, the word *romantic* is often a negative label used to
describe sentimental writing. The word is particularly applied
to bestselling paperback "romances" about love—a subject that
many people mistakenly think the Romantic poets popularized.
130 As a historical term, however, *romantic* has at least three useful
meanings, all of them relevant to the Romantic poets.

■ A Child's Sense of Wonder

First, the term *romantic* signifies a fascination with youth and
innocence, particularly the freshness and wonder of a child's
perception of the world. This perception seemed to resemble the
age's sense of a "new dawn" and what Wordsworth saw in his
first experience in France as "human nature being born again."

■ Social Idealism

Second, the term *romantic* refers to a view of the cyclical develop-
140 ment of human societies. This is the stage when people need to
question tradition and authority in order to imagine better—
that is, happier, fairer, and healthier—ways to live. *Romantic* in
this sense is associated with idealism. (The 1966–1975 period in
the United States might be called a romantic era.)

■ Adaptation to Change

Finally, the term *romantic* suggests an ability to adapt to change—
an acceptance of change rather than a rigid rejection of it. In the
so-called Romantic period of the first half of the nineteenth
century (up to the Civil War in America), Western societies met
150 the conditions necessary for industrialization. This demanded

CLARIFY

How is the word *romantic*
often used today (lines
126–129)?

_____

_____

_____

_____

_____

_____

_____

_____

_____

_____

_____

_____

_____

_____

_____

_____

IDENTIFY

Re-read lines 132–150. In
each of the three sections,
underline the main words
and phrases that define the
word *romantic,* as it applies
to the Romantic period.

that people acquire a stronger and stronger awareness of change, and that they try to find ways to adapt to it. In this sense, we still live with the legacy of the Romantic period.

A New Kind of Poetry

Lyrical Ballads did not remain unnoticed or anonymous for long. In 1800, with Coleridge looking over his shoulder, Wordsworth composed the Preface for the expanded collection. In it he declared that he was writing a new kind of poetry. The subject matter would be different from that of earlier poets like

160 Alexander Pope, who used poetry to satirize, or to persuade the reader with argumentative techniques. For Wordsworth, good poetry was "the spontaneous overflow of powerful feelings." Such poetry should use simple, unadorned language to deal with commonplace subjects. Furthermore, Wordsworth focused on rural life instead of city life; he believed that there is a permanent and interactive bond between the human mind and nature. Wordsworth reveals and celebrates this bond in "Tintern Abbey" (page 169).

The Mystery of Imagination

170 It is a mistake to think of the Romantics as "nature poets." They were "mind poets" who sought a deeper understanding of the bond between human beings and the world of the senses. Their search led them to a third, more mysterious element present in both the mind and nature. The Romantics identified this power as the imagination, which was superior to human reasoning.

Each of the Romantics had his or her own special view of the imagination. But all of them seem to have believed that the imagination could be stimulated by both nature and the mind itself. They had a strong sense of nature's mysterious forces.

180 Romantic poems usually present imaginative experiences as very powerful or moving. This suggests that the human imagination

COMPARE & CONTRAST

How was Wordsworth's "new kind of poetry" different from that of earlier poets (lines 155–168)? Underline words and phrases that describe Wordsworth's poetry; circle words and phrases that describe earlier poetry.

IDENTIFY

Re-read lines 170–183. What important things did the Romantics believe about the human imagination? Underline that information.

is also a kind of desire—a motive that drives the mind to discover things that it cannot learn by rational or logical thinking.

The Romantic Poet

In the Preface, Wordsworth makes it clear that the poet is a special person, "endowed with more lively sensibility, more enthusiasm and tenderness . . . a greater knowledge of human nature, and a more comprehensive soul, than are supposed to be common among mankind." Though the word *supposed*
190   (meaning "thought") may suggest that Wordsworth thought his fellow citizens had too low an estimate of much of humankind, all of the Romantic poets described the poet in such lofty terms.

For William Blake, for example, the poet was the bard, an inspired revealer and teacher. The poet, wrote Coleridge, "brings the whole soul of man into activity" by employing "that synthetic and magical power . . . the imagination." Shelley called poets "the unacknowledged legislators of the world." Keats wrote that a poet is a "physician" to all humanity and "pours out a balm upon the world." The poet, in other words,
200   is someone human beings and society cannot do without.

The Sleeping Princess
(19th century) by Sir Edward Burne-Jones.

CONNECT

Circle words and phrases that describe the Romantic view of the poet's role (lines 185–200). Do you agree that "human beings and society cannot do without" poets? Why?

_____

_____

_____

_____

_____

_____

GENERATE QUESTIONS

Think about the Romantic beliefs and ideas discussed in this essay. What question about the Romantics would you like answered? How would you go about finding an answer to it? *(Grade 9–10 Review)*

_____

_____

_____

_____

_____

_____

_____

Lines Composed a Few Miles Above Tintern Abbey

by William Wordsworth

LITERARY FOCUS: BLANK VERSE

Blank verse is a natural-sounding, flowing style of poetry that echoes the rhythms of everyday speech. The lines do not rhyme, and each line contains five *iambic feet.* (A *foot* is a unit of measurement used in poetry.) An *iambic foot* consists of an unstressed syllable followed by a stressed syllable, as in the word *today.* Blank verse is formally defined as poetry written in unrhymed **iambic pentameter,** meaning that each line is five iambs long.

Wordsworth composed poetry in his head while he walked—he spoke the words aloud to memorize them and to get the rhythm right. "Tintern Abbey" was the first time Wordsworth used blank verse to achieve a more "conversational," natural rhythm in his poetry. He wrote many more poems in which he explored and refined this style.

READING SKILLS: RECOGNIZING PATTERNS OF ORGANIZATION

Wordsworth organizes his poem into **stanzas,** or verse units, by splitting some lines and indenting the second part of each line to signal the beginning of a new section. If you glance over the poem, you can easily spot these stanza breaks; they fall in lines 22, 49, and 111. A stanza break that does not follow this pattern occurs at line 58.

Within each stanza, Wordsworth repeats key words or details in order to develop an idea. For example:

- In stanza one (lines 1–22), the repetition of the word *again* in lines 4, 9, and 14 places emphasis on the idea of the passage of time.

- In stanza two (lines 22–49), the details paint contrasts between city life and rural beauty.

Use the Skill   As you read each stanza, underline or highlight details that help you to identify its main ideas.

Lines Composed a Few Miles Above Tintern Abbey

On Revisiting the Banks of the Wye During a Tour. July 13, 1798

William Wordsworth

> **BACKGROUND**
> Tintern Abbey, mentioned in the poem's title, was the ruins of an abbey, or church building. The poem records Wordsworth's reflections after he and his sister, Dorothy, took a vigorous walking tour in southern Wales. Wordsworth wrote the poem in his head over the period of four to five days as he and his sister left the area near Tintern Abbey to walk to Bristol. The poem was published almost immediately after Wordsworth wrote it down on paper. To this day the poem remains an important statement of the ideas of the Romantic movement and is an inspiration to many poets—and readers.

Five years have past; five summers, with the length

Of five long winters! and again I hear

These waters, rolling from their mountain springs

With a soft inland murmur.—Once again

5   Do I behold these steep and lofty cliffs,

That on a wild secluded scene impress

Thoughts of more deep seclusion; and connect

The landscape with the quiet of the sky.

The day is come when I again repose

10   Here, under this dark sycamore, and view

These plots of cottage ground, these orchard tufts,

Which at this season, with their unripe fruits,

Are clad in one green hue, and lose themselves

CLARIFY

According to the first four lines, how long has it been since the speaker last stood on the banks of the Wye River?

_____

_____

_____

IDENTIFY

Underline key words in lines 1–18 that tell what the speaker hears, and circle key words that show what he sees.

_____

_____

_____

_____

_____

_____

_____

CLARIFY

What are the "beauteous forms" the speaker refers to (line 22)? Read on to line 41, and underline how those beauteous forms have affected the speaker's life away from that place.

_____

_____

_____

_____

_____

IDENTIFY

Re-read lines 41–49, in which the speaker describes the calm, trancelike state that visions of nature create. What special insight does he say we can gain from this "serene and blessed mood"? Circle that information.

'Mid groves and copses.¹ Once again I see

15   These hedgerows,² hardly hedgerows, little lines

Of sportive wood run wild: these pastoral³ farms,

Green to the very door; and wreaths of smoke

Sent up, in silence, from among the trees!

With some uncertain notice, as might seem

20   Of vagrant dwellers in the houseless woods,

Or of some Hermit's cave, where by his fire

The Hermit sits alone.

                                    These beauteous forms,

Through a long absence, have not been to me

As is a landscape to a blind man's eye:

25   But oft, in lonely rooms, and 'mid the din

Of towns and cities, I have owed to them

In hours of weariness, sensations sweet,

Felt in the blood, and felt along the heart;

And passing even into my purer mind,

30   With tranquil restoration:—feelings too

Of unremembered pleasure: such, perhaps,

As have no slight or trivial influence

On that best portion of a good man's life,

His little, nameless, unremembered acts

35   Of kindness and of love. Nor less, I trust,

To them I may have owed another gift,

Of aspect more sublime; that blessed mood,

In which the burden of the mystery,

In which the heavy and the weary weight

40   Of all this unintelligible world,

Is lightened:—that serene and blessed mood,

In which the affections⁴ gently lead us on,—

Until, the breath of this corporeal⁵ frame

_____

1. **copses** *n. pl.:* areas densely covered with shrubs and small trees.
2. **hedgerows** *n. pl.:* rows of bushes, shrubs, and small trees that serve as fences.
3. **pastoral** *adj.:* relating to herds or flocks, pasture land, and country life.
4. **affections** *n. pl.:* feelings.
5. **corporeal** *adj.:* bodily.

And even the motion of our human blood

45 Almost suspended, we are laid asleep

In body, and become a living soul:

While with an eye made quiet by the power

Of harmony, and the deep power of joy,

We see into the life of things.

                              If this

50 Be but a vain belief, yet, oh! how oft—

In darkness and amid the many shapes

Of joyless daylight; when the fretful stir

Unprofitable, and the fever of the world,

Have hung upon the beatings of my heart—

55 How oft, in spirit, have I turned to thee,

O sylvan[6] Wye! thou wanderer through the woods,

How often has my spirit turned to thee!

   And now, with gleams of half-extinguished thought,

With many recognitions dim and faint,

60 And somewhat of a sad perplexity,

The picture of the mind[7] revives again:

While here I stand, not only with the sense

Of present pleasure, but with pleasing thoughts

That in this moment there is life and food

65 For future years. And so I dare to hope,

Though changed, no doubt, from what I was when first

I came among these hills; when like a roe[8]

I bounded o'er the mountains, by the sides

Of the deep rivers, and the lonely streams,

70 Wherever nature led: more like a man

Flying from something that he dreads, than one

Who sought the thing he loved. For nature then

(The coarser pleasures of my boyish days,

And their glad animal movements all gone by)

75 To me was all in all.—I cannot paint

---

6. **sylvan** *adj.*: associated with the forest or woodlands.
7. **picture of the mind**: primarily the picture in the mind, but also the picture the individual mind has of itself.
8. **roe** *n.*: deer.

Lines Composed a Few Miles Above Tintern Abbey   **171**

ANALYZE

What visual clue signals that a new stanza is beginning in line 49? How does the speaker's **tone** change in the new stanza? *(Grade 9–10 Review)*

_____

_____

_____

_____

_____

CLARIFY

The speaker talks directly to an element of nature in lines 49–57. Who—or what—is the "wanderer through the woods" (line 56) that the speaker addresses?

_____

_____

ANALYZE

In lines 65–75, the speaker recalls his youth, when he could bound over the mountains like a young deer. At that time, what was it that he loved about nature?

_____

_____

_____

_____

_____

_____

_____

A shift occurs in lines 83–88.
Circle two things from the
past that the speaker says
are gone now. Restate in
your own words how the
speaker feels about this loss.

_____

_____

_____

_____

_____

_____

_____

INTERPRET

Re-read lines 93–102. What is
the "presence" in line 94
that the speaker describes?

_____

_____

_____

_____

_____

_____

FLUENCY

Read the boxed passage
aloud, using the punctuation
as a guide. Read the passage
several times until you
feel you have captured
the natural rhythm of the
blank verse.

What then I was. The sounding cataract[9]
Haunted me like a passion: the tall rock,
The mountain, and the deep and gloomy wood,
Their colors and their forms, were then to me
80   An appetite; a feeling and a love,
That had no need of a remoter charm,[10]
By thought supplied, nor any interest
Unborrowed from the eye.—That time is past,
And all its aching joys are now no more.
85   And all its dizzy raptures. Not for this
Faint[11] I, nor mourn nor murmur; other gifts
Have followed; for such loss, I would believe,
Abundant recompense.[12] For I have learned
To look on nature, not as in the hour
90   Of thoughtless youth; but hearing oftentimes
The still, sad music of humanity,
Nor harsh nor grating, though of ample power
To chasten and subdue. And I have felt
A presence that disturbs me with the joy
95   Of elevated thoughts; a sense sublime
Of something far more deeply interfused,
Whose dwelling is the light of setting suns,
And the round ocean and the living air,
And the blue sky, and in the mind of man:
100   A motion and a spirit, that impels
All thinking things, all objects of all thought,
And rolls through all things. Therefore am I still
A lover of the meadows and the woods,
And mountains; and of all that we behold
105   From this green earth; of all the mighty world
Of eye, and ear—both what they half create,
And what perceive; well pleased to recognize

---

9. **cataract** *n.:* waterfall.
10. **remoter charm:** appeal other than the scene itself.
11. **faint** *v.:* become weak; lose heart.
12. **recompense** *n.:* repayment.

In nature and the language of the sense

The anchor of my purest thoughts, the nurse,

110   The guide, the guardian of my heart, and soul

Of all my moral being.

                  Nor perchance,

If I were not thus taught, should I the more

Suffer[13] my genial[14] spirits to decay:

For thou art with me here upon the banks

115   Of this fair river; thou my dearest Friend,[15]

My dear, dear Friend; and in thy voice I catch

The language of my former heart, and read

My former pleasures in the shooting lights

Of thy wild eyes. Oh! yet a little while

120   May I behold in thee what I was once,

My dear, dear Sister! and this prayer I make,

Knowing that Nature never did betray

The heart that loved her; 'tis her privilege,

Through all the years of this our life, to lead

125   From joy to joy: for she can so inform

The mind that is within us, so impress

With quietness and beauty, and so feed

With lofty thoughts, that neither evil tongues,

Rash judgments, nor the sneers of selfish men,

130   Nor greetings where no kindness is, nor all

The dreary intercourse[16] of daily life,

Shall e'er prevail against us, or disturb

Our cheerful faith, that all which we behold

Is full of blessings. Therefore let the moon

135   Shine on thee in thy solitary walk;

And let the misty mountain winds be free

To blow against thee: and, in after years,

When these wild ecstasies shall be matured

---

13. **suffer** *v.:* allow.
14. **genial** *adj.:* creative.
15. **my dearest Friend:** Wordsworth's sister, Dorothy.
16. **intercourse** *n.:* dealings; social contacts.

IDENTIFY

Re-read lines 114–121. What shift occurs in this stanza in terms of the speaker's focus?

_____

_____

_____

_____

_____

_____

COMPARE & CONTRAST

The speaker compares his sister to how he once was (lines 116–121). How is she similar?

_____

_____

_____

_____

_____

_____

IDENTIFY

The speaker offers a prayer for his sister that runs from line 121 to the end of the poem. In lines 134–142, underline three blessings he asks nature to bestow upon her.

The ruins of Tintern Abbey today.

Into a sober pleasure; when thy mind
140   Shall be a mansion for all lovely forms,
      Thy memory be as a dwelling place
      For all sweet sounds and harmonies; oh! then,
      If solitude, or fear, or pain, or grief,
      Should be thy portion, with what healing thoughts
145   Of tender joy wilt thou remember me,
      And these my exhortations![17] Nor, perchance—
      If I should be where I no more can hear
      Thy voice, nor catch from thy wild eyes these gleams
      Of past existence—wilt thou then forget
150   That on the banks of this delightful stream
      We stood together; and that I, so long
      A worshipper of Nature, hither came
      Unwearied in that service: rather say
      With warmer love—oh! with far deeper zeal
155   Of holier love. Nor wilt thou then forget
      That after many wanderings, many years
      Of absence, these steep woods and lofty cliffs,
      And this green pastoral landscape, were to me
      More dear, both for themselves and for thy sake!

---

17. **exhortations** *n. pl.:* strong advice.

IDENTIFY

Re-read lines 146–159. What things does the speaker wish his sister to always remember, even after the speaker has died? Underline those things.

Lines Composed a Few Miles Above Tintern Abbey

Reading Skills: Recognizing Patterns of Organization   Wordsworth's thoughts flow from stanza to stanza in the same way ideas flow in conversation. The **mood** of the poem also shifts several times, just as it might in a discussion.

In the chart below, write a sentence or two stating the main ideas Wordsworth expresses in each stanza. Then, write a few words describing the mood created by Wordsworth's word choice. In the space provided below the chart, evaluate the effect the use of blank verse has on you, the reader.

Stanza 1 (lines 1–22)	Ideas: Mood:
Stanza 2 (lines 22–49)	Ideas: Mood:
Stanza 3 (lines 49–57)	Ideas: Mood:
Stanza 4 (lines 58–111)	Ideas: Mood:
Stanza 5 (lines 111–159)	Ideas: Mood:

Evaluate   Re-read passages from "Tintern Abbey." What effect does Wordsworth's use of **blank verse** have on you, the reader?

_____

_____

_____

☑ Check your Standards Mastery at the back of this book.

Kubla Khan by Samuel Taylor Coleridge

Reading Standard 3.4
Analyze ways in which poets use imagery, personification, figures of speech and sounds to evoke readers' emotions.

Reading Standard 3.7 (Grade 9–10 Review)
Recognize and understand the significance of various literary devices, including figurative language, imagery, allegory, and symbolism, and explain their appeal.

LITERARY FOCUS: ALLITERATION

Alliteration is the repetition of consonant sounds in words that are near each other. It occurs most often at the beginnings of words, but it can also happen within words. When writers use alliteration, it is the sound rather than the spelling that matters. For example, the sound repeated in "**cack**ling chi**ck**ens" is the **k** sound. This technique creates musical effects in a poem and makes certain lines easy to remember.

In "Kubla Khan," Coleridge uses alliteration for a variety of purposes. The repeated sounds create a mood of enchantment, establish rhythm, give the poem a musical quality, and emphasize images or ideas. In line 25, the repeated **m** sounds even suggest the lazy, wandering movement of a river: "Five **m**iles **m**eandering with a **m**azy **m**otion."

Tongue Twisters & Cartoon Characters   Have you ever tried saying "**r**ubber **b**aby **b**uggy **b**umpers" three times fast? Think of examples that use alliteration to create some kind of an effect. It could be a tongue twister, the names of cartoon characters (there are lots of them), the title or lyrics of a song, a nursery rhyme, an advertising slogan, the name of a product or business—or some made-up examples of your own. Write your examples below, and then circle or highlight the sounds that are repeated.

Examples of Alliteration

READING SKILLS: IDENTIFYING IMAGERY

Imagery is language that appeals to the senses. Although most imagery appeals to the sense of sight, imagery may appeal to any of the five senses (sight, hearing, taste, touch, smell). The phrase "caverns measureless to man" (line 4 in "Kubla Khan"), for example, brings forth a powerful visual image. In this poem you will encounter vivid images that evoke everything from a sense of peace to a feeling of wild disorder.

Use the Skill   As you read, underline or highlight words and phrases that create sensory images.

KUBLA KHAN

Samuel Taylor Coleridge

BACKGROUND
The historical Kubla Khan (c. 1216–1294) was the Mongol conqueror of China and a grandson of the famous Genghis Khan. What is fascinating about Coleridge's "Kubla Khan" is how much the poem resembles a fantastical dream. Images in the poem collide and overlap as they do in dreams, and the story is interrupted before it reaches a real conclusion. In fact, Coleridge says that the poem came to him after he read a passage in a seventeenth-century travel book and fell into a daydream. Upon awaking, Coleridge began writing his poem/dream but was interrupted by a visitor. By the time the visitor left, the poem was gone from Coleridge's mind.

In Xanadu did Kubla Khan
A stately pleasure-dome decree:
Where Alph,[1] the sacred river, ran
Through caverns measureless to man
5   Down to a sunless sea.
So twice five miles of fertile ground
With walls and towers were girdled round:
And there were gardens bright with sinuous rills,[2]
Where blossomed many an incense-bearing tree;
10 And here were forests ancient as the hills,
Enfolding sunny spots of greenery.

---

1. **Alph:** probably a reference to the Greek river Alpheus, which flows into the Ionian Sea, and whose waters are fabled to rise up again in Sicily.
2. **sinuous** (sin′yo͞o·əs) **rills:** winding streams.

FLUENCY

Read aloud the boxed passage, containing the famous opening lines of the poem. (Pronounce the word *Xanadu* as if it began with a *z*.) Practice reading the lines until you feel you have achieved a smooth, mysterious effect.

IDENTIFY

Re-read lines 6–11. Underline the visual **imagery** the speaker uses to describe the setting. Circle imagery that appeals to other senses. What effect do these images create? *(Grade 9–10 Review)*

_____

_____

_____

_____

_____

_____

_____

_____

_____

_____

IDENTIFY

In lines 17–24, the speaker uses **personification** to describe the earth, a **metaphor** to describe a volcano, and **similes** to describe the volcano's eruption. Underline the example of personification, circle the metaphor, and draw boxes around the two similes.

IDENTIFY

Re-read lines 25–28, which contain a lot of **alliteration**. Circle the letters that make the alliterative sounds.

But oh! that deep romantic chasm which slanted

Down the green hill athwart a cedarn cover![3]

A savage place! as holy and enchanted

15 As e'er beneath a waning moon was haunted

By woman wailing for her demon-lover!

And from this chasm, with ceaseless turmoil seething,

As if this earth in fast thick pants were breathing,

A mighty fountain momently[4] was forced:

20 Amid whose swift half-intermitted burst

Huge fragments vaulted like rebounding hail,

Or chaffy grain beneath the thresher's flail:[5]

And 'mid these dancing rocks at once and ever

It flung up momently the sacred river.

25 Five miles meandering with a mazy[6] motion

Through wood and dale the sacred river ran,

Then reached the caverns measureless to man,

And sank in tumult to a lifeless ocean:

And 'mid this tumult Kubla heard from far

30 Ancestral voices prophesying war!

  The shadow of the dome of pleasure

  Floated midway on the waves;

  Where was heard the mingled measure[7]

  From the fountain and the caves.

35 It was a miracle of rare device,

A sunny pleasure-dome with caves of ice!

  A damsel with a dulcimer[8]

  In a vision once I saw:

  It was an Abyssinian[9] maid,

3. **athwart a cedarn cover:** crossing diagonally under a covering growth of cedar trees.
4. **momently** *adv.:* at each moment.
5. **thresher's flail:** heavy, whiplike tool used to thresh, or beat, grain in order to separate the kernels from their chaff, or husks.
6. **mazy** *adj.:* like a maze; having many turns.
7. **measure** *n.:* rhythmic sound.
8. **dulcimer** *n.:* musical instrument that is often played by striking the strings with small hammers.
9. **Abyssinian:** Ethiopian. Ethiopia is in northeast Africa.

A young woman playing a dulcimer.

INTERPRET

Re-read lines 37–47. Underline who the speaker sees in his vision. What connection does he make between his memory of her and his dream-vision of the pleasure dome?

_____

_____

_____

_____

_____

40 And on her dulcimer she played,

Singing of Mount Abora.[10]

Could I revive within me

Her symphony and song,

To such a deep delight 'twould win me,

45 That with music loud and long,

I would build that dome in air,

That sunny dome! those caves of ice!

And all who heard should see them there,

And all should cry, Beware! Beware!

50 His flashing eyes, his floating hair!

Weave a circle round him thrice,

And close your eyes with holy dread,

For he on honeydew hath fed,

And drunk the milk of Paradise.

INTERPRET

What do you think the pleasure dome—"that dome in air" (line 46)—**symbolizes**? *(Grade 9–10 Review)*

_____

_____

_____

_____

_____

_____

IDENTIFY

Coleridge believed that a poet's creativity and imagination were both to be celebrated and regarded with awe, a fearful reverence. In lines 48–54, locate and underline the **imagery** that supports that idea. *(Grade 9–10 Review)*

_____

10. Mount Abora: probably a reference to John Milton's (1608–1674) *Paradise Lost,* in which Mount Amara, in Ethiopia, is a mythical, earthly paradise.

Kubla Khan

Reading Skills: Identifying Imagery   "Kubla Khan" is so memorable, in part, because of its vivid images and its frequent use of alliteration. Read the passage from the poem below. Circle instances of alliteration you find within it. Then, underline the images. Above each image, write the sense (or senses) that it appeals to (sight, hearing, touch, taste, smell).

from "Kubla Khan"
A damsel with a dulcimer
In a vision once I saw:
It was an Abyssinian maid,
And on her dulcimer she played,
Singing of Mount Abora.
Could I revive within me
Her symphony and song,
To such a deep delight 'twould win me,
That with music loud and long,
I would build that dome in air,
That sunny dome! those caves of ice!
And all who heard should see them there,
And all should cry, Beware! Beware!
His flashing eyes, his floating hair!

 Check your Standards Mastery at the back of this book.

Ozymandias by Percy Bysshe Shelley

LITERARY FOCUS: IRONY

Irony is created when expectations and reality do not match up. "Ozymandias" (äz'ə·män'dē·əs) contains a kind of irony called **situational irony.** Situational irony occurs when what happens is the opposite of what we expect to happen.

In "Ozymandias" you'll meet the speaker, a traveler, and a king who lived centuries ago. As you read, identify which of the poem's characters expects one thing to happen and would be shocked at the way events actually turn out. Then, think about the **theme** that this use of irony conveys.

Reversals of Fortune   Imagine a young warrior in ancient times who has grand dreams of fame. Read about the warrior's dream, and jot down two things that could happen to make his dream turn out the opposite of what he expects.

The Warrior's Dream	Ironic Reversals
One day I will become the most powerful king in history and lead my country to greatness and glory. I'll conquer other rulers who stand in my way, and the riches of their kingdoms will be mine. I'll build fantastic monuments, and I'll be remembered as the greatest king who ever lived!	

READING SKILLS: COMPARING AND CONTRASTING

The details in a story or poem can tell you what a character looks like, thinks about, says, or does. Details can also tell you about the **setting**—the time and place of the action—and what has happened there. As you read "Ozymandias," pay close attention to the details that describe King Ozymandias and his works—in both the past and present. Comparing and contrasting those details will help you recognize the situational irony in the poem.

Use the Skill   As you read the poem, look for words and phrases that describe King Ozymandias and give clues about what he hoped to achieve. Read the poem a second time, and find words and phrases that describe how travelers view Ozymandias many centuries later.

Reading Standard 3.3 Analyze ways in which irony, tone, mood, author's style, and the "sound" of language achieve specific rhetorical or aesthetic purposes.

Reading Standard 3.8 (Grade 9–10 Review) Interpret and evaluate the impact of ambiguities, subtleties, contradictions, ironies, and incongruities in a text.

OZYMANDIAS

Percy Bysshe Shelley

BACKGROUND

"Ozymandias" was inspired by fragments from ancient Egypt that had just been exhibited at the British Museum. Some of the fragments were from the empire of one of Egypt's greatest pharaohs, or kings, Ramses II. Ozymandias is the Greek name for Ramses II.

INTERPRET

Re-read lines 4–11. What do Ozymandias's face and words tell you about his character and ambitions?

_____

_____

_____

_____

INTERPRET

Re-read lines 2–4 and 12–14. Draw a box around descriptions of the statue and the scene around it. What is **ironic** about the contrast between this description and the words on the pedestal (lines 10–11)? *(Grade 9–10 Review)*

_____

_____

_____

I met a traveler from an antique land
Who said: Two vast and trunkless legs[1] of stone
Stand in the desert . . . Near them, on the sand,
Half sunk, a shattered visage[2] lies, whose frown,
5   And wrinkled lip, and sneer of cold command,
Tell that its sculptor well those passions read
Which yet survive, stamped on these lifeless things,
The hand that mocked them, and the heart[3] that fed;
And on the pedestal these words appear:
10   "My name is Ozymandias, king of kings:
Look on my works, ye Mighty, and despair!"
Nothing beside remains. Round the decay
Of that colossal wreck, boundless and bare
The lone and level sands stretch far away.

---

1. **trunkless legs:** that is, the legs without the rest of the body.
2. **visage** *n.:* face.
3. **the hand . . . heart:** the hand of the sculptor who, with his art, ridiculed the passions to which Ozymandias gave himself wholeheartedly.

Ozymandias

Reading Skills: Comparing and Contrasting   In the chart below, list in column one any details that help you infer what King Ozymandias was like. In column two, list details describing what the traveler finds many centuries later. Then, in the space below the chart, examine how those contrasting details create **situational irony.**

King Ozymandias	What the Traveler Finds

Evaluate   What **situational irony** do you find in "Ozymandias"? How does the use of situational irony help reveal the poem's **theme**? How would you state the theme?

_____

_____

_____

_____

_____

_____

_____

_____

Check your Standards Mastery at the back of this book.

Jade Flower Palace; Night Thoughts Afloat by Tu Fu

REVIEW SKILLS

As you read these poems by Tu Fu, look for the themes they express.

THEME
The central idea or insight about life revealed in a work of literature.

LITERARY FOCUS: MOOD

Mood is the overall feeling, or atmosphere, in a literary work. Mood can usually be described in a single word, such as *cheerful, gloomy, thoughtful,* or *wistful.* Authors use descriptive details and vivid language to create mood. A horror story, for example, may create an *eerie* mood with details such as whipping winds, creaking doors, and unearthly moans. In "Jade Flower Palace," the Chinese poet Tu Fu (dōō fōō) describes the ruins of a once-beautiful palace. What kind of mood do you think such a scene might call to mind?

Setting the Right Mood   How good are you at creating mood, or atmosphere? Imagine that you are in charge of special effects for a television drama. List some effects—sounds, sights, camera shots—that you would use to create the different moods for the setting described below.

Scene: Classroom in High School

Mood: Joyful	Mood: Gloomy

Reading Standard 3.3
Analyze the ways in which irony, tone, mood, author's style, and the "sound" of language achieve specific rhetorical or aesthetic purposes.

Reading Standard 3.5 (Grade 9–10 Review)
Compare works that express a universal theme and provide evidence to support the ideas expressed in each work.

READING SKILLS: MAKING CONNECTIONS BETWEEN TEXTS

Works of literature—even those created in vastly different times and places—may have similar moods, settings, or themes. Works by a single writer or poet are even more likely to share some of these elements. As you read the poems by Tu Fu that follow, look for ways in which their moods and themes are similar and different.

Use the Skill   Read Tu Fu's poetry once for basic comprehension and pleasure. Then, read the poems a second time. Think about ways in which the poems share literary elements and explore similar ideas.

Jade Flower Palace

Tu Fu, *translated by* Kenneth Rexroth

Re-read lines 1–10. Circle the vivid verbs, and underline the adjectives. How would you describe the **mood** that these words create?

The stream swirls. The wind moans in
The pines. Gray rats scurry over
Broken tiles. What prince, long ago,
Built this palace, standing in
5   Ruins beside the cliffs? There are
Green ghost fires in the black rooms.
The shattered pavements are all
Washed away. Ten thousand organ
Pipes whistle and roar. The storm
10   Scatters the red autumn leaves.

CLARIFY

Who does the "his" in line 11 refer to? Read on to line 14. What has happened to his palace and his people?

His dancing girls are yellow dust.
Their painted cheeks have crumbled
Away. His gold chariots
And courtiers are gone. Only
15   A stone horse is left of his
Glory. I sit on the grass and
Start a poem, but the pathos of
It overcomes me. The future
Slips imperceptibly away.
20   Who can say what the years will bring?

ANALYZE

Re-read lines 16–20, in which the speaker is overcome by sadness. What does the question at the end of the poem suggest about its **theme**? *(Grade 9–10 Review)*

Night Thoughts Afloat

Tu Fu, *translated by* Arthur Cooper

ANALYZE

Circle details and images in lines 1–8 that describe the setting. How do these details contribute to the **mood**?

_____

_____

INTERPRET

At line 9, the poet shifts from describing the scene to expressing his feelings. What regrets does he express (lines 9–16)?

_____

_____

EVALUATE

Underline the comparison the poet makes in the last stanza (lines 13–16). What do these lines reveal about the poem's **theme**?

_____

_____

_____

_____

_____

By bent grasses
in a gentle wind
   Under straight mast
I'm alone tonight,

5   And the stars hang
above the broad plain
   But moon's afloat
in this Great River:

   Oh, where's my name
10   among the poets?
   Official rank?
"Retired for ill health."

   Drifting, drifting,
what am I more than
15   A single gull
between sky and earth?

Jade Flower Palace; Night Thoughts Afloat

Reading Skills: Making Connections Between Texts   In the chart below, list descriptive details from the two poems that you find most striking or revealing. Then, examine the details you recorded and describe the **mood** or moods they create. Finally, describe the **themes** of the poems and how they are similar.

	Jade Flower Palace	Night Thoughts Afloat
Descriptive Details		
Mood		

Evaluate   In several of their works, poets may explore a single idea or closely related ideas. This is true of Tu Fu, who, in many of his poems, examined the purpose or meaning of life. Review the poems. What **theme** do they share?

_____

_____

_____

Check your Standards Mastery at the back of this book.

When I Have Fears by John Keats

BEFORE YOU READ

LITERARY FOCUS: SONNET

A **sonnet** is a fourteen-line poem that usually has two parts. The first part often presents a problem, a question, or an idea. The second part then resolves the problem, answers the question, or emphasizes the idea.

There are two main types of sonnet. The **Petrarchan,** or Italian, form is divided into an octave (eight-line section) and a sestet (six-line section). "When I Have Fears" is written in the **Shakespearean** sonnet form. The first part of a Shakespearean sonnet contains three four-line sections, or quatrains, in which the first and third lines rhyme, and the second and fourth lines rhyme. The second part of the poem consists of two rhyming lines called a **couplet.**

Sonnets are usually written in **iambic pentameter.** An iambic foot consists of an unstressed syllable followed by a stressed syllable, as in the word *behold.* The word *pentameter* means that five feet appear in each line.

READING SKILLS: READING INVERTED SYNTAX

The sonnet form requires precise patterns of rhyme and rhythm. In order to make rhymes and rhythms work out correctly, poets sometimes have to use unusual syntax, or word order. For example, the normal pattern for a sentence in English is subject-verb-complement, but a poet may switch the subject and the verb in order to create a specific rhyme. This switch in normal word order is called **inversion.**

Here are some examples of inversions from a Keats poem titled "On First Looking into Chapman's Homer."

Passage Containing Inverted Syntax	Standard Word Order
"Much have I traveled in the realms of gold" (line 1)	I have traveled much in the realms of gold
"And many goodly states and kingdoms seen" (line 2)	And seen many goodly states and kingdoms

Use the Skill   As you come across examples of inverted syntax in "When I Have Fears," look for the subject and verb of each to find its basic meaning.

Reading Standard 3.1
Analyze characteristics of subgenres that are used in poetry, prose, plays, novels, short stories, essays, and other basic genres.

When I Have Fears

John Keats

John Keats by Charles Armitage Brown.
By courtesy of the National Portrait Gallery, London.

WORD STUDY

Garners in line 4 means "granaries," or buildings that store grain. In what way are books like granaries?

_____

_____

_____

ANALYZE

Re-read lines 1–12. What three things does the speaker fear he may never live to see?

_____

_____

_____

_____

_____

_____

PARAPHRASE

Re-read lines 12–14. Restate the speaker's concluding thoughts in your own words.

_____

_____

_____

_____

When I have fears that I may cease to be
   Before my pen has gleaned my teeming brain,
Before high-pilèd books, in charact'ry,[1]
   Hold like rich garners the full-ripened grain;
5 When I behold, upon the night's starred face,
   Huge cloudy symbols of a high romance,
And think that I may never live to trace
   Their shadows, with the magic hand of chance;
And when I feel, fair creature of an hour,
10   That I shall never look upon thee more,
Never have relish in the fairy[2] power
   Of unreflecting love!—then on the shore
Of the wide world I stand alone, and think
Till Love and Fame to nothingness do sink.

---

1. **charact'ry** *n.:* the characters of the alphabet.
2. **fairy** *adj.:* supernatural; unearthly.

When I Have Fears

Reading Skills: Reading Inverted Syntax Poets sometimes switch the order of subjects and verbs and complements to achieve a specific rhyme or rhythm. In the left-hand column of the chart below, you will find passages from "When I Have Fears" that contain inverted syntax. In the right-hand column, rewrite those lines in normal English word order. The first one has been done for you.

Passages Containing Inverted Syntax	Normal Word Order
"books . . . / Hold like rich garners the full-ripened grain" (lines 3–4)	books . . . / Hold the full-ripened grain like rich garners
"When I behold, upon the night's starred face, / Huge cloudy symbols of a high romance" (lines 5–6)	
"I shall never look upon thee more" (line 10)	
"on the shore / Of the wide world I stand alone" (lines 12–13)	
"Till Love and Fame to nothingness do sink" (line 14)	

☑ Check your Standards Mastery at the back of this book.

Ode on a Grecian Urn by John Keats

LITERARY FOCUS: METAPHOR

A **metaphor** is a figure of speech that compares two unlike things without using a connecting word such as *like* or *as*. Often a metaphor describes one thing as if it were another. Notice how two dissimilar objects are compared in the metaphors below.

Object 1: dancer	Object 2: gazelle
Metaphor: She was a gazelle, leaping with ease and joy across the stage.	
Object 1: bratty child	**Object 2:** a king
Metaphor: "His highness is ready for his bottle now."	

Keats begins this poem with three metaphors that describe a Greek urn. In line 1, he calls the urn a "still unravished bride of quietness." By comparing the urn with a virgin bride, he implies that the urn has remained untouched through the ages. By adding "of quietness," he implies that it has been silent through the centuries and long awaited contact with the world. As you read, look for other metaphors that describe the urn.

READING SKILLS: VISUALIZING IMAGERY

Imagery is language that appeals to the senses. Most images appeal to the senses of sight and hearing, but they may also appeal to the senses of touch, taste, or smell. Poets often use imagery to bring their subject matter to life. When you visualize imagery, you create mental pictures of what's being described—people, objects, settings, or experiences.

Use the Skill   As you read "Ode on a Grecian Urn," look for imagery that helps you to visualize the scenes painted on the urn. Try reading parts of the poem aloud. Stop after stanzas 1–3 and then after stanza 4, and write a few sentences describing the urn's decorations as you see them.

REVIEW SKILLS

As you read "Ode on a Grecian Urn," notice how the use of figurative language and imagery helps you visualize the object that Keats is describing.

FIGURATIVE LANGUAGE
Words and phrases that describe one thing in terms of another and are not meant to be understood literally. Figurative language includes all **figures of speech,** such as metaphors.

IMAGERY
Language that appeals to the senses.

Reading Standard 3.4
Analyze ways in which poets use imagery, personification, figures of speech, and sounds to evoke reader's emotions.

Reading Standard 3.7 (Grade 9–10 Review)
Recognize and understand the significance of various literary devices, including figurative language, imagery, allegory, and symbolism, and explain their appeal.

ODE ON A GRECIAN URN

John Keats

> **BACKGROUND**
> Like other Romantic poets, Keats wrote a number of odes. An **ode** is a type of long poem that presents a reflection on a serious subject. The speaker in "Ode on a Grecian Urn" studies a beautiful urn, or vase, and thinks about its meaning.

Youth singing and playing the kithara, attributed to the Berlin Painter. Terra-cotta amphora (c. 490), said to be from Nola.

The Metropolitan Museum of Art, New York. Fletcher Fund, 1956 (56.171.38).

INTERPRET

Re-read lines 1–3. Underline the three **metaphors** Keats uses to describe the urn. What do these metaphors tell you about the urn? *(Grade 9–10 Review)*

VISUALIZE

What kind of scene do you visualize from the **imagery** in this description (lines 5–10)? *(Grade 9–10 Review)*

1

Thou still unravished bride of quietness,
　　Thou foster child of silence and slow time,
Sylvan[1] historian, who canst thus express
　　A flowery tale more sweetly than our rhyme:
5　What leaf-fringed legend haunts about thy shape
　　Of deities or mortals, or of both,
　　　In Tempe or the dales of Arcady?[2]
　　What men or gods are these? What maidens loath?[3]
What mad pursuit? What struggle to escape?
10　　What pipes and timbrels?[4] What wild ecstasy?

---

1. **sylvan** *adj.:* of the forest. (The urn is decorated with a rural scene.)
2. **Tempe** (tem′pē) . . . **Arcady** (är′kə·dē): valleys in ancient Greece; ideal types of rural beauty.
3. **loath** *adj.:* reluctant.
4. **timbrels** *n. pl.:* tambourines.

2

Heard melodies are sweet, but those unheard

    Are sweeter; therefore, ye soft pipes, play on;

Not to the sensual ear, but, more endeared,

    Pipe to the spirit ditties[5] of no tone:

15   Fair youth, beneath the trees, thou canst not leave

    Thy song, nor ever can those trees be bare;

      Bold Lover, never, never canst thou kiss,

Though winning near the goal—yet, do not grieve;

    She cannot fade, though thou hast not thy bliss,

20   Forever wilt thou love, and she be fair!

3

Ah, happy, happy boughs! that cannot shed

    Your leaves, nor ever bid the Spring adieu;[6]

And, happy melodist, unwearied,

    Forever piping songs forever new;

25   More happy love! more happy, happy love!

    Forever warm and still to be enjoyed,

      Forever panting, and forever young;

All breathing human passion far above,

    That leaves a heart high-sorrowful and cloyed,[7]

30   A burning forehead, and a parching tongue.

4

Who are these coming to the sacrifice?

    To what green altar, O mysterious priest,

Lead'st thou that heifer lowing[8] at the skies,

    And all her silken flanks[9] with garlands dressed?

35   What little town by river or seashore,

    Or mountain-built with peaceful citadel,[10]

---

5. **ditties** *n. pl.*: short, simple songs.
6. **adieu** (à·dyö′): French for "goodbye."
7. **cloyed** (kloid) *adj.*: filled; satisfied; wearied with excess.
8. **lowing** *v.* used as *adj.*: mooing.
9. **flanks** *n. pl.*: sides between the ribs and the hips.
10. **citadel** (sit′ə·del′) *n.*: fortress.

INTERPRET

Re-read lines 11–12. What point is the speaker making?

_____

_____

_____

_____

_____

CLARIFY

What observation does the speaker make about the "Bold Lover" in line 17? What consolation does the speaker offer him (lines 18–20)?

_____

_____

_____

_____

_____

_____

_____

FLUENCY

Read the boxed stanza aloud once. Then, circle key words that are repeated. Think about the effect of this repetition, and read the stanza aloud a second time, using your voice to emphasize the speaker's enthusiasm.

ANALYZE

Re-read lines 41–45, in which the speaker's **tone** seems to change. Describe the change in the speaker's attitude.

_____

_____

_____

_____

_____

_____

_____

_____

_____

IDENTIFY

Re-read lines 46–50. What does the speaker say will happen to the urn? Underline the explanation that he gives. Circle the words that the urn, "a friend to man" (line 48), will say.

_____

_____

_____

_____

_____

_____

_____

_____

Is emptied of this folk, this pious morn?

And, little town, thy streets forevermore

    Will silent be; and not a soul to tell

40   Why thou art desolate, can e'er return.

5

O Attic[11] shape! Fair attitude![12] with brede[13]

    Of marble men and maidens overwrought,[14]

With forest branches and the trodden weed;

    Thou, silent form, dost tease us out of thought

45 As doth eternity: Cold Pastoral![15]

    When old age shall this generation waste,

       Thou shalt remain, in midst of other woe

    Than ours, a friend to man, to whom thou say'st,

"Beauty is truth, truth beauty,"—that is all

50   Ye know on earth, and all ye need to know.

---

11. **Attic:** Athenian; classically elegant.
12. **attitude** *n.:* disposition or feeling conveyed by the postures of the figures on the urn.
13. **brede** *n.:* interwoven design.
14. **overwrought** *adj.:* decorated to excess; also, in reference to the men and maidens, overexcited.
15. **Pastoral** *n.:* artwork depicting idealized rural life.

Attic vase painting, showing transport of amphoras.

Louvre, Paris.

Ode on a Grecian Urn

Reading Skills: Visualizing Imagery   "Ode on a Grecian Urn" contains imagery that helps you visualize the scenes painted on the urn. Fill in the left-hand column below by listing at least four vivid words or phrases that helped you create a mental picture of the **images.** Most of those words or phrases will appeal to the sense of sight, but some of them will also appeal to another sense, such as hearing or touch. Then, in the right-hand column, describe in your own words how you visualize the scenes on the urn.

Scenes on the Urn	How I Visualize the Scenes
Imagery in stanzas 1–3 (lines 1–30):	
Imagery in stanzas 4–5 (lines 31–50):	

Check your Standards Mastery at the back of this book.

The Victorian Period

(1832–1901)

Paradox and Progress

A gathering of scientists. From left to right,
English physicist and chemist Michael Faraday (1791–1867),
English biologist Thomas Huxley (1825–1895),
English physicist Sir Charles Wheatley (1802–1875),
Scottish physicist Sir David Brewster (1781–1868),
and Irish physicist John Tyndall (1820–1893).

© Hulton Archive.

The Victorian Period
(1832–1901)

Donald Gray

The following essay provides highlights of the historical period.
For a more detailed version of this essay,
see *Holt Literature and Language Arts,* pages 678–693.

Reading Standard 3.7c
Evaluate the philosophical, political, religious, ethical, and social influences of the historical period.

Reading Standard 2.3 (Grade 9–10 Review)
Generate relevant questions about readings on issues that can be researched.

Many Victorians thought of themselves as living in a time of great change. They were right, but the changes during Queen Victoria's long reign (1837–1901) occurred in a period of relative political and social stability, and many were the result of conditions that began before Victoria and most of her subjects were born.

Peace and Economic Growth: Britannia Rules

After Napoleon's defeat at Waterloo in 1815, Britain was not involved in a major European war until World War I began in 1914. The empire that had begun in the seventeenth and eighteenth centuries with British interests in India and North America grew steadily, until by 1900, Victoria was queen-empress of more than 200 million people living outside Great Britain.

At the same time the Industrial Revolution of the eighteenth century greatly expanded. Over the course of the century it steadily created new towns, new goods, new wealth, and new jobs for tens of thousands of people. These social and economic changes were expressed in gradual political reforms. Piece by piece, middle-class and, ultimately, working-class politicians and voters achieved political power while leaving the monarchy and aristocracy in place.

IDENTIFY CAUSE & EFFECT

Re-read lines 14–21. What changes resulted from the expansion of the Industrial Revolution? Underline your answer.

Notes

PARAPHRASE

Pause at line 36. What did progress mean to Macaulay?

_____

_____

_____

_____

DRAW CONCLUSIONS

Re-read lines 28–36. What must the city have been like before the reforms Macaulay proposed?

_____

_____

_____

CLARIFY

Why was the period of the 1840s called the Hungry Forties (lines 42–47)?

_____

_____

_____

_____

_____

_____

_____

_____

_____

The Idea of Progress

The English historian Thomas Babington Macaulay voiced the middle-class Victorian attitude toward government, history, and civilization. For Macaulay, history meant progress, and progress largely meant material improvement that could be seen and touched, counted and measured. Macaulay admired cleanliness and order. He wanted the London streets free of garbage, drained and paved, lighted at night, and patrolled by a sober

30   police force. He wanted the city planned so that residents of respectable neighborhoods did not live next to slums and were not annoyed by beggars and peddlers. He wanted the houses numbered and a population literate enough to read signs. His amazement at the disorder and poverty of the past conveyed his sense of progress: How could those people have lived like that? How different we are; how far we have come.

Many Victorians regretted or disputed Macaulay's confident tone and materialistic standards. However, in his satisfaction with the improvements that the empire had brought to England,

40   his views were typical of those of his contemporaries.

The Hungry Forties

The first decade of Victoria's reign was troubled—in fact, the period came to be known as the Hungry Forties. Victoria came to the throne in the first year of a depression that by 1842 had put 1.5 million unemployed workers and their families (in a population of sixteen million in England and Wales) on some form of poverty relief.

■ Poor Working Conditions

Government commissions investigating working conditions learned

50   of children mangled when they fell asleep at machines at the end of a twelve-hour working day. They discovered young girls and boys hauling sledges of coal through narrow mine tunnels, working shifts so long that in winter they saw the sun only on Sundays.

A poor woman supports her starving child as they wander through the snow outside a factory building. An illustration from Henry Colburn's publication of Frances Trollope's "The Life and Times of Michael Armstrong, the Factory Boy" (1839).
© Hulton Archive.

■ The Potato Famine

In Ireland the potato blight (1845–1849) caused a famine that killed perhaps a million people and forced two million others—more than 25 percent of Ireland's population—to emigrate. Some went to English cities, where they lived ten or twelve to a room in slums that had two toilets for every 250 people.

60 ### ■ Pollution and Filth

The rapid growth of cities often made them filthy and disorderly. Nearly two million people lived in London during the 1840s, and commercial and industrial cities such as Manchester and Liverpool expanded rapidly. In Manchester in the 1840s, 40 percent of the streets were still unpaved. The Thames River in London was polluted with sewage, industrial waste, and the drainage from graveyards, where bodies were buried in layers six or eight deep. In the 1850s, Parliament sometimes had to adjourn from its new riverside building because of the stench
70 from the Thames.

WORD STUDY

The word *emigrate* (em'i·grāt'), line 57, contains another word within it that gives a clue to its meaning. Circle the clue. Using this clue and the information in the next sentence of the paragraph, make a guess about what *emigrate* means.

IDENTIFY CAUSE & EFFECT

What were some of the negative effects of the rapid growth of cities (lines 61–70)? Underline that information.

INFER

Re-read lines 73–81. Circle the reason that political rallies were held in the 1840s. Why do you think the British government prepared the army when reformers petitioned Parliament?

_____

_____

_____

_____

_____

_____

IDENTIFY CAUSE & EFFECT

Pause at line 91. Underline what caused the price of food to drop after the mid-1800s. Circle the effects of this drop in food prices.

IDENTIFY

What three reforms helped to improve the quality of people's lives in Victorian England (lines 93–103)?

_____

_____

_____

_____

_____

_____

_____

Violence broke out at massive political rallies in the 1840s. These rallies protested government policies that kept the price of bread and other food high and deprived most working men (and all women) of the vote and representation in Parliament. In 1848, a year of revolution in Europe, nervous British politicians got the army ready. They armed the staffs of museums and government offices when working-class political reformers organized what they called a monster rally in London to petition Parliament and the queen.

■ **Improvements in Diet**

Still, most middle-class Victorians believed that things were better than in the past and that they were going to be better yet in the future. Their opinion was in part founded on a steady improvement in living conditions. The price of food dropped after midcentury, largely because of increased trade with other countries and the growing empire. Diet improved as meat, fruit, and margarine began to appear regularly in working-class households. Factories and railroads made postage, newspapers, clothing, furniture, travel, and other goods and services cheap.

■ **The Reform Bills**

A series of political reforms gave the vote to almost all adult males by the last decades of the century. (Decades of striving by Victorian women for the right to vote succeeded only in the next century.) A series of factory acts limited child labor and reduced the usual working day to ten hours, with a half-holiday on Saturday. State-supported schools were established in 1870, were made compulsory in 1880, and were made free in 1891. In 1859, 40 percent of the couples getting married could not write their names on their marriage certificates. By 1900, using that simple definition of literacy, more than 90 percent of the population was literate.

"Blushing Cheeks": Decorum and Prudery

Many Victorians thought of themselves as progressing morally and intellectually, as well as materially. In fact, the powerful, mostly middle-class obsession with gentility and decorum has made *prudery* almost a synonym for *Victorianism.* Book publishers and magazine editors deleted or altered words and episodes that might, in the phrase of the day, bring "a blush to the cheek" of a young person. In art and popular fiction, sex, birth, and death were shown as tender courtships, joyous motherhoods, and touching deathbed scenes. In the real world, people were arrested for distributing information about sexually transmitted diseases. Victorian society regarded seduced or adulterous women (but not their male partners) as "fallen" and pushed them to the margins of society.

Authoritarian Values

Victorians also had powerful ideas about authority. Many were uneasy about giving strong authority to a central government. In private life, however, the autocratic father of middle-class households is a vivid figure in both fact and fiction.

Women were subject to male authority. Middle-class women especially were expected to marry and make comfortable homes for their husbands. Women who did not marry had few occupations open to them. Working-class women could find jobs as servants, while unmarried middle-class ladies could become governesses or teachers. Life for unmarried women was painful.

The cruelties and hypocrisies of these repressions were obvious to many Victorians, but the social codes changed slowly because they were part of the ideology of progress. Prudery and social order were intended to control the immorality and sexual excesses that Victorians associated with the violent political revolutions of the eighteenth century and with the social corruption of the regency of George IV (1811–1820).

WORD STUDY

Gentility (jen·til'i·tē) and *decorum* (di·kôr·əm), line 107, are nouns meaning "showing refinement and elegance" and "good taste in behavior and dress." Why might the middle-class people of Victorian England have valued these qualities so much?

_____

_____

_____

_____

_____

_____

_____

_____

_____

COMPARE & CONTRAST

In lines 126–128, circle the kinds of jobs available to unmarried working-class women. Underline jobs available to unmarried middle-class women.

IDENTIFY

According to the information in lines 129–135, Victorian prudery and social order were a reaction to what historical events in England and Europe? Underline that information.

INFER

Pause at line 141. How might improvements in education and living conditions have contributed to intellectual advances in the Victorian period?

_____

_____

_____

_____

_____

_____

_____

_____

CLARIFY

How did Thomas Huxley and other Victorian reformers believe the world's problems could be solved (lines 152–158)?

_____

_____

_____

_____

_____

_____

_____

IDENTIFY

Underline three questions or doubts voiced by Victorian writers (lines 160–165).

Intellectual Progress: The March of the Mind

The intellectual advances of the Victorian period were dramatically evident to those living in it. Humans began to understand more and more about the earth, its creatures, and its natural laws.

140 The industrialization of England depended on and supported science and technology, especially chemistry and engineering.

Thomas Huxley and the Game of Science

Those who made and used scientific and technological knowledge had a confidence of their own. Thomas Huxley, a variously accomplished scientist who wrote and lectured frequently on the necessity of scientific education, imagined science as an exhilarating, high-stakes chess game with the physical universe.

> "The chessboard is the world, the pieces are the
> phenomena of the universe, the rules of the game
150 > are what we call the laws of Nature. The player on
> the other side is hidden from us. . . ."

Huxley resembles those confident Victorians who built railways and sewers, organized markets and schools, and pushed through electoral reforms and laws regulating the conditions of work. These reformers believed that the world offered a challenging set of problems that could be understood by human intelligence and solved by science, government, and other human institutions.

Questions and Doubts

160 Despite the confidence of the age, the Victorian period was filled with voices asking questions and raising doubts. Victorian writers asked whether material comfort fully satisfied human needs and wishes. They questioned the cost of exploiting the earth and human beings to achieve such comfort. They protested or mocked codes of decorum and authority.

In the first half of the period, some writers complained that materialist ideas of reality completely overlooked the spirit or soul that made life beautiful and just. Later in the century, some writers thought that the current ideas of history and nature pre-supposed a coherence that did not really exist. Victorian literature often reassured its readers that, rightly perceived, the universe made sense. However, some writers unsettled their readers by asking them to consider whether human life and the natural world made as much sense as the conventional view told them.

The Popular Mr. Dickens

Charles Dickens, the most popular and most important figure in Victorian literature, is a case in point. The son of a debt-ridden clerk, Dickens lived out one of the favorite myths of the age. Through his own enormous talents and energy, he rose from poverty to become a wealthy and famous man. His success was peculiarly Victorian. It was made possible by increasing wealth and literacy, which gave him a large reading public, and by improved printing and distribution, which made book publishing a big business.

English novelist Charles Dickens (ca. 1860).
© Hulton Archive.

WORD STUDY

The word *coherence* (kō·hir′əns), line 170, means "agreement or unity between all the parts of a whole." In your own words tell what "presupposed a coherence" means. (Use your knowledge of prefixes to figure out the meaning of *presupposed*.)

_____

_____

_____

_____

_____

_____

_____

_____

_____

_____

_____

_____

IDENTIFY CAUSE & EFFECT

Re-read lines 179–184. What two factors helped lead to Dickens's success? Circle that information.

GENERATE
QUESTIONS

Pause at line 201. What question do you have about Dickens's life or books? How would you go about finding an answer to your question? *(Grade 9–10 Review)*

_____

_____

_____

_____

_____

_____

_____

_____

_____

_____

_____

_____

_____

WORD STUDY

A clue to the meaning of *transcendental* (lines 202 and 203) can be found in lines 204–206. Underline the clue.

IDENTIFY

What conditions or views of the world in midcentury England saddened some writers (lines 207–219)? Underline that information.

The conventional happy endings of Dickens's novels satisfied his readers', and probably his own, conviction that things usually work out well for decent people. Still, many of Dickens's most memorable scenes show decent people neglected, abused, and exploited. In his later novels, Dickens created char-
190   acters and scenes to show that even the wealthy had reason to be as desperate and unhappy as the poor.

      Attacks like Dickens's on the hollowness, glitter, superficiality, and excesses of Victorian affluence were common in Victorian literature. Dickens also raised questions about the costs of progress in his descriptions of the huddle and waste of cities and the smoke and fire of industrial landscapes. In 1871, the art historian and social critic John Ruskin noted a new phenomenon that we call smog; he called it the plague wind, or "the storm-cloud of the nineteenth century." He concluded, chillingly, ". . . [M]ere
200   smoke would not blow to and fro in that wild way. It looks more to me as if it were made of dead men's souls."

Trust in the Transcendental—and Skepticism

Trust in a transcendental power was characteristic of the early Victorian writers. The highest purpose of a poet, of any writer, was to make readers aware of the connection between earth and heaven, body and soul, material and ideal.

      Still, with some exceptions—Gerard Manley Hopkins is one and Christina Rossetti another—younger writers found it increasingly difficult to believe in an infinite power and order
210   that made sense of material and human existence. Other writers at midcentury, sometimes reacting to explanations of the world that excluded the spiritual, were saddened by what seemed to them to be the withdrawal of the divine from the world. The dominant note of much mid-Victorian writing was struck by Matthew Arnold in his poem "Dover Beach" (see page 220): "The Sea of Faith," Arnold wrote, had ebbed. There was no certainty; or if there was, what was certain was that existence

was not governed by a benevolent intelligence that cared for its creatures.

220   By the end of the century, this skepticism and denial had become widespread in the works of Thomas Hardy, A. E. Housman, and others. Early and mid-Victorian novelists such as Dickens and George Eliot had dramatized a human ideal achieved through sympathy and unselfishness. Their heroes and heroines learned to find happiness in nurturing marriages and in small communities of family and friends. There were few such marriages and communities in the fiction and poetry of Hardy and Housman. These late-Victorian writers told stories of lovers and friends betrayed by unfaithfulness, war, and the other troubles
230   that humans add to the natural trials of mortal life.

Reflections of a Culture

It is important to remember that the readers of Victorian literature were living Victorian lives. Many of the people who read Dickens settled down with his books after dining in elaborately decorated rooms. People who were making a lot of money listened to Carlyle and Ruskin telling them that they were foolish and damned. People who were disturbed by how much money was being made listened to Macaulay reminding them that a century or so before they might not have been able to afford, or even to read, his book.

240   Victorian literature needs to be read not just as a comment on the complexity of its culture, but also as an important part of that culture. Its writers sent their words to work in the world to alter, to reinforce, to challenge, to enlarge, or to temper the ideas and feelings with which their contemporaries managed their lives.

COMPARE & CONTRAST

Re-read lines 220–230. How were the attitudes of early and mid-Victorian writers different from those of writers near the end of the century?

_____

_____

_____

_____

_____

_____

_____

_____

CLARIFY

How was Victorian literature a part of the culture and not merely a reflection of it (lines 240–244)?

_____

_____

_____

_____

_____

_____

_____

_____

_____

Ulysses by Alfred, Lord Tennyson

Reading Standard 3.2
Analyze the ways in which the theme or meaning of a selection represents a view or comment on life, using textual evidence to support the claim.

Reading Standard 3.11 (Grade 9–10 Review)
Evaluate the aesthetic qualities of style, including the impact of diction and figurative language on tone, mood, and theme, using the terminology of literary criticism.

LITERARY FOCUS: THEME

In works of literature, most writers focus on communicating a central idea or insight about a subject. This central idea is called the **theme.** As you look for the theme of a text, remember that it is different from the text's **subject.** A subject can be summed up in a word or two, such as *love* or *change.* A theme, however, is a complete idea that can be stated in a sentence—for example: *True love is precious and rare,* or *Change is painful but can lead to growth and discovery.*

The subject of "Ulysses," as you will see, is old age. As you read the poem, look for the theme, or idea, Tennyson expresses about this subject. How might this theme represent a view of life?

Subject Versus Theme   In the left-hand column below, list the titles of two books, short stories, poems, or movies that you know well. In the middle column, write down a word or two that sums up its subject. In the final column, write a short sentence that states its theme.

Title	Subject	Theme

READING SKILLS: SUMMARIZING

When you **summarize** a story or poem, you briefly restate its main events and ideas in your own words. A summary is always much shorter than the original text. For a long and challenging poem like "Ulysses," you should pause to summarize the thoughts and ideas that are presented in each section.

Use the Skill   A summarizing chart appears on page 210 of this book. You may fill in the chart as you read the poem, or you may prefer to fill it in after you've read the entire poem first.

Ulysses

Alfred, Lord Tennyson

> **BACKGROUND**
> In ancient mythology, Ulysses (called *Odysseus* in Greek) is one of the Greek leaders who fought in the Trojan War, which lasted for ten years. It then took ten years for Ulysses to make his way back home to Ithaca after the war ended. On his journey to his island home, Ulysses and his men experienced many adventures. In Tennyson's poem, the old king (Ulysses) is at last reunited with his wife and son, Penelope and Telemachus (tə·lem'ə·kəs). At home and at rest, though, Ulysses finds that he yearns to leave yet again on a final voyage.

It little profits that an idle king,
By this still hearth, among these barren crags,
Matched with an aged wife, I mete and dole[1]
Unequal laws unto a savage race,
5   That hoard, and sleep, and feed, and know not me.
I cannot rest from travel; I will drink
Life to the lees.[2] All times I have enjoyed
Greatly, have suffered greatly, both with those
That loved me, and alone; on shore, and when
10   Through scudding drifts the rainy Hyades[3]
Vexed the dim sea. I am become a name;
For always roaming with a hungry heart
Much have I seen and known,—cities of men
And manners, climates, councils, governments,
15   Myself not least, but honored of them all,—
And drunk delight of battle with my peers,
Far on the ringing plains of windy Troy.

CLARIFY

Re-read lines 1–7. The speaker, Ulysses, describes himself as an "idle king," meaning that he feels useless and inactive. What does he want to do instead of staying at home?

_____

_____

INTERPRET

Re-read lines 11–17. What was Ulysses' life like before?

_____

_____

_____

_____

_____

---

1. **mete and dole:** measure and give out.
2. **lees** *n.:* dregs or sediment.
3. **Hyades** (hī'ə·dēz'): stars that were thought to indicate rainy weather.

SUMMARIZE

In lines 22–32, Ulysses shares his thoughts on life and how he wants to live his life now. Summarize what he says.

_____

_____

_____

_____

_____

_____

ANALYZE

In lines 33–43, circle the words and phrases Ulysses uses to describe Telemachus. What do these words reveal about his feelings toward his son?

_____

_____

_____

_____

IDENTIFY

Re-read lines 44–53, in which Ulysses describes his "mariners" (line 45), the sailors who accompanied him on his voyages. What does Ulysses think they can all gain in their old age?

_____

_____

_____

_____

I am a part of all that I have met;

Yet all experience is an arch wherethrough

20 Gleams that untraveled world whose margin fades

Forever and forever when I move.

How dull it is to pause, to make an end,

To rust unburnished, not to shine in use!

As though to breathe were life! Life piled on life

25 Were all too little, and of one to me

Little remains; but every hour is saved

From that eternal silence, something more,

A bringer of new things; and vile it were

For some three suns to store and hoard myself,

30 And this gray spirit yearning in desire

To follow knowledge like a sinking star,

Beyond the utmost bound of human thought.

    This is my son, mine own Telemachus,

To whom I leave the scepter and the isle,[4]—

35 Well-loved of me, discerning to fulfill

This labor, by slow prudence to make mild

A rugged people, and through soft degrees

Subdue them to the useful and the good.

Most blameless is he, centered in the sphere

40 Of common duties, decent not to fail

In offices of tenderness, and pay

Meet[5] adoration to my household gods,

When I am gone. He works his work, I mine.

    There lies the port; the vessel puffs her sail;

45 There gloom the dark, broad seas. My mariners,

Souls that have toiled, and wrought, and thought with me,—

That ever with a frolic welcome took

The thunder and the sunshine, and opposed

Free hearts, free foreheads,—you and I are old;

50 Old age hath yet his honor and his toil.

---

4. **isle** _n.:_ Ithaca, Ulysses' island kingdom off the west coast of Greece.
5. **meet** _adj.:_ proper.

Death closes all; but something ere the end,

Some work of noble note, may yet be done,

Not unbecoming men that strove with Gods.

> The lights begin to twinkle from the rocks;
>
> 55 The long day wanes; the slow moon climbs; the deep
>
> Moans round with many voices. Come, my friends,
>
> 'Tis not too late to seek a newer world.
>
> Push off, and sitting well in order smite
>
> The sounding furrows;[6] for my purpose holds
>
> 60 To sail beyond the sunset, and the baths
>
> Of all the western stars, until I die.
>
> It may be that the gulfs will wash us down;
>
> It may be we shall touch the Happy Isles,[7]
>
> And see the great Achilles,[8] whom we knew.
>
> 65 Though much is taken, much abides; and though
>
> We are not now that strength which in old days
>
> Moved earth and heaven, that which we are, we are,—
>
> One equal temper of heroic hearts,
>
> Made weak by time and fate, but strong in will
>
> 70 To strive, to seek, to find, and not to yield.

---

6. **smite . . . furrows:** row against the waves.
7. **Happy Isles:** in Greek mythology, Elysium (ē·liz′ē·əm), where dead heroes lived for eternity.
8. **Achilles** (ə·kil′ēz′): Greek warrior and leader in the Trojan War.

EVALUATE

Re-read lines 57–64, which describe Ulysses' feelings about his voyage. How would you describe the **tone** of this passage? *(Grade 9–10 Review)*

_____

_____

_____

_____

ANALYZE

In lines 65–70, circle words and phrases that describe aging in a negative way. Underline words that describe aging in a positive way. How do these positive and negative words relate to the **theme** of the poem?

_____

_____

_____

_____

_____

_____

_____

FLUENCY

Read the boxed passage aloud twice. Use your voice to convince your listeners, the sailors, to leave home on another long, dangerous journey.

Ulysses

Reading Skills: Summarizing   In the chart below, write one or two sentences that **summarize** each section of the poem. The first one has been done for you.

Sections of the Poem	Summary Sentences
Stanza 1 Lines 1–5	Ulysses is tired of staying at home, where all he does is spend time with his wife and try to govern difficult people.
Lines 6–17	
Lines 18–32	
Stanza 2 Lines 33–43	
Stanza 3 Lines 44–70	

Evaluate   Review the summary sentences you wrote above. Write a short statement below that summarizes the **theme,** or central idea, of the poem.

_____

_____

✓ Check your Standards Mastery at the back of this book.

My Last Duchess by Robert Browning

BEFORE YOU READ

LITERARY FOCUS: DRAMATIC MONOLOGUE

If you simply let someone keep talking, he or she will often reveal astounding information without even realizing it. In "My Last Duchess," that very thing happens. This poem is one of Browning's most popular dramatic monologues. A **dramatic monologue** is a poem in which a character, who is not the poet, addresses one or more listeners who remain silent. The poet sets a scene in which the speaker reveals information about himself or herself, the other characters, and the situation by dropping indirect clues that we must piece together.

READING SKILLS: DRAWING INFERENCES FROM TEXTUAL CLUES

Sometimes you must draw inferences in order to understand things a writer has not stated directly. An **inference** is a guess you make based on information in the text and on your own knowledge and experience. To draw an inference, focus on important details in the text and then combine that information with what you already know.

Use the Skill   As you read, look for details from the poem that provide clues to the questions given below. Those details will help you infer answers to these questions after you read the poem.

Questions
What kind of a person is the Duke?
What impression of the Duchess does the Duke give in his description of her?
What happened to the Duke's "last Duchess"?

REVIEW SKILLS

As you read "My Last Duchess," look for ways in which Browning uses characterization.

CHARACTERIZATION
The process by which a writer reveals the personality of a character. The writer may reveal character directly (telling us what a character is like) or by using several indirect methods (for example, describing how a character looks and acts).

Reading Standard 3.1
Analyze characteristics of subgenres that are used in poetry, prose, plays, novels, short stories, essays, and other basic genres.

Reading Standard 3.4 (Grade 9–10 Review)
Determine characters' traits by what the characters say about themselves in narration, dialogue, dramatic monologue, and soliloquy.

My Last Duchess

Robert Browning

BACKGROUND

The speaker in "My Last Duchess" is not named, but Browning identified him as Alfonso II, the fifth Duke of Ferrara, who was a powerful
nobleman in Renaissance Italy. The first of the Duke's three wives was
a young girl. Shortly after his marriage, the Duke left for two years. His
wife died in 1561, about a year after his return. Many believed that she
had been poisoned. In "My Last Duchess," the Duke is making plans to
marry the daughter of a Count, and he is making arrangements with
the Count's representative.

IDENTIFY

What clues in lines 1–7 tell
you that this is a **dramatic
monologue**—that the speaker
is addressing a listener who
does not speak?

_____

_____

_____

_____

**IDENTIFY
CAUSE & EFFECT**

From his description of the
Duchess in lines 13–21, what
does the Duke think caused
the "spot of joy" on his
wife's face?

_____

_____

That's my last Duchess painted on the wall,
Looking as if she were alive. I call
That piece a wonder, now; Frà Pandolf's[1] hands
Worked busily a day, and there she stands.
5 Will 't please you sit and look at her? I said
"Frà Pandolf" by design, for never read
Strangers like you that pictured countenance,
The depth and passion of its earnest glance,
But to myself they turned (since none puts by
10 the curtain I have drawn for you, but I)
And seemed as they would ask me, if they durst,
How such a glance came there; so, not the first
Are you to turn and ask thus. Sir, 'twas not
Her husband's presence only, called that spot
15 Of joy into the Duchess' cheek; perhaps

---

1. **Frà Pandolf's:** Brother Pandolf, a fictitious painter and monk.

Frà Pandolf chanced to say, "Her mantle[2] laps

Over my lady's wrist too much," or, "Paint

Must never hope to reproduce the faint

Half flush that dies along her throat." Such stuff

20   Was courtesy, she thought, and cause enough

For calling up that spot of joy. She had

A heart—how shall I say?—too soon made glad,

Too easily impressed; she liked whate'er

She looked on, and her looks went everywhere.

25   Sir, 'twas all one! My favor[3] at her breast,

The dropping of the daylight in the West,

The bough of cherries some officious fool

Broke in the orchard for her, the white mule

She rode with round the terrace—all and each

30   Would draw from her alike the approving speech,

Or blush, at least. She thanked men—good! but thanked

Somehow—I know not how—as if she ranked

My gift of a nine-hundred-years-old name

With anybody's gift. Who'd stoop to blame

35   This sort of trifling? Even had you skill

In speech—(which I have not)—to make your will

Quite clear to such an one, and say, "Just this

Or that in you disgusts me; here you miss,

Or there exceed the mark"—and if she let

40   Herself be lessoned so, nor plainly set

Her wits to yours, forsooth,[4] and made excuse,

—E'en then would be some stooping; and I choose

Never to stoop. Oh sir, she smiled, no doubt,

Whene'er I passed her; but who passed without

45   Much the same smile? This grew; I gave commands;

Then all smiles stopped together. There she stands

As if alive. Will 't please you rise? We'll meet

---

2. **mantle** *n.:* cloak.
3. **favor** *n.:* gift; token of love.
4. **forsooth** *adv.:* archaic for "in truth."

INFER

Re-read lines 21–31. What inferences can you make about the Duchess's **character** from the information given? *(Grade 9–10 Review)*

_____

_____

_____

_____

_____

_____

_____

_____

FLUENCY

Read the boxed passage aloud several times. Focus on conveying the Duke's **tone**—his attitude toward the Duchess—as you read.

INFER

Pause at line 47. What do you suspect happened to the Duchess?

_____

_____

_____

_____

_____

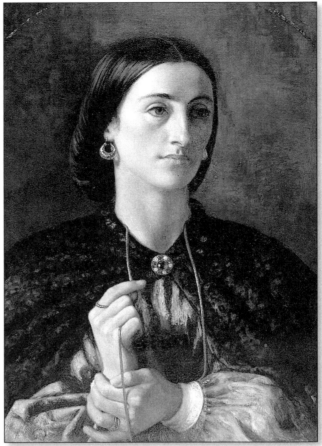

A Lady with a Gold Chain and Earrings (1861)
by Robert Braithwaite Martineau.
Oil on panel (14" x 10").
© Manchester City Art Galleries, England.

INFER

Re-read lines 48–53. What does the Duke say is his object as he negotiates to marry the Count's daughter? Circle that information. What else can you infer he is interested in?

CONNECT

After reading this poem, what are your thoughts or impressions of the Duke's character? *(Grade 9–10 Review)*

The company below, then. I repeat,

The Count your master's known munificence[5]

50 Is ample warrant[6] that no just pretense

Of mine for dowry will be disallowed;

Though his fair daughter's self, as I avowed

At starting, is my object. Nay, we'll go

Together down, sir. Notice Neptune,[7] though,

55 Taming a seahorse, thought a rarity,

Which Claus of Innsbruck[8] cast in bronze for me!

---

5. **munificence** *n.:* generosity.
6. **warrant** *n.:* guarantee.
7. **Neptune:** in Roman mythology, god of the sea.
8. **Claus of Innsbruck:** imaginary sculptor.

My Last Duchess

Reading Skills: Drawing Inferences from Textual Clues   Browning's poem contains details that provide clues about the Duke and his last Duchess. Answer the questions below by listing details from the text that help you find the answers. Then, answer each question by drawing inferences. Write your inferences in the column on the right.

Questions	Details in the Text	My Inferences
What kind of a person is the Duke?		
What impression of the Duchess does the Duke give in his description of her?		
What happened to the Duke's "last Duchess"?		

Check your Standards Mastery at the back of this book.

Sonnet 43 by Elizabeth Barrett Browning

BEFORE YOU READ

LITERARY FOCUS: PETRARCHAN SONNET

Sonnet 43, like all of the poems in *Sonnets from the Portuguese,* is a Petrarchan sonnet. A **Petrarchan,** or Italian, sonnet is divided into two parts: an eight-line **octave** that poses a question, and a six-line **sestet** that answers the question. Sonnet 43, however, does not have the usual **turn,** or break in thought, between the octave and the sestet. Instead, the poem is broken into short units of thought. A traditional Petrarchan sonnet is written in iambic pentameter and rhymes in the following way: *abbaabba* (the octave) and *cdcdcd* (the sestet).

READING SKILLS: PARAPHRASING

When you **paraphrase** a poem, you restate every line using your own words. You do not use quotations from the work. A paraphrase is often as long as, or even longer than, the original text. (A paraphrase differs from a summary, which is shorter than the original text and includes only its main ideas.) A sample paraphrase of the first three lines of Shakespeare's Sonnet 116 is shown below.

Lines from Sonnet 116	Paraphrase
"Let me not to the marriage of true minds Admit impediments. Love is not love Which alters when it alteration finds, . . ."	I will not allow any obstacles to stand in the way of true love. True love is not changeable.

Use the Skill

Read Sonnet 43 at least twice. As you read, pause from time to time to paraphrase Browning's words.

Elizabeth Barrett Browning (1806–1861), wife of Robert Browning.
© Hulton Archive.

Reading Standard 3.1 Analyze characteristics of subgenres that are used in poetry, prose, plays, novels, short stories, essays, and other basic genres.

SONNET 43

Elizabeth Barrett Browning

> **BACKGROUND**
> Before her marriage, Elizabeth Barrett Browning wrote a group of love
> poems addressed to her future husband, Robert Browning. Two years
> passed before she gave him the poems she had written during their
> courtship. The poems revealed such personal feelings that she at first
> hesitated to publish them. At last, she developed a plan that allowed
> her to share her sonnets with the public and save a little privacy for
> herself. She called her collection of poems *Sonnets from the Portuguese,*
> a title that suggested she had not written the poems herself, but had
> merely translated them from Portuguese into English.

How do I love thee? Let me count the ways.
I love thee to the depth and breadth and height
My soul can reach, when feeling out of sight
For the ends of Being and ideal Grace.
5 I love thee to the level of everyday's
Most quiet need, by sun and candlelight.
I love thee freely, as men strive for Right;
I love thee purely, as they turn from Praise.
I love thee with the passion put to use
10 In my old griefs, and with my childhood's faith.
I love thee with a love I seemed to lose
With my lost saints°—I love thee with the breath,
Smiles, tears, of all my life!—and, if God choose,
I shall but love thee better after death.

IDENTIFY

Circle the question the
speaker poses at the beginning of the poem. Underline
what she intends to do.

ANALYZE

Circle the line that begins
the **sestet** of this Petrarchan
sonnet. Then, underline the
ccc rhymes, and circle the
ddd rhymes.

INFER

Re-read the final thought
in the sonnet (lines 12–14).
What do you learn about
Browning's religious faith
from these lines?

_____

_____

_____

° **lost saints:** childhood faith.

Sonnet 43

Reading Skills: Paraphrasing   In the chart below, "count the ways" of Browning's love in your own words by paraphrasing the lines from the poem.

Passages from the Poem	My Paraphrases
"I love thee to the depth and breadth and height / My soul can reach, when feeling out of sight / For the ends of Being and ideal Grace."	
"I love thee to the level of everyday's / Most quiet need, by sun and candlelight."	
"I love thee freely, as men strive for Right; / I love thee purely, as they turn from Praise."	
"I love thee with the passion put to use / In my old griefs, and with my childhood's faith."	
"I love thee with a love I seemed to lose / With my lost saints"	
"I love thee with the breath, / Smiles, tears, of all my life!"	

☑ Check your Standards Mastery at the back of this book.

Dover Beach by Matthew Arnold

LITERARY FOCUS: MOOD

Mood is the atmosphere created by the writer's choice of descriptive details, images, and sounds. Mood can usually be described in a single word, such as *peaceful, gloomy, optimistic,* or *threatening.* In "Dover Beach," Matthew Arnold creates a mood that shifts at certain points in the poem like the ebb and flow of the tide he describes.

In the Mood   Below are descriptions of two very different scenes. List some words and phrases that you think describe the mood of each.

Passage	Description of Mood
It is late afternoon, and dark clouds gather overhead. Rugged cliffs tower over a rocky, windswept beach. The echoing screeches of seagulls fill the air.	
Morning sunlight filters into the child's room through delicate, lace curtains. The child begins to wake as her mother quietly puts away toys and tidies up the room.	

READING SKILLS: USING PUNCTUATION CLUES

"Dover Beach" builds meaning as the speaker develops an important idea in each of the four stanzas. One way to follow the speaker's train of thought is to look for and use punctuation clues. Here are some tips to help you identify each complete thought in the poem:

- The end of a line does not mean the end of a sentence unless there is a period. Keep reading past the line breaks until you reach a period or other end punctuation. Although each new poetic line begins with a capital letter, it does not always signal the beginning of a new sentence.

- Read the semicolons and dash (line 3) as if they were periods, thus signaling the end of one thought and the beginning of another.

Use the Skill   As you read the poem, look for punctuation clues. You may want to circle or highlight end punctuation. Once you find a complete sentence, re-read to be sure you've identified its subject and the verb(s).

REVIEW SKILLS

As you read "Dover Beach," pay special attention to how the poet uses figurative language to develop his ideas.

FIGURATIVE LANGUAGE
Words and phrases that describe one thing in terms of another and that are not meant to be understood literally. Figurative language includes all **figures of speech,** such as metaphors.

Reading Standard 3.3 Analyze the ways in which irony, tone, mood, the author's style, and the "sound" of language achieve specific rhetorical or aesthetic purposes.

Reading Standard 3.11 (Grade 9–10 Review) Evaluate the aesthetic qualities of style, including the impact of diction and figurative language on tone, mood, and theme, using the terminology of literary criticism.

Dover Beach

Matthew Arnold

BACKGROUND

In 1851, Matthew Arnold and his wife honeymooned on the English coast, spending the night at the seaside city of Dover. Looking across the English Channel, they could see—on a clear day—the coastline of France. During their visit they would also have seen the famous White Cliffs of Dover, a chalk formation that forms a natural defense of the English coastline. Dover has been the site of battles fought by Roman soldiers; William the Conqueror; and the French emperor, Napoleon Bonaparte.

Dover Beach, like many of the beaches in the British Isles, consists of round, gray pebbles, not sand. Arnold describes the sound of the sea receding over the pebbles as a "grating roar."

ANALYZE

The first six lines of the poem establish a setting and **mood.** Circle descriptive details that create this mood. How would you describe it?

_____

_____

_____

_____

_____

_____

_____

_____

The sea is calm tonight.
The tide is full, the moon lies fair
Upon the straits[1]—on the French coast the light
Gleams and is gone; the cliffs of England stand,
5   Glimmering and vast, out in the tranquil bay.
Come to the window, sweet is the night air!
Only, from the long line of spray
Where the sea meets the moon-blanched land,
Listen! you hear the grating roar
10 Of pebbles which the waves draw back, and fling,
At their return, up the high strand,[2]

---

1. **straits** *n. pl.:* Strait of Dover, a body of water separating southeastern England and northwestern France.
2. **strand** *n.:* shore.

Pegwell Bay, Kent—A Recollection of October 5, 1858
(1859–1860) by William Dyce.

Tate Gallery, London.

IDENTIFY
CAUSE & EFFECT

Pause at line 14. A shift in **mood** occurs in the second half of the first stanza (lines 1–14). What does the speaker hear that causes the mood to change? Circle the details that tell you. Then, explain how this sound affects the speaker.

Begin, and cease, and then again begin,

With tremulous cadence slow, and bring

The eternal note of sadness in.

WORD STUDY

The word *turbid* (line 17) is an adjective based on the Latin verb *turbare,* meaning "to throw into disorder or confusion." A turbid stream, for example, would be muddy and thick with swirling sediment. Here, *turbid* refers to a state of disturbance.

15   Sophocles³ long ago

Heard it on the Aegean,⁴ and it brought

Into his mind the turbid ebb and flow

Of human misery; we

Find also in the sound a thought,

20   Hearing it by this distant northern sea.

The Sea of Faith

Was once, too, at the full, and round earth's shore

Lay like the folds of a bright girdle⁵ furled.

INTERPRET

Re-read lines 21–23, in which the speaker uses a **metaphor** to compare the sea with religious beliefs ("The Sea of Faith"). Underline the **simile** he uses to describe the Sea of Faith. What is the speaker saying about the positive effects of faith on the world? *(Grade 9–10 Review)*

---

3. **Sophocles** (säf′ə·klēz′) (c. 496–406 B.C.): writer of tragedies in ancient Greece.
4. **Aegean** (ē·jē′ən): sea between Greece and Turkey.
5. **girdle** *n.:* belt.

In lines 24–28, the speaker compares what has happened to people's faith to the movements of the sea. What observation is the speaker making through this figurative comparison? *(Grade 9–10 Review)*

_____

_____

_____

_____

_____

_____

_____

_____

_____

_____

IDENTIFY

What does the speaker urge his loved one to do in the last stanza? Underline that information.

FLUENCY

Read the boxed passage aloud three times. Circle the marks of punctuation that signal the end of one thought and the beginning of another. With each reading, improve your interpretation of the speaker's feelings of urgency and fear.

But now I only hear

25 Its melancholy, long, withdrawing roar,

Retreating, to the breath

Of the night wind, down the vast edges drear

And naked shingles[6] of the world.

Ah, love, let us be true

30 To one another! for the world, which seems

To lie before us like a land of dreams,

So various, so beautiful, so new,

Hath really neither joy, nor love, nor light,

Nor certitude, nor peace, nor help for pain;

35 And we are here as on a darkling plain

Swept with confused alarms of struggle and flight,

Where ignorant armies clash by night.

_____

6. **shingles** *n. pl.:* here, beaches covered with pebbles.

Dover Beach

Literary Focus: Mood   Think about how words, details, and punctuation clues helped you identify the ideas in the poem and the points at which the **mood,** or atmosphere, shifts. Refer to the poem as you answer the questions below.

What words, details, and punctuation clues signal a change of mood in the first stanza?

How would you describe the mood in the second half of the first stanza?

In the second stanza, how does the use of punctuation help to emphasize the mood?

How are the moods expressed in the third stanza similar to the moods in the first stanza?

**Arnold claimed that "Dover Beach" was mainly a love poem.
Does the overall mood of the poem remind you of a love poem, or something else?**

✓ Check your Standards Mastery at the back of this book.

The Bet by Anton Chekhov

BEFORE YOU READ

REVIEW SKILLS

As you read "The Bet," pay special attention to how conflict drives the characters and plot.

CONFLICT
A struggle or clash between characters, forces, or emotions. A character who experiences **external conflict** struggles against an outside force, such as society, another character, or nature. When characters face **internal conflicts,** they struggle with opposing emotions, needs, or desires within themselves.

Reading Standard 3.2
Analyze the way in which the theme or meaning of a selection represents a view or comment on life, using textual evidence to support the claim.

Reading Standard 3.3 (Grade 9–10 Review)
Analyze interactions between main and subordinate characters in a literary text (e.g., internal and external conflicts, motivations, relationships, influences) and explain the way those interactions affect the plot.

LITERARY FOCUS: THEME

The **theme** of a story is its central idea, or insight, that usually expresses a view or comment on life. In some stories, the themes are directly stated, but in most stories it is up to the reader to piece together details that provide clues about the theme.

Some stories, like "The Bet," present more than one theme or present an ambiguous theme. Readers must consider the story's different elements in order to decide on its overall meaning. Figuring out a theme requires that readers accept a certain degree of ambiguity—not every story will have one simple explanation. "The Bet" is just such a story, raising more questions than it answers.

READING SKILLS: MAKING PREDICTIONS

A **prediction** is a special kind of **inference**—an educated guess about what will happen in the future. When you make a prediction about a story's outcome, you forecast what might happen next as a result of particular actions or events. Predictions are based on your own knowledge and experience and on information that is stated or implied. As you continue to read and gather information, your predictions may change.

What Happens Next?   Read the information in the left-hand column below. In the next column, make a prediction about what will happen, drawing on your own knowledge and experience.

Situation	My Prediction
A man decorates his dining table with a tall vase of flowers for a dinner party. He then puts the smoked salmon appetizer on the table and goes back to the kitchen to finish preparing the main dish. A cat crawls out from under the sofa and sniffs the air.	

Use the Skill   As you read "The Bet," identify details that provide clues about what will happen to the characters later in the story. Then, make predictions based on these clues. Highlight or underline details that help you make predictions, as well as further details that cause you to change your predictions.

The Bet

Anton Chekhov *translated by* Constance Garnett

BACKGROUND

Anton Chekhov (1860–1904) was born in a seaport town in the south of Russia. He was the grandson of a farm laborer and the son of a shopkeeper. Chekhov (che′kôf′) attended medical school on a scholarship and began writing comic stories for periodicals to support himself and his family.

Chekhov's stories often emphasize character and mood rather than plot. The theme of many of his works is the individual's alienation from others. His characters may often be sensitive and intelligent, but also foolish, detached from the world, and dishonest with themselves about their real feelings. In addition to many fine short stories, Chekhov wrote a number of plays that today are considered masterpieces. His life was cut short by tuberculosis, and he died at the age of forty-four, at the height of his creativity.

1

It was a dark autumn night. The old banker was walking up and down his study and remembering how, fifteen years before, he had given a party one autumn evening. There had been many clever men there, and there had been interesting conversations. Among other things, they had talked of capital punishment. The majority of the guests, among whom were many journalists and intellectual men, disapproved of the death penalty. They considered that form of punishment out of date, immoral, and unsuitable for Christian states.[1] In the opinion of some of them, the death penalty ought

10　to be replaced everywhere by imprisonment for life.

"I don't agree with you," said their host, the banker. "I have not tried either the death penalty or imprisonment for life, but if

CLARIFY

The story opens with a long **flashback,** a storytelling technique in which the present action of the plot is interrupted to show events that happened at an earlier time. Re-read lines 1–5, and underline details that tell you these events happened earlier.

WORD STUDY

Find the context clue in line 7 that suggests the meaning of the phrase *capital punishment.* Circle it.

1.　**Christian states:** countries in which Christianity is the main religion.

**COMPARE &
CONTRAST**

Pause at line 18. How do the
banker's views on capital
punishment differ from the
views of most of his guests?

_____

_____

_____

_____

_____

_____

_____

PREDICT

Re-read lines 40–50.
Underline the words and
phrases the banker uses to
try to talk the lawyer out
of the bet. Explain whether
or not you think the lawyer
will be convinced by the
banker's argument.

_____

_____

_____

_____

_____

_____

_____

_____

_____

_____

one may judge a priori,[2] the death penalty is more moral and
more humane than imprisonment for life. Capital punishment
kills a man at once, but lifelong imprisonment kills him slowly.
Which executioner is the more humane, he who kills you in a
few minutes or he who drags the life out of you in the course
of many years?"

"Both are equally immoral," observed one of the guests, "for
20 they both have the same object—to take away life. The state is
not God. It has not the right to take away what it cannot restore
when it wants to."

Among the guests was a young lawyer, a young man of five-
and-twenty. When he was asked his opinion, he said: "The death
sentence and the life sentence are equally immoral, but if I had
to choose between the death penalty and imprisonment for life,
I would certainly choose the second. To live anyhow is better
than not at all."

A lively discussion arose. The banker, who was younger
30 and more nervous in those days, was suddenly carried away by
excitement; he struck the table with his fist and shouted at the
young man: "It's not true! I'll bet you two million you wouldn't
stay in solitary confinement for five years."

"If you mean that in earnest," said the young man, "I'll take
the bet, but I would stay not five, but fifteen years."

"Fifteen? Done!" cried the banker. "Gentlemen, I stake two
million!"

"Agreed! You stake your millions and I stake my freedom!"
said the young man.

40 And this wild, senseless bet was carried out! The banker,
spoiled and **frivolous,** with millions beyond his reckoning, was
delighted at the bet. At supper he made fun of the young man
and said: "Think better of it, young man, while there is still time.
To me two million is a trifle, but you are losing three or four of
the best years of your life. I say three or four, because you won't

---

2. **a priori** (ā′prī·ôr′ī) *adv.:* here, on the basis of theory rather
than experience.

stay longer. Don't forget either, you unhappy man, that voluntary confinement is a great deal harder to bear than **compulsory.** The thought that you have the right to step out in liberty at any moment will poison your whole existence in prison. I am sorry for you."

50

And now the banker, walking to and fro, remembered all this and asked himself: "What was the object of that bet? What is the good of that man's losing fifteen years of his life and my throwing away two million? Can it prove that the death penalty is better or worse than imprisonment for life? No, no. It was all nonsensical and meaningless. On my part it was the **caprice** of a pampered man, and on his part simple greed for money. . . ."

Then he remembered what followed that evening. It was decided that the young man should spend the years of his cap-

60

tivity under the strictest supervision in one of the lodges in the banker's garden. It was agreed that for fifteen years he should not be free to cross the threshold of the lodge, to see human beings, to hear the human voice, or to receive letters and newspapers. He was allowed to have a musical instrument and books and was allowed to write letters, to drink wine, and to smoke. By the terms of the agreement, the only relations he could have with the outer world were by a little window made purposely for that object. He might have anything he wanted—books, music, wine, and so on—in any quantity he desired, by writing an

70

order, but could receive them only through the window. The agreement provided for every detail and every trifle that would make his imprisonment strictly solitary, and bound the young man to stay there exactly fifteen years, beginning from twelve o'clock of November 14, 1870, and ending at twelve o'clock of November 14, 1885. The slightest attempt on his part to break the conditions, if only two minutes before the end, released the banker from the obligation to pay him two million.

For the first year of his confinement, as far as one could judge from his brief notes, the prisoner suffered severely from

80

loneliness and depression. The sounds of the piano could be

VOCABULARY

frivolous (friv′ə·ləs) *adj.:* light-minded; lacking seriousness.

compulsory (kəm·pul′sə·rē) *adj.:* required; enforced.

caprice (kə·prēs′) *n.:* sudden notion or desire.

ANALYZE

Re-read lines 51–57, and circle words that indicate the banker's feelings about the bet as he thinks about it now. What **conflict** is the banker experiencing, and what kind of conflict is it— internal or external? *(Grade 9–10 Review)*

_____

_____

_____

_____

IDENTIFY

Pause at line 65. Underline the things the lawyer may not do or have during his imprisonment. Circle the things he is allowed.

IDENTIFY CAUSE & EFFECT

Pause at line 77. What happens if the lawyer breaks the conditions of the agreement? Underline that information.

What **inner conflicts** does the prisoner experience during the first year of his confinement (lines 78–87)? *(Grade 9–10 Review)*

_____

_____

_____

_____

_____

_____

_____

What changes occur in the prisoner's behavior in the fifth year of his confinement (lines 89–96)? Underline those details.

zealously (zel′əs·lē) *adv.:* fervently; done with intense emotion, passion, or enthusiasm.

Pause at line 112. After reading this letter from the prisoner, predict whether or not he will stay in prison for fifteen years and win the bet. Underline details that helped you make your prediction.

_____

_____

heard continually day and night from his lodge. He refused wine and tobacco. Wine, he wrote, excites the desires, and desires are the worst foes of the prisoner; and besides, nothing could be more dreary than drinking good wine and seeing no one. And tobacco spoiled the air of his room. In the first year the books he sent for were principally of a light character—novels with a complicated love plot, sensational and fantastic stories, and so on.

In the second year the piano was silent in the lodge, and the prisoner asked only for the classics. In the fifth year music
90   was audible again, and the prisoner asked for wine. Those who watched him through the window said that all that year he spent doing nothing but eating and drinking and lying on his bed, frequently yawning and talking angrily to himself. He did not read books. Sometimes at night he would sit down to write; he would spend hours writing and in the morning tear up all that he had written. More than once he could be heard crying.

In the second half of the sixth year the prisoner began **zealously** studying languages, philosophy, and history. He threw himself eagerly into these studies—so much so that the banker
100 had enough to do to get him the books he ordered. In the course of four years, some six hundred volumes were procured at his request. It was during this period that the banker received the following letter from his prisoner:

"My dear Jailer, I write you these lines in six languages. Show them to people who know the languages. Let them read them. If they find not one mistake, I implore you to fire a shot in the garden. That shot will show me that my efforts have not been thrown away. The geniuses of all ages and of all lands speak different languages, but the same flame burns in them all. Oh,
110 if you only knew what unearthly happiness my soul feels now from being able to understand them!" The prisoner's desire was fulfilled. The banker ordered two shots to be fired in the garden.

Then, after the tenth year, the prisoner sat immovably at the table and read nothing but the Gospels. It seemed strange to the banker that a man who in four years had mastered six hundred learned volumes should waste nearly a year over one thin book easy of comprehension. Theology[3] and histories of religion followed the Gospels.

In the last two years of his confinement, the prisoner read 120 an immense quantity of books quite **indiscriminately.** At one time he was busy with the natural sciences; then he would ask for Byron or Shakespeare. There were notes in which he demanded at the same time books on chemistry, and a manual of medicine, and a novel, and some treatise on philosophy or theology. His reading suggested a man swimming in the sea among the wreckage of his ship and trying to save his life by greedily clutching first at one spar[4] and then at another.

2

The old banker remembered all this and thought: "Tomorrow at twelve o'clock he will regain his freedom. By our arrangement I 130 ought to pay him two million. If I do pay him, it is all over with me: I shall be utterly ruined."

Fifteen years before, his millions had been beyond his reckoning; now he was afraid to ask himself which were greater, his debts or his assets. Desperate gambling on the Stock Exchange, wild speculation, and the excitability which he could not get over even in advancing years had by degrees led to the decline of his fortune, and the proud, fearless, self-confident millionaire had become a banker of middling rank, trembling at every rise and fall in his investments. "Cursed bet!" muttered the old man, 140 clutching his head in despair. "Why didn't the man die? He is only forty now. He will take my last penny from me, he will marry, will enjoy life, will gamble on the Exchange, while I shall look at him with envy like a beggar and hear from him every day the same sentence: 'I am indebted to you for the happiness of my life; let me help you!' No, it is too much! The one means of being saved from bankruptcy and disgrace is the death of that man!"

---

3. **theology** (thē·äl′ə·jē) *n.:* the study of religious teachings concerning God and God's relation to the world.
4. **spar** *n.:* pole that supports or extends a ship's sail.

VOCABULARY

indiscriminately
(in′di·skrim′i·nit·lē) *adv.:*
without making careful
distinctions; randomly.

PREDICT

Pause at line 127. Do you
need to revise your previous
prediction? Why or why not?

_____

_____

CLARIFY

Pause at line 131. What
happens at this point in the
story in terms of the time
frame of the events? Underline details that tell you.

_____

_____

_____

_____

ANALYZE

What **external** and **internal**
conflicts is the banker
experiencing at this point in
the story (lines 132–146)?
(Grade 9–10 Review)

_____

_____

_____

_____

PREDICT

Pause at line 152. What do you predict will happen after the banker leaves the house? What possible clue is in the previous paragraph? Circle it. (As you read further, underline details that confirm your prediction or cause you to revise it.)

_____

_____

_____

_____

_____

_____

_____

_____

INFER

Re-read lines 153–162. What do you think the old banker wants to do?

_____

_____

_____

_____

_____

_____

_____

_____

_____

_____

It struck three o'clock. The banker listened; everyone was asleep in the house, and nothing could be heard outside but the rustling of the chilled trees. Trying to make no noise, he took

150 from a fireproof safe the key of the door which had not been opened for fifteen years, put on his overcoat, and went out of the house.

It was dark and cold in the garden. Rain was falling. A damp, cutting wind was racing about the garden, howling and giving the trees no rest. The banker strained his eyes but could see neither the earth nor the white statues, nor the lodge, nor the trees. Going to the spot where the lodge stood, he twice called the watchman. No answer followed. Evidently the watchman had sought shelter from the weather and was now asleep

160 somewhere either in the kitchen or in the greenhouse.

"If I had the pluck to carry out my intention," thought the old man, "suspicion would fall first upon the watchman."

The Verandah at Liselund (1916) by Peter Ilsted.
Oil on canvas.
Courtesy of Adelson Galleries, New York.

He felt in the darkness for the steps and the door and went into the entry of the lodge. Then he groped his way into a little passage and lighted a match. There was not a soul there. There was a bedstead with no bedding on it, and in the corner there was a dark cast-iron stove. The seals on the door leading to the prisoner's rooms were intact.

When the match went out, the old man, trembling with emotion, peeped through the little window. A candle was burning dimly in the prisoner's room. He was sitting at the table. Nothing could be seen but his back, the hair on his head, and his hands. Open books were lying on the table, on the two easy chairs, and on the carpet near the table.

Five minutes passed and the prisoner did not once stir. Fifteen years' imprisonment had taught him to sit still. The banker tapped at the window with his finger, and the prisoner made no movement whatever in response. Then the banker cautiously broke the seals off the door and put the key in the keyhole. The rusty lock gave a grating sound and the door creaked. The banker expected to hear at once footsteps and a cry of astonishment, but three minutes passed and it was as quiet as ever in the room. He made up his mind to go in.

At the table a man unlike ordinary people was sitting motionless. He was a skeleton with the skin drawn tight over his bones, with long curls like a woman's, and a shaggy beard. His face was yellow with an earthy tint in it, his cheeks were hollow, his back long and narrow, and the hand on which his shaggy head was propped was so thin and delicate that it was dreadful to look at it. His hair was already streaked with silver, and seeing his emaciated, aged-looking face, no one would have believed that he was only forty. He was asleep. . . . In front of his bowed head there lay on the table a sheet of paper, on which there was something written in fine handwriting.

"Poor creature!" thought the banker, "he is asleep and most likely dreaming of the millions. And I have only to take this half-dead man, throw him on the bed, stifle him a little with the pillow,

INFER

Pause at line 178. Why hasn't the prisoner stirred or moved at the banker's entrance?

DRAW CONCLUSIONS

From the description of the lawyer's appearance in lines 184–194, what can you conclude about what he endured during his imprisonment?

INTERPRET

What does the banker's comment in lines 195–199 reveal about his character?

_____

_____

_____

_____

ethereal (ē·thir′ē·əl) *adj.*: light and delicate; unearthly.

Re-read lines 207–224, in which the prisoner describes what he experienced in all the books he read. Circle the action verbs that tell what he did in his imagination. How did reading books help the prisoner cope with his lack of freedom?

_____

_____

_____

_____

_____

Read the boxed passage aloud two times. Focus on conveying the rich life that the prisoner experienced while apart from the world.

and the most conscientious expert would find no sign of a violent death. But let us first read what he has written here. . . ."

200   The banker took the page from the table and read as follows:

"Tomorrow at twelve o'clock I regain my freedom and the right to associate with other men, but before I leave this room and see the sunshine, I think it necessary to say a few words to you. With a clear conscience I tell you, as before God, who beholds me, that I despise freedom and life and health and all that in your books is called the good things of the world.

"For fifteen years I have been intently studying earthly life. It is true I have not seen the earth or men, but in your books I have drunk fragrant wine, I have sung songs, I have hunted stags
210   and wild boars in the forests, I have loved women. . . . Beauties as **ethereal** as clouds, created by the magic of your poets and geniuses, have visited me at night and have whispered in my ears wonderful tales that have set my brain in a whirl. In your books I have climbed to the peaks of Elburz and Mont Blanc,[5] and from there I have seen the sun rise and have watched it at evening flood the sky, the ocean, and the mountaintops with gold and crimson. I have watched from there the lightning flashing over my head and cleaving the storm clouds. I have seen green forests, fields, rivers, lakes, towns. I have heard the singing of the sirens,[6]
220   and the strains of the shepherds' pipes; I have touched the wings of comely devils who flew down to converse with me of God. . . . In your books I have flung myself into the bottomless pit, performed miracles, slain, burned towns, preached new religions, conquered whole kingdoms. . . .

"Your books have given me wisdom. All that the unresting thought of man has created in the ages is compressed into a small compass in my brain. I know that I am wiser than all of you.

---

5. **Elburz** (el·bŏŏrz′) and **Mont Blanc** (mōn blän′): Elburz is a mountain range in northern Iran; Mont Blanc, in France, is the highest mountain in the Alps.
6. **sirens** *n. pl.*: in Greek mythology, partly human female creatures who lived on an island and lured sailors to their deaths with their beautiful singing.

"And I despise your books, I despise wisdom and the blessings of this world. It is all worthless, fleeting, **illusory,** and deceptive, like a mirage. You may be proud, wise, and fine, but death will wipe you off the face of the earth as though you were no more than mice burrowing under the floor, and your **posterity,** your history, your immortal geniuses will burn or freeze together with the earthly globe.

"You have lost your reason and taken the wrong path. You have taken lies for truth and hideousness for beauty. You would marvel if, owing to strange events of some sort, frogs and lizards suddenly grew on apple and orange trees instead of fruit or if roses began to smell like a sweating horse; so I marvel at you who exchange heaven for earth. I don't want to understand you.

"To prove to you in action how I despise all that you live by, I **renounce** the two million of which I once dreamed as of paradise and which now I despise. To deprive myself of the right to the money, I shall go out from here five minutes before the time fixed and so break the compact. . . ."

When the banker had read this, he laid the page on the table, kissed the strange man on the head, and went out of the lodge, weeping. At no other time, even when he had lost heavily on the Stock Exchange, had he felt so great a contempt for himself. When he got home, he lay on his bed, but his tears and emotion kept him for hours from sleeping.

Next morning the watchmen ran in with pale faces and told him they had seen the man who lived in the lodge climb out of the window into the garden, go to the gate, and disappear. The banker went at once with the servants to the lodge and made sure of the flight of his prisoner. To avoid arousing unnecessary talk, he took from the table the writing in which the millions were renounced and, when he got home, locked it up in the fireproof safe.

VOCABULARY

illusory (i·lōō′sə·rē) *adj.*: not real; false.

posterity (päs·ter′ə·tē) *n.*: descendants; future generations.

renounce (ri·nouns′) *v.*: formally give up; reject.

INTERPRET

Pause at line 235. What does the prisoner's letter imply about the **theme** of the story?

_____

_____

IDENTIFY

What decision has the lawyer come to (lines 241–245)?

_____

_____

_____

INFER

Underline details in lines 246–259 that reveal the banker's response to the letter. Why does the banker lock it in a safe?

_____

_____

_____

_____

_____

The Bet

Reading Skills: Making Predictions   As you read "The Bet," what predictions did you make? Were they on target most of the time, or did Chekhov's characters surprise you? In the first column of the chart, state four major predictions that you made as you read. In the second column, tell whether or not your predictions came true, and list the details on which you based your predictions. At the bottom of the chart, explain how the characters' actions in the story helped you to formulate the story's theme.

My Predictions	Details

Evaluate   Review your story predictions and think about what the characters' actions and words reveal about their views of the world. What **theme** or themes might Chekhov be conveying in this story?

_____

_____

The Bet

VOCABULARY IN CONTEXT

DIRECTIONS: Write vocabulary words from the Word Box to complete the paragraph below. Not all words from the box will be used.

Word Box

frivolous
compulsory
caprice
zealously
indiscriminately
ethereal
illusory
posterity
renounce

A promise made between friends or family members is a serious matter. It is not a (1) _____ or silly business to be started as a whim or in a moment of (2) _____. Because a promise is usually a verbal agreement, there may be no rules or laws to enforce it. Therefore, fulfilling a promise may not be (3) _____. After careful thought, it might be best to (4) _____ promises that were made in haste. Friends, however, should never carelessly or (5) _____ break important agreements; such behavior may cause distrust and hard feelings for years to come.

SYNONYMS: SHADES OF MEANING

Words that have similar meanings are called **synonyms**. Dictionaries usually give one or more synonyms for each word. You can also find synonyms in a **thesaurus.** Synonyms have subtle differences in meaning and are not always interchangeable. A synonym should suit the **context**—the surrounding words, phrases, and sentences.

DIRECTIONS: Below are vocabulary words followed by synonyms. In the sentences that follow, fill in the blank with the word best suited to the context of the sentence.

1. **ethereal,** *syn.:* **delicate**

   a. The _____ piano music that could be heard day and night coming from the lodge had an eerie and unsettling effect on the watchman.

   b. The stranger outside the window peered through the _____ lace curtains into the dimly lit room where the prisoner sat slumped in a chair.

2. **illusory,** *syn.:* **deceptive**

   a. The host of the dinner party gave the _____ impression that he was in favor of the death penalty.

   b. It is _____ to think that wealth and power give a person true wisdom and happiness.

 Check your Standards Mastery at the back of this book.

The Bet 235

The Modern World

(1900 to the Present)

A Remarkable Diversity

British service men and women and civilians celebrate the end of World War I on Armistice Day, November 11, 1918.

The Modern World (1900 to the Present)

Reading Standard 3.7c
Evaluate the philosophical, political, religious, ethical, and social influences of the historical period that shaped the characters, plots, and settings.

John Leggett *and* David Adams Leeming

The following essay provides highlights of the historical period.
For a more detailed version of this essay,
see *Holt Literature and Language Arts,* pages 804–818.

Change on the Horizon

If we had lived in the era of Victoria or during the nine-year reign of her son Edward VII, we would have believed that Britain's moral and economic dominance of the world would continue forever.

But even during this long, fairly stable period in Great Britain, profound changes were taking place. Several major colonies—Australia, South Africa, and New Zealand—gained their independence in the first decade of the twentieth century. Also, Britain was experiencing social reforms that were to have

10 far-reaching consequences. The rise in literacy, the growing power and influence of the Labour party, the widespread interest in socialist ideology—all would dramatically change Great Britain and the world.

Darwin, Marx, and Freud: Undermining Victorian Ideas

Many of the social and intellectual changes that were taking place in the early years of the twentieth century had their roots in the nineteenth-century work of three men: Charles Darwin (1809–1882), Karl Marx (1818–1883), and Sigmund Freud

20 (1856–1939).

Darwin's *Origin of Species* (1895) sets forth a theory of the evolution of animal species based on natural selection. The theory

IDENTIFY

Underline the major changes that occurred in Great Britain during the reigns of Victoria and Edward VII (lines 5–13).

_____

_____

_____

_____

_____

_____

_____

IDENTIFY

Pause at line 20. According to the text, which three men had a profound influence on the changes taking place in the early twentieth century?

_____

_____

_____

_____

IDENTIFY

Re-read lines 21–33. How was Darwin's theory of natural selection misused? Underline the answer.

CLARIFY

Pause at line 49. What, according to Sigmund Freud, is the cause of most human behavior? What differing views did Victorians have about Freud's theory?

_____

_____

_____

_____

_____

_____

_____

_____

_____

_____

_____

_____

_____

IDENTIFY

Pause at line 54. How did the work of Darwin, Marx, and Freud affect British society? Underline that information.

of natural selection claims that those species that successfully adapt to their environments survive and reproduce; those that do not become extinct. This theory, which seems to contradict the Biblical account of the special creation of each species exactly as the species exists on earth today, fueled a debate that continues to the present. So-called **social Darwinism,** the notion that in human society, as in nature, only the fittest should survive and
30 flourish, was a nasty extension of Darwin's scientific theories. Social Darwinism was used to justify rigid class distinctions, indifference to social problems, and even doctrines of racial superiority.

Karl Marx was a German philosopher and political economist who spent the last thirty years of his life in London. In *Das Kapital* (1867), he advocates doing away with private property and argues that workers should own the means of production. His theories revolutionized political thought and eventually led to sweeping changes in many governments and economic systems,
40 including those of Britain.

The psychological theories of Sigmund Freud, a doctor in Vienna, were equally revolutionary and far-reaching in their effects. In *The Interpretation of Dreams* (1900) and later works, Freud finds the motives for human behavior in the irrational and sexually driven realm of the unconscious, which is revealed mainly in our dreams. Conservative Victorians were outraged by Freud's claims that sexual drives motivated their behavior, but many artists and writers were strongly influenced by the notion of the unconscious and its mysterious, illogical workings.
50 The work of these three thinkers helped to undermine the political, religious, and psychological assumptions that had served as the foundation of British society and the British Empire for generations. With the calamity of the Great War and the events that followed, that foundation was largely swept away.

The Great War: "A War to End All Wars"

The truly great disaster of the first half of the century was the breakdown of the European balance of power. In 1914, Britain, France, and Russia, bound by treaties, became locked in opposition to Germany and Austria-Hungary. When the German army

60 invaded Belgium, all of Europe was plunged into World War I— the Great War.

The Victorian writer Rudyard Kipling celebrated the British character as essentially patriotic, and he was right. When Britain declared war on Germany in 1914, young Britons crowded to the recruiting stations to enlist. Six months later hordes of them lay slaughtered in the miserable, rainsoaked, vermin-infested trenches of France. Over the course of four years, an entire generation of young Englishmen was fed to the insatiable furnace of the war.

With the armistice in 1918, a new cynicism arose. Britons

70 gradually recognized that the results of the war were negative: a weakened economy, a shaky colonial empire, and a loss of life equal to that caused by the plagues of the past. Out of disillusionment came a pessimism about the state and the individual's relation to society. A new realism swept in, a response to the "romantic nonsense" of the past and, in particular, to the propaganda machine that had led a whole people into war.

Experimentation in the Arts: Shocking in Form and Content

The decade before the war had seen the beginnings of a trans-

80 formation in all the arts, especially on the Continent. In Paris, Henri Matisse and other new painters exhibiting in 1905 were called *les fauves* (the wild beasts) by critics for their bold, new use of line and color. In 1913, Igor Stravinsky's revolutionary music for the ballet *The Rite of Spring,* which was marked by strong, primitive (that is, "sexual") rhythms and dissonant harmonies, caused a riot at its première in Paris. The year after that, James Joyce's *Dubliners,* containing stories written up to a

Imperial War Museum, London.

IDENTIFY

Re-read lines 62–68. What was one devastating effect of Britain's entry into World War I?

_____

_____

_____

IDENTIFY

An *armistice* (line 69) is a temporary cease-fire, or stop to warfare, usually preceding the signing of a treaty. Why did a new cynicism arise with the armistice of 1918? Underline the answer.

CONNECT

Pause at line 86. How would you describe the art and music that was created at the century's beginning?

_____

_____

_____

IDENTIFY

Pause at line 90. How were the arts of the twentieth century different from earlier forms? Underline this information.

WORD STUDY

The word *introspection* (line 93) comes from the Latin *intro–,* meaning "within," and *specere,* meaning "to see; to spy." *Introspection* means "looking into one's own mind or feelings."

IDENTIFY

Pause at line 112. Who was the most influential English-language writer of the early twentieth century? Why?

_____

_____

_____

_____

_____

_____

_____

_____

_____

_____

_____

_____

_____

_____

decade before, finally found an Irish publisher brave enough to publish it. All these works challenged traditional values of

90 beauty and order and opened new avenues of expression.

A Revolution in Literature

The novelists of the twentieth century moved from a concern with society to a focus on introspection. Some novelists, including Virginia Woolf, even rejected traditional chronological order in storytelling. Experimenting with the novel's structure, with a shifting point of view, and with a style called **stream of consciousness,** Woolf probed the human mind with the delicacy of a surgeon, examining all its shifts of moods and impressions.

In his novels, D. H. Lawrence was expressing his own strong
100 resentment against British society. Lawrence shocked the British with his glorification of the senses and his heated descriptions of relations between the sexes. His novel *Lady Chatterley's Lover* (1928), about an affair between an upper-class woman and her gamekeeper, is explicitly sexual, and its full publication was banned in England until 1960.

Most influential of all was the Irish poet and novelist James Joyce, whose controversial novel *Ulysses* appeared in 1922. In this retelling of the story of Odysseus's wanderings, Joyce drew on myth and symbol, on Freudian explorations of sexuality, and on
110 new conceptions of time and the workings of human consciousness. Literary critics called this experimentation with form and content **modernism.**

The Rise of Dictatorships: Origins of World War II

The Great War, which had been called a war to end all wars, ironically led to another war. A worldwide economic depression that began in 1929 gave rise to dictators in Germany, Italy, and Russia. In general, these dictatorial governments are called totalitarian, meaning that only one political party has control of the
120 state and all opposition is banned.

In Italy and Germany the form of totalitarianism that developed was **fascism,** a type of government that is rigidly nationalistic and that relies on the rule of a single dictator whose power is absolute and backed by force. Benito Mussolini, a fascist who came to power in Italy in 1922, held control through brutality and manipulation. Adolf Hitler and the Nazi party capitalized on Germany's economic woes to convince many Germans that their problems were caused by Jews, Communists, and immigrants.

130   Russia's totalitarian government, based on the political theories of the economist Karl Marx, was Communist. Its founder, Vladimir Lenin, had sought in the 1920s to create a society without a class system, one in which the state would distribute the country's wealth equally among the people. In reality, the new government became as repressive as the rule of the czars had been. After Lenin's death in 1924, Joseph Stalin took power. Under Stalin's rule, as many as fifteen million people were exiled to the gulag, or system of forced-labor and detention camps.

By 1939, the Nazis were sweeping through Europe. Hitler's
140   plan for the systematic destruction of the Jews and other minorities resulted in the deaths of millions of innocent men, women, and children—including the six million Jews who were killed in the Holocaust. In 1940, Germany defeated France and then prepared to invade Britain by launching devastating air attacks against London and other cities. Prime Minister Winston Churchill declared: "We shall go on to the end." The British *did* persevere, but only after the Soviet Union and the United States entered the war did Germany's defeat become inevitable. For Japan, which had allied itself with Germany and Italy, the war
150   ended in the ultimate horror. On August 6, 1945, the entire city of Hiroshima, Japan, was wiped out by a single atomic bomb dropped from an American plane. Small wonder, then, that much of the literature following the Second World War was dark and pessimistic.

INTERPRET

Why, according to lines 115–154, was the literature following World War II so dark and pessimistic?

IDENTIFY

Pause at line 164. Why couldn't Britain hold on to its colonies?

_____

_____

_____

_____

_____

_____

_____

_____

IDENTIFY

Re-read lines 166–169. What did the Angry Young Men criticize? Underline that information.

_____

_____

_____

_____

_____

_____

_____

_____

_____

_____

Britain After World War II: The End of an Empire

After the war ended in Europe, Winston Churchill and his Conservative party were defeated by the Labour party, and Britain was transformed into a welfare state. The government assumed
160 responsibility for providing medical care and other basic benefits for its citizens. While recovering from the war and rebuilding its own economy, Great Britain could not hold on to its many colonies. Most of them—including India, the "jewel in the crown"— became independent nations. The British Empire was gone.

British Writing Today

After the war a group of young novelists and playwrights emerged who became known as the Angry Young Men. These writers criticized the pretensions of intellectuals and the boring lives of the newly prosperous middle class. One of the major works of the
170 period was Kingsley Amis's novel *Lucky Jim* (1953), a scathing satire of British university life. Much of the work written in England since World War II is considered **postmodern** and often deals, either directly or indirectly, with issues of women's rights, multiculturalism, the environment, and nuclear destruction.

The Growth of World Literature: A Remarkable Diversity

Though our world isn't really a global village, innovations in technology and transportation have linked us in ways our ancestors couldn't have imagined. Ideas travel as fast as electronic
180 channels can carry them, and one writer may influence another writer living continents away. When important British, Asian, African, Middle Eastern, European, or Latin American writers publish in their native languages, translations are soon available for eager readers in other parts of the world.

Seeking Cultural Identity: Postcolonial Literature

Current world literature, more so than British literature of the past, frequently focuses on political and social problems. Literally hundreds of writers from former British colonies explore issues
190 of personal identity and the effects of cultural domination and racism. Literary critics call their work **postcolonial literature.** These writers have seen their local cultures uprooted by colonialism or foreign influence, and they have had to ask themselves whether they are to celebrate their native traditions, imitate foreign models, or create new modes of expression. Further complicating their situation is the spread of English around the world, resulting in a kind of linguistic dominance. To reach the largest literate audience, some writers from other countries often feel obligated to write in English even if English fails to convey
200 adequately the subtleties of their native language.

African Expressions

In Africa one response to colonial oppression of native cultures was a literary movement called **negritude,** which encouraged black writers to turn to precolonial African culture, art, and history as a source of inspiration and pride. Although some writers believed that negritude was a necessary response to years of imperialism, others, like the Nigerians Chinua Achebe and Wole Soyinka, felt that negritude tended to idealize or cloak Africa's precolonial past in nostalgia or innocence. They felt that
210 African literature must instead examine that past more critically and realistically. Soyinka quipped that "A tiger does not shout its tigritude." Though both Achebe and Soyinka write in English, Achebe has succeeded in grafting the oral tradition of Igbo storytellers and their idiom onto his novels.

IDENTIFY

Pause at line 191. What is postcolonial literature?

Haitian village scene (20th century) by Antoine Montas. Collection of Manu Sassoonian, New York.

CLARIFY

Pause at line 214. How do Achebe and Soyinka feel about the negritude movement?

INFER

Pause at line 231. Why do you think some writers may view India as a chaotic patchwork—"two worlds or ten"?

_____

_____

_____

_____

_____

_____

_____

_____

_____

_____

_____

_____

_____

_____

IDENTIFY

Pause at line 245. What has the Egyptian writer Naguib Mahfouz used his writing for? Underline this information.

Liberal white writers in Africa face another kind of identity crisis as they confront racism and social inequality. The South African writer Nadine Gordimer says, "One has an immense sense of shame." Several of Gordimer's novels are such powerful indictments of racist government policies that they have been

220   banned in her country.

"Two Worlds or Ten": Literature in India

In India, despite nearly one hundred years of British rule, English is only one of a diverse number of languages used by Indian writers. Two of the best known and established Indian novelists writing in English are R. K. Narayan and Anita Desai. Narayan is perhaps India's greatest modern fiction writer. His characters often reveal a sort of pluck or stubbornness that is peculiar to India. Desai, who excels at creating characters who must contend with an array of bewildering social forces vying

230   for their attention, speaks of the chaotic patchwork that is India as "two worlds or ten."

Other Postcolonial Explorations

The Nobel Prize winner V. S. Naipaul, from Britain's former West Indies colony of Trinidad, takes an unrelentingly satirical, pessimistic view of postcolonial nations. One of his characters sums up the raw struggle for existence in a developing nation: "We lack order. Above all we lack power, and we do not understand that we lack power."

The Egyptian novelist Naguib Mahfouz, who writes in

240   Arabic, helped to establish and perfect the Arabic novel. In such works as the *Cairo Trilogy,* this Nobel Prize–winning writer has used the novel form to depict the struggles of Egyptians expelling foreign invaders; he also uses his writing to criticize the social conditions, suffering, and spiritual emptiness in modern Egypt during and after British control.

Latin America and Magic Realism

In Latin America, writers have responded to their changing societies in different ways. The Chilean poet Pablo Neruda was greatly influenced by the modernist movement, but his epic work, *The Heights of Machu Picchu (Alturas de Machu Picchu)*, published in 1944, reconciles the poet to his country's ancient Indian heritage. The Mexican poet Octavio Paz writes about cultural questions involving the effect of history on the present in his country. The Argentine writer Jorge Luis Borges writes fiction that has stories within stories, character doubles, labyrinths, mysterious libraries filled with unreadable books, and parallel worlds that confuse and fascinate his narrators—all in the service of exploring the nature of time and reality. Borges's works, which he called *fantástico,* foreshadowed **magic realism,** a literary style that combines realistic details with incredible events recounted in a matter-of-fact tone. Magic realists hope to startle readers and create doubt in their perceptions of reality.

Women's Voices: A "Second Sex" No More

Political concerns in postwar world literature are not the sole domain of nations and cultures; one of the strongest voices to emerge in the postwar world is that of women.

Feminist writers dramatize women's lack of power in a world controlled by men. In the influential feminist work *The Second Sex* (1949), French author Simone de Beauvoir analyzes women's secondary status in society and denounces the male middle class for perceiving women as objects. The Nigerian feminist Buchi Emecheta has influenced numerous women writers from various African countries and uses motherhood (but not marriage) as a symbol for artistic creativity in her fiction. In *The Handmaid's Tale* (1985), the Canadian novelist Margaret Atwood serves up a grim cautionary tale, warning readers of a possible future by creating a world in which a puritanical dictatorship seeks to repress and control women.

IDENTIFY

What is **magic realism** (lines 258–262)? Underline the answer.

CLARIFY

Pause at line 278. What issues are dealt with by many women writers today?

IDENTIFY

Re-read lines 281–284. Why
has so much modern literature been a response to war
and repression?

_____

_____

_____

_____

_____

_____

_____

_____

_____

*Lone protestor standing
in front of tanks at
Tiananmen Square (1989).*

IDENTIFY

Pause at line 311. According
to Solzhenitsyn, what can art
and literature do? Underline
the answer.

Never Forget: Responses to War and Government Repression

280

Since the beginning of the twentieth century, world history has been marked by periods of widespread warfare interspersed with periods of uneasy peace. Not surprisingly, then, much of modern world literature has been a direct and blistering response to war. In *All Quiet on the Western Front* (1928), the German author Erich Maria Remarque described the physical and psychological horrors of World War I. This harrowing war novel paled beside the personal trauma of World War II's Holocaust as described by the Italian writer Primo Levi, interned at Auschwitz, and the

290

Romanian writer Elie Wiesel, who has spent a lifetime serving as a witness to the atrocities of the Holocaust. Few modern Japanese writers could avoid addressing World War II. Writers in the former Soviet Union—such as Aleksandr Solzhenitsyn and Anna Akhmatova—made an art out of defying government attempts to regulate their writing. Even though Communist China's government set out to "reeducate" its stubborn writers, some, like Ha Jin—who left China after seeing the Tiananmen Square massacre in 1989—explore the troubling, unequal relationships between the state and the individual.

300

A "Marvelous Capacity": The Promise of World Literature

In literature as in history, many different stories can proceed at the same time. Such a variety of writing can only broaden and deepen our understanding of the human condition. As Solzhenitsyn commented in his Nobel Prize acceptance speech, "The only substitute for what we ourselves have not experienced is art and literature. They have the marvelous capacity of trans-mitting from one nation to another—despite differences in language, customs, and social structure—practical experience,

310

the harsh national experience of many decades never tasted by the other nation."

The Hollow Men by T. S. Eliot

LITERARY FOCUS: ALLUSION

An **allusion** is a reference to a person, a place, an event, or a quotation from literature, history, mythology, politics, religion, sports, science, and so on. Readers must understand allusions in order to understand fully the meaning of a text. When writers make allusions, they expect readers to draw on their own knowledge and fill in the details.

Here are some of the allusions that T. S. Eliot uses in "The Hollow Men":

- The line right under the title, "Mistah Kurtz—he dead," is an allusion to the main character of Joseph Conrad's novel *Heart of Darkness.* Kurtz journeys to the interior of Africa and rapidly loses his humanity. This allusion sets a bleak tone for the poem.

- Eliot's next line, "A penny for the Old Guy," refers to the notorious Gunpowder Plot, an event from British history. On November 5, 1605, Guy Fawkes and others tried to kill King James I (and other leaders) by setting off an explosion in the cellar of the Parliament building. The plot failed, and Guy Fawkes was brutally executed.

  Even today, every November scarecrow-like images of Guy Fawkes (the "stuffed men" of the poem) are thrown into bonfires all over England. Children join the fun by carrying small "guys" and begging passersby to give them "a penny for the guy" so they can buy fireworks.

- "The Hollow Men" also contains allusions to Shakespeare's *The Tragedy of Julius Caesar* and to Dante's great epic *The Divine Comedy.* Be on the lookout, too, for an allusion to the Lord's Prayer and an allusion to a familiar children's rhyme.

READING SKILLS: ANALYZING PHILOSOPHICAL VIEWS

In 1923, Eliot wrote an essay that speaks of "the immense panorama of futility and anarchy which is contemporary history." This line expresses his philosophical view about the times in which he lived. He believed these times were marked by pointlessness ("futility") and lawlessness ("anarchy"). Occasionally, Eliot directly states his views about contemporary history. At other times you have to use evidence in his poems to infer his attitudes.

Use the Skill   As you read the poem, highlight or underline words, phrases, images, and allusions that reveal the nature of "the hollow men" and the world they live in. What inferences can you make about the hollow men and what they reflect about Eliot's opinion of human history?

Reading Standard 3.4 Analyze ways in which poets use figures of speech to evoke readers' emotions.

Reading Standard 3.9 Analyze the philosophical arguments presented in literary works to determine whether the authors' positions have contributed to the quality of each work and the credibility of the characters.

Reading Standard 3.7 (Grade 9–10 Review) Recognize and understand the significance of various literary devices, including figurative language, imagery, allegory, and symbolism, and explain their appeal.

The Hollow Men

T. S. Eliot

BACKGROUND
T. S. Eliot was one of the most influential poets of the twentieth century. Born in 1888 in St. Louis, Missouri, he spent most of his life in England. Eliot was a remote, disciplined, and self-possessed man who created the most influential poetry written in English over a span of three decades. He was also an editor, a critic, and a playwright. Eliot became internationally famous at an early age, and in 1948 he was awarded the Nobel Prize in literature. Not long before his death, in 1965, so many people wanted to see and hear him read his poetry that one reading was held in a football stadium.

Eliot published "The Hollow Men" in 1925. At the time, he believed that humanity was suffering from a loss of will and faith. The complex poem describes a world filled with despair and empty of religion or the promise of salvation.

INFER

Circle **images** in lines 1–10 that give you clues about the character of the hollow men. What does having a head-piece filled with straw tell you about the hollow men?
(Grade 9–10 Review)

_____

_____

_____

_____

_____

_____

_____

_____

Mistah Kurtz—he dead.

A penny for the Old Guy

I

We are the hollow men[1]

We are the stuffed men

Leaning together

Headpiece filled with straw. Alas!

5   Our dried voices, when

We whisper together

Are quiet and meaningless

---

1. **hollow men:** allusion to Shakespeare's *Julius Caesar* (Act IV, Scene 2, lines 23–27): "hollow men . . . sink in the trial" (that is, fail when put to the test).

As wind in dry grass

Or rats' feet over broken glass

10   In our dry cellar.

    Shape without form, shade without color,

Paralyzed force, gesture without motion;

    Those who have crossed

With direct eyes, to death's other Kingdom[2]

15   Remember us—if at all—not as lost

Violent souls, but only

As the hollow men

The stuffed men.

II

Eyes I dare not meet in dreams

20   In death's dream kingdom

These do not appear:

There, the eyes are

Sunlight on a broken column

There, is a tree swinging

25   And voices are

In the wind's singing

More distant and more solemn

Than a fading star.

    Let me be no nearer

30   In death's dream kingdom

Let me also wear

Such deliberate disguises

Rat's coat, crowskin, crossed staves[3]

In a field

---

2. **Those . . . Kingdom:** Those with "direct eyes" have crossed from the
   world of the hollow men into Paradise. The allusion is to Dante's
   Paradiso.
3. **staves** *n. pl.:* rods or staffs; "crossed staves / In a field" form a scarecrow.

FLUENCY

Read Section I of the poem aloud at least twice. Plan where you will pause and where you will make full stops. On your second reading, think about what mood you want to create in your reading.

INTERPRET

A **paradox** is an apparent contradiction that is actually true. Lines 11–12 list four paradoxes, one right after another. What does the paradox "paralyzed force" tell you about the hollow men?

_____

_____

_____

INTERPRET

In line 18, the speaker asks the reader to remember the hollow men as "stuffed men." How can hollow men also be "stuffed" men?

_____

_____

_____

_____

IDENTIFY

Re-read lines 19–28. Underline the **images** that help you see and hear "death's dream kingdom." *(Grade 9–10 Review)*

INTERPRET

Pause at line 38. Why does the speaker want to wear disguises and avoid "that final meeting / In the twilight kingdom"?

_____

_____

_____

IDENTIFY

Underline the **images** in lines 39–44 that describe the hollow men's world. *(Grade 9–10 Review)*

INTERPRET

The image of the star (line 44) is an **allusion** to Dante's use of a star to represent God. Why do you think Eliot refers to "a fading star" (line 44) and "dying stars" (line 54)? *(Grade 9–10 Review)*

_____

_____

_____

INTERPRET

Re-read lines 52–67. Underline the references to eyes and sight. Why is it fitting that the hollow men are also blind, or sightless?

_____

_____

_____

35   Behaving as the wind behaves
No nearer—

    Not that final meeting
In the twilight kingdom

III

This is the dead land
40   This is cactus land
Here the stone images
Are raised, here they receive
The supplication[4] of a dead man's hand
Under the twinkle of a fading star.

45   Is it like this
In death's other kingdom
Waking alone
At the hour when we are
Trembling with tenderness
50   Lips that would kiss
Form prayers to broken stone.

IV

The eyes are not here
There are no eyes here
In this valley of dying stars
55   In this hollow valley
This broken jaw of our lost kingdoms

---

4. **supplication** *n.:* humble plea.

In this last of meeting places

We grope together

And avoid speech

60   Gathered on this beach of the tumid river[5]

Sightless, unless

The eyes reappear

As the perpetual star

Multifoliate rose[6]

65   Of death's twilight kingdom

The hope only

Of empty men.

V

Here we go round the prickly pear[7]

Prickly pear prickly pear

70   *Here we go round the prickly pear*

At five o'clock in the morning.

Between the idea

And the reality

Between the motion

75   And the act[8]

Falls the Shadow

CONNECT

Pause at line 71. In the old rhyme, children dance around a mulberry bush, not a prickly pear. The mulberry bush was a traditional symbol of fertility. What makes going around a prickly pear—a cactus—so strange?

_____

_____

_____

_____

_____

_____

_____

_____

INTERPRET

Psalm 23 includes the line "Yea, though I walk through the valley of the shadow of death I will fear no evil." What might "the Shadow" be in lines 76, 82, and 90?

_____

_____

_____

_____

_____

_____

_____

5.   **tumid river:** Hell's swollen ("tumid") river, the Acheron (ak'ər·än'), in Dante's *Inferno.* The damned must cross this river to enter the land of the dead.

6.   **multifoliate rose:** Dante describes Paradise as a rose of many leaves (*Paradiso,* Canto 32).

7.   **prickly pear:** cactus.

8.   **between . . . act:** reference to Shakespeare's *Julius Caesar:* "Between the acting of a dreadful thing / And the first motion, all the interim is / Like a phantasma or a hideous dream" (Act II, Scene 1, lines 63–65).

Between the conception

And the creation

80   Between the emotion

And the response

Falls the Shadow

Life is very long

Between the desire

85   And the spasm

Between the potency[10]

And the existence

Between the essence

And the descent[11]

90   Falls the Shadow

For Thine is the Kingdom

For Thine is

Life is

For Thine is the

95   *This is the way the world ends*

This is the way the world ends

This is the way the world ends

Not with a bang but a whimper.

INTERPRET

The last four lines of the poem continue the **parody** of the children's rhyme. (The original words are "This is the way we clap our hands.") What does it mean for the world to end with a "whimper" instead of with a "bang"?

---

9. **For . . . Kingdom:** closing lines of the Lord's Prayer: "For thine is the kingdom, and the power, and the glory, forever and ever."

10. **potency** *n.:* strength; power.

11. **between . . . descent:** The Greek philosopher Plato defined "the essence" as an unattainable ideal and "the descent" as its imperfect expression in material or physical reality.

The Hollow Men

Reading Skills: Analyzing Philosophical Views   In "The Hollow Men," T. S. Eliot characterizes people of his time as "hollow." The chart below presents three general statements that express Eliot's philosophical views about the modern world. In the right-hand column, list at least three passages from the poem that support each generalization. When you've filled in the chart, complete the Evaluate exercise below.

Statements	Supporting Evidence from the Poem
Modern people do not think or feel, and language is meaningless.	
Modern people live in a sterile, meaningless world without love or religious faith.	
Modern people are powerless to take action.	

Evaluate   In your opinion, do the allusions in "The Hollow Men" add to the meaning and emotional impact of the poem, or do they make it more difficult to understand its ideas and theme?

_____

_____

_____

✓ Check your Standards Mastery at the back of this book.

Blood, Sweat, and Tears by Winston Churchill

LITERARY FOCUS: PERSUASION

Persuasion is the use of language to convince an audience to act or think in a certain way. Advertisers use persuasion to convince people to buy their products, and politicians use persuasion to convince people to vote for them. Famous examples of persuasion from American history include the Declaration of Independence and Patrick Henry's speech "Give me liberty, or give me death."

In "Blood, Sweat, and Tears," Winston Churchill uses the following **persuasive techniques** to convince the English people that they must be victorious in the war against Germany.

- **Logical appeals** offer facts and reasons as evidence to support an argument. Writers use logical appeals to demonstrate credibility, or reliability.

- **Emotional appeals** use rousing language that creates an emotional response in the audience.

- **Rhetorical devices,** such as repetition, word choice, and stirring calls to action, help arouse emotional responses.

READING SKILLS: IDENTIFYING AND CRITIQUING AN AUTHOR'S ARGUMENT

An **argument** is the series of persuasive details used to convince an audience to think or act in a certain way. Churchill begins his argument by listing the methodical, reasonable steps he has taken to form a new government during a time of war. He then appeals to his audience's emotions by using charged words such as *ordeal, struggle,* and *tyranny.*

Use the Skill   As you read the speech, highlight or underline words that build Churchill's argument. Then, decide which appeals he makes to reason (logic) and which he makes to emotion (feelings).

BLOOD, SWEAT, AND TEARS

Winston Churchill

BACKGROUND
When Hitler's army invaded Poland on September 1, 1939, World War II officially began. Two days later Britain declared war on Germany and began to manufacture weapons, ships, and planes. Over the next few months, Germany overran Holland and Belgium, and moved into France. By May 13, 1940, when Churchill gave this speech, it was clear that Germany's next target was Britain.

Churchill was the newly elected prime minister, or head of the British government (which is referred to as Parliament). He had just formed a new government that included all the political parties, even those that had opposed him. This speech, in which he addressed the Houses of Parliament, was broadcast on the radio. Churchill knew he had to unite the country to meet this terrible threat and inspire people to believe in their ability to survive and to triumph. No one who heard Churchill's radio speeches during the war ever forgot them.

On Friday evening last I received His Majesty's Commission[1] to form a new Administration. It was the evident wish and will of Parliament and the nation that this should be conceived on the broadest possible basis and that it should include all Parties, both those who supported the last Government and also the Parties of the Opposition.[2] I have completed the most important part of this task. A War Cabinet has been formed of five Members, representing, with the Opposition Liberals,[3] the unity of the nation. The three Party Leaders have agreed to serve, either in

Notes

1. **His Majesty's Commission:** The king at the time was George VI; after his party is elected, the Prime Minister is officially appointed by the monarch.
2. **Parties of the Opposition:** political parties in the parliament other than the one(s) making up the ruling administration.
3. **Opposition Liberals:** Churchill was a member of the Conservative Party; those belonging to the Liberal Party were in the opposition, not the government.

IDENTIFY

Re-read lines 11–18. Circle words and phrases that relate to the time and the sequence of Churchill's actions. Underline the reason he must move quickly.

IDENTIFY

Pause at line 29. Underline what Churchill wants his audience, the House, to approve.

ANALYZE

Re-read lines 19–29. Is Churchill using appeals to **logic** or appeals to **emotion**?

_____

_____

_____

_____

_____

VOCABULARY

rigor (rig′ər) *n.:* extreme severity.

provision (prə·vizh′ən) *n.:* arrangement or preparation beforehand.

grievous (grēv′əs) *adj.:* outrageous; horrible.

lamentable (lə·men′tə·bəl) *adj.:* regrettable; unfortunate.

buoyancy (boi′ən·sē) *n.:* lightness of spirit; cheerfulness.

Our Heritage (1943) by Robert Austin. The poster first appeared in the London Underground, or subway.
London Transit Museum.

10 the War Cabinet or in high executive office. The three Fighting Services have been filled. It was necessary that this should be done in one single day, on account of the extreme urgency and **rigor** of events. A number of other key positions were filled yesterday, and I am submitting a further list to His Majesty tonight. I hope to complete the appointment of the principal Ministers during tomorrow. The appointment of the other Ministers usually takes a little longer, but I trust that, when Parliament meets again, this part of my task will be complete in all respects.

I considered it in the public interest to suggest that the
20 House should be summoned to meet today. Mr. Speaker agreed, and took the necessary steps, in accordance with the powers conferred[4] upon him by the Resolution of the House. At the end of the proceedings today, the Adjournment of the House will be proposed until Tuesday, 21st May, with, of course, **provision** for earlier meeting if need be. The business to be considered during that week will be notified to Members at the earliest opportunity. I now invite the House, by the Resolution which stands in my name, to record its approval of the steps taken and to declare its confidence in the new Government.[5]

4. **conferred** *v.:* granted.
5. **the new Government:** the recently elected administration led by Churchill.

30   To form an Administration of this scale and complexity is a serious undertaking in itself, but it must be remembered that we are in the preliminary stage of one of the greatest battles in history, that we are in action at many points in Norway and in Holland, that we have to be prepared in the Mediterranean, that the air battle is continuous, and the many preparations have to be made here at home. In this crisis I hope I may be pardoned if I do not address the House at any length today. I hope that any of my friends and colleagues, or former colleagues, who are affected by the political reconstruction, will make all allowance for any lack

40   of ceremony with which it has been necessary to act. I would say to the House, as I said to those who have joined this Government: "I have nothing to offer but blood, toil, tears, and sweat."

    We have before us an ordeal of the most **grievous** kind. We have before us many, many long months of struggle and of suffering. You ask, What is our policy? I will say: "It is to wage war, by sea, land and air, with all our might and with all the strength that God can give us: to wage war against a monstrous tyranny, never surpassed in the dark, **lamentable** catalogue of human crime. That is our policy." You ask, What is our aim? I can answer

50   in one word: Victory—victory at all costs, victory in spite of all terror, victory however long and hard the road may be; for without victory there is no survival. Let that be realized; no survival for the British Empire; no survival for all that the British Empire has stood for; no survival for the urge and impulse of the ages, that mankind will move forward towards its goal. But I take up my task with **buoyancy** and hope. I feel sure that our cause will not be suffered to fail among men. At this time I feel entitled to claim the aid of all, and I say, "Come, then, let us go forward together with our united strength."

EVALUATE

How would you describe the **tone** of Churchill's remarks in this paragraph, particularly in lines 36–42? *(Grade 9–10 Review)*

_____

_____

_____

_____

_____

FLUENCY

Read the boxed passage aloud three times. Each time, increase the force and effectiveness of your delivery.

IDENTIFY

Churchill uses a rhetorical device called **parallelism,** the repetition of grammatical structures to emphasize key words and ideas. Re-read lines 43–59, and underline the repeated words and phrases.

ANALYZE

Re-read the final paragraph, in which Churchill uses **emotional appeals.** What powerful point does he make about the connection between "victory" and "survival"?

_____

_____

_____

Blood, Sweat, and Tears

Reading Skills: Identifying and Critiquing an Author's Argument   Look back over the **logical** and **emotional** appeals you highlighted or underlined in Churchill's speech. Use your notes to answer the questions in the chart below.

1. What appeals to reason or logic does Churchill use in the first two paragraphs of his speech?	
2. What appeals to feeling or emotion does Churchill use in the final paragraph? List words and phrases that carry strong emotional overtones.	
3. How does Churchill establish his credibility and strength as a leader?	
4. What is Churchill's purpose in this speech? Did you find his argument effective and convincing, or not?	

Blood, Sweat, and Tears

VOCABULARY IN CONTEXT

DIRECTIONS: Write a word from the Word Box in each blank to complete the paragraph below. Use each word only once.

Word Box

rigor

provision

grievous

lamentable

buoyancy

It is a sorry and (1) _____ fact that nations often resort to war to achieve their goals. During World War II, Germany launched invasions and made (2) _____ attacks upon neighboring countries. Winston Churchill recognized the threat to England and made suitable (3) _____ for his country to protect itself. He knew that victory would require extreme discipline and (4) _____, but that the English people would unite and face the challenges ahead with great (5) _____ of spirit.

ANALOGIES

In an **analogy,** the words in one pair relate to each other in the same way as the words in a second pair. Two of the most common relationships used in analogies are **synonyms** (words having similar meanings) and **antonyms** (words having opposite meanings). In the analogy below, for example, the words in each pair are synonyms. Read each colon (:) as "is to" and the double colon (::) as "as." The sequence below therefore translates to "*harsh* is to *severe* as *opulent* is to *lavish.*"

HARSH : SEVERE :: opulent : lavish

DIRECTIONS: Study each incomplete analogy below to determine whether the word pairs are synonyms and antonyms. Then, fill each blank with the appropriate word from the Word Box above.

1. TERROR : DREAD :: cheerfulness : _____

2. HAPPY : SAD :: laziness : _____

3. ACTIVE : PASSIVE :: admirable : _____

4. FAME : RENOWN :: outrageous : _____

5. HOPE : OPTIMISM :: preparation : _____

Reading Standard 1.3 Discern the meaning of analogies encountered, analyzing specific comparisons as well as relationships and inferences.

 Check your Standards Mastery at the back of this book.

In the Shadow of War by Ben Okri

LITERARY FOCUS: POINT OF VIEW

Point of view is the vantage point from which a story is told. Ben Okri uses a point of view called **limited third person,** in which the narrator, who is outside the story, tells the story from the vantage point of only one character, a boy named Omovo. Thus, the point of view helps us see war not as an adult would, but through the eyes of a child.

Through Omovo's eyes, we learn that war is frightening and confusing. Our challenge as readers is to balance the child's perspective with other things we know about war and about human behavior. It's up to us to decide whether the soldiers are good or bad, and what the veiled woman is really doing. By limiting the viewpoint to that of a child, Okri deepens the mysteries and uncertainties of life during wartime.

READING SKILLS: MAKING PREDICTIONS

Instead of factual information about where and when the story takes place, we are given a vivid picture of what the child, Omovo, sees and hears. Early in the story, we read about Omovo's impressions of the soldiers, of his father's words, and of a woman in a yellow dress. Use these details to make **predictions** about what might happen to the story's characters. Here are some questions you might ask yourself:

- Should Omovo treat any characters with suspicion?
- Which characters seem to present the most danger, and to whom?
- Which details provide clues about things Omovo can observe but cannot fully understand?

Use the Skill   As you read the story, jot down your predictions. Highlight or underline details that helped you make your predictions. Be prepared to change your predictions, if necessary, while you read.

IN THE SHADOW OF WAR

Ben Okri

BACKGROUND

This story takes place during the Nigerian Civil War (1967–1970). Nigeria gained its independence from Great Britain in 1960, but because the population is made up of more than 250 different ethnic or tribal groups, Nigeria had trouble forming a stable government. In 1966, a bitter civil war broke out when the Hausa-Fulani people established a military power. Another major group, the Ibo people, declared their region an independent republic, which they called Biafra. Thousands were killed or starved to death before the Biafrans surrendered in 1970. For many people during those years, the very mention of Biafra conjured up horrible images of starving children with swollen bellies.

That afternoon three soldiers came to the village. They scattered the goats and chickens. They went to the palm-frond bar and ordered a calabash[1] of palm wine. They drank amidst the flies.

Omovo watched them from the window as he waited for his father to go out. They both listened to the radio. His father had bought the old Grundig[2] cheaply from a family that had to escape the city when the war broke out. He had covered the radio with a white cloth and made it look like a household fetish.[3] They listened to the news of bombings and air raids in the interior of the country. His father combed his hair, parted it carefully, and slapped some after-shave on his unshaven face. Then he struggled into the shabby coat that he had long outgrown.

IDENTIFY

Pause at line 3. Who arrives in the village on the day the story begins?

_____

_____

_____

_____

_____

_____

_____

_____

_____

INFER

Re-read lines 13–17. Circle details that describe the woman and her actions. Why does Omovo wait for her to appear?

_____

_____

_____

PREDICT

Re-read lines 18–30. Underline what the radio announcer says will happen that night. Make a **prediction** about what might take place. Circle details that helped you make your prediction.

_____

_____

_____

_____

INFER

What do you learn about the father's **character** in lines 18–40?

_____

_____

_____

_____

_____

_____

_____

Omovo stared out of the window, irritated with his father. At that hour, for the past seven days, a strange woman with a black veil over her head had been going past the house. She went up the village paths, crossed the Express road, and disappeared into the forest. Omovo waited for her to appear.

The main news was over. The radio announcer said an eclipse of the moon was expected that night. Omovo's father
20 wiped the sweat off his face with his palm and said, with some bitterness:

"As if an eclipse will stop this war."

"What is an eclipse?" Omovo asked.

"That's when the world goes dark and strange things happen."

"Like what?"

His father lit a cigarette.

"The dead start to walk about and sing. So don't stay out late, eh."

Omovo nodded.
30 "Heclipses hate children. They eat them."

Omovo didn't believe him. His father smiled, gave Omovo his ten kobo[4] allowance, and said:

"Turn off the radio. It's bad for a child to listen to news of war."

Omovo turned it off. His father poured a libation[5] at the doorway and then prayed to his ancestors. When he had finished he picked up his briefcase and strutted out briskly. Omovo watched him as he threaded his way up the path to the bus stop at the main road. When a danfo bus[6] came, and his father went
40 with it, Omovo turned the radio back on. He sat on the window-sill and waited for the woman. The last time he saw her she had glided past with agitated flutters of her yellow smock. The children stopped what they were doing and stared at her. They had said that she had no shadow. They had said that her feet

---

4. **kobo** (käb′ō) *n.:* Nigerian monetary unit.
5. **libation** (lī·bā′shən): liquid poured onto the ground as a sacrifice to the gods.
6. **danfo bus:** small bus. In the region surrounding Lagos, *danfo* means "in disrepair."

never touched the ground. As she went past, the children began to throw things at her. She didn't flinch, didn't quicken her pace, and didn't look back.

The heat was **stupefying.** Noises dimmed and lost their edges. The villagers stumbled about their various tasks as if they
50 were sleepwalking. The three soldiers drank palm wine and played draughts[7] beneath the sun's **oppressive** glare. Omovo noticed that whenever children went past the bar the soldiers called them, talked to them, and gave them some money. Omovo ran down the stairs and slowly walked past the bar. The soldiers stared at him. On his way back one of them called him.

"What's your name?" he asked.

Omovo hesitated, smiled mischievously, and said:

"Heclipse."

The soldier laughed, spraying Omovo's face with spit. He had
60 a face crowded with veins. His companions seemed uninterested. They swiped flies and concentrated on their game. Their guns were on the table. Omovo noticed that they had numbers on them. The man said:

"Did your father give you that name because you have big lips?"

His companions looked at Omovo and laughed. Omovo nodded.

"You are a good boy," the man said. He paused. Then he asked, in a different voice:
70 "Have you seen that woman who covers her face with a black cloth?"

"No."

The man gave Omovo ten kobo and said:

"She is a spy. She helps our enemies. If you see her, come and tell us at once, you hear?"

Omovo refused the money and went back upstairs. He repositioned himself on the windowsill. The soldiers occasionally looked at him. The heat got to him and soon he fell asleep in a

---

7. **draughts** (drafts) *n.:* British game of checkers.

IDENTIFY

Underline details that describe the woman from the **point of view** of Omovo and the other children (lines 40–47). How do the children treat her?

_____

_____

_____

VOCABULARY

stupefying (stoo′pə·fī′iŋ) *adj.:* dulling the mind and senses; bringing on a state of lethargy, or great drowsiness and lack of energy.

oppressive (ə·pres′iv) *adj.:* hard to bear.

INFER

Re-read lines 50–76. From what Omovo notices about the soldiers and from his behavior in this scene, what can you tell about his feelings toward them?

_____

_____

_____

_____

_____

_____

_____

succumbed (sə·kumd') *v.:*
yielded; gave way to.

Re-read lines 85–100.
Underline details that
describe the soldiers, and
circle details that describe
the woman. How do you
think Omovo feels about
the woman?

_____

_____

_____

_____

_____

ostentatious (äs'ten·tā'shəs)
adj.: showy.

Underline details that describe
the scene that Omovo comes
upon (lines 101–105) but is
not able to fully understand.
What do these details suggest
about what is going on in
the area Omovo is walking
through? *(Grade 9–10
Review)*

_____

_____

_____

_____

_____

80

90

100

110

sitting position. The cocks, crowing dispiritedly, woke him up.
He could feel the afternoon softening into evening. The soldiers
dozed in the bar. The hourly news came on. Omovo listened
without comprehension to the day's casualties. The announcer
succumbed to the stupor, yawned, apologized, and gave further
details of the fighting.

Omovo looked up and saw that the woman had already
gone past. The men had left the bar. He saw them weaving
between the eaves of the thatch houses, stumbling through the
heat-mists. The woman was further up the path. Omovo ran
downstairs and followed the men. One of them had taken off
his uniform top. The soldier behind had buttocks so big they
had begun to split his pants. Omovo followed them across the
Express road. When they got into the forest the men stopped
following the woman, and took a different route. They seemed
to know what they were doing. Omovo hurried to keep the
woman in view.

He followed her through the dense vegetation. She wore
faded wrappers and a gray shawl, with the black veil covering
her face. She had a red basket on her head. He completely forgot
to determine if she had a shadow, or whether her feet touched
the ground.

He passed unfinished estates, with their flaking, **ostentatious**
signboards and their collapsing fences. He passed an empty
cement factory: Blocks lay crumbled in heaps and the workers'
sheds were deserted. He passed a baobab[8] tree, under which was
the intact skeleton of a large animal. A snake dropped from a
branch and slithered through the undergrowth. In the distance,
over the cliff edge, he heard loud music and people singing war
slogans above the noise.

He followed the woman till they came to a rough camp on
the plain below. Shadowy figures moved about in the half-light
of the cave. The woman went to them. The figures surrounded
her and touched her and led her into the cave. He heard their

---

8. **baobab** (bā'ō·bab') *n.:* thick-trunked African tree; often called
"upside-down tree" because its branches look like roots.

weary voices thanking her. When the woman reappeared she was without the basket. Children with kwashiorkor[9] stomachs and women wearing rags led her halfway up the hill. Then, reluctantly, touching her as if they might not see her again, they went back.

He followed her till they came to a muddied river. She moved as if an invisible force were trying to blow her away. Omovo saw capsized canoes and trailing, waterlogged clothes on the dark water. He saw floating items of sacrifice: loaves of bread in polythene[10] wrappings, gourds of food, Coca-Cola cans. When he looked at the canoes again they had changed into the shapes of swollen dead animals. He saw outdated currencies on the riverbank. He noticed the terrible smell in the air. Then he heard the sound of heavy breathing from behind him, then someone coughing and spitting. He recognized the voice of one of the soldiers urging the others to move faster. Omovo crouched in the shadow of a tree. The soldiers strode past. Not long afterward he heard a scream. The men had caught up with the woman. They crowded round her.

"Where are the others?" shouted one of them.

The woman was silent.

"You dis witch! You want to die, eh? Where are they?"

She stayed silent. Her head was bowed. One of the soldiers coughed and spat toward the river.

"Talk! Talk!" he said, slapping her.

The fat soldier tore off her veil and threw it to the ground. She bent down to pick it up and stopped in the attitude of kneeling, her head still bowed. Her head was bald, and disfigured with a deep corrugation.[11] There was a livid gash along the side of her face. The bare-chested soldier pushed her. She fell on her face and lay still. The lights changed over the forest and for the first

---

9. **kwashiorkor** (kwä′shē·ôr′kôr′): severe disease of young children, caused by deficiency of protein and calories and marked by stunted growth and a protruding belly.
10. **polythene** (päl′i·thēn′): term used in most English-speaking countries other than the United States for *polyethylene* (päl′ē·eth′ə·lēn′), a synthetic substance used to make tough, lightweight plastics, films, and the like.
11. **corrugation** (kôr′ə·gā′shən) *n.:* groove or furrow.

INFER

What can you infer about why the woman has been going into the forest (lines 109–116)?

_____

_____

_____

_____

_____

_____

_____

_____

_____

FLUENCY

Read the boxed passage aloud at least twice. With each reading, try to bring to life the **imagery** that describes what Omovo is seeing. Look for clues that explain what the "capsized canoes" and "swollen dead animals" might really be.

WORD STUDY

"You dis witch!" (line 133) is dialect, possibly meaning "You're this witch." The word *eh* (line 133) means, roughly, "right?" Nigeria is a former British colony, and use of this British term there would be fairly common.

PREDICT

Pause at line 145. Circle the lines that explain what Omovo really saw earlier. What might happen next?

_____

_____

_____

_____

VOCABULARY

dementedly (dē·ment′id·lē) _adv.:_ madly; wildly.

EVALUATE

The **point of view** of this story allows us to see and hear only what Omovo sees and hears. What effect does this point of view have on you? _(Grade 9–10 Review)_

_____

_____

_____

_____

INTERPRET

At the end of the story, why is Omovo's father so friendly toward the soldiers?

_____

_____

_____

_____

time Omovo saw that the dead animals on the river were in fact the corpses of grown men. Their bodies were tangled with river-weed and their eyes were bloated. Before he could react, he heard another scream. The woman was getting up, with the veil in her hand. She turned to the fat soldier, drew herself to her fullest height, and spat in his face. Waving the veil in the air, she began to howl **dementedly.** The two other soldiers backed away.

150 The fat soldier wiped his face and lifted the gun to the level of her stomach. A moment before Omovo heard the shot a violent beating of wings just above him scared him from his hiding place. He ran through the forest screaming. The soldiers tramped after him. He ran through a mist which seemed to have risen from the rocks. As he ran he saw an owl staring at him from a canopy of leaves. He tripped over the roots of a tree and blacked out when his head hit the ground.

When he woke up it was very dark. He waved his fingers in front of his face and saw nothing. Mistaking the darkness for

160 blindness he screamed, thrashed around, and ran into a door. When he recovered from his shock he heard voices outside and the radio crackling on about the war. He found his way to the balcony, full of wonder that his sight had returned. But when he got there he was surprised to find his father sitting on the sunken cane chair, drinking palm wine with the three soldiers. Omovo rushed to his father and pointed frantically at the three men.

"You must thank them," his father said. "They brought you back from the forest."

Omovo, overcome with delirium, began to tell his father

170 what he had seen. But his father, smiling apologetically at the soldiers, picked up his son and carried him off to bed.

In the Shadow of War

Reading Skills: Making Predictions   Look back over the story details that helped you make predictions. In the first column of the chart, cite three predictions you made. In the second column, list the details on which you based your predictions. In the final column, explain which predictions were correct and which you had to revise as you read on.

My Predictions	Details from the Story	Correct or Needed Revising?

In the Shadow of War

VOCABULARY IN CONTEXT

DIRECTIONS: Write a word from the Word Box in each blank to complete each sentence. Use each word only once.

Word Box

stupefying

oppressive

succumbed

ostentatious

dementedly

1. Because of the _____ military regime, people could not come and go freely.

2. The effect of the heat in the small room was so _____ I could not think clearly.

3. During the epidemic, thousands _____ to the virus.

4. The unhappy child howled _____, as if she were crazy.

5. The people trying to impress the boss made an _____ display of their wealth.

ANGLO-SAXON AFFIXES

Many English words contain word parts that come from Anglo-Saxon, or Old English. Learning Anglo-Saxon **affixes** can help you discover the meaning of unfamiliar words.

Anglo-Saxon Affixes	Meanings	Examples
a–	in; on; of; up; to	ashore; aside
un–	not; the opposite of	untrue; unknown
–ness	quality; state	kindness; tenderness

DIRECTIONS: Using the information in the chart and context clues, write the meaning of each boldface word.

1. "They drank **amidst** the flies."

   _____

2. "His father . . . slapped some after-shave on his **unshaven** face."

   _____

3. "Omovo's father . . . said, with some **bitterness**: 'As if an eclipse will stop this war.'"

   _____

Reading Standard 1.2
Apply knowledge of Greek, Latin, and Anglo-Saxon roots and affixes to draw inferences concerning the meaning of scientific and mathematical terminology.

 Check your Standards Mastery at the back of this book.

Shakespeare's Sister by Virginia Woolf

BEFORE YOU READ

LITERARY FOCUS: ESSAY

An **essay** is a short piece of nonfiction writing that examines a single subject from a limited point of view. Formal essays are usually serious in tone, full of facts, and tightly organized. **Informal essays,** on the other hand, clearly reflect the beliefs, feelings, and attitudes of the author. Their language and structure are more casual and informal, and their tone may be humorous. Despite their informality, informal essays like this one by Virginia Woolf often deal with controversial issues or serious subjects.

READING SKILLS: IDENTIFYING THE AUTHOR'S BELIEFS

Woolf's essay presents thought-provoking ideas about an aspect of society that she found very troubling: gender differences. The essay analyzes the gender differences Woolf sees in her own world and in the world of Shakespeare, 350 years earlier. Woolf is not concerned with the obvious biological differences between men and women. Instead, she focuses on cultural realities—the gender roles that society as a whole views as normal or acceptable.

In "Shakespeare's Sister," Woolf imagines that Shakespeare had a talented sister, a literary genius like her famous brother. What would have become of the talented woman of that time?

Use the Skill   As you read the essay, watch for beliefs that Woolf states directly and other beliefs that she only hints at. Each time you identify one of Woolf's convictions or opinions, write it in the list below. (You may discover fewer than five beliefs, or more than five.) When you are finished, place a check mark next to the belief you think is central to the essay.

Virginia Woolf believes that . . .
1.
2.
3.
4.
5.

As you read "Shakespeare's Sister," think about Virginia Woolf's tone.

TONE
The attitude a writer takes toward the reader, a subject, or a character. Tone is conveyed through the writer's choice of words and details.

Reading Standard 2.5 Analyze an author's implicit and explicit philosophical assumptions and beliefs about a subject.

Reading Standard 2.8 (Grade 9–10 Review) Evaluate the credibility of an author's argument or defense of a claim by critiquing the relationship between generalizations and evidence, the comprehensiveness of evidence, and the way in which the author's intent affects the structure and tone of the text (e.g., in professional journals, editorials, political speeches, primary source material).

Shakespeare's Sister

from A Room of One's Own

Virginia Woolf

BACKGROUND

In 1929, Virginia Woolf published a collection of essays called *A Room of One's Own,* from which this essay is taken. In it, Woolf uncovers forgotten women writers and reveals how gender affects subjects, themes, and even style.

Woolf begins this essay by asking questions about the lives of women in sixteenth-century England, when Elizabeth I was on the throne, a period known as the Elizabethan Age. It was also the age of Shakespeare, when men were writing some of the most important plays and poems in the English language. Why then, asks Woolf, were women not writing poetry, too?

IDENTIFY

Re-read lines 1–14. Underline the facts that lead Woolf to conclude it would have been "extremely odd" (line 9) for women to have written the plays of Shakespeare.

INFER

What belief is implied in the "old gentleman's" statement that it is "impossible for any woman . . . to have the genius of Shakespeare" (lines 12–14)?

_____

_____

_____

_____

_____

Here am I asking why women did not write poetry in the Elizabethan age, and I am not sure how they were educated; whether they were taught to write; whether they had sitting rooms to themselves; how many women had children before they were twenty-one; what, in short, they did from eight in the morning till eight at night. They had no money evidently; according to Professor Trevelyan[1] they were married whether they liked it or not before they were out of the nursery, at fifteen or sixteen very likely. It would have been extremely odd, even

10 upon this showing, had one of them suddenly written the plays of Shakespeare, I concluded, and I thought of that old gentleman, who is dead now, but was a bishop, I think, who declared that it was impossible for any woman, past, present, or to come, to have the genius of Shakespeare. He wrote to the papers about it. He

---

1. **Professor Trevelyan:** G. M. Trevelyan, author of *The History of England* (1926).

also told a lady who applied to him for information that cats do not as a matter of fact go to heaven, though they have, he added, souls of a sort. How much thinking those old gentlemen used to save one! How the borders of ignorance shrank back at their approach! Cats do not go to heaven. Women cannot write the plays of Shakespeare.

Be that as it may, I could not help thinking, as I looked at the works of Shakespeare on the shelf, that the bishop was right at least in this; it would have been impossible, completely and entirely, for any woman to have written the plays of Shakespeare in the age of Shakespeare. Let me imagine, since facts are so hard to come by, what would have happened had Shakespeare had a wonderfully gifted sister, called Judith, let us say. Shakespeare himself went, very probably—his mother was an heiress—to the grammar school, where he may have learnt Latin—Ovid, Virgil, and Horace—and the elements of grammar and logic. He was, it is well known, a wild boy who poached rabbits, perhaps shot a deer, and had, rather sooner than he should have done, to marry a woman in the neighborhood, who bore him a child rather quicker than was right. That escapade sent him to seek his fortune in London. He had, it seemed, a taste for the theater; he began by holding horses at the stage door. Very soon he got work in the theater, became a successful actor, and lived at the hub of the universe, meeting everybody, knowing everybody, practicing his art on the boards, exercising his wits in the streets, and even getting access to the palace of the queen. Meanwhile his extraordinarily gifted sister, let us suppose, remained at home. She was as adventurous, as imaginative, as agog to see the world as he was. But she was not sent to school. She had no chance of learning grammar and logic, let alone of reading Horace and Virgil. She picked up a book now and then, one of her brother's perhaps, and read a few pages. But then her parents came in and told her to mend the stockings or mind the stew and not moon about with books and papers. They would

ANALYZE

Re-read lines 14–20, in which Woolf discredits the opinions of the bishop. How would you describe the **tone** of this passage? *(Grade 9–10 Review)*

_____

_____

_____

INTERPRET

Re-read lines 21–25. Underline the statement in which Woolf agrees with the bishop in one respect. Then, based on the facts you underlined in the first paragraph, tell why Woolf agrees.

_____

_____

_____

_____

IDENTIFY

Pause at line 27. What imaginary person does Woolf conjure up? Circle that information.

COMPARE & CONTRAST

Re-read lines 41–48. How did Judith's education compare to her brother's? Underline that information. Circle the jobs that her parents would have expected her to do.

Pause at line 62. Woolf
speculates that Judith didn't
want to hurt her father, but
that a powerful reason
caused her to leave home.
State the reason in your
own words.

_____

_____

_____

_____

_____

_____

_____

_____

_____

_____

_____

_____

_____

_____

_____

_____

CLARIFY

Woolf imagines that Shakespeare's sister met a tragic
fate after she went up to
London to seek her fortune
(lines 76–83). Underline what
happened to her.

have spoken sharply but kindly, for they were substantial people
who knew the conditions of life for a woman and loved their
daughter—indeed, more likely than not she was the apple of
her father's eye. Perhaps she scribbled some pages up in an apple
loft on the sly, but was careful to hide them or set fire to them.
Soon, however, before she was out of her teens, she was to be
betrothed to the son of a neighboring wool stapler.[2] She cried
out that marriage was hateful to her, and for that she was severely
beaten by her father. Then he ceased to scold her. He begged her
instead not to hurt him, not to shame him in this matter of her
marriage. He would give her a chain of beads or a fine petticoat,
he said; and there were tears in his eyes. How could she disobey
him? How could she break his heart? The force of her own gift
alone drove her to it. She made up a small parcel of her belong-
ings, let herself down by a rope one summer's night, and took
the road to London. She was not seventeen. The birds that sang
in the hedge were not more musical than she was. She had the
quickest fancy, a gift like her brother's, for the tune of words.
Like him, she had a taste for the theater. She stood at the stage
door; she wanted to act, she said. Men laughed in her face. The
manager—a fat, loose-lipped man—guffawed. He bellowed
something about poodles dancing and women acting—no
woman, he said, could possibly be an actress. He hinted—you
can imagine what. She could get no training in her craft. Could
she even seek her dinner in a tavern or roam the streets at midnight? Yet her genius was for fiction and lusted to feed abun-
dantly upon the lives of men and women and the study of their
ways. At last—for she was very young, oddly like Shakespeare
the poet in her face, with the same gray eyes and rounded
brows—at last Nick Greene the actor-manager took pity on her;
she found herself with child by that gentleman and so—who
shall measure the heat and violence of the poet's heart when
caught and tangled in a woman's body?—killed herself one

---

2. **wool stapler:** dealer in wool, a product sorted according to its fiber,
   or "staple."

winter's night and lies buried at some crossroads where the omnibuses now stop outside the Elephant and Castle.[3]

That, more or less, is how the story would run, I think, if a woman in Shakespeare's day had had Shakespeare's genius. But for my part, I agree with the deceased bishop, if such he was— it is unthinkable that any woman in Shakespeare's day should have had Shakespeare's genius. For genius like Shakespeare's is not born among laboring, uneducated, **servile** people. It was

90 not born in England among the Saxons and the Britons. It is not born today among the working classes. How, then, could it have been born among women whose work began, according to Professor Trevelyan, almost before they were out of the nursery, who were forced to it by their parents and held to it by all the power of law and custom? Yet genius of a sort must have existed among women as it must have existed among the working classes. Now and again an Emily Brontë or a Robert Burns blazes out and proves its presence. But certainly it never got itself onto paper. When, however, one reads of a witch being

100 ducked, of a woman possessed by devils, of a wise woman selling herbs, or even of a very remarkable man who had a mother, then I think we are on the track of a lost novelist, a **suppressed** poet, of some mute and inglorious[4] Jane Austen, some Emily Brontë who dashed her brains out on the moor or mopped and mowed about the highways crazed with the torture that her gift had put her to. Indeed, I would venture to guess that Anon, who wrote so many poems without signing them, was often a woman. It was a woman Edward Fitzgerald,[5] I think, suggested who made the ballads and the folk songs, crooning

110 them to her children, beguiling her spinning with them, or the length of the winter's night.

---

3. **buried . . . Elephant and Castle:** Suicides, who were for years not permitted church burials, were commonly buried at a crossroads as a kind of punishment, perhaps to ensure that their souls would wander forever. The Elephant and Castle is a pub at a busy crossroads in south London.
4. **mute and inglorious:** allusion to line 59 of Thomas Gray's poem "Elegy Written in a Country Churchyard."
5. **Edward Fitzgerald** (1809–1883): English translator and poet.

VOCABULARY

servile (sur′vīl) *adj.:* like or characteristic of a slave; submissive; yielding.

suppressed (sə·prest′) *v.* used as *adj.:* kept from being known.

INTERPRET

Pause at line 98. Woolf mentions the English novelist and poet Emily Brontë and the Scottish poet Robert Burns (line 97), who was a farmer. What belief of Woolf's do these two examples support? Underline that information.

WORD STUDY

Anon (line 107) is an abbreviation for *anonymous,* which comes from the Greek *an–,* meaning "without," and *onyma,* meaning "name." Works of literature for which the name of the author is unknown or withheld carry the word *anonymous* to designate unknown authorship.

FLUENCY

Read the boxed passage aloud twice. Woolf's style in this informal essay is easier to understand when you hear it aloud. Note the long, conversational sentences that contain side remarks set off by dashes or commas. Try to capture Woolf's biting, critical **tone** as well as her meaning. *(Grade 9–10 Review)*

PARAPHRASE

What does Woolf say is "true" in her story (lines 112–127)? Restate it in your own words.

_____

_____

_____

_____

_____

_____

_____

_____

_____

_____

IDENTIFY

Re-read lines 134–138. If a woman in the sixteenth century had survived and written, what two things does Woolf say would have been true of her writing? Underline them.

This may be true or it may be false—who can say?—but what is true in it, so it seemed to me, reviewing the story of Shakespeare's sister as I had made it, is that any woman born with a great gift in the sixteenth century would certainly have gone crazed, shot herself, or ended her days in some lonely cottage outside the village, half witch, half wizard, feared and mocked at. For it needs little skill in psychology to be sure that a highly gifted girl who had tried to use her gift for poetry would have

120   been so thwarted and hindered by other people, so tortured and pulled asunder by her own contrary instincts, that she must have lost her health and sanity to a certainty. No girl could have walked to London and stood at a stage door and forced her way into the presence of actor-managers without doing herself a violence and suffering an anguish which may have been irrational—for chastity may be a fetish invented by certain societies for unknown reasons—but were nonetheless inevitable. Chastity had then, it has even now, a religious importance in a woman's life, and has so wrapped itself round with nerves and

130   instincts that to cut it free and bring it to the light of day demands courage of the rarest. To have lived a free life in London in the sixteenth century would have meant for a woman who was poet and playwright a nervous stress and dilemma which might well have killed her. Had she survived, whatever she had written would have been twisted and deformed, issuing from a strained and morbid imagination. And undoubtedly, I thought, looking at the shelf where there are no plays by women, her work would have gone unsigned. That refuge she would have sought certainly. It was the relic of the sense of chastity that dictated anonymity

140   to women even so late as the nineteenth century. Currer Bell, George Eliot, George Sand,[6] all the victims of inner strife as their writings prove, sought ineffectively to veil themselves by

---

6. **Currer Bell, George Eliot, George Sand:** male pseudonyms for the female writers Charlotte Brontë, Mary Ann Evans, and Amantine-Aurore-Lucile Dupin.

using the name of a man. Thus they did homage to the convention, which if not implanted by the other sex was liberally encouraged by them (the chief glory of a woman is not to be talked of, said Pericles,[7] himself a much-talked-of man), that publicity in women is detestable. Anonymity runs in their blood. The desire to be veiled still possesses them. They are not even now as concerned about the health of their fame as men are,

150 and, speaking generally, will pass a tombstone or a signpost without feeling an irresistible desire to cut their names on it, as Alf, Bert, or Chas. must do in obedience to their instinct, which murmurs if it sees a fine woman go by, or even a dog, *Ce chien est à moi.*[8] And, of course, it may not be a dog, I thought, remembering Parliament Square, the Sieges Allee,[9] and other avenues; it may be a piece of land or a man with curly black hair. It is one of the great advantages of being a woman that one can pass even a very fine negress without wishing to make an Englishwoman of her.

160 That woman, then, who was born with a gift of poetry in the sixteenth century, was an unhappy woman, a woman at strife against herself. All the conditions of her life, all her own instincts, were hostile to the state of mind which is needed to set free whatever is in the brain. But what is the state of mind that is most **propitious** to the act of creation, I asked. Can one come by any notion of the state that furthers and makes possible that strange activity? Here I opened the volume containing the Tragedies of Shakespeare. What was Shakespeare's state of mind, for instance, when he wrote *Lear* and *Antony and Cleopatra*? It

170 was certainly the state of mind most favorable to poetry that there has ever existed. But Shakespeare himself said nothing about it. We only know casually and by chance that he "never blotted a line." Nothing indeed was ever said by the artist

---

7. **Pericles** (c. 495–429 B.C.): Athenian legislator and general.
8. *Ce chien est à moi* (sə shē·en′ ät ä mwä): French for "This dog is mine."
9. **Sieges Allee** (zē′gəs ä·lā′): busy thoroughfare in Berlin. The name—more commonly written as one word, *Siegesallee*—is German for "Avenue of Victory."

ANALYZE

Pause at line 159. What impulse in regard to "fame" does Woolf attribute to men but not to women?

_____

_____

_____

VOCABULARY

propitious (prō·pish′əs) *adj.:* favorable.

IDENTIFY

Pause at line 167. Draw a box around the questions that Woolf now begins to explore.

WORD STUDY

"Never blotted a line" (lines 172–173) refers to the use of pens filled from ink wells. Back in Shakespeare's day, people made corrections not by erasing but by covering mistakes with blots, or globs, of ink. What does this reference tell you about Shakespeare's writing process?

_____

_____

_____

_____

VOCABULARY

prodigious (prō·dij′əs) *adj.:* enormous.

notorious (nō·tôr′ē·əs) *adj.:* widely but unfavorably known; infamous.

ANALYZE

Re-read lines 186–204. Circle the "material circumstances" (line 190) that hinder or go against a writer's act of creation. What general belief about writing a work of genius does Woolf express here?

_____

_____

_____

_____

_____

_____

_____

_____

_____

_____

_____

_____

_____

_____

_____

himself about his state of mind until the eighteenth century perhaps. Rousseau[10] perhaps began it. At any rate, by the nineteenth century self-consciousness had developed so far that it was the habit for men of letters to describe their minds in confessions and autobiographies. Their lives also were written, and their letters were printed after their deaths. Thus, though

180 we do not know what Shakespeare went through when he wrote *Lear,* we do know what Carlyle went through when he wrote *The French Revolution;* what Flaubert went through when he wrote *Madame Bovary;* what Keats was going through when he tried to write poetry against the coming of death and the indifference of the world.

And one gathers from this enormous modern literature of confession and self-analysis that to write a work of genius is almost always a feat of **prodigious** difficulty. Everything is against the likelihood that it will come from the writer's mind

190 whole and entire. Generally material circumstances are against it. Dogs will bark; people will interrupt; money must be made; health will break down. Further, accentuating all these difficulties and making them harder to bear is the world's **notorious** indifference. It does not ask people to write poems and novels and histories; it does not need them. It does not care whether Flaubert finds the right word or whether Carlyle scrupulously verifies this or that fact. Naturally, it will not pay for what it does not want. And so the writer, Keats, Flaubert, Carlyle, suffers, especially in the creative years of youth, every form of distraction

200 and discouragement. A curse, a cry of agony, rises from those books of analysis and confession. "Mighty poets in their misery dead"[11]—that is the burden of their song. If anything comes through in spite of all this, it is a miracle, and probably no book is born entire and uncrippled as it was conceived.

---

10. **Rousseau:** Jean-Jacques Rousseau (1712–1778), French author whose candid, autobiographical *Confessions* began a vogue in literature for confessional accounts.

11. **Mighty poets . . . dead:** line from William Wordsworth's poem "Resolution and Independence."

But for women, I thought, looking at the empty shelves, these difficulties were infinitely more **formidable.** In the first place, to have a room of her own, let alone a quiet room or a soundproof room, was out of the question, unless her parents were exceptionally rich or very noble, even up to the beginning of the nineteenth

210 century. Since her pin money,[12] which depended on the goodwill of her father, was only enough to keep her clothed, she was debarred from such alleviations[13] as came even to Keats or Tennyson or Carlyle, all poor men, from a walking tour, a little journey to France, from the separate lodging which, even if it were miserable enough, sheltered them from the claims and tyrannies of their families. Such material difficulties were formidable; but much worse were the immaterial. The indifference of the world which Keats and Flaubert and other men of genius have found so hard to bear was in her case not indiffer-

220 ence but hostility. The world did not say to her as it said to them, Write if you choose; it makes no difference to me. The world said with a **guffaw,** Write? What's the good of your writing?

---

12. pin money: small allowance given for personal expenses.
13. alleviations (ə·lē′vē·ā′shənz): *n. pl.:* things that lighten, relieve, or make easier to bear.

A Corner of the Artist's Room, Paris (late 19th or early 20th century) by Gwen John.
Sheffield City Art Galleries, England.

Shakespeare's Sister

Reading Skills: Identifying the Author's Beliefs   Woolf's concerns, principles, and beliefs are directly reflected in this **informal essay.** The left-hand column below lists some of her beliefs about the special difficulties faced by women writers. Look back over the essay, and complete the chart with details, examples, or other evidence Woolf uses to express and support her beliefs.

Woolf's Beliefs	Evidence from the Essay
Sixteenth-century women lacked the education, money, privacy, and time to become writers.	
A woman who tried to write would have suffered great personal misery and public scorn.	
Women probably wrote most of the works that are marked "Anonymous."	
All writing demands a prodigious amount of work and is largely unappreciated.	
Society is hostile, not just indifferent, toward women writers.	

Shakespeare's Sister

VOCABULARY DEVELOPMENT

VOCABULARY IN CONTEXT

DIRECTIONS: Write a word from the Word Box in each blank to complete the paragraph below. Not all words from the box will be used.

Word Box

- servile
- suppressed
- propitious
- prodigious
- notorious
- formidable
- guffaw

Virginia Woolf imagines the role of sixteenth-century women as primarily (1) _____: cooking, cleaning, and sewing. She observes that society did not create (2) _____ circumstances to support women who had literary talent. In any era, even male writers face huge obstacles and need to exert (3) _____ effort to write anything worthwhile. In the sixteenth century, however, women faced obstacles so (4) _____ that most of them probably (5) _____ the urge to write—or settled for composing ballads to sing to their children.

CONNOTATIONS: DISTINGUISHING SHADES OF MEANING

A word's **denotation** is its dictionary definition. Some words also have **connotations,** the attitudes or emotional overtones that they suggest. For example, the words *firm* and *rigid* have similar denotations. *Rigid* is a negative word, and suggests someone who is fixed in his or her opinions. *Firm* suggests strength of character.

DIRECTIONS: Answer the following questions about words and their connotations.

1. Would you rather be **famous** or **notorious**? Why?

   _____

   _____

2. Which is a more pleasant sound, a **guffaw** or a **laugh**? Why?

   _____

   _____

3. If a character is described as **servile,** would he or she be likely to be the hero of a story? Why or why not?

   _____

   _____

Reading Standard 1.2 (Grade 9–10 Review) Distinguish between the denotative and connotative meanings of words and interpret the connotative power of words.

 Check your Standards Mastery at the back of this book.

Shooting an Elephant by George Orwell

REVIEW SKILLS

As you read "Shooting an Elephant," notice how irony makes the story both compelling and surprising.

IRONY
The contrast between our expectations and what actually happens.

LITERARY FOCUS: IRONY

Irony is a discrepancy between expectations and reality or between appearances and reality. Irony is a dominant feature in works of literature written in the twentieth century. In this essay, George Orwell uses **verbal irony:** He says one thing and means something else, often just the opposite. He also points out **situational irony:** events that are completely different from what we expect or what we think is appropriate.

In this essay, Orwell describes a troubling event that happened while he was a police officer in the British colony of Burma in the 1920s. He is called upon to deal with a rampaging elephant, a spectacle that draws a large crowd of Burmese people. Orwell suddenly finds himself caught in a conflict between what the crowd expects, what he himself believes is right, and his role as an agent of the British Empire.

READING SKILLS: IDENTIFYING THE AUTHOR'S PURPOSE

Orwell's purpose in this informal essay is twofold: to reveal his own personal dilemma and to reveal the cultural dilemma presented by colonialism itself. As an officer in the Indian Imperial Police, Orwell did not just symbolize foreign control of Burma—he was responsible for enforcing it. His awareness of being an enemy within another culture created enormous conflicts in him, and, as you will see, it forced him to act against his conscience.

Use the Skill   As you read the essay, mark words and phrases that describe Orwell's thoughts and feelings about British imperialism, about the Burmese people, and about his job.

Reading Standard 2.4
Make warranted and reasonable assertions about the author's arguments by using elements of the text to defend and clarify interpretations.

Reading Standard 3.3
Analyze the way in which irony achieves specific rhetorical purposes.

Reading Standard 3.8 (Grade 9–10 Review)
Interpret and evaluate the impact of ambiguities, subtleties, contradictions, ironies, and incongruities in a text.

Shooting an Elephant

George Orwell

> **BACKGROUND**
> Great Britain practiced colonialism; that is, it ruled over groups of people in geographically distant lands and benefited from the raw materials and cheap labor those lands provided. Burma, a country in Southeast Asia, became a British colony in the 1880s. Under colonialism, the British government imposed its culture, religion, and language upon the Burmese people. In 1948, Burma became an independent country and is now called the Union of Myanmar.
> In this essay, Orwell uses the term *imperialism* rather than *colonialism* to emphasize the tyranny and oppression of British rule. *Imperialism* suggests a powerful empire's control over another country's people and resources. No matter how long the British lived in a country they controlled, they generally remained a minority of outsiders holding power over a resentful people.

In Moulmein, in Lower Burma, I was hated by large numbers of people—the only time in my life that I have been important enough for this to happen to me. I was subdivisional police officer of the town, and in an aimless, petty kind of way anti-European feeling was very bitter. No one had the guts to raise a riot, but if a European woman went through the bazaars alone somebody would probably spit betel juice over her dress. As a police officer I was an obvious target and was baited whenever it seemed safe to do so. When a nimble Burman tripped me up on the football
10 field and the referee (another Burman) looked the other way, the crowd yelled with hideous laughter. This happened more than once. In the end the sneering yellow faces of young men that met me everywhere, the insults hooted after me when I was at a safe distance, got badly on my nerves. The young Buddhist priests were the worst of all. There were several thousands of

INTERPRET

In the opening paragraph, underline words and phrases that Orwell uses to describe the Burmese people and their attitude toward Europeans. How would you characterize his feelings about the Burmese?

_____

_____

_____

_____

_____

_____

_____

Re-read lines 18–24. Compared to his statements in the first paragraph, what surprising admission does Orwell make regarding his feelings about the Burmese and his attitude toward British imperialism?

_____

_____

_____

_____

_____

_____

VOCABULARY

supplant (sə·plant′) *v.:* replace; take the place of.

IDENTIFY

Orwell begins to tell a story that identifies the topic for the entire essay (lines 44–47). What is his topic? Underline that information.

WORD STUDY

Orwell uses the adjective *despotic* (line 47) to describe a government that has unlimited powers, such as a government run by a tyrant. The word *despot,* or "absolute ruler," comes from *dems-potis,* an Indo-European compound word meaning "house-master." We find the root *dems,* or "house," in words such as *domestic. Potis,* or "powerful," is the root of the words *power* and *potent.*

them in the town and none of them seemed to have anything to do except stand on street corners and jeer at Europeans.

All this was perplexing and upsetting. For at that time I had already made up my mind that imperialism was an evil thing and the sooner I chucked up my job and got out of it the better. Theoretically—and secretly, of course—I was all for the Burmese and all against their oppressors, the British. As for the job I was doing, I hated it more bitterly than I can perhaps make clear. In a job like that you see the dirty work of Empire at close quarters. The wretched prisoners huddling in the stinking cages of the lockups, the gray, cowed faces of the long-term convicts, the scarred buttocks of the men who had been flogged with bamboos—all these oppressed me with an intolerable sense of guilt. But I could get nothing into perspective. I was young and ill-educated and I had had to think out my problems in the utter silence that is imposed on every Englishman in the East. I did not even know that the British Empire is dying, still less did I know that it is a great deal better than the younger empires that are going to **supplant** it. All I knew was that I was stuck between my hatred of the empire I served and my rage against the evil-spirited little beasts who tried to make my job impossible. With one part of my mind I thought of the British Raj[1] as an unbreakable tyranny, as something clamped down, *in saecula saeculorum,*[2] upon the will of prostrate peoples; with another part I thought that the greatest joy in the world would be to drive a bayonet into a Buddhist priest's guts. Feelings like these are the normal by-products of imperialism; ask any Anglo-Indian official, if you can catch him off duty.

One day something happened which in a roundabout way was enlightening. It was a tiny incident in itself, but it gave me a better glimpse than I had had before of the real nature of imperialism—the real motives for which despotic governments act.

---

1. **Raj** (räj): rule over India. The word is derived from *rajya,* Hindi for "kingdom."
2. *in saecula saeculorum* (in sē′kōō·lə sē′kōō·lôr′əm): Latin for "forever and ever" (literally, "into ages of ages").

Early one morning the subinspector at a police station the other end of the town rang me up on the phone and said that an

50 elephant was ravaging the bazaar. Would I please come and do something about it? I did not know what I could do, but I wanted to see what was happening and I got on to a pony and started out. I took my rifle, an old .44 Winchester and much too small to kill an elephant, but I thought the noise might be useful *in terrorem.*[3] Various Burmans stopped me on the way and told me about the elephant's doings. It was not, of course, a wild elephant, but a tame one which had gone "must."[4] It had been chained up, as tame elephants always are when their attack of "must" is due, but on the previous night it had broken its chain and escaped. Its mahout,[5]

60 the only person who could manage it when it was in that state, had set out in pursuit, but had taken the wrong direction and was now twelve hours' journey away, and in the morning the elephant had suddenly reappeared in the town. The Burmese population had no weapons and were quite helpless against it. It had already destroyed somebody's bamboo hut, killed a cow, and raided some fruit stalls and devoured the stock; also it had met the municipal rubbish van and, when the driver jumped out and took to his heels, had turned the van over and inflicted violences upon it.

The Burmese subinspector and some Indian constables

70 were waiting for me in the quarter where the elephant had been seen. It was a very poor quarter, a **labyrinth** of **squalid** bamboo huts, thatched with palm leaf, winding all over a steep hillside. I remember that it was a cloudy, stuffy morning at the beginning of the rains. We began questioning the people as to where the elephant had gone and, as usual, failed to get any definite information. That is invariably the case in the East; a story always sounds clear enough at a distance, but the nearer you get to the scene of events the vaguer it becomes. Some of the people said

---

3. *in terrorem* (in ter·ôr′əm): Latin for "for terror." In other words, the gun might serve to frighten the elephant.
4. **must** *n.*: state of frenzy in animals. The word comes from *mast,* Hindi for "intoxicated."
5. **mahout** (mə·hout′) *n.*: elephant keeper. The word derives from *mahaut,* Hindi for "great in measure" and, thus, "important officer."

WORD STUDY

The word *subinspector* (line 48) uses the prefix *sub–,* which means "below" or "under." Can you guess what a subinspector's role in the police hierarchy would be? The word *constables* in line 69 is British for "police officers."

_____

_____

_____

ANALYZE

Orwell's **tone** in lines 55–68 could be described as suspenseful or humorous. Underline words and phrases that create a suspenseful tone or a humorous one, or both.

VOCABULARY

labyrinth (lab′ə·rinth′) *n.*: maze; complex or confusing arrangement.

squalid (skwäl′id) *adj.*: foul or unclean; wretched.

INFER

Orwell says that "as usual" he has difficulty getting information from the people in Burma (line 75). Why might Burmese people hesitate to give information to a British police officer?

_____

_____

_____

EVALUATE

Underline the details in lines 88–102 that describe the dead man. What **purpose** might such a vivid description serve?

_____

_____

_____

_____

_____

_____

_____

_____

_____

_____

_____

INFER

Why does Orwell send for an elephant rifle as soon as he sees the dead man (lines 102–105)?

_____

_____

_____

_____

_____

_____

_____

80 that the elephant had gone in one direction, some said that he had gone in another, some professed not even to have heard of any elephant. I had almost made up my mind that the whole story was a pack of lies, when we heard yells a little distance away. There was a loud, scandalized cry of "Go away, child! Go away this instant!" and an old woman with a switch in her hand came round the corner of the hut, violently shooing away a crowd of naked children. Some more women followed, clicking their tongues and exclaiming; evidently there was something that the children ought not to have seen. I rounded the hut and saw a man's dead body sprawling in the mud. He was an Indian,

90 a black Dravidian coolie,[6] almost naked, and he could not have been dead many minutes. The people said that the elephant had come suddenly upon him round the corner of the hut, caught him with its trunk, put its foot on his back, and ground him into the earth. This was the rainy season and the ground was soft, and his face had scored a trench a foot deep and a couple of yards long. He was lying on his belly with arms crucified and head sharply twisted to one side. His face was coated with mud, the eyes wide open, the teeth bared and grinning with an expression of unendurable agony. (Never tell me, by the way, that the dead

100 look peaceful. Most of the corpses I have seen looked devilish.) The friction of the great beast's foot had stripped the skin from his back as neatly as one skins a rabbit. As soon as I saw the dead man I sent an orderly to a friend's house nearby to borrow an elephant rifle. I had already sent back the pony, not wanting it to go mad with fright and throw me if it smelled the elephant.

The orderly came back in a few minutes with a rifle and five cartridges, and meanwhile some Burmans had arrived and told us that the elephant was in the paddy fields below, only a few hundred yards away. As I started forward practically the whole

110 population of the quarter flocked out of the houses and followed

---

6. **Dravidian** (drə·vid′ē·ən) **coolie:** *Dravidian* denotes any of several intermixed races living chiefly in southern India and northern Sri Lanka. A coolie is an unskilled laborer. The word is derived from *quli,* Hindi for "hired servant," and has become offensive.

me. They had seen the rifle and were all shouting excitedly that I was going to shoot the elephant. They had not shown much interest in the elephant when he was merely ravaging their homes, but it was different now that he was going to be shot. It was a bit of fun to them, as it would be to an English crowd; besides they wanted the meat. It made me vaguely uneasy. I had no intention of shooting the elephant—I had merely sent for the rifle to defend myself if necessary—and it is always unnerving to have a crowd following you. I marched down the hill, looking and feeling a

120 fool, with the rifle over my shoulder and an ever-growing army of people jostling at my heels. At the bottom, when you got away from the huts, there was a metaled[7] road and beyond that a miry waste of paddy fields a thousand yards across, not yet plowed but soggy from the first rains and dotted with coarse grass. The elephant was standing eight yards from the road, his left side toward us. He took not the slightest notice of the crowd's approach. He was tearing up bunches of grass, beating them against his knees to clean them, and stuffing them into his mouth.

I had halted on the road. As soon as I saw the elephant

130 I knew with perfect certainty that I ought not to shoot him. It is a serious matter to shoot a working elephant—it is comparable to destroying a huge and costly piece of machinery—and obviously one ought not to do it if it can possibly be avoided. And at that distance, peacefully eating, the elephant looked no more dangerous than a cow. I thought then and I think now that his attack of "must" was already passing off; in which case he would merely wander harmlessly about until the mahout came back and caught him. Moreover, I did not in the least want to shoot him. I decided that I would watch him for a little while to make sure

140 that he did not turn savage again, and then go home.

But at that moment I glanced round at the crowd that had followed me. It was an immense crowd, two thousand at the least and growing every minute. It blocked the road for a long distance on either side. I looked at the sea of yellow faces above the garish

---

7. **metaled** v. used as adj.: paved with cinders, stones, or the like.

PREDICT

Orwell reveals that he does not want to shoot the elephant (lines 116–117). Do you think he will shoot the animal or not?

_____

_____

_____

_____

_____

ANALYZE

Lines 116–128 contain two examples of **irony**. One involves Orwell, and the other involves the elephant. Describe the events. (**Grade 9–10 Review**)

_____

_____

_____

_____

_____

_____

_____

_____

_____

EVALUATE

Circle words and phrases in Orwell's description of the elephant (lines 129–140) that affect your feelings for the animal.

CLARIFY

Pause at line 152. What realization does Orwell come to, and why? Underline that information.

ANALYZE

Circle words and phrases that describe the reality of "the white man's dominion," or power (lines 152–165). What is ironic about the Europeans who control the colonial government of Burma? (Grade 9–10 Review)

_____

_____

_____

_____

_____

_____

_____

_____

_____

IDENTIFY

According to Orwell, what will happen if he does not shoot the elephant (lines 168–172)?

_____

_____

_____

_____

_____

clothes—faces all happy and excited over this bit of fun, all certain that the elephant was going to be shot. They were watching me as they would watch a conjurer about to perform a trick. They did not like me, but with the magical rifle in my hands I was momentarily worth watching. And suddenly I realized that I 150 should have to shoot the elephant after all. The people expected it of me and I had got to do it; I could feel their two thousand wills pressing me forward, irresistibly. And it was at this moment, as I stood there with the rifle in my hands, that I first grasped the hollowness, the futility of the white man's dominion in the East. Here was I, the white man with his gun, standing in front of the unarmed native crowd—seemingly the leading actor of the piece; but in reality I was only an absurd puppet pushed to and fro by the will of those yellow faces behind. I perceived in this moment that when the white man turns tyrant it is his own 160 freedom that he destroys. He becomes a sort of hollow, posing dummy, the conventionalized figure of a sahib.[8] For it is the condition of his rule that he shall spend his life in trying to impress the "natives," and so in every crisis he has got to do what the "natives" expect of him. He wears a mask, and his face grows to fit it. I had got to shoot the elephant. I had committed myself to doing it when I sent for the rifle. A sahib has got to act like a sahib; he has got to appear resolute, to know his own mind and do definite things. To come all that way, rifle in hand, with two thousand people marching at my heels, and then to trail feebly 170 away, having done nothing—no, that was impossible. The crowd would laugh at me. And my whole life, every white man's life in the East, was one long struggle not to be laughed at.

But I did not want to shoot the elephant. I watched him beating his bunch of grass against his knees, with that preoccupied grandmotherly air that elephants have. It seemed to me that it would be murder to shoot him. At that age I was not squeamish about killing animals, but I had never shot an elephant and never wanted to. (Somehow it always seems worse to kill a _large_ animal.)

---

8. **sahib** (sä'ib') _n._: master; sir. In colonial India, the title was used as a sign of respect for a European gentleman.

Besides, there was the beast's owner to be considered. Alive, the elephant was worth at least a hundred pounds; dead, he would only be worth the value of his tusks, five pounds, possibly. But I had got to act quickly. I turned to some experienced-looking Burmans who had been there when we arrived, and asked them how the elephant had been behaving. They all said the same thing: He took no notice of you if you left him alone, but he might charge if you went too close to him.

It was perfectly clear to me what I ought to do. I ought to walk up to within, say, twenty-five yards of the elephant and test his behavior. If he charged, I could shoot; if he took no notice of me, it would be safe to leave him until the mahout came back. But also I knew that I was going to do no such thing. I was a poor shot with a rifle and the ground was soft mud into which one would sink at every step. If the elephant charged and I missed him, I should have about as much chance as a toad under a steamroller. But even then I was not thinking particularly of my own skin, only of the watchful yellow faces behind. For at that moment, with the crowd watching me, I was not afraid in the ordinary sense, as I would have been if I had been alone. A white man mustn't be frightened in front of "natives"; and so, in general, he isn't frightened. The sole thought in my mind was that if anything went wrong those two thousand Burmans would see me pursued, caught, trampled on, and reduced to a grinning corpse like that Indian up the hill. And if that happened it was quite probable that some of them would laugh. That would never do. There was only one alternative. I shoved the cartridges into the magazine and lay down on the road to get a better aim.

The crowd grew very still, and a deep, low, happy sigh, as of people who see the theater curtain go up at last, breathed from innumerable throats. They were going to have their bit of fun after all. The rifle was a beautiful German thing with cross-hair sights. I did not then know that in shooting an elephant one would shoot to cut an imaginary bar running from earhole to

IDENTIFY

Re-read lines 173–186. Underline the reasons Orwell gives for not shooting the elephant. What **conflict** is he feeling?

_____

_____

_____

_____

_____

_____

INTERPRET

Re-read lines 187–195. Underline the colorful **figure of speech** that describes what might happen to Orwell if the elephant charged.

IDENTIFY

Orwell says he is not really concerned about his own safety (lines 195–206). Underline the real reason he decides he must shoot the elephant.

WORD STUDY

The word *innumerable* (line 209) is built on the word "number." It contains the prefix *in–*, which means "not," and the suffix *–able*, meaning "able to be." Thus, the word *innumerable* means "not able to be numbered." It describes things too numerous to count.

Orwell describes the crowd's reaction as a "devilish roar of glee" (line 218). What does this description suggest about his feelings toward the Burmese?

_____

_____

_____

_____

WORD STUDY

The word *senility* (line 227) is built on the Latin word *senex,* meaning "old man." Circle the context clue in the next sentence that suggests the meaning of *senility.* The word *senate,* which originally referred to a council of elders, comes from the same Latin root, as does the word *senior.*

INTERPRET

Underline details in lines 229–239 that describe the elephant's struggle. What feelings about the elephant's death does this description evoke?

_____

_____

_____

_____

_____

earhole. I ought, therefore, as the elephant was sideways on, to have aimed straight at his earhole; actually I aimed several inches in front of this, thinking the brain would be further forward.

When I pulled the trigger I did not hear the bang or feel the kick—one never does when a shot goes home—but I heard the devilish roar of glee that went up from the crowd. In that
220 instant, in too short a time, one would have thought, even for the bullet to get there, a mysterious, terrible change had come over the elephant. He neither stirred nor fell, but every line of his body had altered. He looked suddenly stricken, shrunken, immensely old, as though the frightful impact of the bullet had paralyzed him without knocking him down. At last, after what seemed a long time—it might have been five seconds, I dare say—he sagged flabbily to his knees. His mouth slobbered. An enormous senility seemed to have settled upon him. One could have imagined him thousands of years old. I fired again into the same spot. At the second shot he did not collapse but climbed
230 with desperate slowness to his feet and stood weakly upright, with legs sagging and head drooping. I fired a third time. That was the shot that did for him. You could see the agony of it jolt his whole body and knock the last remnant of strength from his legs. But in falling he seemed for a moment to rise, for as his hind legs collapsed beneath him he seemed to tower upward like a huge rock toppling, his trunk reaching skyward like a tree. He trumpeted, for the first and only time. And then down he came, his belly toward me, with a crash that seemed to shake the ground even where I lay.
240 I got up. The Burmans were already racing past me across the mud. It was obvious that the elephant would never rise again, but he was not dead. He was breathing very rhythmically with long rattling gasps, his great mound of a side painfully rising and falling. His mouth was wide open—I could see far down into caverns of pale pink throat. I waited a long time for him to die, but his breathing did not weaken. Finally I fired my two

remaining shots into the spot where I thought his heart must be. The thick blood welled out of him like red velvet, but still he did not die. His body did not even jerk when the shots hit him, the tortured breathing continued without a pause. He was dying, very slowly and in great agony, but in some world remote from me where not even a bullet could damage him further. I felt that I had got to put an end to that dreadful noise. It seemed dreadful to see the great beast lying there, powerless to move and yet powerless to die, and not even to be able to finish him. I sent back for my small rifle and poured shot after shot into his heart and down his throat. They seemed to make no impression. The tortured gasps continued as steadily as the ticking of a clock.

In the end I could not stand it any longer and went away. I heard later that it took him half an hour to die. Burmans were bringing dahs[9] and baskets even before I left, and I was told they had stripped his body almost to the bones by the afternoon.

Afterward, of course, there were endless discussions about the shooting of the elephant. The owner was furious, but he was only an Indian and could do nothing. Besides, legally I had done the right thing, for a mad elephant has to be killed, like a mad dog, if its owner fails to control it. Among the Europeans opinion was divided. The older men said I was right, the younger men said it was a damn shame to shoot an elephant for killing a coolie, because an elephant was worth more than any damn Coringhee[10] coolie. And afterward I was very glad that the coolie had been killed; it put me legally in the right and it gave me a sufficient **pretext** for shooting the elephant. I often wondered whether any of the others grasped that I had done it solely to avoid looking a fool.

IDENTIFY

Re-read lines 263–271. Underline the racist remark made by the younger men. What does the remark reveal about the attitudes many Europeans had toward the Burmese?

VOCABULARY

pretext (prē′tekst′) *n.:* excuse.

---

9. **dahs** (däz) *n. pl.:* large carving knives.
10. **Coringhee** (kôr·iŋ′ē): port in southeastern India.

Shooting an Elephant

Reading Skills: Identifying the Author's Purpose   Read the excerpts from the essay in the left-hand column below. Then, in the right-hand column, explain why each excerpt is ironic and what it reveals about Orwell's purpose.

Examples of Irony	Orwell's Purpose
"For at that time I had already made up my mind that imperialism was an evil thing and the sooner I chucked up my job and got out of it the better. Theoretically—and secretly, of course—I was all for the Burmese and all against their oppressors, the British."	
"I perceived in this moment that when the white man turns tyrant it is his own freedom that he destroys. He becomes a sort of hollow, posing dummy. . . . For it is the condition of his rule that he shall spend his life in trying to impress the 'natives,' and so in every crisis he has got to do what the 'natives' expect of him."	
"I did not then know that in shooting an elephant one would shoot to cut an imaginary bar running from earhole to earhole. I ought, therefore, as the elephant was sideways on, to have aimed straight at his earhole; actually I aimed several inches in front of this, thinking the brain would be further forward."	
"And afterward I was very glad that the coolie had been killed; it put me legally in the right and it gave me a sufficient pretext for shooting the elephant. I often wondered whether any of the others grasped that I had done it solely to avoid looking a fool."	

Shooting an Elephant

VOCABULARY
DEVELOPMENT

VOCABULARY IN CONTEXT

DIRECTIONS: Write words from the Word Box in the blanks to complete the paragraph below. Use each word only once.

Word Box

supplant
labyrinth
squalid
pretext

To add to its mighty empire, Great Britain would (1) _____ an existing government, often taking it over with military force. Countries with colonial empires argue that they provide native peoples with modern medicine and technology. They claim to improve unhealthful, (2) _____ conditions. However, bringing humanitarian aid may be only a (3) _____ for gaining control of a country's resources. Controlling native peoples created personal and political difficulties for the British. British residents who lived in colonial territories had to work through a (4) _____ of confusing social customs and laws.

POLITICAL SCIENCE AND HISTORICAL TERMS

DIRECTIONS: The **etymology** of a word traces its history back to its original use. Match each boldface term from political science and history to its word history.

_____ **1.** Orwell came to believe that British **imperialism** was oppressive and wrong.

    a. from Greek *monos,* "alone," and *archein,* "to rule"

_____ **2.** Orwell fought against the government of a **fascist** dictator in the Spanish Civil War.

    b. from Latin *imperialis,* "empire"

_____ **3.** British citizens working in colonial territories remained loyal to the British **monarchy.**

    c. from Latin *fascis,* "political group"

Reading Standard 1.1
Trace the etymology of significant terms used in political science and history.

 Check your Standards Mastery at the back of this book.

No Witchcraft for Sale by Doris Lessing

BEFORE YOU READ

REVIEW SKILLS

As you read "No Witchcraft for Sale," notice how the historical context of the story affects the characters' actions and feelings.

HISTORICAL CONTEXT
The cultural and political events occurring at a specific time and place that influence a literary work.

Reading Standard 3.2
Analyze the way in which the theme or meaning of a selection represents a view or comment on life, using textual evidence to support the claim.

Reading Standard 3.7b
Relate literary works and authors to the major themes and issues of their eras.

Reading Standard 3.12 (Grade 9–10 Review)
Analyze the way in which a work of literature is related to the themes and issues of its historical period.

LITERARY FOCUS: THEME

The **theme** of a story is the insight it reveals to us about human experience. In a few stories the themes are directly stated, but most writers want readers to piece together key details and decide what theme the story reveals to them.

To identify theme, ask yourself these questions:

- What did the main character (or you) discover by the end of the story? Very often, this discovery can be stated as the story's theme.
- Does the title of the story illuminate the story's theme?
- Do any key passages state something important about life?

READING SKILLS: IDENTIFYING HISTORICAL CONTEXT

The time and place in which a writer lives often have a direct influence on his or her themes—even if the work itself is set in a different time or place. This tale from Doris Lessing's *African Stories* takes place in Southern Rhodesia, a country in South Africa. Lessing's work is written within the **historical context** of Southern Rhodesia's racial and political struggles. Here are some historical connections to keep in mind as you read:

- The story is set at a time when Southern Rhodesia was still part of the British Empire. When Lessing wrote the story in 1964, however, Southern Rhodesia was demanding independence from Britain.
- When the British established a colony in the country they called Rhodesia, they took the most fertile farmland for themselves. The Rhodesian people were removed from their ancestral homes and sent to communal lands with poor soil that made raising crops difficult. As a result, those who had previously made a living on the land now became a source of cheap labor in cities and were more dependent upon the white minority for their livelihood.
- After Southern Rhodesia declared independence from Britain in 1965, the white minority was eager to establish its own government—a government that would continue the policy of denying rights to black citizens.

Use the Skill As you read the story, highlight or underline references to the Rhodesian language, culture, and history. In addition, mark sections that describe interactions between black and white Rhodesians. Consider how the political climate in which Lessing wrote this story may have influenced her portrayal of the earlier time period.

No Witchcraft for Sale

Doris Lessing

> **BACKGROUND**
>
> Doris Lessing was born in 1919 and grew up on a three-thousand-acre farm in Southern Rhodesia, a country now called Zimbabwe. Her family employed about fifty black African workers who earned the equivalent of $1.50 per month and lived in mud huts with no sanitation. Southern Rhodesia was a colony of Great Britain, but both its black and its white residents wanted independence. The white minority wanted to establish a government that continued to limit black citizens' political participation. Black citizens wanted a government in which the black majority would rule. Civil war broke out in the country after it declared independence from Britain in 1965, and more than 25,000 people were killed before the country gained self-rule in 1980.

The Farquars had been childless for years when little Teddy was born; and they were touched by the pleasure of their servants, who brought presents of fowls and eggs and flowers to the homestead when they came to rejoice over the baby, exclaiming with delight over his downy golden head and his blue eyes. They congratulated Mrs. Farquar as if she had achieved a very great thing, and she felt that she had—her smile for the lingering, admiring natives was warm and grateful.

10 Later, when Teddy had his first haircut, Gideon the cook picked up the soft gold tufts from the ground, and held them **reverently** in his hand. Then he smiled at the little boy and said: "Little Yellow Head." That became the native name for the child. Gideon and Teddy were great friends from the first. When Gideon had finished his work, he would lift Teddy on his shoulders to the shade of a big tree, and play with him there, forming curious little toys from twigs and leaves and grass, or shaping

INTERPRET

Pause at line 8. What do you learn about the relationship between the Farquars and their servants?

VOCABULARY

reverently (rev′ə·rənt′lē) *adv.:* with deep respect, or awe, as for something sacred.

"No Witchcraft for Sale" from *African Stories* by Doris Lessing. Copyright © 1951, 1953, 1954, 1957, 1958, 1962, 1963, 1964, 1965, 1972, 1981 by Doris Lessing. Reprinted by permission of **Simon & Schuster.** Electronic format by permission of **Jonathan Clowes Ltd.**

ANALYZE

Pause at line 21. How would you describe Gideon's feelings about Teddy? Underline the text that explains Mrs. Farquar's feelings about Gideon.

_____

_____

_____

_____

INFER

Re-read lines 22–30. What does this description of the relationship between the Farquars and their servants reveal about the **historical context** of the story? *(Grade 9–10 Review)*

_____

_____

_____

_____

_____

_____

_____

INTERPRET

What idea about servants and masters does this exchange in lines 36–42 convey?

_____

_____

_____

_____

_____

animals from wetted soil. When Teddy learned to walk it was often Gideon who crouched before him, clucking encouragement, finally catching him when he fell, tossing him up in the
20 air till they both became breathless with laughter. Mrs. Farquar was fond of the old cook because of his love for her child.

There was no second baby; and one day Gideon said: "Ah, missus, missus, the Lord above sent this one; Little Yellow Head is the most good thing we have in our house." Because of that "we" Mrs. Farquar felt a warm impulse toward her cook; and at the end of the month she raised his wages. He had been with her now for several years; he was one of the few natives who had his wife and children in the compound and never wanted to go home to his kraal,[1] which was some hundreds of miles
30 away. Sometimes a small piccanin[2] who had been born the same time as Teddy, could be seen peering from the edge of the bush, staring in awe at the little white boy with his miraculous fair hair and Northern blue eyes. The two little children would gaze at each other with a wide, interested gaze, and once Teddy put out his hand curiously to touch the black child's cheeks and hair.

Gideon, who was watching, shook his head wonderingly, and said: "Ah, missus, these are both children, and one will grow up to be a baas,[3] and one will be a servant"; and Mrs. Farquar smiled and said sadly, "Yes, Gideon, I was thinking the same."
40 She sighed. "It is God's will," said Gideon, who was a mission boy.[4] The Farquars were very religious people; and this shared feeling about God bound servant and masters even closer together.

Teddy was about six years old when he was given a scooter, and discovered the intoxications of speed. All day he would fly around the homestead, in and out of flowerbeds, scattering squawking chickens and irritated dogs, finishing with a wide

---

1. **kraal** (kräl): South African village.
2. **piccanin** (pik′ə·nin): black African child. Derived from *pequeno* (pā·kā′n
oo
), Portuguese for "small," the term is often considered offensive.
3. **baas** (bäs): Afrikaans for "master." Afrikaans, a language developed from seventeenth-century Dutch, is spoken in South Africa.
4. **mission boy:** one educated by Christian missionaries.

dizzying arc into the kitchen door. There he would cry: "Gideon, look at me!" And Gideon would laugh and say: "Very clever, Little Yellow Head." Gideon's youngest son, who was now a

50 herdsboy, came especially up from the compound to see the scooter. He was afraid to come near it, but Teddy showed off in front of him. "Piccanin," shouted Teddy, "get out of my way!" And he raced in circles around the black child until he was frightened, and fled back to the bush.

"Why did you frighten him?" asked Gideon, gravely reproachful.

Teddy said defiantly: "He's only a black boy," and laughed. Then, when Gideon turned away from him without speaking, his face fell. Very soon he slipped into the house and found an

60 orange and brought it to Gideon, saying: "This is for you." He could not bring himself to say he was sorry; but he could not bear to lose Gideon's affection either. Gideon took the orange unwillingly and sighed. "Soon you will be going away to school, Little Yellow Head," he said wonderingly, "and then you will be grown up." He shook his head gently and said, "And that is how our lives go." He seemed to be putting a distance between himself and Teddy, not because of resentment, but in the way a person accepts something **inevitable**. The baby had lain in his arms and smiled up into his face: The tiny boy had swung

70 from his shoulders and played with him by the hour. Now Gideon would not let his flesh touch the flesh of the white child. He was kind, but there was a grave formality in his voice that made Teddy pout and sulk away. Also, it made him into a man: With Gideon he was polite, and carried himself formally, and if he came into the kitchen to ask for something, it was in the way a white man uses toward a servant, expecting to be obeyed.

But on the day that Teddy came staggering into the kitchen with his fists to his eyes, shrieking with pain, Gideon dropped the pot full of hot soup that he was holding, rushed to the child,

80 and forced aside his fingers. "A snake!" he exclaimed. Teddy had

INTERPRET

Re-read lines 55–66. Underline the reason Teddy gives for treating Gideon's son so cruelly. Circle Gideon's responses, including what he says when Teddy brings him the orange.

VOCABULARY

inevitable (in·ev′i·tə·bəl) *adj.:* certain to happen; unavoidable.

IDENTIFY CAUSE & EFFECT

Underline details that describe the changes in Gideon's behavior toward Teddy (lines 68–76). Circle the changes in Teddy's behavior toward Gideon. What permanent effect does the scooter incident have on their relationship?

_____

_____

_____

_____

_____

_____

_____

_____

_____

_____

Neveride Mushwana, a South African "witch doctor,"
in front of his home, with one of his snakes.
Tzaneen, South Africa (March 1997).
Juhan KUUS/SIPA Press.

CLARIFY

Pause at line 90. Why are
Gideon and Mrs. Farquar so
concerned about Teddy's
eyes?

been on his scooter, and had come to a rest with his foot on the
side of a big tub of plants. A tree snake, hanging by its tail from
the roof, had spat full into his eyes. Mrs. Farquar came running
when she heard the commotion. "He'll go blind," she sobbed,
holding Teddy close against her. "Gideon, he'll go blind!"
Already the eyes, with perhaps half an hour's sight left in them,
were swollen up to the size of fists: Teddy's small white face was
distorted by great purple oozing protuberances.[5] Gideon said:
"Wait a minute, missus, I'll get some medicine." He ran off into
90   the bush.

Mrs. Farquar lifted the child into the house and bathed
his eyes with permanganate.[6] She had scarcely heard Gideon's
words; but when she saw that her remedies had no effect at all,

---

5.   **protuberances** (prō·tōō'bər·əns·iz) *n. pl.:* swellings; bulges.
6.   **permanganate** (pər·maŋ'gə·nāt') *n.:* dark purple chemical compound
       used as a disinfectant.

and remembered how she had seen natives with no sight in their eyes, because of the spitting of a snake, she began to look for the return of her cook, remembering what she heard of the **efficacy** of native herbs. She stood by the window, holding the terrified, sobbing little boy in her arms, and peered helplessly into the bush. It was not more than a few minutes before she saw Gideon
100   come bounding back, and in his hand he held a plant.

     "Do not be afraid, missus," said Gideon, "this will cure Little Yellow Head's eyes." He stripped the leaves from the plant, leaving a small white fleshy root. Without even washing it, he put the root in his mouth, chewed it vigorously, and then held the spittle there while he took the child forcibly from Mrs. Farquar. He gripped Teddy down between his knees, and pressed the balls of his thumbs into the swollen eyes, so that the child screamed and Mrs. Farquar cried out in protest: "Gideon, Gideon!" But Gideon took no notice. He knelt over the writhing
110   child, pushing back the puffy lids till chinks of eyeball showed, and then he spat hard, again and again, into first one eye, and then the other. He finally lifted Teddy gently into his mother's arms, and said: "His eyes will get better." But Mrs. Farquar was weeping with terror, and she could hardly thank him: It was impossible to believe that Teddy could keep his sight. In a couple of hours the swellings were gone: The eyes were inflamed and tender but Teddy could see. Mr. and Mrs. Farquar went to Gideon in the kitchen and thanked him over and over again. They felt helpless because of their gratitude: It seemed they could do
120   nothing to express it. They gave Gideon presents for his wife and children, and a big increase in wages, but these things could not pay for Teddy's now completely cured eyes. Mrs. Farquar said: "Gideon, God chose you as an instrument for His goodness," and Gideon said: "Yes, missus, God is very good."

     Now, when such a thing happens on a farm, it cannot be long before everyone hears of it. Mr. and Mrs. Farquar told their neighbors and the story was discussed from one end of the district to the other. The bush is full of secrets. No one can live

VOCABULARY

efficacy (ef'i·kə·sē) *n.*: effectiveness; the ability to accomplish something.

INFER

Circle the words and phrases that describe how Gideon treats the injured Teddy (lines 101–113). What do we learn about Gideon from the way he helps Teddy?

_____

_____

_____

_____

_____

_____

_____

_____

EVALUATE

Why do Teddy's parents feel "helpless because of their gratitude" (line 119)?

_____

_____

_____

_____

_____

_____

_____

Re-read lines 125–134. This passage gives a white person's view of "the black man's heritage" (line 132). What does the description reveal about the Europeans' perspective of the African people? *(Grade 9–10 Review)*

_____

_____

_____

_____

WORD STUDY

Anecdotes (line 133) comes from the Greek word *anekdota,* meaning "unpublished things." *Anecdotes* are short, amusing stories.

ANALYZE

Think about the story's title, "No Witchcraft for Sale." Why wouldn't Africans want to share their secrets about native medicines?

_____

_____

_____

_____

_____

_____

_____

_____

_____

in Africa, or at least on the veld,[7] without learning very soon

130 that there is an ancient wisdom of leaf and soil and season—and, too, perhaps most important of all, of the darker tracts of the human mind—which is the black man's heritage. Up and down the district people were telling anecdotes, reminding each other of things that had happened to them.

"But I saw it myself, I tell you. It was a puff-adder bite. The kaffir's[8] arm was swollen to the elbow, like a great shiny black bladder. He was groggy after a half a minute. He was dying. Then suddenly a kaffir walked out of the bush with his hands full of green stuff. He smeared something on the place, and next

140 day my boy was back at work, and all you could see was two small punctures in the skin."

This was the kind of tale they told. And, as always, with a certain amount of exasperation, because while all of them knew that in the bush of Africa are waiting valuable drugs locked in bark, in simple-looking leaves, in roots, it was impossible to ever get the truth about them from the natives themselves.

The story eventually reached town; and perhaps it was at a sundowner party,[9] or some such function, that a doctor, who happened to be there, challenged it. "Nonsense," he said. "These

150 things get exaggerated in the telling. We are always checking up on this kind of story, and we draw a blank every time."

Anyway, one morning there arrived a strange car at the homestead, and out stepped one of the workers from the laboratory in town, with cases full of test tubes and chemicals.

Mr. and Mrs. Farquar were flustered and pleased and flattered. They asked the scientist to lunch, and they told the story all over again, for the hundredth time. Little Teddy was there too, his blue eyes sparkling with health, to prove the truth of it.

---

7. **veld** *n.:* in South Africa, open country with very few bushes or trees; grassland. *Veld,* also spelled *veldt,* is Afrikaans for "field."
8. **kaffir's** (kaf′ərz): *Kaffir* is a contemptuous term for a black African, derived from *kāfir,* Arabic for "infidel."
9. **sundowner party:** British colloquial term for "cocktail party." The term derives from the British custom of gathering for drinks at sunset.

The scientist explained how humanity might benefit if this new
160   drug could be offered for sale; and the Farquars were even more
pleased: They were kind, simple people, who liked to think of
something good coming about because of them. But when the
scientist began talking of the money that might result, their
manner showed discomfort. Their feelings over the miracle
(that was how they thought of it) were so strong and deep and
religious, that it was distasteful to them to think of money. The
scientist, seeing their faces, went back to his first point, which
was the advancement of humanity. He was perhaps a trifle
perfunctory: It was not the first time he had come salting the
170   tail of a fabulous bush secret.[10]

Eventually, when the meal was over, the Farquars called
Gideon into their living room and explained to him that this
baas, here, was a Big Doctor from the Big City, and he had come
all that way to see Gideon. At this Gideon seemed afraid; he did
not understand; and Mrs. Farquar explained quickly that it was
because of the wonderful thing he had done with Teddy's eyes
that the Big Baas had come.

Gideon looked from Mrs. Farquar to Mr. Farquar, and then
at the little boy, who was showing great importance because of
180   the occasion. At last he said grudgingly: "The Big Baas want to
know what medicine I used?" He spoke incredulously, as if he
could not believe his old friends could so betray him. Mr. Farquar
began explaining how a useful medicine could be made out of
the root, and how it could be put on sale, and how thousands of
people, black and white, up and down the continent of Africa,
could be saved by the medicine when that spitting snake filled
their eyes with poison. Gideon listened, his eyes bent on the
ground, the skin of his forehead puckering in discomfort. When
Mr. Farquar had finished he did not reply. The scientist, who all
190   this time had been leaning back in a big chair, sipping his coffee
and smiling with skeptical good humor, chipped in and explained

---

10. **salting . . . bush secret:** allusion to the ironic advice given to children,
about catching a bird by putting salt on its tail. In other words, the
scientist knows his search may be futile.

How does the scientist's
motivation for finding out
the cure compare with
that of the Farquars (lines
159–170)?

_____

_____

_____

_____

VOCABULARY

perfunctory (pər·fuŋk′tə·rē)
adj.: halfhearted; done
without care, as a routine.

PREDICT

Underline words and phrases
that describe Gideon's
response to the Farquars'
request (lines 178–189). Do
you think Gideon will reveal
which plant he used to treat
Teddy's eyes? Explain your
prediction.

_____

_____

_____

_____

_____

_____

_____

all over again, in different words, about the making of drugs and the progress of science. Also, he offered Gideon a present.

There was silence after this further explanation, and then Gideon remarked indifferently that he could not remember the root. His face was sullen and hostile, even when he looked at the Farquars, whom he usually treated like old friends. They were beginning to feel annoyed; and this feeling **annulled** the guilt that had been sprung into life by Gideon's accusing manner. 200 They were beginning to feel that he was unreasonable. But it was at that moment that they all realized he would never give in. The magical drug would remain where it was, unknown and useless except for the tiny scattering of Africans who had the knowledge, natives who might be digging a ditch for the municipality in a ragged shirt and a pair of patched shorts, but who were still born to healing, hereditary healers, being the nephews or sons of the old witch doctors whose ugly masks and bits of bone and all the uncouth properties of magic were the outward signs of real power and wisdom.

210 The Farquars might tread on that plant fifty times a day as they passed from house to garden, from cow kraal to mealie[11] field, but they would never know it.

But they went on persuading and arguing, with all the force of their exasperation; and Gideon continued to say that he could not remember, or that there was no such root, or that it was the wrong season of the year, or that it wasn't the root itself, but the spit from his mouth that had cured Teddy's eyes. He said all these things one after another, and seemed not to care they were contradictory. He was rude and stubborn. The Farquars could 220 hardly recognize their gentle, lovable old servant in this ignorant, **perversely** obstinate African, standing there in front of them with lowered eyes, his hands twitching his cook's apron, repeating over and over whichever one of the stupid refusals that first entered his head.

VOCABULARY

annulled (ə·nuld′) *v.:* did away with; canceled.

perversely (pər·vurs′lē) *adv.:* disagreeably; with a contrary attitude.

---

11. **mealie** *n.:* corn.

And suddenly he appeared to give in. He lifted his head, gave a long, blank angry look at the circle of whites, who seemed to him like a circle of yelping dogs pressing around him, and said: "I will show you the root."

They walked single file away from the homestead down a
230 kaffir path. It was a blazing December afternoon, with the sky full of hot rain clouds. Everything was hot: The sun was like a bronze tray whirling overhead, there was a heat shimmer over the fields, the soil was scorching underfoot, the dusty wind blew gritty and thick and warm in their faces. It was a terrible day, fit only for reclining on a veranda with iced drinks, which is where they would normally have been at that hour.

From time to time, remembering that on the day of the snake it had taken ten minutes to find the root, someone asked: "Is it much further, Gideon?" And Gideon would answer over
240 his shoulder, with angry politeness: "I'm looking for the root, baas." And indeed, he would frequently bend sideways and trail his hand among the grasses with a gesture that was insulting in its perfunctoriness. He walked them through the bush along unknown paths for two hours, in that melting destroying heat, so that the sweat trickled coldly down them and their heads ached. They were all quite silent: the Farquars because they were angry, the scientist because he was being proved right again; there was no such plant. His was a tactful silence.

At last, six miles from the house, Gideon suddenly decided
250 they had had enough; or perhaps his anger evaporated at that moment. He picked up, without an attempt at looking anything but casual, a handful of blue flowers from the grass, flowers that had been growing plentifully all down the paths they had come.

He handed them to the scientist without looking at him, and marched off by himself on the way home, leaving them to follow him if they chose.

When they got back to the house, the scientist went to the kitchen to thank Gideon: He was being very polite, even though there was an amused look in his eyes. Gideon was not there.

INFER

Pause at line 224. The Farquars say that they hardly recognize Gideon because he acts "ignorant" and "stupid." Why do you think Gideon's behavior has changed?

_____

_____

_____

_____

_____

_____

_____

_____

_____

_____

_____

INFER

Why is Gideon taking so long to find the root (lines 237–246)?

_____

_____

_____

_____

_____

260   Throwing the flowers casually into the back of his car, the eminent visitor departed on his way back to his laboratory.

Gideon was back in his kitchen in time to prepare dinner, but he was sulking. He spoke to Mr. Farquar like an unwilling servant. It was days before they liked each other again.

The Farquars made inquiries about the root from their laborers. Sometimes they were answered with distrustful stares. Sometimes the natives said: "We do not know. We have never heard of the root." One, the cattle boy, who had been with them a long time, and had grown to trust them a little, said: "Ask your

270   boy in the kitchen. Now, there's a doctor for you. He's the son of a famous medicine man who used to be in these parts, and there's nothing he cannot cure." Then he added politely: "Of course, he's not as good as the white man's doctor, we know that, but he's good for us."

After some time, when the soreness had gone from between the Farquars and Gideon, they began to joke: "When are you going to show us the snake root, Gideon?" And he would laugh and shake his head, saying, a little uncomfortably: "But I did show you, missus, have you forgotten?"

280   Much later, Teddy, as a schoolboy, would come into the kitchen and say: "You old rascal, Gideon! Do you remember that time you tricked us all by making us walk miles all over the veld for nothing? It was so far my father had to carry me!"

And Gideon would double up with polite laughter. After much laughing, he would suddenly straighten himself up, wipe his old eyes, and look sadly at Teddy, who was grinning mischievously at him across the kitchen: "Ah, Little Yellow Head, how you have grown! Soon you will be grown up with a farm of your own. . . ."

No Witchcraft for Sale

Reading Skills: Identifying Historical Context   By looking at story details, you can learn about what life was like in a certain time and place. Match each passage from the story with information it reveals about life in Southern Rhodesia during the period of British control. Write the letter of each passage before the item of historical information it exemplifies.

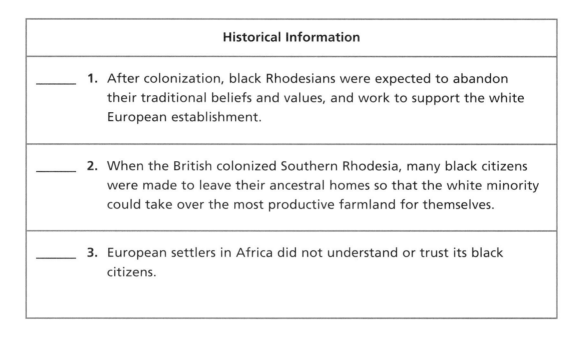

Historical Information

_____ 1. After colonization, black Rhodesians were expected to abandon their traditional beliefs and values, and work to support the white European establishment.

_____ 2. When the British colonized Southern Rhodesia, many black citizens were made to leave their ancestral homes so that the white minority could take over the most productive farmland for themselves.

_____ 3. European settlers in Africa did not understand or trust its black citizens.

Story Passages

a. "Mrs. Farquar felt a warm impulse toward her cook. . . . He had been with her now for several years; he was one of the few natives who had his wife and children in the compound and never wanted to go home to his kraal, which was some hundreds of miles away." (lines 25–30)

b. "The bush is full of secrets. No one can live in Africa, or at least on the veld, without learning very soon that there is an ancient wisdom of leaf and soil and season—and, too, perhaps most important of all, of the darker tracts of the human mind—which is the black man's heritage." (lines 128–132)

c. "The magical drug would remain where it was, unknown and useless except for the tiny scattering of Africans who had the knowledge, natives who might be digging a ditch for the municipality in a ragged shirt and a pair of patched shorts, but who were still born to healing. . . ." (lines 201–206)

No Witchcraft for Sale

VOCABULARY IN CONTEXT

DIRECTIONS: Write a vocabulary word from the Word Box in each blank to complete this paragraph. Not all words will be used.

Word Box

reverently
inevitable
efficacy
perfunctory
annulled
perversely

Doris Lessing writes about African native cultures almost
(1) _____, with respect for their traditions and way of
life. Although it is (2) _____ that people from different
cultures occasionally have misunderstandings, they must show mutual respect.
The (3) _____ of Lessing's writings about racism has been
proven. Her books have brought about greater awareness of the injustices of
European colonial rule.

CONTEXT CLUES

When you come across a word you do not know, you can often figure out its meaning by examining its **context,** the surrounding words, phrases, and sentences.

DIRECTIONS: In each sentence below, circle the words or phrases that give a clue to the meaning of the underlined vocabulary word from "No Witchcraft for Sale."

1. The Farquars adored their new baby and treated him <u>reverently.</u>

2. Because Gideon's father was a great medicine man, it was <u>inevitable</u> that Gideon would learn about healing, too.

3. The <u>efficacy</u> of the drug was plain to see; it was so effective the child soon began to recover.

4. We hoped his response to the offer would be enthusiastic, but he gave only a <u>perfunctory</u> reply.

 Check your Standards Mastery at the back of this book.

The Second Coming by William Butler Yeats

BEFORE YOU READ

LITERARY FOCUS: THEME

The title of Yeats's poem alludes to the Christian prophecy of the Second Coming of Christ that appears in the Book of Revelation in the Bible. (An **allusion** is a reference to something that is known from literature, religion, politics, and so on.) The Second Coming refers to the belief that Jesus will one day return to earth to usher in an era of peace and justice. The "First Coming" was the birth of Jesus in Bethlehem more than two thousand years ago.

The poem's **theme** also relies upon this allusion to the Second Coming, but Yeats turns it inside out. As you read, ask yourself why Yeats reverses the Christian prophecy to portray an end-time of chaos and bloodshed.

READING SKILLS: VISUALIZING

When you visualize a text, you create mental images of what is being described—characters, settings, events. Below are some phrases from "The Second Coming." Read each phrase, and describe what you visualize.

Images	What I Visualize
"Turning and turning in the widening gyre" (line 1)	
"The blood-dimmed tide is loosed" (line 5)	
"A shape with lion body and the head of a man" (line 14)	

Use the Skill As you read the poem, underline or highlight words and phrases that help you form mental images. How do the images help convey the poem's central themes?

THE SECOND COMING

William Butler Yeats

BACKGROUND

"The Second Coming" addresses Yeats's personal view of history. Yeats saw human history as cyclical. Each cycle, known as a gyre, begins in a rational state and then dissolves into chaos and irrationality. The poem repeats a question that Yeats asks in his book *A Vision:* "What if the irrational returns?" Yeats wrote this poem in 1921, after the horrors unleashed by World War I and by the Russian Revolution of 1917. He wonders if—like the falconer who can't control his falcon—humankind is spinning out of control and into chaos.

INTERPRET

Underline words and phrases in lines 1–8 that describe the disorder that the speaker sees in the world. What idea about civilization do these words suggest?

_____

_____

_____

_____

_____

_____

_____

_____

_____

_____

Turning and turning in the widening gyre

The falcon cannot hear the falconer;

Things fall apart; the center cannot hold;

Mere anarchy is loosed upon the world,

5   The blood-dimmed tide is loosed, and everywhere

The ceremony of innocence is drowned;

The best lack all conviction, while the worst

Are full of passionate intensity.

Surely some revelation is at hand;

10   Surely the Second Coming is at hand.

The Second Coming! Hardly are those words out

When a vast image out of Spiritus Mundi°

Troubles my sight: somewhere in sands of the desert

A shape with lion body and the head of a man,

° **Spiritus Mundi:** Latin for "the world's soul or spirit"; for Yeats, the collective reservoir of human memory from which artists draw their images.

15   A gaze blank and pitiless as the sun,
      Is moving its slow thighs, while all about it
      Reel shadows of the indignant desert birds.
      The darkness drops again; but now I know
      That twenty centuries of stony sleep
20   Were vexed to nightmare by a rocking cradle,
      And what rough beast, its hour come round at last,
      Slouches towards Bethlehem to be born?

ANALYZE

Re-read lines 13–16. Circle **images** that describe the shape that the speaker sees in the desert. **(Grade 9–10 Review)**

EVALUATE

Re-read lines 18–22. From the description of the beast about to be born, what kind of future do you think the speaker envisions?

The Second Coming

Reading Skills: Visualizing   The poem's central ideas are listed in the left-hand column below. In the right-hand column, list images that you think support these ideas.

Ideas	Images
Like the falcon and the falconer, people can't control events happening around them.	
The world is in a state of chaos during times of war. War is bloody and violent and destroys innocence.	
There is no hope of future salvation, because the Second Coming won't be the return of Christ but of some awful beast.	

Check your Standards Mastery at the back of this book.

Araby by James Joyce

LITERARY FOCUS: EPIPHANY

An **epiphany** is a moment of insight or revelation. Before James Joyce applied the term to literature, the word *epiphany* referred to a religious experience, one in which a human being learned a spiritual truth. The word comes from the Greek and can be translated as "manifestation" or "showing forth."

Here is an excerpt from one of Joyce's early novels, in which a character explains what he means by *epiphany:*

"By an epiphany he meant a sudden spiritual manifestation, whether in the vulgarity of speech or of gesture or in a memorable phase of the mind itself. He believed that it was for the man of letters to record these epiphanies with extreme care, seeing that they themselves are the most delicate and evanescent of moments."

READING SKILLS: COMPARING AND CONTRASTING

In "Araby," the main character has a vivid imagination that leads him to misunderstand the realities of his life. As a result, the way he imagines things is at times different from the way things really are.

Use the Skill   As you read the story, underline or highlight sections in which the character has fantasies about future events. Then, mark the sections in which he actually experiences these events. You may want to keep track of these differences between imagination and reality by listing them in a comparison-contrast chart like the one shown here.

Imagination	Reality

 ARABY

James Joyce

BACKGROUND
James Joyce's "Araby" is built around scenes from his childhood in Ireland. The narrator's house in the story is based on one where his family lived in Dublin. The Joyces' house, like the one in the story, was located on the same street as the Christian Brothers' School, which Joyce himself attended. The bazaar called Araby that the narrator visits was a five-day charity event. The name *Araby* referred to Arabia, which is known for its bazaars, or markets, with long rows of shops. The reference to Arabia, with its deserts and bazaars, would have seemed mysterious and exotic to the children of Ireland, half a world away.

IDENTIFY

Circle **images** in the first paragraph that describe the setting and set a mood. How would you describe the mood? *(Grade 9–10 Review)*

_____

_____

_____

_____

_____

_____

_____

VOCABULARY

imperturbable
(im′pər·tʉr′bə·bəl) *adj.:* calm; not easily excited.

North Richmond Street, being blind, was a quiet street except at the hour when the Christian Brothers' School set the boys free. An uninhabited house of two stories stood at the blind end, detached from its neighbors in a square ground. The other houses of the street, conscious of decent lives within them, gazed at one another with brown **imperturbable** faces.

　　The former tenant of our house, a priest, had died in the back drawing-room. Air, musty from having been long enclosed, hung in all the rooms, and the waste room behind the kitchen

10　was littered with old useless papers. Among these I found a few paper-covered books, the pages of which were curled and damp: *The Abbot,* by Walter Scott, *The Devout Communicant,* and *The Memoirs of Vidocq.*[1] I liked the last best because its leaves were yellow. The wild garden behind the house contained a central

---

1. ***The Abbot . . . Vidocq*** (vē·duk′): in order, a historical romance about Mary, Queen of Scots, by Sir Walter Scott; an 1813 religious manual written by a Franciscan friar; and the memoirs (though not actually written by François Vidocq) of a French criminal who later became a detective.

apple-tree and a few straggling bushes under one of which I found the late tenant's rusty bicycle-pump. He had been a very charitable priest; in his will he had left all his money to institutions and the furniture of his house to his sister.

When the short days of winter came dusk fell before we had well eaten our dinners. When we met in the street the houses had grown **somber.** The space of sky above us was the color of ever-changing violet and toward it the lamps of the street lifted their feeble lanterns. The cold air stung us and we played till our bodies glowed. Our shouts echoed in the silent street. The career[2] of our play brought us through the dark muddy lanes behind the houses where we ran the gauntlet[3] of the rough tribes from the cottages, to the back doors of the dark dripping gardens where odors arose from the ashpits, to the dark odorous stables where a coachman smoothed and combed the horse or shook music from the buckled harness. When we returned to the street light from the kitchen windows had filled the areas. If my uncle was seen turning the corner we hid in the shadow until we had seen him safely housed. Or if Mangan's sister came out on the doorstep to call her brother in to his tea we watched her from our shadow peer up and down the street. We waited to see whether she would remain or go in and, if she remained, we left our shadow and walked up to Mangan's steps resignedly. She was waiting for us, her figure defined by the light from the half-opened door. Her brother always teased her before he obeyed and I stood by the railings looking at her. Her dress swung as she moved her body and the soft rope of her hair tossed from side to side.

Every morning I lay on the floor in the front parlor watching her door. The blind was pulled down to within an inch of the sash so that I could not be seen. When she came out on the

---

2. **career** *n.:* course; path.
3. **gauntlet** (gônt′lit) *n.:* series of challenges. Derived from *gatlopp,* Swedish for "running down a lane," the term originally referred to a form of military punishment in which a wrongdoer had to run between two rows of soldiers who struck him as he passed.

ANALYZE

Pause at line 33. Circle **images** that refer to light and dark. How does this imagery affect the story's mood? *(Grade 9–10 Review)*

_____

_____

_____

_____

_____

_____

_____

_____

_____

_____

_____

_____

WORD STUDY

In medieval monasteries, monks were required to keep silent at certain times. One room, however, was set aside for conversation. This room, the *parlor* (line 43), took its name from the Old French word *parleor,* meaning "to speak."

Re-read lines 53–64. Circle
the **image** (lines 62–63) from
the boy's imagination. How
does this image compare to
the images describing the
market? *(Grade 9–10 Review)*

_____

_____

_____

_____

_____

_____

_____

_____

_____

_____

_____

_____

_____

_____

_____

_____

IDENTIFY

Re-read lines 63–70.
Underline words used by
the narrator to describe his
feelings that have religious
overtones.

doorstep my heart leaped. I ran to the hall, seized my books,
and followed her. I kept her brown figure always in my eye and,
when we came near the point at which our ways diverged, I
quickened my pace and passed her. This happened morning
50 after morning. I had never spoken to her, except for a few
casual words, and yet her name was like a summons to all my
foolish blood.

Her image accompanied me even in places the most hostile
to romance. On Saturday evenings when my aunt went market-
ing I had to go to carry some of the parcels. We walked through
the flaring streets, jostled by drunken men and bargaining
women, amid the curses of laborers, the shrill litanies[4] of shop-
boys who stood on guard by the barrels of pigs' cheeks, the nasal
chanting of street-singers, who sang a *come-all-you* about
60 O'Donovan Rossa,[5] or a ballad about the troubles in our native
land. These noises converged in a single sensation of life for me:
I imagined that I bore my chalice[6] safely through a throng of
foes. Her name sprang to my lips at moments in strange prayers
and praises which I myself did not understand. My eyes were
often full of tears (I could not tell why) and at times a flood from
my heart seemed to pour itself out into my bosom. I thought
little of the future. I did not know whether I would ever speak
to her or not or, if I spoke to her, how I could tell her of my
confused adoration. But my body was like a harp and her words
70 and gestures were like fingers running upon the wires.

One evening I went into the back drawing-room in which
the priest had died. It was a dark rainy evening and there was no
sound in the house. Through one of the broken panes I heard

---

4. **litanies** *n. pl.:* repeated sales cries. Literally, a litany is a prayer
    composed of a series of specific invocations and responses.
5. ***come-all-you . . . Rossa:*** A come-all-you (kum·al'yə) is a type of Irish
    ballad that usually begins "Come all you [young lovers, rebels,
    Irishmen, and so on]." O'Donovan Rossa was Jeremiah O'Donovan
    (1831–1915) from County Cork. He was active in Ireland's struggle
    against British rule in the mid–nineteenth century.
6. **chalice** (chal'is) *n.:* cup; specifically, the cup used for Holy Communion
    wine. Joyce's use of the term evokes the image of a young man on a
    sacred mission.

the rain **impinge** upon the earth, the fine incessant needles of
water playing in the sodden beds. Some distant lamp or lighted
window gleamed below me. I was thankful that I could see so
little. All my senses seemed to desire to veil themselves and,
feeling that I was about to slip from them, I pressed the palms
of my hands together until they trembled, murmuring: *O love!*
80 *O love!* many times.

At last she spoke to me. When she addressed the first words
to me I was so confused that I did not know what to answer. She
asked me was I going to *Araby.* I forget whether I answered yes or
no. It would be a splendid bazaar, she said; she would love to go.

—And why can't you? I asked.

While she spoke she turned a silver bracelet round and
round her wrist. She could not go, she said, because there would
be a retreat that week in her convent.[7] Her brother and two
other boys were fighting for their caps and I was alone at the
90 railings. She held one of the spikes, bowing her head toward me.
The light from the lamp opposite our door caught the white
curve of her neck, lit up her hair that rested there and, falling,
lit up the hand upon the railing. It fell over one side of her
dress and caught the white border of a petticoat, just visible as
she stood at ease.

—It's well for you,[8] she said.

—If I go, I said, I will bring you something.

What innumerable follies laid waste my waking and sleeping
thoughts after that evening! I wished to **annihilate** the tedious
100 intervening days. I chafed against the work of school. At night
in my bedroom and by day in the classroom her image came
between me and the page I strove to read. The syllables of the
word *Araby* were called to me through the silence in which my
soul luxuriated and cast an Eastern enchantment over me. I
asked for leave to go to the bazaar on Saturday night. My aunt

---

7. **retreat . . . convent:** temporary withdrawal from worldly life by
   the students and teachers at the convent school, to devote time
   to prayer, meditation, and studies.
8. **It's well for you:** "You're lucky" (usually said enviously).

VOCABULARY

impinge (im·pinj′) *v.:* strike;
touch.

annihilate (ə·nī′ə·lāt′) *v.:*
destroy; make nonexistent.

PARAPHRASE

Restate what takes place in
lines 81–97 between the narrator and Mangan's sister.

_____

_____

_____

_____

_____

FLUENCY

Read the boxed passage
aloud twice. Try to convey
the narrator's feelings of
excitement and anticipation.

PREDICT

Will Araby be the "Eastern
enchantment" the narrator
imagines (line 104)? Explain.

_____

_____

_____

_____

_____

_____

**COMPARE &
CONTRAST**

Re-read lines 121–133. How
does the narrator's behavior
contrast with the realities of
the scene that is around him?

_____

_____

_____

_____

_____

_____

_____

_____

_____

_____

_____

_____

_____

_____

_____

_____

_____

_____

was surprised and hoped it was not some Freemason[9] affair. I answered few questions in class. I watched my master's face pass from amiability to sternness; he hoped I was not beginning to idle. I could not call my wandering thoughts together. I had hardly any patience with the serious work of life which, now that it stood between me and my desire, seemed to me child's play, ugly **monotonous** child's play.

On Saturday morning I reminded my uncle that I wished to go to the bazaar in the evening. He was fussing at the hall-stand, looking for the hat-brush, and answered me curtly:

—Yes, boy, I know.

As he was in the hall I could not go into the front parlor and lie at the window. I left the house in bad humor and walked slowly toward the school. The air was pitilessly raw and already my heart misgave me.

When I came home to dinner my uncle had not yet been home. Still it was early. I sat staring at the clock for some time and, when its ticking began to irritate me, I left the room. I mounted the staircase and gained the upper part of the house. The high cold empty gloomy rooms liberated me and I went from room to room singing. From the front window I saw my companions playing below in the street. Their cries reached me weakened and indistinct and, leaning my forehead against the cool glass, I looked over at the dark house where she lived. I may have stood there for an hour, seeing nothing but the brown-clad figure cast by my imagination, touched discreetly by the lamp-light at the curved neck, at the hand upon the railings and at the border below the dress.

When I came downstairs again I found Mrs. Mercer sitting at the fire. She was an old **garrulous** woman, a pawnbroker's widow, who collected used stamps for some pious purpose. I had to endure the gossip of the tea-table. The meal was pro-

---

9. **Freemason:** The Freemasons are a secret society whose practices were originally drawn from those of British medieval stonemasons' guilds; its members, almost exclusively Protestant, were often hostile to Catholics. The aunt apparently associates the exotic bazaar with the mysterious practices of Freemasonry.

longed beyond an hour and still my uncle did not come. Mrs. Mercer stood up to go: She was sorry she couldn't wait any longer, but it was after eight o'clock and she did not like to be out late, as the night air was bad for her. When she had gone I began to walk up and down the room, clenching my fists. My aunt said:

—I'm afraid you may put off your bazaar for this night of Our Lord.

At nine o'clock I heard my uncle's latchkey in the halldoor. I heard him talking to himself and heard the hallstand rocking when it had received the weight of his overcoat. I could interpret these signs. When he was midway through his dinner I asked him to give me the money to go to the bazaar. He had forgotten.

—The people are in bed and after their first sleep now, he said.

I did not smile. My aunt said to him energetically:

—Can't you give him the money and let him go? You've kept him late enough as it is.

My uncle said he was very sorry he had forgotten. He said he believed in the old saying: *All work and no play makes Jack a dull boy.* He asked me where I was going and, when I had told him a second time he asked me did I know *The Arab's Farewell to his Steed.*[10] When I left the kitchen he was about to recite the opening lines of the piece to my aunt.

I held a florin[11] tightly in my hand as I strode down Buckingham Street toward the station. The sight of the streets thronged with buyers and glaring with gas recalled to me the purpose of my journey. I took my seat in a third-class carriage of a deserted train. After an intolerable delay the train moved out of the station slowly. It crept onward among ruinous houses and over the twinkling river. At Westland Row Station a crowd of people pressed to the carriage doors; but the porters moved

---

10. *The Arab's . . . Steed:* popular sentimental poem by the English writer Caroline Norton (1808–1877).
11. **florin** *n.:* British coin worth at the time the equivalent of about fifty cents.

EVALUATE

Pause at line 142. Do you think the narrator's uncle is cruel to keep the boy waiting, or is he just forgetful? Explain your response.

IDENTIFY

Read lines 162–175 carefully. Circle details that describe the narrator's journey to Araby.

VOCABULARY

improvised (im′prə·vīzd′)
v. used as *adj.*: made for the
occasion from whatever is
handy.

pervades (pər·vādz′) *v.*:
spreads throughout.

CLARIFY

The narrator has finally
arrived at Araby (lines
176–186). What does he
find there?

_____

_____

_____

_____

_____

_____

COMPARE & CONTRAST

The narrator watches a young
woman flirt with two young
men (lines 189–197). How
does this scene compare with
the narrator's own secret love
for Mangan's sister?

_____

_____

_____

_____

_____

_____

_____

170 them back, saying that it was a special train for the bazaar. I remained alone in the bare carriage. In a few minutes the train drew up beside an **improvised** wooden platform. I passed out on to the road and saw by the lighted dial of a clock that it was ten minutes to ten. In front of me was a large building which displayed the magical name.

I could not find any sixpenny entrance and, fearing that the bazaar would be closed, I passed in quickly through a turnstile, handing a shilling to a weary-looking man. I found myself in a big hall girdled at half its height by a gallery. Nearly all the stalls

180 were closed and the greater part of the hall was in darkness. I recognized a silence like that which **pervades** a church after a service. I walked into the center of the bazaar timidly. A few people were gathered about the stalls which were still open. Before a curtain, over which the words *Café Chantant*[12] were written in colored lamps, two men were counting money on a salver.[13] I listened to the fall of the coins.

Remembering with difficulty why I had come I went over to one of the stalls and examined porcelain vases and flowered tea-sets. At the door of the stall a young lady was talking and

190 laughing with two young gentlemen. I remarked their English accents and listened vaguely to their conversation.

—O, I never said such a thing!

—O, but you did!

—O, but I didn't!

—Didn't she say that?

—Yes. I heard her.

—O, there's a . . . fib!

Observing me the young lady came over and asked me did I wish to buy anything. The tone of her voice was not encourag-

200 ing; she seemed to have spoken to me out of a sense of duty.

---

12. *Café Chantant* (kȧ·fā′ shän′tän′): The name refers to a coffeehouse with musical entertainment.
13. **salver** (sal′vər) *n.*: serving tray.

I looked humbly at the great jars that stood like eastern guards at either side of the dark entrance to the stall and murmured:

—No, thank you.

The young lady changed the position of one of the vases and went back to the two young men. They began to talk of the same subject. Once or twice the young lady glanced at me over her shoulder.

I lingered before her stall, though I knew my stay was useless, to make my interest in her wares seem the more real. Then 210 I turned away slowly and walked down the middle of the bazaar. I allowed the two pennies to fall against the sixpence in my pocket. I heard a voice call from one end of the gallery that the light was out. The upper part of the hall was now completely dark.

Gazing up into the darkness I saw myself as a creature driven and derided by vanity; and my eyes burned with anguish and anger.

St. Patrick's Close, Dublin by Walter Osborne.
© Courtesy of The National Gallery of Ireland.

ANALYZE

Pause at line 203. Why doesn't the narrator buy anything at the young woman's stall?

_____

_____

_____

_____

_____

_____

_____

_____

_____

_____

_____

_____

_____

_____

_____

_____

_____

INTERPRET

What **epiphany** does the narrator experience at the end of the story? Underline the answer.

Araby

Reading Skills: Comparing and Contrasting   Look back over the story details that reveal how the narrator imagines events will be and how he actually experiences those events. In the chart below, list details from the text that show the contrast between what the narrator imagines and what really happens.

	Imagination	Reality
Love		
Religion		
Araby		

Araby

VOCABULARY IN CONTEXT

DIRECTIONS: Write a vocabulary word in each blank to complete the paragraph.
Not all words will be used.

Word Box

imperturbable

somber

impinge

annihilate

monotonous

garrulous

improvised

pervades

Ordinary, everyday life can become (1) _____
when the same events always happen the same way. A kind of boredom
(2) _____ our routine, spreading throughout our
entire daily schedule. If it is not changed occasionally, an everyday routine
can (3) _____ our sense of gaiety and fun, destroying
our ability to do something unplanned or spontaneous. Daily routines
can become (4) _____ or gloomy. Conducting
(5) _____ meetings or unplanned trips can bring
new energy and focus to your work.

PREFIXES AND SUFFIXES

You can unlock the meanings of some unfamiliar words by examining their prefixes
and suffixes. **Prefixes** are placed at the beginning of a word, while **suffixes** are
placed at the end.

DIRECTIONS: Study the prefixes and suffixes listed below and how they are used in
vocabulary words from the story. Find two more words that have the same prefix or
suffix. Enter the words and their definitions in the last column of the chart.

Word Part / Meaning	Example	My Examples and Definitions
im– or *in–*, "not"	*imperturbable:* "not excitable"	1. 2.
–ous, "full of, possessing"	*monotonous:* "full of monotony; having one tone"	1. 2.

Reading Standard 1.1 (Grade 9–10 Review) Identify and use the literal and figurative meanings of words and understand word derivations.

Check your Standards Mastery at the back of this book.

Musée des Beaux Arts by W. H. Auden

REVIEW SKILLS

As you read "Musée des Beaux Arts," identify the speaker's **tone**.

TONE
The attitude a writer takes toward the reader, a subject, or a character.

Reading Standard 3.3
Analyze the ways in which irony, tone, mood, the author's style, and the "sound" of language achieve specific rhetorical or aesthetic purposes or both.

Reading Standard 3.11 (Grade 9–10 Review)
Evaluate the aesthetic qualities of style, including the impact of diction and figurative language on tone, mood, and theme, using the terminology of literary criticism.

LITERARY FOCUS: DICTION

W. H. Auden often combines eloquent, poetic language with colloquial language, the down-to-earth informal language of everyday life. This use of contrasting **diction,** or word choice, has several effects. It surprises the reader, who may be expecting only lofty, formal language. It also creates a **tone** of informality that mirrors the randomness of the "real world." Often, the mixture of dictions reinforces the speaker's sense of irony.

Creating Contrasts   In the statement below, circle the formal language and underline the informal, colloquial words. Then, write two of your own sentences that combine formal and informal language.

The stately, ancient trees towered above the guys catching a few Zs in the shade below.

READING SKILLS: IDENTIFYING THEME

Theme is the insight into human experience revealed by a work of literature. Most works of literature do not state theme directly; instead, writers hope that the reader will discover theme by becoming involved in the details of the story or poem. Remember that theme is not the same as the subject. The subject can be summed up in a word or two, such as *human suffering* or *change.* A theme, however, is a complete idea that must be stated in at least one sentence.

The subject of "Musée des Beaux Arts" is a painting by Pieter Bruegel, based on the myth of Icarus. What does the poem reveal about that story of the drowned boy?

Use the Skill   As you read the poem, underline or highlight key details that seem to make a comment on human suffering.

Musée des Beaux Arts

W. H. Auden

BACKGROUND

This poem was inspired by a famous painting called *The Fall of Icarus,* done by the Renaissance painter Pieter Bruegel. It is on permanent display in the Musée des Beaux Arts (myōō·zā′ dā bō·zàr′), or Fine Arts Museum, in Brussels, Belgium. The painting shows a dramatic moment in the Greek myth about Daedalus and his son, Icarus. The father and son were imprisoned on the island of Crete. Daedalus made wings of feathers and wax so the two could escape. Though they managed to fly over the walls of their prison, Icarus did not heed his father's warning and flew too close to the sun. When the sun melted the wax on his wings, the boy fell to his death in the sea.

The focus of the painting is not the drowning boy, however, but a peasant who is plowing a field. Icarus appears in the lower right-hand corner of the painting, almost as an afterthought. Only his legs are seen splashing into the water, not far from a passing ship.

About suffering they were never wrong,

The Old Masters: how well they understood

Its human position; how it takes place

While someone else is eating or opening a window or just
    walking dully along;

5   How, when the aged are reverently, passionately waiting

For the miraculous birth, there always must be

Children who did not specially want it to happen, skating

On a pond at the edge of the wood:

They never forgot

10   That even the dreadful martyrdom must run its course

Anyhow in a corner, some untidy spot

Where the dogs go on with their doggy life and the torturer's horse

Scratches its innocent behind on a tree.

INTERPRET

Re-read lines 1–4. The "Old Masters" (line 2) are the great artists of the European Renaissance. Circle the word that shows what they understood. What fact is pointed out in lines 3–4?

_____

_____

_____

IDENTIFY

The words "dreadful martyrdom" (line 10) suggest tortured, martyred saints. Underline the ordinary events taking place while the torture goes on.

The Fall of Icarus (16th century) by Pieter Bruegel the Elder.
Musées Royaux des Beaux-Arts, Brussels, Belgium.

_____
_____
_____
_____
_____
_____
_____
_____
_____
_____
_____
_____
_____

> In Bruegel's *Icarus,* for instance: how everything turns away
> 15 Quite leisurely from the disaster; the plowman may
> Have heard the splash, the forsaken cry,
> But for him it was not an important failure; the sun shone
> As it had to on the white legs disappearing into the green
> Water; and the expensive delicate ship that must have seen
> 20 Something amazing, a boy falling out of the sky,
> Had somewhere to get to and sailed calmly on.

Musée des Beaux Arts

Reading Skills: Identifying Theme   Review the key details in the poem that suggest the poem's theme. List five examples below. Then, on the lines under the box, identify the theme.

Key Details That Reveal Theme

Theme   The poem reveals that . . .

_____

_____

_____

_____

☑ Check your Standards Mastery at the back of this book.

Fern Hill by Dylan Thomas

REVIEW SKILLS

As you read "Fern Hill," look for Thomas's use of figurative language.

FIGURATIVE LANGUAGE
Words or phrases that describe one thing in terms of another and that are not meant to be taken literally.

Reading Standard 3.1
Analyze characteristics of subgenres that are used in poetry, prose, plays, novels, short stories, essays, and other basic genres.

Reading Standard 3.4
Analyze ways in which poets use imagery, personification, figures of speech, and sounds to evoke reader's emotions.

Reading Standard 3.11 (Grade 9–10 Review)
Evaluate the aesthetic qualities of style, including the impact of diction and figurative language on tone, mood, and theme, using the terminology of literary criticism.

LITERARY FOCUS: LYRIC POETRY

The focus of **lyric poetry** is on expressing emotions or thoughts, not on telling a story. "Fern Hill" is an example of a lyric poem that uses **sound effects** and **figurative language** to express vivid memories of a young boy's enchanted life in the countryside of Wales. Reflection and experience color the speaker's memories, but it is the enthusiasm of his feelings that makes the strongest claim on our attention.

READING SKILLS: DRAWING INFERENCES

An **inference** is a guess you make based on information in the text and on your own knowledge and experience. To draw an inference, you focus on important details in the text and then combine that information with what you already know. In "Fern Hill," Dylan Thomas describes in detail the joy and beauty of his childhood, but he also delivers a powerful message about the lurking presence of death in life. To find that message, you will have to use your powers of inference.

Use the Skill   As you read the poem, highlight or underline details that reveal the speaker's feelings about his childhood. Watch especially for details that describe how he felt when he was young, and how he feels about the effects of time on a person's life.

Portrait of Dylan Thomas by Augustus John.
National Museum of Wales, Cardiff.
© Courtesy of the Estate of Augustus John.

Fern Hill

Dylan Thomas

BACKGROUND

As a child, Dylan Thomas spent summers with relatives who worked on a farm that he calls Fern Hill in this poem. The farmhouse is made of the whitewashed stucco typical of Wales and is set in an apple orchard. There are several outlying barns for livestock and hay storage. Not far from the sea, the farm looks down upon huge tidal flats that provide good habitat for thousands of waterbirds.

"Fern Hill" is a memory of childhood joy. It describes an earthly paradise, a playground for a boy for whom every day is a magical adventure. Yet this joy has a dark side, which is typical of Thomas's poetry. At first, "time" holds the speaker "green and growing." Toward the end of the poem, however, "time" holds him "green and dying."

Now as I was young and easy under the apple boughs
About the lilting house and happy as the grass was green,
  The night above the dingle[1] starry,
    Time let me hail and climb
5   Golden in the heydays of his eyes,
And honored among wagons I was prince of the apple towns
And once below a time I lordly had the trees and leaves
    Trail with daisies and barley
  Down the rivers of the windfall light.

10 And as I was green and carefree, famous among the barns
About the happy yard and singing as the farm was home,
    In the sun that is young once only,
      Time let me play and be

IDENTIFY

In the first stanza (lines 1–9), underline words that tell where the speaker played, how he felt, and what he pretended to be.

INTERPRET

In line 10, the speaker uses **figurative language**—he describes himself as "green." What does the speaker mean by that expression? *(Grade 9–10 Review)*

_____

_____

_____

_____

---

1. **dingle:** little wooded valley, nestled between steep hills.

FLUENCY

Read the boxed passage aloud twice. Read to understand meaning the first time through. Use punctuation to help you decide where to pause and where to come to a full stop. For your second reading, pay special attention to Thomas's use of **sound effects,** such as **alliteration** (the repetition of consonant sounds in words that are close to one another).

ANALYZE

Underline the **figurative language** that the speaker uses in lines 19–27. What effect does this description create? *(Grade 9–10 Review)*

_____

_____

_____

_____

_____

_____

Golden in the mercy of his means,

15   And green and golden I was huntsman and herdsman, the calves

Sang to my horn, the foxes on the hills barked clear and cold,

And the sabbath rang slowly

In the pebbles of the holy streams.

All the sun long it was running, it was lovely, the hay

20   Fields high as the house, the tunes from the chimneys, it was air

And playing, lovely and watery

And fire green as grass.

And nightly under the simple stars

As I rode to sleep the owls were bearing the farm away,

25   All the moon long I heard, blessed among stables, the nightjars[2]

Flying with the ricks,[3] and the horses

Flashing into the dark.

----

2. **nightjars:** common, gray-brown nocturnal birds named for their jarring cries.
3. **ricks:** haystacks.

And then to awake, and the farm, like a wanderer white

With the dew, come back, the cock on his shoulder: it was all

30   Shining, it was Adam and maiden,

       The sky gathered again

    And the sun grew round that very day.

So it must have been after the birth of the simple light

In the first, spinning place, the spellbound horses walking warm

35   Out of the whinnying green stable

       On to the fields of praise.

And honored among foxes and pheasants by the gay house

Under the new made clouds and happy as the heart was long,

    In the sun born over and over,

40   I ran my heedless ways,

       My wishes raced through the house high hay

And nothing I cared, at my sky blue trades, that time allows

In all his tuneful turning so few and such morning songs

    Before the children green and golden

45   Follow him out of grace,

Nothing I cared, in the lamb white days, that time would take me

Up to the swallow thronged loft by the shadow of my hand,

    In the moon that is always rising,

       Nor that riding to sleep

50   I should hear him fly with the high fields

And wake to the farm forever fled from the childless land.

Oh as I was young and easy in the mercy of his means,

    Time held me green and dying

    Though I sang in my chains like the sea.

INTERPRET

Underline details in lines 28–36 that suggest that the speaker saw Fern Hill as a kind of Garden of Eden.

INTERPRET

Personification is a type of figurative language in which a nonhuman thing or quality is talked about as if it were human. Underline the details in the last two stanzas that personify time.

INFER

What is happening to the boy in the last two stanzas?

_____

_____

_____

_____

_____

_____

_____

_____

_____

_____

_____

_____

_____

Fern Hill

Reading Skills: Drawing Inferences   In the left-hand column below are lines from the poem. Read the lines carefully. Then, in the right-hand column, write your inferences about the speaker's feelings and ideas.

Lines from "Fern Hill"	My Inferences
"I was prince of the apple towns" (line 6)	
"And green and golden I was huntsman and herdsman" (line 15)	
"And the sabbath rang slowly / In the pebbles of the holy streams." (lines 17–18)	
"the spellbound horses walking warm / Out of the whinnying green stable" (lines 34–35)	
"Time held me green and dying / Though I sang in my chains like the sea." (lines 53–54)	

 Check your Standards Mastery at the back of this book.

Games at Twilight by Anita Desai

LITERARY FOCUS: IMAGERY

Imagery is language that creates pictures in our minds; imagery can also appeal to the other senses (hearing, touch, taste, and smell). Almost all writers use imagery to help us picture settings, characters, and actions. In this story, Anita Desai drenches us in the smells, textures, sounds, and colors of a summer afternoon in India. Desai helps us to experience the world through the eyes and ears of her characters, from the bursting open of a door to the crushed silence of a defeated child.

Imagine That!   Close your eyes and imagine a summer afternoon gradually turning into twilight. What might that scene look and feel like? Think of two images to describe it. You can use complete sentences or just phrases. Identify the senses that your images appeal to.

Images	Senses

READING SKILLS: ANALYZING DETAILS

Desai is known for her use of rich imagery and striking details. As you read the story, note how the imagery allows you to imagine a scene and to share a character's feelings and experiences. When you have finished reading, analyze the impressions created by these details. What mood is created by the images? Which single detail did you find the most striking or memorable?

Use the Skill   Underline or highlight details that help you picture a setting or a character, or to smell, taste, feel, or hear something.

Reading Standard 3.4 Analyze ways in which poets use imagery, personification, figures of speech, and sounds to evoke readers' emotions.

Reading Standard 3.6 (Grade 9–10 Review) Analyze and trace an author's development of time and sequence, including the use of complex literary devices (e.g., foreshadowing, flashbacks).

Games at Twilight

Anita Desai

BACKGROUND

This story takes place shortly after India won its independence from Britain in 1947. During the long British rule in India, many upper-class Indian families adopted Western values, behaviors, and customs, including games such as the one played in the story.

IDENTIFY

Re-read the first paragraph. Underline **images** that help you understand the effect of the heat on the children.

VOCABULARY

maniacal (mə·nī′ə·kəl) *adj.:* crazed; wildly enthusiastic.

It was still too hot to play outdoors. They had had their tea, they had been washed and had their hair brushed, and after the long day of confinement in the house that was not cool but at least a protection from the sun, the children strained to get out. Their faces were red and bloated with the effort, but their mother would not open the door, everything was still curtained and shuttered in a way that stifled the children, made them feel that their lungs were stuffed with cotton wool and their noses with dust and if they didn't burst out into the light and see the sun

10 and feel the air, they would choke.

"Please, ma, please," they begged. "We'll play in the veranda and porch—we won't go a step out of the porch."

"You will, I know you will, and then—"

"No—we won't, we won't," they wailed so horrendously that she actually let down the bolt of the front door so that they burst out like seeds from a crackling, overripe pod into the veranda, with such wild, **maniacal** yells that she retreated to her bath and the shower of talcum powder and the fresh sari that were to help her face the summer evening.

20   They faced the afternoon. It was too hot. Too bright. The white walls of the veranda glared **stridently** in the sun. The bougainvillea[1] hung about it, purple and magenta, in livid balloons. The garden outside was like a tray made of beaten brass, flattened out on the red gravel and the stony soil in all shades of metal—aluminum, tin, copper, and brass. No life stirred at this arid time of day—the birds still drooped, like dead fruit, in the papery tents of the trees; some squirrels lay limp on the wet earth under the garden tap. The outdoor dog lay stretched as if dead on the veranda mat, his paws and ears

30   and tail all reaching out like dying travelers in search of water. He rolled his eyes at the children—two white marbles rolling in the purple sockets, begging for sympathy—and attempted to lift his tail in a wag but could not. It only twitched and lay still.

    Then, perhaps roused by the shrieks of the children, a band of parrots suddenly fell out of the eucalyptus tree, tumbled frantically in the still, sizzling air, then sorted themselves out into battle formation and streaked away across the white sky.

    The children, too, felt released. They too began tumbling, shoving, pushing against each other, frantic to start. Start what?

40   Start their business. The business of the children's day which is—play.

    "Let's play hide-and-seek."

    "Who'll be It?"

    "You be It."

    "Why should I? You be—"

    "You're the eldest—"

    "That doesn't mean—"

    The shoves became harder. Some kicked out. The motherly Mira intervened. She pulled the boys roughly apart. There was a

50   tearing sound of cloth, but it was lost in the heavy panting and angry grumbling, and no one paid attention to the small sleeve hanging loosely off a shoulder.

---

1. **bougainvillea** (boo′gən·vil′ē·ə) *n.:* woody, tropical vine with showy, purplish leaves.

VOCABULARY

stridently (strīd″nt·lē) *adv.:* harshly; sharply.

ANALYZE

Re-read lines 20–33. Underline **images** that help you experience the intense heat of the afternoon. What senses do these images appeal to?

_____

_____

_____

IDENTIFY CAUSE & EFFECT

Circle the verbs in lines 34–37 that describe the parrots' actions. What effect do their actions have on the children?

_____

_____

_____

_____

_____

_____

_____

CLARIFY

Re-read lines 48–52. Underline details that describe the **conflict** between the children.

What kind of person is Mira,
judging from her actions
(lines 53–60)?

_____

_____

_____

_____

_____

_____

_____

_____

_____

_____

EVALUATE

Pause at line 71. Underline
the **image** that you feel best
describes the emptiness
after everyone but Raghu
runs away.

ANALYZE

Underline **images** that convey
the tension that Manu is
feeling (lines 72–83).

VOCABULARY

superciliously
(sōō'pər·sil'ē·əs·lē) *adv.:*
disdainfully or scornfully;
haughtily.

"Make a circle, make a circle!" she shouted, firmly pulling
and pushing till a kind of vague circle was formed. "Now clap!"
she roared, and, clapping, they all chanted in melancholy unison:
"Dip, dip, dip—my blue ship—" and every now and then one
or the other saw he was safe by the way his hands fell at the
crucial moment—palm on palm, or back of hand on palm—
and dropped out of the circle with a yell and a jump of relief
60   and jubilation.

Raghu was It. He started to protest, to cry "You cheated—
Mira cheated—Anu cheated—" but it was too late, the others
had all already streaked away. There was no one to hear when he
called out, "Only in the veranda—the porch—Ma said—Ma *said*
to stay in the porch!" No one had stopped to listen, all he saw
were their brown legs flashing through the dusty shrubs, scram-
bling up brick walls, leaping over compost heaps and hedges,
and then the porch stood empty in the purple shade of the
bougainvillea, and the garden was as empty as before; even the
70   limp squirrels had whisked away, leaving everything gleaming,
brassy, and bare.

Only small Manu suddenly reappeared, as if he had
dropped out of an invisible cloud or from a bird's claws, and
stood for a moment in the center of the yellow lawn, chewing
his finger and near to tears as he heard Raghu shouting, with his
head pressed against the veranda wall, "Eighty-three, eighty-five,
eighty-nine, ninety . . ." and then made off in a panic, half of
him wanting to fly north, the other half counseling south.
Raghu turned just in time to see the flash of his white shorts and
80   the uncertain skittering of his red sandals, and charged after him
with such a bloodcurdling yell that Manu stumbled over the
hosepipe, fell into its rubber coils, and lay there weeping, "I
won't be It—you have to find them all—all—All!"

"I know I have to, idiot," Raghu said, **superciliously** kicking
him with his toe. "You're dead," he said with satisfaction, licking
the beads of perspiration off his upper lip, and then stalked off

in search of worthier prey, whistling spiritedly so that the hiders should hear and tremble.

Ravi heard the whistling and picked his nose in a panic, trying
90 to find comfort by burrowing the finger deep—deep into that soft tunnel. He felt himself too exposed, sitting on an upturned flowerpot behind the garage. Where could he burrow? He could run around the garage if he heard Raghu come—around and around and around—but he hadn't much faith in his short legs when matched against Raghu's long, hefty, hairy footballer legs. Ravi had a frightening glimpse of them as Raghu combed the hedge of crotons and hibiscus, trampling delicate ferns under-foot as he did so. Ravi looked about him desperately, swallowing a small ball of snot in his fear.

100 The garage was locked with a great heavy lock to which the driver had the key in his room, hanging from a nail on the wall under his workshirt. Ravi had peeped in and seen him still sprawling on his string cot in his vest and striped underpants, the hair on his chest and the hair in his nose shaking with the vibrations of his phlegm-obstructed snores. Ravi had wished he were tall enough, big enough to reach the key on the nail, but it was impossible, beyond his reach for years to come. He had sidled away and sat dejectedly on the flowerpot. That at least was cut to his own size.

110 But next to the garage was another shed with a big green door. Also locked. No one even knew who had the key to the lock. That shed wasn't opened more than once a year, when Ma turned out all the old broken bits of furniture and rolls of mat-ting and leaking buckets, and the white anthills were broken and swept away and Flit sprayed into the spider webs and rat holes so that the whole operation was like the looting of a poor, ruined, and conquered city. The green leaves of the door sagged. They were nearly off their rusty hinges. The hinges were large

COMPARE & CONTRAST

Pause at line 99. Underline the words and phrases that describe how much bigger Raghu is, compared to Ravi.

_____

_____

_____

_____

_____

_____

_____

_____

IDENTIFY

Re-read lines 110–117. What change in the **sequence of events** occurs here, in the description of the shed? **(Grade 9–10 Review)**

_____

_____

_____

_____

_____

_____

_____

_____

Pause at line 120. How does Ravi get into the shed with the green door?

_____

_____

_____

_____

_____

_____

_____

_____

_____

_____

_____

VOCABULARY

temerity (tə·mer′ə·tē) *n.*: foolish or rash boldness; recklessness.

ANALYZE

What kind of atmosphere does Desai create in the description of the shed (lines 135–152)?

_____

_____

_____

_____

_____

_____

Two young girls, Rajasthan, India.

120 and made a small gap between the door and the walls—only just large enough for rats, dogs, and, possibly, Ravi to slip through.

Ravi had never cared to enter such a dark and depressing mortuary of defunct household goods seething with such unspeakable and alarming animal life but, as Raghu's whistling grew angrier and sharper and his crashing and storming in the hedge wilder, Ravi suddenly slipped off the flowerpot and through the crack and was gone. He chuckled aloud with astonishment at his own **temerity** so that Raghu came out of the hedge, stood silent with his hands on his hips, listening, and finally shouted, "I heard you! I'm coming! *Got* you—" and came

130 charging round the garage only to find the upturned flowerpot, the yellow dust, the crawling of white ants in a mud hill against the closed shed door—nothing. Snarling, he bent to pick up a stick and went off, whacking it against the garage and shed walls as if to beat out his prey.

Ravi shook, then shivered with delight, with self-congratulation. Also with fear. It was dark, spooky in the shed. It had a muffled smell, as of graves. Ravi had once got locked into the linen cupboard and sat there weeping for half an hour before he was rescued. But at least that had been a familiar place, and even

140   smelled pleasantly of starch, laundry, and, reassuringly, of his mother. But the shed smelled of rats, anthills, dust, and spider webs. Also of less definable, less recognizable horrors. And it was dark. Except for the white-hot cracks along the door, there was no light. The roof was very low. Although Ravi was small, he felt as if he could reach up and touch it with his fingertips. But he didn't stretch. He hunched himself into a ball so as not to bump into anything, touch or feel anything. What might there not be to touch him and feel him as he stood there, trying to see in the dark? Something cold, or slimy—like a snake. Snakes! He leapt

150   up as Raghu whacked the wall with his stick—then, quickly realizing what it was, felt almost relieved to hear Raghu, hear his stick. It made him feel protected.

But Raghu soon moved away. There wasn't a sound once his footsteps had gone around the garage and disappeared. Ravi stood frozen inside the shed. Then he shivered all over. Something had tickled the back of his neck. It took him a while to pick up the courage to lift his hand and explore. It was an insect—perhaps a spider—exploring *him*. He squashed it and wondered how many more creatures were watching him, waiting

160   to reach out and touch him, the stranger.

There was nothing now. After standing in that position— his hand still on his neck, feeling the wet splodge of the squashed spider gradually dry—for minutes, hours, his legs began to tremble with the effort, the inaction. By now he could see enough in the dark to make out the large solid shapes of old wardrobes, broken buckets, and bedsteads piled on top of each other around him. He recognized an old bathtub—patches of enamel glimmered at him, and at last he lowered himself onto its edge.

170   He contemplated slipping out of the shed and into the fray. He wondered if it would not be better to be captured by Raghu and be returned to the milling crowd as long as he could be in the sun, the light, the free spaces of the garden, and the familiarity

ANALYZE

Re-read lines 141–160. Underline **images** that appeal to the senses of sight, smell, hearing, and touch. What is most frightening to Ravi about being in the shed?

Pause at line 191. What makes Ravi decide to remain in hiding a while longer?

_____

_____

_____

_____

_____

_____

intoxicating (in·täks′i·kāt′iŋ) *v.* used as *adj.:* causing wild excitement or happiness, often to a point beyond self-control; heady.

dogged (dôg′id) *adj.:* persistent; stubborn.

of his brothers, sisters, and cousins. It would be evening soon. Their games would become legitimate. The parents would sit out on the lawn on cane basket chairs and watch them as they tore around the garden or gathered in knots to share a loot of mulberries or black, teeth-splitting *jamun*[2] from the garden trees. The gardener would fix the hosepipe to the water tap,

180 and water would fall lavishly through the air to the ground, soaking the dry yellow grass and the red gravel and arousing the sweet, the **intoxicating** scent of water on dry earth—that loveliest scent in the world. Ravi sniffed for a whiff of it. He half-rose from the bathtub, then heard the despairing scream of one of the girls as Raghu bore down upon her. There was the sound of a crash, and of rolling about in the bushes, the shrubs, then screams and accusing sobs of "I touched the den—" "You did not—" "I did—" "You liar, you did *not*" and then a fading away and silence again.

190   Ravi sat back on the harsh edge of the tub, deciding to hold out a bit longer. What fun if they were all found and caught— he alone left unconquered! He had never known that sensation. Nothing more wonderful had ever happened to him than being taken out by an uncle and bought a whole slab of chocolate all to himself, or being flung into the soda man's pony cart and driven up to the gate by the friendly driver with the red beard and pointed ears. To defeat Raghu—that hirsute,[3] hoarse-voiced football champion—and to be the winner in a circle of older, bigger, luckier children—that would be thrilling beyond imagi-

200 nation. He hugged his knees together and smiled to himself almost shyly at the thought of so much victory, such laurels.

There he sat smiling, knocking his heels against the bathtub, now and then getting up and going to the door to put his ear to the broad crack and listening for sounds of the game, the pursuer and the pursued, and then returning to his seat with

---

2. **jamun** (jä·mən) *n.:* plumlike fruit.
3. **hirsute** (hur′sōot′) *adj.:* hairy; shaggy.

the **dogged** determination of the true winner, a breaker of records, a champion.

It grew darker in the shed as the light at the door grew softer, fuzzier, turned to a kind of crumbling yellow pollen that turned to yellow fur, blue fur, gray fur. Evening. Twilight. The sound of water gushing, falling. The scent of earth receiving water, slaking its thirst in great gulps and releasing that green scent of freshness, coolness. Through the crack Ravi saw the long purple shadows of the shed and the garage lying still across the yard. Beyond that, the white walls of the house. The bougainvillea had lost its lividity, hung in dark bundles that quaked and twittered and seethed with masses of homing sparrows. The lawn was shut off from his view. Could he hear the children's voices? It seemed to him that he could. It seemed to him that he could hear them chanting, singing, laughing. But what about the game? What had happened? Could it be over? How could it when he was still not found?

It then occurred to him that he could have slipped out long ago, dashed across the yard to the veranda, and touched the "den." It was necessary to do that to win. He had forgotten. He had only remembered the part of hiding and trying to elude the seeker. He had done that so successfully, his success had occupied him so wholly, that he had quite forgotten that success had to be clinched by that final dash to victory and the ringing cry of "Den!"

With a whimper he burst through the crack, fell on his knees, got up, and stumbled on stiff, benumbed legs across the shadowy yard, crying heartily by the time he reached the veranda so that when he flung himself at the white pillar and bawled, "Den! Den! Den!" his voice broke with rage and pity at the disgrace of it all, and he felt himself flooded with tears and misery.

Out on the lawn, the children stopped chanting. They all turned to stare at him in amazement. Their faces were pale and triangular in the dusk. The trees and bushes around them stood inky and sepulchral, spilling long shadows across them. They stared, wondering at his reappearance, his passion, his wild

DRAW CONCLUSIONS

Re-read lines 208–218. Underline details that show the passage of time. How do you know that Ravi has been waiting in the shed a long time? *(Grade 9–10 Review)*

_____

_____

_____

_____

_____

IDENTIFY

Pause at line 222. What makes Ravi suspect that the game might be over?

_____

_____

_____

_____

_____

_____

CLARIFY

Re-read lines 223–235. Why does Ravi start crying?

_____

_____

_____

_____

If All the World Were Paper and All the Waters Ink (1962) by Jess.
The Fine Arts Museum of San Francisco, California. Courtesy of the Odyssia Gallery, New York.

animal howling. Their mother rose from her basket chair and came toward him, worried, annoyed, saying, "Stop it, stop it, Ravi. Don't be a baby. Have you hurt yourself?" Seeing him attended to, the children went back to clasping their hands and chanting, "The grass is green, the rose is red. . . ."

But Ravi would not let them. He tore himself out of his mother's grasp and pounded across the lawn into their midst, charging at them with his head lowered so that they scattered in surprise. "I won, I won, I won," he bawled, shaking his head so 250 that the big tears flew. "Raghu didn't find me. I won, I won—"

It took them a minute to grasp what he was saying, even who he was. They had quite forgotten him. Raghu had found all the others long ago. There had been a fight about who was to be It next. It had been so fierce that their mother had emerged from her bath and made them change to another game. Then they had played another and another. Broken mulberries from the tree and eaten them. Helped the driver wash the car when their father returned from work. Helped the gardener water the beds till he roared at them and swore he would complain to their parents.

260   The parents had come out, taken up their positions on the cane chairs. They had begun to play again, sing and chant. All this time no one had remembered Ravi. Having disappeared from the scene, he had disappeared from their minds. Clean.

"Don't be a fool," Raghu said roughly, pushing him aside, and even Mira said, "Stop howling, Ravi. If you want to play, you can stand at the end of the line," and she put him there very firmly.

The game proceeded. Two pairs of arms reached up and met in an arc. The children trooped under it again and again

270   in a **lugubrious** circle, ducking their heads and intoning

"The grass is green,
The rose is red;
Remember me
When I am dead, dead, dead, dead . . ."

And the arc of thin arms trembled in the twilight, and the heads were bowed so sadly, and their feet tramped to that melancholy refrain so mournfully, so helplessly, that Ravi could not bear it. He would not follow them, he would not be included in this funereal game. He had wanted victory and triumph—not a

280   funeral. But he had been forgotten, left out, and he would not join them now. The **ignominy** of being forgotten—how could he face it? He felt his heart go heavy and ache inside him unbearably. He lay down full length on the damp grass, crushing his face into it, no longer crying, silenced by a terrible sense of his insignificance.

VOCABULARY

lugubrious (lə·go͞o'brē·əs) *adj.:* very solemn or mournful, especially in a way that seems exaggerated or ridiculous.

ignominy (ig'nə·min'ē) *n.:* shame and dishonor.

INTERPRET

Pause at line 285. Underline details in the last paragraph that describe how Ravi feels. Why is Ravi so sad?

_____

_____

_____

_____

_____

_____

_____

_____

FLUENCY

Read the boxed passage aloud twice. The first time around, focus on marks of punctuation that help communicate meaning. During the second reading, pay attention to the feeling you want to express in your reading.

Games at Twilight

Reading Skills: Analyzing Details   Complete this chart with images from the story that you thought were particularly vivid or important. In the right-hand column, identify the mood created by the image, or explain why you think the image is especially significant.

Images	Mood/Significance

Games at Twilight

VOCABULARY IN CONTEXT

DIRECTIONS: Write a vocabulary word from the Word Box in each blank to complete the sentences below. Not all words from the box will be used.

Word Box

maniacal
stridently
superciliously
temerity
intoxicating
dogged
lugubrious
ignominy

1. The excitement surrounding the Winter Games was positively _____, causing all present to feel thrilled and expectant.

2. The bobsled team was _____; nothing would stop them on their quest for a gold medal.

3. Following her fall on the giant slalom, last year's champion placed last. Filled with _____, she bowed her head.

4. The speed skater was known for his _____. No one was surprised when he questioned the judges' decision.

WORD ANALOGIES

In an **analogy** the words in one pair relate to each other in the same way as the words in a second pair. Types of relationships frequently expressed in word analogies are listed below. Read each colon (:) as "is to" and the double colon (::) as "as."

Part to Whole   FINGER : HAND :: stanza : poem
   A *finger* is a part of a *hand,* just as a *stanza* is a part of a *poem.*

Location   ROOT : GROUND :: antifreeze : engine
   A *root* can be found in the *ground,* just as *antifreeze* can be found in an *engine.*

Performer and Related Action   MUSICIAN : PERFORM :: carpenter : build
   A *musician* is someone who *performs,* just as a *carpenter* is someone who *builds.*
   In this type of analogy, the first word is a noun and the second word is a verb.

DIRECTIONS: Study each analogy below to determine the relationship between the word pairs. Fill in each blank with the appropriate type of relationship.

_____   1. PARROT : TREE :: junk : shed

_____   2. BIRD : CHIRP :: fruit : rot

_____   3. VERANDA : HOUSE :: chant : game

_____   4. CAR : GARAGE :: blender : kitchen

Reading Standard 1.3 Discern the meaning of analogies encountered, analyzing specific comparisons as well as relationships and inferences.

 Check your Standards Mastery at the back of this book.

Part Two

Consumer, Workplace, and Public Documents

Academic Vocabulary

These are the terms you should know
as you read and analyze the selections that follow.

Consumer documents Documents used in the selling and buying of
products. Many consumer documents, such as warranties, protect the rights of the purchaser and the seller. Other consumer
documents include advertisements, contracts, instruction manuals, and product information.

Public documents Documents that inform the public. Public documents
are created by governmental, social, religious, or news-gathering
organizations. They include safety information, government
regulations, schedules of events, explanations of services, and
informational articles.

Workplace documents Documents used in offices, factories, and other
work sites to communicate job-related information. These
include business letters, contracts, instruction manuals, memo-
randums, and safety information.

Technical documents Documents used to explain or establish procedures for using technology, such as mechanical, electronic, or
digital products or systems. Technical documents include how-
to instructions, installation instructions, and instructions on
carrying out scientific procedures.

Functional documents Any documents prepared for a specific function,
such as consumer, public, workplace, and technical documents.

Reading Standard 2.3 (Grade 9–10 Review) Generate relevant questions about readings on issues that can be researched.

Reading Standard 2.6 (Grade 9–10 Review) Demonstrate use of sophisticated learning tools by following technical directions (e.g., those found with graphic calculators and specialized software programs and in access guides to World Wide Web sites on the Internet).

Reading Standard 2.7 (Grade 9–10 Review) Critique the logic of functional documents by examining the sequence of information and procedures in anticipation of possible reader misunder-standings.

Warwick Castle Web Site *from* Tussauds Attractions Ltd.

BEFORE YOU READ

If they ever made a movie about Warwick Castle, it would be rated R for violence. The tenth Earl of Warwick seized the favorite of King Edward II, Piers Gaveston, and brought him to the castle to be tried for treason—and beheaded. His great-grandson, the thirteenth Earl, had Joan of Arc burned at the stake. Earls 17 and 18 themselves faced execution as supposed traitors to the throne. Some say the ghost of the later owner Sir Fulke Grenville, stabbed to death by a disgruntled servant, still haunts the tower where he slept.

INFORMATIONAL FOCUS: WEB SITE

If you think of the Internet as a gigantic library, then a Web site is a book in that library, and a Web page is a page in that book. You're about to look at two pages from the Warwick Castle Web site. Here's what you'll see:

- **Text and graphics.** *Text* means written words. *Graphics* are pictures and designs.

- **Menu.** You know that in a restaurant, a menu is a list of available dishes. On a Web site, a menu is a list of available links.

- **Links.** Also known as hyperlinks or "hot spots," links are text and graphics you can click on that will take you to other locations, such as another page in the same site or to another site entirely.

- **Logo.** A symbol that represents a company, place, group, and so on. The logo may be just the name set in a distinctive typeface, or it may include a graphic illustration.

INFORMATIONAL FOCUS: FUNCTIONAL DOCUMENTS

Functional documents are documents used for a particular purpose or function. Three common types are:

- **Consumer documents**—used in the selling and buying of products.

- **Public documents**—used to inform the public.

- **Workplace documents**—used to communicate job-related information.

TERMS TO KNOW

Format—the design and layout of a document.
Typeface—the style or design of the type.
Boldface—dark, heavy type.
Header—a label or heading that begins a section of a document.

Reading Standard 2.1 (Grade 9–10 Review) Analyze the structure and format of functional workplace documents, including the graphics and headers, and explain how authors use the features to achieve their purposes.

WARWICK CASTLE WEB SITE

from Tussauds Attractions Ltd.

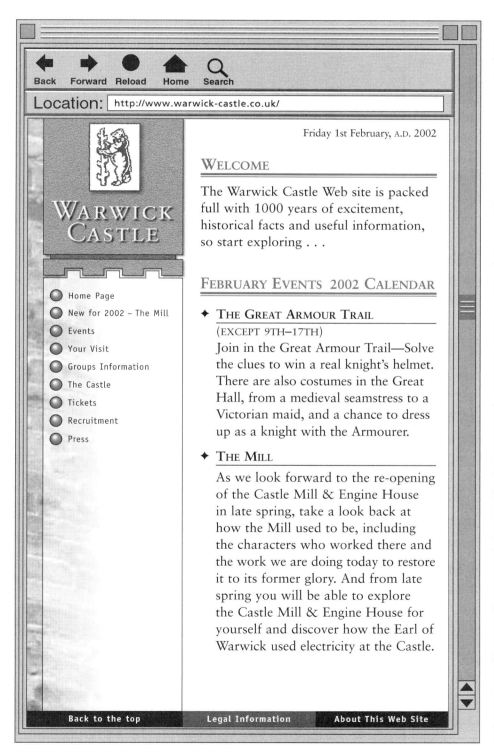

Friday 1st February, A.D. 2002

WELCOME

The Warwick Castle Web site is packed full with 1000 years of excitement, historical facts and useful information, so start exploring . . .

FEBRUARY EVENTS 2002 CALENDAR

✦ **THE GREAT ARMOUR TRAIL**
(EXCEPT 9TH–17TH)
Join in the Great Armour Trail—Solve the clues to win a real knight's helmet. There are also costumes in the Great Hall, from a medieval seamstress to a Victorian maid, and a chance to dress up as a knight with the Armourer.

✦ **THE MILL**
As we look forward to the re-opening of the Castle Mill & Engine House in late spring, take a look back at how the Mill used to be, including the characters who worked there and the work we are doing today to restore it to its former glory. And from late spring you will be able to explore the Castle Mill & Engine House for yourself and discover how the Earl of Warwick used electricity at the Castle.

Navigation menu:
- Home Page
- New for 2002 – The Mill
- Events
- Your Visit
- Groups Information
- The Castle
- Tickets
- Recruitment
- Press

Browser: Back | Forward | Reload | Home | Search

Location: http://www.warwick-castle.co.uk/

Back to the top | Legal Information | About This Web Site

From *Warwick Castle* Web site, accessed on February 1, 2002, at http://www.warwick-castle.co.uk/castle/castle.html. Reprinted by permission of **Tussauds Attractions Limited.**

TEXT FEATURES

Circle the castle **logo**. What is the logo used for?

_____

_____

_____

WORD STUDY

American spelling often varies slightly from the British. In the United States, *armour* would be spelled *armor*. Other examples:

British	American
centre	center
favourite	favorite
paycheque	paycheck

PURPOSE

Recruitment (in the menu on the left side of the Web page) means "hiring." You would click on this menu item if you were looking for a job at the castle. Circle the menu items a tour operator might click on to use this Web site as a **workplace document.**

TEXT FEATURES

Underline the **headers** that draw your attention to upcoming events and attractions at the castle. *(Grade 9–10 Review)*

PURPOSE

PURPOSE

What is the purpose of the **boldface text** under "The Castle" header?

_____

_____

_____

FORMAT

What menu item would you click on to learn about the layout of the castle? What item would you click on to buy something? *(Grade 9–10 Review)*

_____

_____

TEXT FEATURES

Circle two different links you could click on to reach the same Web page.

PURPOSE

Explain why this Web site can be considered both a **consumer document** and a **public document**.

_____

_____

_____

_____

_____

_____

Back   Forward   Reload   Home   Search

Location: http://www.warwick-castle.co.uk/castle/castle.html

Friday 1st February, A.D. 2002

THE CASTLE

Discover 1000 years of history with our **Timeline** or stumble across towers, dungeons and state rooms while **Exploring the Castle.**

- Home Page
- New for 2002 – The Mill
- Events
- Your Visit
- Groups Information
- The Castle
  - Castle History
  - Exploring the Castle
  - The Tussaud's Group
  - Links
- Tickets
- Recruitment
- Press

For enthusiasts, we also have a full Castle History and a chronology of the Earls of Warwick since 1088.

And finally, you can also find information about **The Tussaud's Group** and **Links** to related sites.

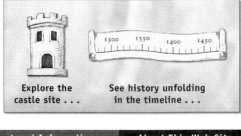

Explore the castle site . . .   See history unfolding in the timeline . . .

Back to the top   Legal Information   About This Web Site

Standards Review

TestPractice Warwick Castle Web Site

Complete the sample test item below by circling the correct answer. Then, read the explanation to the right.

Sample Test Item	Explanation of the Correct Answer
On a Web site, the purpose of **links** is to— A connect you to illustrations B highlight important information C connect you to additional information D teach you how to use the document	The correct answer is *C*. A particular link *could* connect you to illustrations (*A*), highlight important information (*B*), or teach you how to use the document (*D*), but only *C* gives the purpose of all Web-site links.

DIRECTIONS: Circle the letter of each correct response.

1. "Warwick Castle" can be considered a **workplace document** because it—

   A describes job openings

   B contains interesting graphics

   C is interactive

   D recounts historic events

2. All of the following are graphic elements of the Web site *except*—

   F the photographs of the castle

   G the time-line link

   H text describing the mill

   J the castle logo

3. The **menu** on this Web site is a list of—

   A links to additional information

   B events happening at the castle

   C ticket prices for group tours

   D dishes available for lunch

4. This Web site could be considered a **consumer document** because it—

   F lists a schedule of events

   G sells tickets to events

   H displays photographs

   J tells about castle history

Reading Standard 2.1 (Grade 9–10 Review) Analyze the structure and format of functional workplace documents, including the graphics and headers, and explain how authors use the features to achieve their purposes.

Europe in the Middle Ages *from* World History: People and Nations

Imagine: You are a teenager in the year 3000, and today is "21st Century Day" at your school. Everyone is dressed up as someone rich and famous. Your best friend has come as a movie star, and your teacher is a president of the United States. A typical 21st-century scene? Not for most of us. The same is true of the Middle Ages. If you lived back then, you were more likely to have been a peasant sweating in the fields than a knight in shining armor or a princess in a castle.

INFORMATIONAL FOCUS: TEXTBOOK

On the next pages you'll read the beginning of a chapter from a world-history textbook. Textbooks can be challenging to read, because they're packed with information. Fortunately, they're organized to help you find and understand that information. Some organizational features you'll find are—

- **Introduction.** The section labeled "Chapter 10 Focus" introduces the information you will find in the chapter. It shows a **time line** of the period covered and gives a brief **overview,** called "Significance." The chapter focus also lists key terms, people, and places to look for as you read.

- **Headers.** Sections of text are introduced or highlighted by labels, or headers. The two **main heads** in this selection are "Chapter 10 Focus" and "**1** Frankish Rulers Governed Much of Western Europe for Centuries." The other headers are **subheads,** because they come under the main heads.

INFORMATIONAL FOCUS: LOGICAL SEQUENCE

To be clear, information has to be organized in a **logical sequence**—an order that makes sense. Some common organizational patterns are—

- **point-by-point sequence**—items are listed in no particular order. A report on breeds of dogs would probably be in point-by-point order.

- **step-by-step sequence**—items are listed first, second, third, and so on. Directions and recipes are usually in step-by-step order.

- **chronological sequence**—items are listed in the time order in which they occurred. Most histories and narratives are in chronological order.

- **spatial sequence**—items are listed in the order they appear in a space. A description of a setting is likely to be in spatial order.

TERMS TO KNOW

Boldface—dark, heavy type.
Italic—type that slants to the right.
Format—the design and layout of a document.

Reading Standard 2.2
Analyze the way in which clarity of meaning is affected by the patterns of organization, hierarchical structures, repetition of the main ideas, syntax, and word choice in the text.

Europe in the Middle Ages

from World History: People and Nations

CHAPTER 10 FOCUS

Place Western Europe

Time

432–1328

3.7 mil. B.C.   4000 B.C.   A.D. 2100

Compare the date span in the time line to the dates given for the Middle Ages in lines 11–13. What do you learn about the period called the Middle Ages from these two sets of information?

_____

_____

_____

_____

_____

_____

_____

_____

Significance

While the Byzantine and Muslim empires flourished in the East, no strong empire emerged in what had been the western part of the Roman Empire. The Roman Empire did not end with a sudden crash, however. Rather, it slipped away a little at a time. A border fort would be abandoned. Mail would no longer come to a city. Slowly, what had been a magnificent empire became

10   splintered ruins.

The period in western European history following the collapse of the Roman Empire, from about 500 to about 1500, is called the *Middle Ages,* or the *medieval* period. (The word *medieval* comes from the Latin words *medius,* meaning "middle," and *aevum,* meaning "age.")

The people of that time never thought of themselves as living in a "middle age." They thought of human history as a chain of events that had begun in the Biblical era and continued to their own time. Although these people had little understanding of the

20   past, they developed new customs and institutions to suit the conditions under which they lived.

PURPOSE

What is the purpose of the section labeled "Significance"?

_____

_____

_____

_____

_____

_____

_____

Terms to Define

Middle Ages	feudalism	Inquisition
serf	manor	Magna Carta

Where in the selection would you expect to find information about the topics listed under the **subheads** "Terms to Define," "People to Identify," "Places to Locate," and "Questions to Guide Your Reading"? (Note that this selection includes only the beginning of the chapter.) *(Grade 9–10 Review)*

_____

_____

_____

_____

_____

_____

_____

_____

_____

_____

FORMAT

Why do you think the section on peasants is set off in **italic** type?

_____

_____

_____

_____

_____

_____

_____

People to Identify

Charlemagne   William the Conqueror

Vikings   Hugh Capet

Places to Locate

Papal States   Hastings

30   Normandy   Worms

Questions to Guide Your Reading

1. How did Frankish rulers gain control of western Europe?

2. Why was medieval life organized around feudalism and the manorial system?

3. What was the role of the church during the Middle Ages?

4. What prompted conflict between kings and nobles in France and England?

5. Why did popes and emperors clash over Germany and Italy?

In the Middle Ages, most Europeans were peasants who eked out
40   *a meager living in the fields, often working from dawn to dusk.*
As one historian noted:

" *The sun rose early, . . . but not much earlier than the peasants of the little village of Belcombe. . . . Within most of the houses men were stirring . . . taking a look at the sky before they ate a brief meal . . . of a lump of bread and a draught of ale. . . . Then they . . . fetched their scythes and rakes from the sheds, and started off. . . . On entering the field the peasants broke up in little groups, some going to one and some to another part of the meadow. . . .*

In one corner of the field John Wilde and his two sons,
50   *Richard and Roger, kept to their tasks for some time without pause.*
. . . All three continued until the sun was getting well up into the heavens, when they stopped their work and left the field together with many others. As they passed the church John glanced at the

Mass clock on its wall near the door, and saw by the shadow . . .
that they had good time before the service, as it was
not yet eight. **"**

These hardworking peasants formed the backbone of a society
attempting to restore order out of the chaos that followed the
collapse of the Roman Empire in the West. In time a new social
60 *and political order emerged.*

1 Frankish Rulers Governed Much of Western Europe for Centuries

After the Roman Empire in the West collapsed, many Germanic
tribes, including Visigoths, Vandals, Burgundians, and Ostrogoths,
plundered Europe and established several small kingdoms. Most
tribes, however, did not create strong governments. Of all the
Germanic tribes the Franks played the greatest role in European
history. The Franks first entered the Roman Empire near the
mouth of the Rhine River in the A.D. 300s. They settled in the
70 area of northern Gaul that corresponds roughly to the present-
day nations of Belgium and the Netherlands.

Clovis and the Merovingians

In 481, an able ruler named Clovis became king of one of the
Frankish tribes. He and his successors were called Merovingians
because Clovis traced his family back to an ancestor named
Meroveg. Although brutal, cruel, and apparently without a
conscience, Clovis excelled as a military leader. His troops
conquered the other Frankish tribes and soon controlled all
of northern Gaul.

80   Later, Clovis seized southwestern Gaul from the Visigoths.
Even though he ruled most of what is today France (which
took its name from the Franks), Clovis failed to pass on to his
successors either his strong leadership qualities or his united
kingdom. In accordance with Frankish custom, Clovis's sons
divided the kingdom among themselves.

FORMAT

What can you infer from
the number "1" in the
header "**1** Frankish Rulers
Governed . . ."?

_____

_____

_____

_____

_____

_____

_____

SEQUENCE

How can you tell that the
information in lines 63–85 is
in **chronological order**? Circle
clues you find in the text.
(Grade 9–10 Review)

_____

_____

_____

_____

_____

_____

_____

_____

_____

_____

Standards Review

TestPractice **Europe in the Middle Ages**

Complete the sample test item below by circling the correct answer. Then, read the explanation to the right.

Sample Test Item	Explanation of the Correct Answer
The beginning of the Middle Ages dates from the collapse of which empire? A Muslim B Byzantine C Roman D Frankish	*C* is the correct answer, as is stated in the text: "The period in western European history following the collapse of the Roman Empire . . . is called the Middle Ages." The Muslim (*A*) and Byzantine (*B*) empires flourished in the East during that time, and Frankish (*D*) rulers came to power in the West but never had an empire.

DIRECTIONS: Circle the letter of each correct response.

Reading Standard 2.2
Analyze the way in which clarity of meaning is affected by the patterns of organization, hierarchical structures, repetition of the main ideas, syntax, and word choice in the text.

1. Under which **subhead** would you look for a listing of important historical figures covered in this chapter?

    A "Significance"

    B "Terms to Define"

    C "People to Identify"

    D "Places to Locate"

2. All of the following are used in the selection to highlight or identify a section of text *except*—

    F headers

    G different type styles

    H numbers

    J pictures

3. Under which **header** do you find information to answer number 1 under "Questions to Guide Your Reading"?

    A "Chapter 10 Focus"

    B "Places to Locate"

    C "Questions to Guide Your Reading"

    D "1 Frankish Rulers Governed Much of Western Europe for Centuries"

4. The main history text is presented in which type of **sequence**?

    F point by point

    G step by step

    H chronological

    J spatial

Managing Money in Britain

from TravelBritain (British Tourist Authority)

An American who travels to Great Britain won't get far without noticing some interesting differences. The British put their steering wheel on the left side of the car, and they drive on the left side of the road. They call apartments *flats* and elevators *lifts.* Our cookies are their *biscuits;* our french fries are their *chips;* our potato chips are their *crisps.* Their favorite meals have names like Toad in the Hole, Bubble and Squeak, Bangers and Mash. If someone *nicks your brolly* (steals your umbrella), you'll be sorry—in Britain, it rains more often than in most parts of America.

INFORMATIONAL FOCUS: FUNCTIONAL DOCUMENTS

A travel guide is an example of a **functional document.** Its function, or purpose, is to provide information a traveler needs: what to see, where to stay, or—as in the following pages—how to use money in another country. In this article, look for:

- Information broken up into small, manageable chunks

- **Headers** allowing readers to skim quickly for specific topics

- Simple, straightforward language meant to explain clearly

- **Graphic illustrations** showing some of the items discussed

As you read the document, think about how clear it is and what you might change to prevent reader misunderstandings.

Reading Standard 2.7 (Grade 9–10 Review) Critique the logic of functional documents by examining the sequence of information and procedures in anticipation of possible reader misunderstandings.

Managing Money in Britain

from TravelBritain (British Tourist Authority)

British money.

ANALYZE

Read the section called "Spending Money." What have you learned, and what do you still need to learn before you spend money in Great Britain?

_____

_____

_____

_____

_____

_____

Spending Money

There are no restrictions on the amount of money you can bring into Britain (in any currency or any form); however, only the pound sterling is valid for payment. In other words, dollar bills or dollar travelers checks must be exchanged into pounds either before you leave the USA or upon arrival. Travelers checks can be purchased from your bank in either dollars or sterling (or ask your travel agent where they are available in your area). It is advisable to arrive with some sterling currency for tipping

10   and other incidentals.

What's What?

There are 100 pence to the pound sterling, and the different colored notes come in £50, £20, £10 and £5 values (£1 notes are still issued in Scotland and though most places should accept them, it may be better to change them to £1 coins before you leave Scotland). All coins bear HM The Queen's head on one side, but the £1 coins have different flip-sides to reflect the different countries of Britain: lions for England, a thistle for Scotland and a leek for Wales are just a few . . . See how many
20   different ones you can find! A new £2.00 coin has recently been introduced, in two-tone, with a silver coin bordered by gold.

Banks & Bureaux de Change

Most banks are open from 9:30 A.M. until 4:30 P.M., Monday to Friday, with some of the main branches open an extra hour and for a few hours on Saturday mornings. Many branches have 24-hour banking lobbies where a range of services can be obtained through ATMs.

      Bureaux de Change, also found in travel agencies, larger department stores, and some post offices in London and
30   Northern Ireland, are often open even in the evenings, and there is a 24-hour service at major airports. Always check the exchange rate and any commission charges in advance.

Exchange Rates, May 22, 2002

	U.S.$	U.K.£	SFranc	¥en	Euro
Euro	1.0808	1.5764	0.6881	0.0087	—
Japan	124.21	181.27	79.095	—	114.93
Switzerland	1.5701	2.2910	—	0.0126	1.4533
U.K.	0.6856	—	0.4365	0.0055	0.6343
U.S.	—	1.4587	0.6369	0.0081	0.9252

EVALUATE

"What's What?" is a very general header. Why do you think the writer chose it? How could you make it clearer or more specific?

_____

_____

_____

_____

_____

_____

_____

WORD STUDY

Pence (line 12) are pennies or cents (p = pence). *Notes* (line 13) are bills. British notes are in pounds, as ours are in dollars (£ = pounds). *HM* (line 16) stands for "Her Majesty."

Bureaux de Change (line 28) is French for Bureaus of Exchange—places to exchange one country's currency for another.

PURPOSE

What is the purpose of the table at the bottom of the page?

_____

_____

_____

_____

The euro, the new European currency.

EVALUATE

Pause at line 45. Does the section labeled "The Euro" make clear the role of the euro in Great Britain? Why or why not? *(Grade 9–10 Review)*

_____

_____

_____

_____

_____

_____

_____

_____

ANALYZE

What information is unclear in the section entitled "Tipping"? *(Grade 9–10 Review)*

_____

_____

_____

_____

_____

_____

_____

_____

_____

_____

The Euro

The new common currency of Europe was introduced on January 1, 1999. To date, eleven European Union countries are introducing the euro, as the new currency is called, with the objective of easing transactions between European countries. The countries are: Austria, Belgium, Finland, France, Germany, the Republic of Ireland, Italy, Luxembourg, Netherlands,

40 Portugal and Spain. There are plans for the UK to join at a later date.

New euro notes and coins will circulate alongside national currencies, with exchange rates posted for both. The goal is to replace the national currencies of participating countries by July 1, 2002.

Tipping

Service is often included in your hotel, restaurant or bar bill, but if it isn't, a tip of 10–15% is customary. A higher tip for exceptional service is at your discretion. The only other times

50 a tip is expected is for a taxi ride—10–15%, a bell boy—£1 per

bag, or at a beauty salon. Theater, movie, petrol (gas) station, and bar staff do not expect one.

TAX/VAT Refunds

American visitors to Britain can reclaim the 17.5% VAT, minus the administrative fee, on purchases over a minimum limit (check with the store for their limit—usually £50–£100). Look for the "Tax Free Shopping" sign in the windows of participating stores. All you have to do is fill out the form, which the sales assistant will give you, keep the goods in your hand luggage and

60 show both goods and forms to the VAT desk at the airport or seaport on your departure. A customs officer will check the goods and validate the refund voucher. You can receive your refund on the spot at some airports, otherwise you should mail the validated form back to the store in the envelope provided, and a refund check will be sent to you by mail. You can also have the refund credited to your credit card account. Please be patient, refunds can take up to three months to be processed. Any queries should be taken up with the store where you purchased the goods. Don't forget that VAT refunds cannot

70 be processed after you arrive back home in the USA.

VAT, just like American sales tax, is charged on almost everything, but please remember that refunds only apply to goods being taken out of the country, not services.

IDENTIFY

In lines 53–58, circle the information that tells you VAT is a sales tax.

EVALUATE

Underline the sentence in lines 69–70. Based on information earlier in this section, what is unclear about this sentence? How could the sentence be written more clearly? *(Grade 9–10 Review)*

_____

_____

_____

_____

_____

_____

_____

_____

_____

_____

_____

_____

_____

_____

_____

_____

_____

_____

_____

_____

Standards Review

 **Managing Money in Britain**

Complete the sample test item below by circling the correct answer. Then, read the explanation to the right.

Sample Test Item	Explanation of the Correct Answer
According to the travel guide, how much money are you allowed to bring into Great Britain? **A** none **B** only pounds sterling **C** up to $1000 per person **D** as much as you like	*D* is the correct answer. The guide states: "There are no restrictions on the amount of money you can bring into Britain (in any currency or any form)," so *A*, *B*, and *C* are incorrect. Only pounds sterling are valid for payment, but you can bring in any currency and any amount.

DIRECTIONS: Circle the letter of each correct response.

Reading Standard 2.7 (Grade 9–10 Review) Critique the logic of functional documents by examining the sequence of information and procedures in anticipation of possible reader misunderstandings.

1. Which section gives you the most information about the pound sterling?

   A "Spending Money"

   B "What's What?"

   C "Banks & Bureaux de Change"

   D "The Euro"

2. The section labeled "The Euro" is about—

   F kinds of British currency

   G a new European currency

   H what things are called

   J the names of banks

3. All of the following countries have already introduced the euro *except*—

   A Germany

   B Ireland

   C Italy

   D Great Britain

4. Which "Tipping" tip is unclear?

   F what to tip bellboys

   G how much to tip for a taxi ride

   H whether to tip at a bar

   J whether to buy gas or petrol

Jobs at the British Broadcasting Corporation (BBC) *from* BBC Online

The BBC is Great Britain's national TV and radio network. Listeners around the world turn to BBC radio for high-quality news reporting day and night. When it first started transmission in the 1920s, however, the BBC broadcast news only after 7:00 P.M. They didn't want to upset the press, which sold papers by getting the news out first. The BBC doesn't sell advertising to pay for programming. Instead, it charges a license fee. In 2002, the household fee was about 28.5 pence a day, or around 43 cents.

INFORMATIONAL FOCUS: WORKPLACE DOCUMENT

How would you like to work as a broadcast journalist in the BBC radio newsroom in London? This job listing will help you decide. The information given in a job listing has two main purposes:

- to explain the qualifications (experience, skills, education) you need to get the job, and
- to describe the work you would do if you were hired.

As you read through the job listing, think of questions you might want to ask the person who interviews you or that you might want to research yourself before you even apply for the job.

Reading Standard 2.3 **(Grade 9–10 Review)** Generate relevant questions about readings on issues that can be researched.

Jobs at the British Broadcasting Corporation (BBC)

Broadcast Journalists BBC News
BBC Radio Newsroom Location/London

IDENTIFY

What information is included in the "Summary Information" section?

_____

_____

_____

_____

_____

_____

QUESTION

Imagine you have applied for this job. For each item under "Job Purpose," write a question you might ask the interviewer. *(Grade 9–10 Review)*

1. _____

_____

2. _____

_____

3. _____

_____

4. _____

_____

Summary Information

- **The BBC radio newsroom . . .**
  . . . provides news for five national networks and News Online. The newsroom meets more than a hundred deadlines a day.

- **Originate material, write scripts, produce packages . . .**
  . . . using radio production techniques. Broadcast news reports and summaries where appropriate.

- **Experience in journalism . . .**
  . . . and proven ability to select, originate, prepare and develop story ideas as essential as good broadcasting voice. Thorough and in-depth knowledge of domestic and world news and good awareness of Parliament crucial.

10

More Information

Job Purpose

1. Working for Senior Broadcast Journalists and Editors.
2. To prepare items and packages for BBC News programmes.
3. To work as appropriate in a multi-skilled manner in Radio and/or Television.
4. To broadcast as necessary.

20 ### Accountabilities

1. To attend the pre-programme conferences and planning meetings as required, and offer programme ideas and stories.
2. To research stories, checking factual details; undertaking background research as required and obtaining further information from all sources.

From "Job Listing for the BBC" *from BBC Online,* accessed March 11, 2002 at http://www.bbc.co.uk/jobs/e54388.shtml. Copyright **British Broadcasting Corporation.** Reprinted by permission of the publisher.

3. To write the story to the required specification maintaining professional journalistic standards of accuracy, impartiality and fair dealing while adhering to the BBC's Producer and Factual program guidelines.

30 4. To work on a developing story, following through the coverage, amending and updating the material as required. To work with resource staff ensuring that final scripts contain all necessary instructions, cues, and information, and that the timing conforms to the program planning requirements.

5. To produce packages making use of the appropriate Radio or TV production techniques and to undertake pre or post production and studio work according to individual skills and times available.

40 6. To field produce and report on a wide range of news stories and issues and undertake operational duties as appropriate.

7. To observe and carry out any requirement outlined in the BBC News safety policy and specifically to conduct risk assessments when appropriate.

Knowledge and Experience

1. Postholders will be professional journalists or have equivalent experiences combined with demonstrable commitment to BBC News. Good writing skills are essential, as is the potential to originate and develop program stories.

50 2. Must have an understanding of the editorial aims and policies of BBC News output and must be able to exercise an appropriate degree of editorial judgement and to take responsibility for any brief that might be assigned by a program newsroom or a newsgathering editor.

3. Knowledge of production techniques and facilities in both Radio and/or Television and the ability to develop bi-media production skills. Knowledge of information sources.

EXTEND

Pause at line 25. Where might you do research for a news story? List at least three sources. *(Grade 9–10 Review)*

_____

_____

_____

CONNECT

In line 40, "field produce" means to produce stories where the news is happening, rather than in a newsroom. What would be an "operational duty" (line 41) a journalist might have to undertake in the field?

_____

_____

_____

EXTEND

How could you get "an understanding of the editorial aims and policies of BBC News output" (lines 50–51)?

_____

_____

_____

_____

_____

Standards Review

 TestPractice : **Jobs at the BBC**

Complete the sample test item below by circling the correct answer. Then, read the explanation to the right.

Sample Test Item	Explanation of the Correct Answer
What would be the best preparation for a position as a BBC broadcast journalist? A starring in your school play B writing for your school newspaper C taking pictures for your senior yearbook D running for student council	*B* is the correct answer. A broadcast journalist needs strong writing skills and experience reporting stories. Acting (*A*), photography (*C*), and political skills (*D*) are not requirements for a broadcast journalist.

DIRECTIONS: Circle the letter of each correct response.

Reading Standard 2.3 (Grade 9–10 Review) Generate relevant questions about readings on issues that can be researched.

1. According to the job listing, a successful applicant needs all of the following *except*—

   A journalism experience

   B good writing skills

   C an attractive appearance

   D knowledge of the BBC

2. If as a journalist you most enjoyed broadcasting on air, which question would you most likely ask during an interview for this job?

   F How long do pre-program conferences take?

   G How often would I be called on to broadcast?

   H What assistance will I get in researching stories?

   J Which senior staff members will I be working with?

3. BBC broadcast journalists need to generate research questions when—

   A undertaking background research

   B interviewing people involved in the news

   C working on a developing story

   D all of the above

4. A risk assessment would most likely be appropriate when covering—

   F a natural disaster

   G Parliamentary proceedings

   H tennis at Wimbledon

   J all of the above

Building a Model Chunnel Train *from* TGVweb

The Channel Tunnel, or "Chunnel," opened in 1994. It runs 39 kilometers—a little over 24 miles—under the English Channel, connecting France and England. It is the longest undersea tunnel in the world. A few facts and figures:

- In its first six years of operation, 57 million people traveled through the Chunnel via high-speed rail. That's equivalent to the entire population of Great Britain.

- Chunnel train locomotives (also called "power cars" or "power units") are the most powerful locomotives in the world. Running on electricity, they haul trains of up to 2,400 tons at speeds of up to 140 kilometers per hour (87 mph).

- If you rode on the Chunnel train, you would be about 40 meters (over 131 feet) *below the ocean floor.*

INFORMATIONAL FOCUS: TECHNICAL DIRECTIONS

Every Chunnel train has two power cars, front and back, one pulling and one pushing. The train changes direction without turning around: the front simply becomes the back, and vice versa. Power cars have a distinctive aerodynamic nose. On the following pages, you'll find directions for building a model power car. These directions have three distinct types of information:

Steps. Numbered directions to be followed in the order they are written.
Figures. Pictures showing what is meant by the directions at specific points. The figures appear near steps that refer to them.
Illustrations. A smaller copy of the actual paper model shows parts of the model, which are numbered 1–6, and flaps, which are lettered A–V.

Always read directions the whole way through before beginning.

TERMS TO KNOW

Cross-reference—text that directs you to another section of the document or to another document entirely. Cross-references are often placed in parentheses.
Cross-section—an illustration showing how something would appear if cut down the middle.
Step-by-step sequence—a sequence that lists items first, second, third, and so on. Directions, recipes, and any other information that has to be followed in a particular order are usually presented in step-by-step sequence.

Reading Standard 2.6 **(Grade 9–10 Review)** Demonstrate use of sophisticated learning tools by following technical directions (e.g., those found with graphic calculators and specialized software programs and in access guides to World Wide Web sites on the Internet).

Building a Model Chunnel Train

from TGVweb

Read these important assembly instructions before starting! To preview the parts for the power car assembly, turn to page 368.

Step 1 Cut out the base of the power unit (part number 2) leaving about 5 mm (1/4 inch) margin around the edge of the part.

Step 2 Find a piece of cardboard slightly larger than the part you just cut out. A cereal box will do nicely. The cardboard will stiffen the base of the model and ensure that it is straight. Glue the part from step 1 to the cardboard. When it is dry, cut out around the edge of the part (cutting off the margin you left earlier).

Step 3 Score the main body (part number 1) at each place indicated by the arrows.

Step 4 Cut out the main body. Where the small scissors symbol is indicated, cut along the black line until you reach the base of the cab windows.

Step 5 Mark the folds on the main body. All the folds are "peak" folds.

Step 6 Score the roof (part number 4) at the places indicated by the arrows and along the base of each flap (F, G, H, J).

Step 7 Cut out the roof and mark the folds. All folds are "peak" folds.

DRAW CONCLUSIONS

Read through the instructions. Why do you think the directions appear in a **step-by-step sequence**?

_____

_____

_____

WORD STUDY

Steps 3, 6, 16, 21, and 24 call for *scoring* along lines to be folded. To *score* means to use a sharp tool and a straight edge to make a scratch or groove, without actually cutting through the paper. Scoring makes folding easier.

INTERPRET

What is meant by "peak folds" (Steps 5, 7, 17, and 25) and "valley folds" (Step 17)?

_____

_____

_____

_____

_____

_____

"Build Your Own Power Car" from "Power Car Instructions" by Clem Tillier from TGVweb, accessed on February 12, 2002, at http://mercurio.iet.unipi.it/tgv/models/motatlinst.html. Reprinted by permission of **Clem Tillier.**

Step 8 Apply glue to flap F and glue it to the edge of the roof on the main body. The roof should now form one continuous surface along the entire length of the power unit. Apply glue to flaps G and glue them to the edges of part 1, the main body. Make sure you don't do this on a flat surface since the front section of the roof slopes downward very slightly.

30 **Step 9** Apply glue to flaps H and glue them to the edge of the cab roof (just above the side windows). The roof profile should follow the profile of the body side, as it slopes down from the top of the unit onto the cab.

Step 10 Apply glue to flap E and glue it to the opposite side of the body so that the windshield now forms the front of the unit. Next, from inside the body (underneath), apply glue to flaps J and glue them to the back of the two windshield windows. The front of the unit should now look like Figure 1 below.

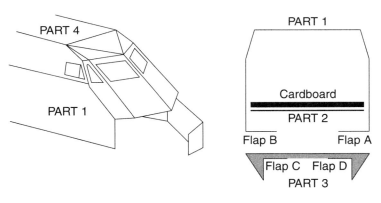

Figure 1   **Figure 2**

40 **Step 11** Apply glue to the back side of flap A. Glue flap A onto the base (part 1) so that it wraps around the bottom of the base (see Figure 2). Make sure that the marks on flap A align with the marks on part 2. This alignment is very important; if you don't get it right the model will be twisted or bent.

TEXT FEATURES

A **cross-reference** is text that directs the reader to another section of the document or to another document. Circle the cross-reference in Step 11.

WORD STUDY

Align (line 42) means "to line up, or place in the correct position." (See Step 11.) Why is it important to *align* parts correctly before gluing them? Underline what happens if you don't get the alignment right.

_____

_____

_____

_____

_____

_____

TEXT FEATURES

Figure 2 shows a **cross-section** of the model. What makes this figure a cross-section?

_____

_____

_____

_____

_____

TEXT FEATURES

Sometimes directions save space by instructing you to repeat a step described earlier. Re-read steps 12–19. Find three examples, and underline them.

IDENTIFY

Re-read the text in parentheses in lines 63 and 72. What kind of information do the parentheses contain?

_____

_____

_____

_____

_____

_____

_____

_____

_____

_____

_____

_____

_____

_____

_____

_____

_____

Also make sure that you don't glue part 2 backwards; it is labeled "front" and "rear." Pressing down on flaps A and B is difficult; try holding the base (part 2) by the edges.

Step 12 Repeat Step 11 for flap B.

Step 13 Glue flaps T, U, and V to close the ends of the body.

50 **Step 14** Fold flap S onto part 2 and glue it down. Make sure the alignment marks are lined up. Since it's difficult to press down on this area, temporarily insert a piece of cardboard crosswise in the space under part 2 to press against.

Step 15 Repeat the procedure for flap R.

Step 16 Score part 3, the underbody. Score along its entire length at the six places indicated by arrows, and cut it out.

Step 17 Mark the folds on the underbody. In the order from flap C to flap D, the first and last fold should be "valley" folds and the four others should be "peak" folds. Refer to the shaded part 60 of Figure 2.

Step 18 Apply glue to the back side of flap C. Glue flap C onto the back side of the underbody so that you form the shape shown on the shaded part of Figure 2 (seen from the end). The shaded part of the underbody should slope inwards at an angle of about 30 degrees.

Step 19 Repeat the last step for flap D.

Step 20 Apply glue to the top of the underbody and glue it to the underside of the main body. The underbody should cover flaps A and B. Make sure the underbody is centered, both 70 lengthwise and crosswise.

Step 21 Score and cut out the nose, part 5. Bend the hood (where the headlights are) into a hump, just like the shape of a fingernail.

Step 22 Bend the sides of the nose around and glue them to the hood using flaps K. Next, bend the underside of the nose (the two curved sections) and glue them together at the small white flap. Finally, glue the underside of the nose to flap M. The assembled nose is shown in Figure 3.

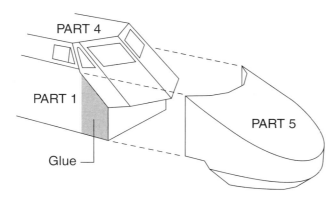

Figure 3

Step 23 Apply glue to the front edge of the sides, as shown in the gray shaded area on Figure 3. (Do one side after the other.) Glue the nose to the main body, making sure everything lines up (use the white strip for reference).

Step 24 Score part 6, the wheels, according to the arrows. Also score on the lines beneath flaps Q.

Step 25 Cut out part 6 and fold it. All folds are "peak" folds. Fold the bottom flaps (unlabeled) to the back of the wheels. These flaps are not glued to anything and are used only for stiffness.

Step 26 Glue flap P so that part 6 forms a box. Fold flaps Q inward, and glue one wheelset to each spot on part 4 (one in front, one in the rear).

This completes the assembly of the TGV power unit.

What do the dotted lines mean in Figure 3?

INFER

Why do you think the parts to be cut out are numbered, while the flaps are lettered?

_____

_____

_____

_____

_____

_____

_____

_____

_____

_____

_____

_____

_____

_____

_____

_____

_____

_____

_____

TEXT FEATURES

Illustrations are often drawn to **scale**—that is, they have the same proportions as the original but a different size. Circle where you learn what the scale of the illustration is.

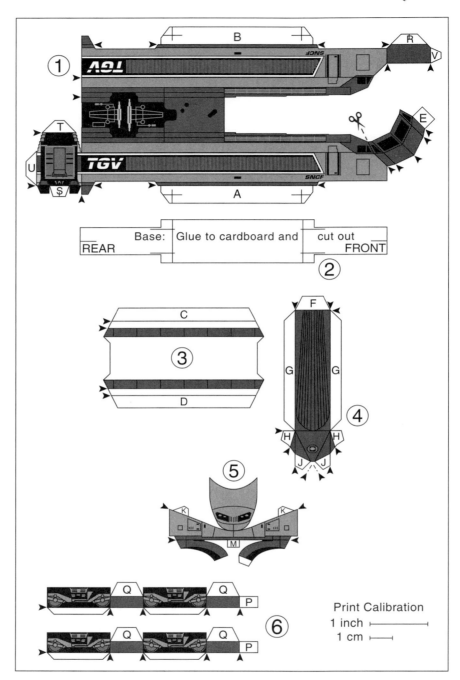

Standards Review

 **Building a Model Chunnel Train**

Complete the sample test item below by circling the correct answer. Then, read the explanation to the right.

Sample Test Item	Explanation of the Correct Answer
You should do all of the following steps before assembling a model power car *except*— **A** Collect all the tools and materials you will need. **B** Read through the instructions. **C** Cut out all the parts and glue them to a cardboard backing. **D** Look over the figures and the parts to be cut out.	*C* is the correct answer. According to the instructions, only the base is glued to cardboard, and the parts are cut out one by one, not all at once. Going over the instructions (*B*) and pictures (*D*) *before* you start a project, and making sure everything you need is at hand (*A*), will make assembly smoother and easier.

DIRECTIONS: Circle the letter of each correct response.

1. According to the instructions, which part should be cut out and assembled *first*?

   A the main body

   B the base

   C the underbody

   D the roof

2. According to the instructions, which part should be cut out and assembled *last*?

   F the main body

   G the base

   H the nose

   J the wheels

3. Figure 3 illustrates the instructions for—

   A Steps 21–22

   B Steps 24–25

   C Step 11

   D None of the above

4. Which figure shows the entire assembled power car?

   F Figure 1

   G Figure 2

   H Figure 3

   J None of the above

Reading Standard 2.6 (Grade 9–10 Review) Demonstrate use of sophisticated learning tools by following technical directions (e.g., those found with graphic calculators and specialized software programs and in access guides to World Wide Web sites on the Internet).

Checklist for Standards Mastery

Each time you read, you learn something new. Track your growth as a reader and your progress toward success by checking off skills you have acquired. If you read all the selections in this book and complete the sidenote questions and activities, you will be able to check off, at least once, all the standards for success listed below.

✓	California Reading Standard (Grade 9–10 Review)	Selection
☐	**1.1** Identify and use the literal and figurative meanings of words and understand word derivations.	
☐	**1.2** Distinguish between the denotative and connotative meanings of words and interpret the connotative power of words.	
☐	**2.1** Analyze the structure and format of functional workplace documents, including the graphics and headers, and explain how authors use the features to achieve their purposes.	
☐	**2.3** Generate relevant questions about readings on issues that can be researched.	
☐	**2.5** Extend ideas presented in primary or secondary sources through original analysis, evaluation, and elaboration.	
☐	**2.6** Demonstrate use of sophisticated learning tools by following technical directions (e.g., those found with graphic calculators and specialized software programs and in access guides to World Wide Web sites on the Internet).	
☐	**2.7** Critique the logic of functional documents by examining the sequence of information and procedures in anticipation of possible reader misunderstandings.	

✓	California Reading Standard (Grade 9–10 Review)	Selection
☐	**2.8** Evaluate the credibility of an author's argument or defense of a claim by critiquing the relationship between generalizations and evidence, the comprehensiveness of evidence, and the way in which the author's intent affects the structure and tone of the text (e.g., in professional journals, editorials, political speeches, primary source material).	
☐	**3.3** Analyze interactions between main and subordinate characters in a literary text (e.g., internal and external conflicts, motivations, relationships, influences) and explain the way those interactions affect the plot.	
☐	**3.4** Determine characters' traits by what the characters say about themselves in narration, dialogue, dramatic monologue, and soliloquy.	
☐	**3.5** Compare works that express a universal theme and provide evidence to support the ideas expressed in each work.	
☐	**3.6** Analyze and trace an author's development of time and sequence, including the use of complex literary devices (e.g., foreshadowing, flashbacks).	
☐	**3.7** Recognize and understand the significance of various literary devices, including figurative language, imagery, allegory, and symbolism, and explain their appeal.	
☐	**3.8** Interpret and evaluate the impact of ambiguities, subtleties, contradictions, ironies, and incongruities in a text.	
☐	**3.9** Explain how voice, persona, and the choice of a narrator affect characterization and the tone, plot, and credibility of a text.	

✓	California Reading Standard (Grade 9–10 Review)	Selection
☐	**3.11** Evaluate the aesthetic qualities of style, including the impact of diction and figurative language on tone, mood, and theme, using the terminology of literary criticism. (Aesthetic approach)	
☐	**3.12** Analyze the way in which a work of literature is related to the themes and issues of its historical period. (Historical approach)	

✓	California Grades 11–12 Reading Standard	Selection
☐	**1.1** Trace the etymology of significant terms used in political science and history.	
☐	**1.2** Apply knowledge of Greek, Latin, and Anglo-Saxon roots and affixes to draw inferences concerning the meaning of scientific and mathematical terminology.	
☐	**1.3** Discern the meaning of analogies encountered, analyzing specific comparisons as well as relationships and inferences.	
☐	**2.1** Analyze both the features and the rhetorical devices of different types of public documents (e.g., policy statements, speeches, debates, platforms) and the way in which authors use those features and devices.	
☐	**2.2** Analyze the way in which clarity of meaning is affected by the patterns of organization, hierarchical structures, repetition of the main ideas, syntax, and word choice in the text.	

✓	California Grades 11–12 Reading Standard	Selection
☐	**2.4** Make warranted and reasonable assertions about the author's arguments by using elements of the text to defend and clarify interpretations.	
☐	**2.5** Analyze an author's implicit and explicit philosophical assumptions and beliefs about a subject.	
☐	**2.6** Critique the power, validity, and truthfulness of arguments set forth in public documents; their appeal to both friendly and hostile audiences; and the extent to which the arguments anticipate and address reader concerns and counterclaims (e.g., appeal to reason, to authority, to pathos and emotion).	
☐	**3.1** Analyze characteristics of subgenres (e.g., satire, parody, allegory, pastoral) that are used in poetry, prose, plays, novels, short stories, essays, and other basic genres.	
☐	**3.2** Analyze the way in which the theme or meaning of a selection represents a view or comment on life, using textual evidence to support the claim.	
☐	**3.3** Analyze the ways in which irony, tone, mood, the author's style, and the "sound" of language achieve specific rhetorical or aesthetic purposes or both.	
☐	**3.4** Analyze ways in which poets use imagery, personification, figures of speech, and sounds to evoke readers' emotions.	
☐	**3.6** Analyze the way in which authors through the centuries have used archetypes drawn from myth and tradition in literature, film, political speeches, and religious writings (e.g., how the archetypes of banishment from an ideal world may be used to interpret Shakespeare's tragedy *Macbeth*).	

✓	California Grades 11–12 Reading Standard	Selection

☐	**3.7** Analyze recognized works of world literature from a variety of authors:
	  a. Contrast the major literary forms, techniques, and characteristics of the major literary periods (e.g., Homeric Greece, medieval, romantic, neoclassic, modern).
	  b. Relate literary works and authors to the major themes and issues of their eras.
	  c. Evaluate the philosophical, political, religious, ethical, and social influences of the historical period that shaped the characters, plots, and settings.	

☐	**3.8** Analyze the clarity and consistency of political assumptions in a selection of literary works or essays on a topic (e.g., suffrage, women's role in organized labor). (Political approach)	
☐	**3.9** Analyze the philosophical arguments presented in literary works to determine whether the authors' positions have contributed to the quality of each work and the credibility of the characters. (Philosophical approach)	

Index of Authors and Titles

Vocabulary Development

Pronunciation guides, in parentheses, are provided for the vocabulary words in this book. The following key will help you use those pronunciation guides.

As a practice in using a pronunciation guide, sound out the words used as examples in the list that follows. See if you can hear the way the same vowel might be sounded in different words. For example, say "at" and "ate" aloud. Can you hear the difference in the way "a" sounds?

The symbol ə is called a **schwa.** A schwa is used by many dictionaries to indicate a sort of weak sound like the "a" in "ago." Some people say that the schwa sounds like "eh." A vowel sounded like a schwa is never accented.

The vocabulary words in this book are also provided with a part-of-speech label. The parts of speech are *n.* (noun), *v.* (verb), *pro.* (pronoun), *adj.* (adjective), *adv.* (adverb), *prep.* (preposition), *conj.* (conjunction), and *interj.* (interjection). To learn about the parts of speech, consult the *Holt Handbook.*

To learn more about the vocabulary words, consult your dictionary. You will find that many of the words defined here have several other meanings.

---

at, āte, cär; ten, ēve; is, īce; gō, hôrn, look, tool; oil, out; up, fur; ə *for unstressed vowels, as* a *in* ago, u *in* focus; ' *as in* Latin (lat''n); chin; she; zh *as in* azure (azh'ər); thin, *the*; ŋ *as in* ring (riŋ)

Picture Credits